The Fastest Game in the World

SPORT IN WORLD HISTORY

Edited by Susan Brownell, Robert Edelman, Wayne Wilson, and Christopher Young

This University of California Press series explores the story of modern sport from its recognized beginnings in the nineteenth century to the current day. The books present to a wide readership the best new scholarship connecting sport with broad trends in global history. The series delves into sport's intriguing relationship with political and social power, while also capturing the enthusiasm for the subject that makes it so powerful.

1. *Empire in Waves: A Political History of Surfing,* by Scott Laderman
2. *Country of Football: Soccer and the Making of Modern Brazil,* by Roger Kittleson
3. *Skiing into Modernity: A Cultural and Environmental History,* by Andrew Denning
4. *ABC Sports: The Rise and Fall of Network Sports Television,* by Travis Vogan
5. *The Sportsworld of the Hanshin Tigers: Professional Baseball in Modern Japan,* by William W. Kelly
6. *The Fastest Game in the World: Hockey and the Globalization of Sports,* by Bruce Berglund

The Fastest Game in the World

HOCKEY AND THE GLOBALIZATION OF SPORTS

Bruce Berglund

UNIVERSITY OF CALIFORNIA PRESS

*The publisher and the University of California Press
Foundation gratefully acknowledge the generous support of the
Ahmanson Foundation Endowment Fund in Humanities.*

University of California Press
Oakland, California

© 2021 by Bruce Berglund

Library of Congress Cataloging-in-Publication Data

Names: Berglund, Bruce R., author.
Title: The fastest game in the world : hockey and the globalization of sports /
    Bruce Berglund.
Other titles: Sport in world history ; 6.
Description: Oakland, California : University of California Press, [2021] |
    Series: Sport in world history ; 6 | Includes bibliographical references
    and index.
Identifiers: LCCN 2020030586 (print) | LCCN 2020030587 (ebook)
    ISBN 9780520303720 (hardcover) | ISBN 9780520303737 (paperback) |
    ISBN 9780520972858 (ebook)
Subjects: LCSH: Hockey. | Sports and globalization.
Classification: LCC GV847 .B44 2021 (print) | LCC GV847 (ebook) |
    DDC 796.356—dc23
LC record available at https://lccn.loc.gov/2020030586
LC ebook record available at https://lccn.loc.gov/2020030587

29 28 27 26 25 24 23 22 21
10 9 8 7 6 5 4 3 2 1

*To Megan,
my best friend,
my wife,
my person*

CONTENTS

List of Illustrations ix

Introduction 1

1 · Up from the Ice 19

2 · Into the Arena 50

3 · Out of the Storm 82

4 · Toward New Directions 112

5 · On the Brink 145

6 · In the Money 174

7 · Around the World 206

Epilogue 239

Acknowledgments 251
Notes 255
Bibliography 299
Index 317

ILLUSTRATIONS

MAPS

1. Canada in 1894 and locations of Stanley Cup challengers, 1892–1914 *47*
2. Hockey in 1930s Europe *75*
3. New hockey arenas in North America and Europe, 1990–2015 *217*

FIGURES

1. Fans cheer the unified Korean women's team against Sweden, 2018 Winter Olympics *9*
2. The Edmonton Ladies' Team promoting Starr skates, 1899 *20*
3. Women and men playing bandy in St. Moritz, 1910 *25*
4. A game at the ice stadium in Davos, 1928 *67*
5. Poster illustrated by Paul Ordner for the grand opening of the Palais des Sports, October 1931 *78*
6. Bohumil Modrý returning to Prague after winning the 1949 world championship *105*
7. Schedule for the 1961–62 season of *Hockey Night in Canada* *115*
8. Tabletop hockey for Soviet boomers *123*
9. "The Goalie," 1961, photograph by Vladimir Lagrange *124*
10. Fans at the 1963 world championship in Stockholm *129*
11. Opening of the 1965 world championship at Hakametsä Ice Hall in Tampere *132*

12. The Winnipeg Jets' high-scoring Swedish forwards celebrate winning the 1976 WHA championship *163*
13. Bob Johnson, coaching the University of Wisconsin Badgers *170*
14. Justine Blainey at age twelve, taking her case to court *194*
15. International migration of players during the 2000s *209*
16. Bobby Orr at Boston Garden, 1974, and Tomáš Tatar at Joe Louis Arena, 2017 *214*
17. Pregame introductions at the home arena of CSKA Moscow *225*
18. A Russian fan at the 2018 Winter Olympics, wearing a jersey with Putin's name *244*

Introduction

BY THE TIME I ARRIVED HOME that Friday afternoon my dad was already there, listening to the game. I found him in the kitchen, leaning over the small RCA solid state radio. The game was scheduled to be shown on television later that night, on tape delay. But true fans, dedicated fans, heard the live call over the radio that afternoon.

The date was February 22, 1980.

The "Miracle on Ice" has been celebrated as an upset without equal. *Sports Illustrated* dubbed it the greatest event in sports history, surpassing Ali and Foreman, Jesse Owens in Berlin, and Roger Bannister's four-minute mile. For my dad and me, among the relatively few Americans who experienced the game live, there was a sense that something special was happening. I cannot remember any specific words of radio announcer Curt Chaplin, nothing like Al Michael's iconic call on TV later that night—"Do you believe in miracles? Yes!" I do recall that we were riveted. We did believe in miracles. As late afternoon gave way to the darkness of a winter evening, we stayed in the kitchen—him leaning against the counters, me sitting on the linoleum floor—listening out of a belief in the impossible.

At the same time, we were surprised the game was so close. We didn't understand why Soviet goaltender Vladislav Tretiak was on the bench after the first period, but we knew that it helped the Americans' chances. We were relieved that the Soviets led by just one goal after the second period and held hope for a comeback. Still, after Mark Johnson's tying goal midway through the third period and then, just over a minute later, the go-ahead goal by Mike Eruzione, we were stunned. They could actually beat the Soviets. I remember our nervousness in the final minutes, waiting for the clock to run down, hoping they could hold the lead. At the same time, I remember that the anxiety was mixed with exhilaration, with the realization we were listening to history being made.

And our celebration? I don't remember. I can't recall what we did or said when the final horn sounded. My dad had to leave shortly after the game ended. He refereed high school and college hockey in the area and there was a game that night. I often went along when he officiated, but not this Friday. I stayed for the delayed TV broadcast of the game, to watch what I had just heard. Already knowing the outcome, I could watch with joyful anticipation. That feeling stuck with me as I watched the US team defeat Finland on Sunday morning to win the gold and then the medal ceremony later that day, when Eruzione called his teammates to the podium after the anthem. I eagerly read the newspaper and magazine stories. When the new issue of *Sports Illustrated* arrived later that week, its cover went up on my bedroom wall: Heinz Kluetmeier's famous photograph of the players in their white USA jerseys celebrating after the win over the Soviets. Even ten months later, when I unwrapped my own USA hockey jersey for Christmas, my joy had barely diminished. No one in my neighborhood had a jersey like that.

Why was this game so meaningful to me? First, I understood its political importance. Even at age eleven, my path to becoming a historian was ordained. I was a news junkie who watched Walter Cronkite every evening and pored over issues of *Time* and *Newsweek*. I knew of the American hostages held in Iran, the Soviet invasion of Afghanistan, and the emerging Abscam corruption scandal swirling around members of Congress. When the 2004 film *Miracle* told the story of the 1980 Olympic team, it opened with a montage of news clips from the 1970s: Nixon's resignation, the fall of Saigon, inflation, fuel shortages. The montage closes with Jimmy Carter's televised address from July 1979, his warning that the United States was facing a "crisis of confidence." All accounts of the US team's victory at Lake Placid paint the same background: the country was at a low point in winter 1980. This was true—at least from the viewpoint of a precocious fifth-grader. The hockey team's win over the Soviets, America's Cold War rival, was a needed dose of good news.

But the gold medal at Lake Placid was important to me for more personal reasons. At the time, hockey had limited, regional appeal in the United States. Among the four major team sports in America, hockey was firmly in fourth place, behind football, baseball, and basketball. The rare times the sport gained national attention were when Snoopy and Woodstock faced off on a frozen birdbath in the comics pages. Even the TV broadcast of the US-Soviet game did not draw that large of an audience. Yes, it's one of the most-watched hockey games in American television history, but that's not saying much. In the Nielsen ratings, that night's Olympic programming ranked only twelfth. The latest episode of *Diff'rent Strokes* and the movie of the week, *Harper Valley P.T.A.*, earned higher ratings than the Miracle on Ice.[1]

Hockey was not America's game. But it was my game. When the *Sports Illustrated* cover went on my bedroom wall, it joined team pennants and hockey cards, featuring the likes of Guy Lafleur, Bryan Trottier, and Marcel Dionne. Thanks to my subscription to *Hockey Digest*, I knew the game's records and lore. My dad made me watch the Hartford Whalers when they were on TV, just so someday I could say that I had seen Gordie Howe play. He told me of the time he sat next to Bobby Orr at a bar. I never saw Orr play, but I knew that was important.

I learned the game from my dad. He had old hockey gloves of soft leather and a wool sweater he kept at the bottom of his dresser drawer, its numbers coming unstitched at the corners. He and I usually had our first skate in November, when the ice on the bay was so smooth that the puck would glide forever, off in the direction of the big ore ships frozen at their docks. We moved to the neighborhood rink once it was ready. I spent the winter months there, either in practices for my park team or in Saturday-afternoon pickup games. But often I was there with my dad, who would get me away from the TV by telling me to grab my skates. Our annual ritual was to go for a skate on Christmas morning, after the presents had been unwrapped. The ice was ours alone, and I usually had a new stick that had been leaning near the tree that morning.

Hockey was a niche attraction in the United States in 1980. But I was among the initiated. The Olympic team's win was important to me because I had been raised on the game. More than that, I was a hockey player from Minnesota. As an eleven-year-old, I was aware that I lived in a remote part of the country. The places I would see on television—New York, Washington, Los Angeles, Chicago—seemed a world away. Whenever my hometown was mentioned in popular media, it was usually as a joke. Duluth was synonymous with the distant, frozen North. People who live in the Duluths of the world, the marginal places, often take pride in being set apart; we like to tell ourselves that we have a different ethic than those who live in centers of wealth and power. At the same time, there is a longing for recognition from those at the center. This is a constant theme in Canadian culture as well. As novelist Douglas Coupland writes, Canadian popular media regularly tries to stir national pride by listing all of the actors and athletes who have become successful in the United States. "Does Illinois torture itself about how many famous actors come from Illinois?" Coupland asks. "No. But Canada cares about how many Canadian actors come from Canada."[2] So does Minnesota.

For many people in the state, including me, the Olympic team's triumph was an instance of fellow Minnesotans stepping onto the world stage. This was our team. Of the twenty players on the Olympic team, twelve were from Minnesota, as was the team's coach, Herb Brooks. They were from towns and neighborhoods we knew. Newspaper articles told of the celebrations of parents and siblings, uncles and aunts, high school classmates and college roommates. Reporters visited Brooks's parents, Herbert and Pauline, at their home on St. Paul's East Side. "Herb has come a long way from Hastings Pond," his mother said. "I remember when he was 10 or 11 and my husband said he would help him learn to play hockey. And now he's brought a lot of honor to our country."[3]

When the coach and his Minnesota-raised players returned home after their visit to the White House, they were paraded through the streets of St. Paul and Minneapolis. Local papers printed photos of fans lining the parade route and described the players as humble, hometown boys. "This is better than going to Washington," Mike Ramsey told a reporter. "In Washington, there was the president and everything. But being here and seeing all the real people is unbelievable."[4] Ramsey and his teammates spoke of their Olympic triumph in awestruck, appreciative terms. They were grateful to have been part of such a historic event. But now they were happy to be home—soon to be out of the limelight. "There's a point of getting too much attention," Ramsey said. A few of the players from towns in northern Minnesota skipped the parade altogether. They chose instead to get home right away.

One of these players, Phil Verchota, lived in my hometown. A few months after the Olympics, my dad and I had the chance to meet him at his family's home. I remember being struck by the fact that his house was an ordinary house. His parents were ordinary parents. And Verchota himself was an ordinary guy. But he had been part of something extraordinary. I saw his gold medal. I saw the white USA jersey he and his teammates had worn in the game against the Soviets. This was someone from the place where I lived, who played the sport I played, who had gone on to accomplish the remarkable. Maybe, I dreamed as an eleven-year-old, maybe I could do something remarkable, too.

At age eleven, I dreamed of being an Olympian. At age twelve, I reached my peak. I was a short, stocky forward, but I made up for it by being slow. I ended up having more success as a historian than as a hockey player.

I did make it to the Olympics, though, as a spectator at the 2018 Pyeongchang games. A lot had changed in hockey by that time. The Soviet Union no longer existed, yet the Russians were still the strongest team in the tournament. They were also still cast as villains, after multiple investigations had revealed a massive doping program in Russian sport. No longer was the United States represented by a team of college players; instead, pros were allowed to compete. But for the first time since 1998, the National Hockey League (NHL) did not pause the season and allow its players to participate. With revenue topping $4.5 billion, Commissioner Gary Bettman and league owners no longer saw the benefit of players risking injury while their arenas sat empty. As a result, attendance was disappointing at the new arenas in Gangneung, on South Korea's northeast coast.

Yet even without NHL stars, Olympic hockey still drew a big audience back home. Since being introduced at the 1998 Nagano games, women's hockey had become one of the marquee events of the Winter Olympics, and the rivalry between the Canadian and American national teams was touted as one of the best in sports. Team USA's shootout win over Canada for the gold medal set records for late-night TV ratings in the United States. In Canada, the game was the second-most-watched program of the year, beating out the Academy Awards, the World Cup final, and the Maple Leafs in the playoffs.

But I was not at the 2018 games to watch the traditional powers of women's and men's hockey. Instead, I was following the Koreans. For the first time ever, South Korea's men's and women's teams were playing in the Olympics. The International Ice Hockey Federation (IIHF) had made the unprecedented decision to grant the host nation an automatic bid to the Olympic tournament, rather than requiring the normal qualification process. To hockey fans in North America and Europe, the addition was surprising. "They play hockey in Korea?" plenty of people asked me. The answer was yes—just as they play hockey in Mexico, Australia, and South Africa.

In his travelogue of the world's unlikely hockey nests, journalist Dave Bidini writes that sport, "like dandelion seeds sown on the wind, has the tendency to settle where you least expect it."[5] The seeds of hockey had first settled in Korea in the 1920s, carried over by American missionaries and teachers. After the war, hockey took root in high schools and universities in the South. The South Korean national men's team first competed in 1979, and the women's team in 2004. Although speed skating is Korea's most popular winter sport, hockey has gained a dedicated following. Pro teams compete in the Asian League against opponents from Japan and the Russian

Far East. One of the league's top teams, Anyang Halla, is made up mostly of Korean players, with a handful of Canadians and Americans—coached by a Czech.

Korea's small hockey community is avid. The problem was, with a pool of only three thousand registered players, the national teams were not strong enough to compete in the Olympics. The men's and women's teams regularly competed in the second or third tiers of world hockey. Jumping to the Olympics and playing the likes of Canada and Russia would be potentially embarrassing. To prepare for the sport's biggest stage, the Korean Ice Hockey Association turned to Jim Paek as director of hockey operations and coach of the men's team. Paek, born in Seoul, had been raised in the Toronto suburbs after his parents emigrated. He started skating at the park across from his family's home in Etobicoke and climbed the ladder of Canadian minor hockey. Eventually joining the Pittsburgh Penguins, Paek became the first Korean-born player to have his name inscribed on the Stanley Cup. After a sixteen-year playing career, he coached for the Red Wings' farm team in Grand Rapids before taking the position in Korea. In interviews, he spoke of returning to his family's home country as an honor.[6]

The Korean federation imported players as well as coaches to strengthen its teams. When the men's team took the ice at the Olympics, the roster included five Canadians and one American. But these were not sons of immigrants; instead, they were big white guys who were naturalized as Korean citizens. Korea's North American players drew plenty of attention. On the ice, they towered over their teammates. Off the rink, there were a few raised eyebrows. "They thought I was representing North Korea," said goalie Matt Dalton of the questions he got back home. "They just didn't know the difference."[7] In Korea as well, where national identity had long been linked to a notion of ethnic homogeneity, the idea of blonde, white North Americans representing the country was perplexing.[8] The addition of the foreign players was made possible by a 2011 change in citizenship laws, allowing people with special skills to fast-track through the process. One aim of the law was to improve the country's performance in international sports, and among the first naturalized citizens were an African-American basketball player, a Kenyan marathoner, and a German luger. Still, citizenship was not easy to earn. Candidates had to read and write in Hangul characters and sing the national anthem in Korean.

For the North American hockey players, Korean citizenship brought a once-in-a-lifetime opportunity. As journeymen pros, they knew chances were slim of playing in the Olympics for their home countries. At the same time, as Dalton explained to me, their new passports provided something else that was rare for pro athletes—stability. Like each of his naturalized teammates, Dalton had taken a meandering path through the hockey world before landing in the Asian League: from his hometown in rural Ontario to junior teams in Montana and Iowa; college hockey in Bemidji, Minnesota; farm teams in Pennsylvania and Providence; a brief stop in Boston with the Bruins; and then Podolsk and Nizhnekamsk in Russia's Kontinental Hockey League—eight teams in nine seasons. After signing with Anyang Halla, Dalton and his wife quickly appreciated life in the Seoul suburb where the team was based. The money was good, his team won, and he became a fan favorite. The decision to become a citizen ensured a steady place for the first time in his hockey career. He was no longer designated an import player, at risk of being cut if the team's fortunes turned.[9]

By contrast, the players imported for the South Korean women's team all had family connections to the country. Former Princeton player Caroline Park was a first-generation Korean-Canadian from Brampton, Ontario. Randi Griffin, who played college hockey at Harvard, grew up in North Carolina with her Korean mother and white father. The player who drew the most media attention before the games was Marissa Brandt, who had been adopted from Korea by a Minnesota couple when she was a baby. Brandt played as a member of the Korean team, while her sister Hannah played for Team USA. Unlike the naturalized players on the men's team, who had all played pro hockey in Korea for years, the imported women received surprise invitations to join the national team. Many thought their days of organized hockey had ended after college. Park, who was in medical school, dismissed the Korean federation's email as some joke from her father. Weeks later, she was at tryouts in Korea.[10]

For two and a half years, the mix of Koreans and North American imports trained together for the games. Then, just three weeks before the opening ceremony, the news broke: twelve players from North Korea would be added to the South Korean team. For the first time since Korea was divided after World War II, athletes from North and South would compete together in the Olympics. The International Olympic Committee and the IIHF had discussed the possibility of a unified team for five years. After Moon Jae-in became president in 2017, South Korea had a leader willing to make such a gesture to the North. Public opinion, however, was at first strongly opposed. According to one survey, more than 80 percent of young Koreans opposed the inclusion of North Korean players. Critics derided the move as a propaganda stunt for the North's benefit. Others called out the apparent sexism—that officials would have never dared add North Koreans to the men's team.[11]

Despite the initial criticism, the atmosphere was charged for the unified team's first Olympic game. Outside the Kwandong Hockey Centre, volunteers handed out thousands of small white flags with the same logo as the team's new jerseys: a blue image of the Korean Peninsula, with no boundaries. Behind the arena, I found hundreds of people lining the service entrance, waving their flags and singing in anticipation of the expected dignitaries—President Moon of South Korea and Kim Yo-jong, sister of North Korean leader Kim Jong-un.

Along with a delegation of officials, North Korea also sent a troop of more than two hundred cheerleaders. These carefully screened young women, all from families with impeccable Communist Party credentials, were regularly sent abroad to cheer North Korean teams at international sporting events. There were no short skirts, pom-poms, or acrobatic routines. Instead, the North Korean women dressed demurely in matching track suits and sat together in large groups, filling entire rows of the arena. They sang traditional songs, accompanied by synchronized swaying and arm movements. Occasionally, a woman in each group performed a dance routine in a *hanbok*, the traditional Korean gown.

Other than the noodle bowls for sale at concession stands, the Kwandong Hockey Centre was much like any other arena in the hockey world. A handful of Koreans wore team jerseys. I met one father and daughter dressed in Anyang Halla jerseys with Matt Dalton's name on the back. As in arenas in North America or Europe, hard rock blasted during breaks in play. What stood out were the North Korean cheerleaders. As an AC/DC or Metallica riff sounded, the smiling women performed their choreographed songs. When the familiar "stomp-stomp-clap, stomp-stomp-clap" of Queen's "We Will Rock You" thundered over the speakers, the crowd instinctively joined in. But the cheerleaders sat still. They did not know the song. Or they were forbidden to know it. Later in the game, I caught sight of a cheerleader clapping along to a pop song during a stoppage. Her neighbor gave a discrete elbow. She put her hands in her lap.

Even without the cheerleaders and dignitaries, the unified team's contests were more like political rallies than hockey games. During the team's second match, against Sweden, I sat among a pro-unification group whose members had traveled from as far away as Pusan, on Korea's southern tip. Like many

Fans cheer the unified Korean women's team against Sweden, 2018 Winter Olympics (photo by author).

Americans in 1980, they were watching their first game. But they were not there for hockey. Instead, they were there for what the hockey team represented. Even as Sweden scored goal after goal in a one-sided game, people sitting around me, young and old, waved their flags and cheered fervently. The score ended up 8–0, but no one left early. They did not come to see a miracle on ice, but the miracle of Korean unity. Said a fan at one of the team's games, "I just want to cheer for them and see them work together."[12]

The players felt this electricity in the arena. "When I first stepped onto the ice, I felt like I was dreaming," Marissa Brandt later recalled.[13] Yet they also bore the weight of high expectations. After the South Korean players had trained together for years, the addition of the North Koreans undermined their play on the rink and their morale off the ice. "We had humble goals, but we were serious about them," Randi Griffin explained. Once the team became a political symbol, it was harder to keep those goals in sight. Some players accepted that they were part of history; others resented being pawns and having to watch every word for fear of starting an international incident. "It was very hard to concentrate on hockey," Griffin told me. "I think we were all overwhelmed, confused, and concerned the entire time."[14]

In the end, the Koreans finished the tournament in last place. The experiment of building an Olympic-caliber team did not succeed. In the lead-up to the winter games, there was an increase in Korean girls playing hockey, but the total number remains small. Sports do scatter like dandelion seeds, but even dandelions need soil to grow. The question remains as to whether women's hockey will find a place in the sports culture of South Korea. As for the political experiment of the unified team, that did appear to have some effect. Two months after the Olympics, President Moon met Kim Jong-un at the Demilitarized Zone, the first summit between leaders of North and South in eleven years. In November 2018, the two governments announced plans to have their athletes march together at the Tokyo Olympics and then submit a joint bid for the 2032 summer games. Whether just a dramatic gesture or a real catalyst for improved relations, the unified hockey team helped break the peninsula out of growing hostility.

Local. National. Global. For fans and players, ice hockey has different meanings at each level. There is a rich body of writing examining the sport in each of these different contexts. Numerous popular chronicles and academic studies have traced hockey's growth in late nineteenth-century cities and towns, through the rise of the NHL, to the epic clashes of the Cold War.[15] Much of this writing focuses on hockey at the national level, specifically hockey in one nation: Canada. Journalists, historians, sociologists, economists, poets, politicians, and literary scholars have examined Canadian hockey from all angles, plumbing the sport's important place in the life of the country.[16] Two of the game's most respected interpreters, journalist Roy MacGregor and former player and politician Ken Dryden, sum it up eloquently: "Hockey is Canada's game. It may also be Canada's national theatre.... It is a place where the monumental themes of Canadian life are played out—English and French, East and West, Canada and the U.S., Canada and the world, the timeless tensions of commerce and culture, our struggle to survive and civilize winter."[17]

Canada still has more registered hockey players than any other country. Its men's and women's teams remain among the best in the world. The sport is vital to Canadian national identity. But hockey has a long history in other parts of the world as well. In parts of Europe and the United States, skaters have been playing the puck as long as Brazilians have been kicking soccer balls. Yet while it would be hard to write the history of soccer without Brazil, there are many books on hockey history that pay scant attention to the

Russians, Czechs, Swedes, and Finns. Without question, Canada has a large and essential place in the history of hockey. But hockey is bigger than Canada. As Dryden observed in one of his other books, the acclaimed memoir *The Game:* "A game we treat as ours isn't ours. It is part of our national heritage, and pride, part of us; but we can't control it."[18]

Admittedly, taking on the history of world hockey is daunting. At the start of their global history of the sport, Stephen Hardy and Andrew Holman acknowledge that the book is not "a comprehensive account of hockey's total history"—even at an encyclopedic five hundred pages.[19] This book also doesn't dare to encompass the whole of world hockey. Instead, it is a history of the hockey world. This term, "the hockey world," is often used to describe the global network of people connected by the game—players, coaches, scouts, executives, journalists, fans.[20] It appeared, for example, in North American coverage of the 2011 plane crash that killed forty-five players and coaches with the Russian team Lokomotiv Yaroslavl. With nine different countries represented among the victims, the crash was, in Gary Bettman's words, "a catastrophic loss to the hockey world." Conversely, we don't often hear of a "baseball world" or a "basketball world." Both of these sports are global, but they do not have the same volume of back-and-forth movement between North America and other world regions as there is in hockey. Soccer certainly has extensive migration of players and managers, within networks that are vast and complex. The hockey world, by comparison, has been described as small, like a community. No one would call the soccer world small.

Researchers studying globalization use the concept of "imagined worlds" to understand links between people in distant places who regard themselves as part of the same community, bound by shared beliefs, interests, or activities. Barbara Keys applied the concept in her study of international sport during the 1930s, the period when soccer's World Cup began and the Olympics became a global movement. "The imagined world of sport," she wrote, "was governed by distinctive laws and practices, linked by its own repertoire of invented symbols and traditions, referring to a common past and common heroes."[21] Of course, hockey was one part of this imagined world. The men who organized the sport's governing body were from the same class of European amateur sportsmen as those who led the International Olympic Committee and FIFA. The Ligue Internationale de Hockey sur Glace was a founding participant in the Winter Olympics and organized an annual world championship, beginning in 1930.

Yet hockey was also distinct from this larger world of international sport. We can think of hockey at the time as its own proto-world, still in the process of formation. During the interwar years, the hockey cultures of North America and Europe had tenuous links, but they were divided by their respective laws and practices, symbols and traditions. Europeans, Canadians, and Americans played the same game with skates, sticks, and pucks, but on different rinks, according to different strategies, and with different institutional structures. There was little common tradition, and no common heroes: the NHL stars of Canada and the United States were largely unknown in Europe, while the best European players did not register even a blip of attention in North America.

The hockey world of today is much different. Players begin traveling the globe as children, carrying the same high-tech branded equipment in the same branded bags. In the world's premier professional league, the NHL, over a quarter of players come from outside North America, representing more than a dozen countries. Meanwhile, hundreds of Canadians and Americans—women and men—play each year in leagues around the world. Along with importing players and coaches, these leagues have adopted other features of North American hockey, such as postseason playoffs, privately owned franchises, and arenas with luxury seating. Even the pregame introductions and cartoon logos of menacing beasts are the same. One example is Eisbären Berlin. Founded in 1954 as SC Dynamo Berlin, the club was part of the athletics organization affiliated with the East German state police, the dreaded Stasi. Its affiliation with the Stasi long in the past, the team is owned by the Los Angeles–based Anschutz Entertainment Group, which has a stake in more than a dozen other teams and arenas in Europe and North America. The roster is stocked with Germans, Canadians, and Americans. And before each home game, in front of packed crowds in Berlin's new Mercedes-Benz Arena, players skate onto the ice through the fangs of a giant polar bear.

In charting the formation of today's hockey world, this book looks first to the local level. In the course of my research, I visited libraries and archives in places like Edmonton and Winnipeg, Helsinki and Bratislava. I paged through plans for local arenas, game programs, school yearbooks, and the scrapbooks and letters of young men who played the game and then became shop owners and middle managers. I spoke with former players and coaches, with local journalists and librarians, hoping to understand the game's history in specific places. I started my investigation of the sport's global development "from below," so to speak. As historian Lynn Hunt suggests in her book

Writing History in the Global Era, this approach allows us to see the unique histories of different communities, as well as how these "histories of diverse places become connected and interdependent."[22] Following Hunt's advice, this book brings readers to the box rinks of Soviet apartment blocks and the local arenas of North American suburbs. We will hear the stories of players like Randi Griffin and Matt Dalton—young men and women who move from country to country. As we will see, the history of global sport is revealed just as much in their travels as in the careers of international stars like Dominik Hašek or Alexander Ovechkin.

The first question in my research was basic: Why were people in various communities drawn to this sport? To be sure, climate and the natural landscape were essential to hockey's early development, but they were not the only factors that spurred its growth and popularity. For example, the states of Minnesota and Wisconsin have similar populations and climates, yet in Minnesota there are three times as many children under age ten registered for hockey as in Wisconsin. Colorado, a state well known for its winter sports, has had only thirteen players reach the NHL, compared to more than two hundred from Massachusetts. We see similar regional differences in Europe. There are more than three times as many boys and girls playing hockey in Switzerland, with its snow and mountains and population of eight million people, as there are in Austria, with its snow and mountains and population of eight million people. Why have some communities, in some cold-weather regions of Europe and North America, made hockey part of their winter routine, part of their local culture? As the book shows, this process didn't just *happen.*

In investigating hockey's growth (as well as its decline in places), this book steers in directions some might find surprising. This is not a book about Gordie Howe, Rocket Richard, and other NHL legends. Their stories have been told elsewhere. Instead, this is a book about marketing and television. It is a book about American suburbs and European social welfare. It is a book about domestic and international politics, economics and the environment. Above all, this is a book about how we raise up young people. From its beginnings, hockey—like all team sports—was viewed as beneficial for young people, specifically young men of particular social standing. This motivation has been present throughout the game's history, wherever it was played. Today, we sign up our kids for hockey because it's fun, but also because we think it's good for them, that it helps prepare them, in some way, for life in today's world.

As historian and former Olympic athlete Bruce Kidd states, "It is impossible to describe modern life without some account of sports."[23] Turning Kidd's statement around, we might also say that we cannot describe the history of sports without an account of modern life. The imagined world of hockey is not insulated from politics, culture, and economics. These broader developments and their impact on the hockey world are the subject of this book. The aim is to gain some understanding of the place of hockey and other sports in contemporary society and the reasons we devote so much of our time, money, and emotions to them.

As the title states, this is a book about the globalization of sports. What does *globalization* mean, and how does it affect sports in general and hockey in particular? Although specific definitions are notoriously slippery, scholars of contemporary politics, economics, and culture typically point to four developments that characterize globalization.[24]

First, globalization involves greater movement of goods, services, money, and people across boundaries and world regions. Second, institutions and social relations have expanded around the world. Business firms and nonprofit organizations extend their activities and tap into talent far beyond their home countries, and in the process diffuse their practices and values across the globe. Third, advances in technology and communications have accelerated worldwide social and cultural change. Lastly, globalization has brought a change in how we understand ourselves and our horizons. We are aware that we are global. We know that developments across the world shape our national politics, the makeup of our communities, and our individual livelihoods. The COVID-19 pandemic made this clear.

These characteristics of globalization are evident in the world of sport. Athletes travel the world for better competition, better training, and better paychecks. Wealthy owners now hold sports assets around the world, with Russian oligarchs and Persian Gulf sheikhs investing in Europe and North America. Sports institutions also have global reach. Matches of the English Premier League are televised on Saturday mornings in the United States, while European networks broadcast NFL games on Sunday evenings. Even individual athletes like LeBron and Messi are global brands.

Our global awareness also shapes our relationship to sports. We can follow any sport, any team, in any part of the world. Any piece of fan gear we desire, from this year's Arsenal third shirt to a retro Brooklyn Dodgers cap, can be delivered across an ocean to our mailbox in days. Our global awareness also means that a young hockey player knows there are opportunities to play around the world, whether for an American college, a European club, or an emerging pro team in China.

Some who follow sports, however, resist these globalizing trends. Opponents typically frame their stand as a defense of tradition or community values. In some instances, this resistance to globalization in sports has spawned racist and xenophobic movements. But the desire to maintain local allegiances and practices cannot be dismissed entirely as reactionary. Sports are important in shaping family relationships, community belonging, and individual identity. The defense of local sports cultures against globalizing trends taps into the very DNA of sport: the legacy of long-past football matches between neighboring towns, weekend baseball on the village green, and games of shinny on a frozen river.

In looking at this dynamic between the local and the global, ice hockey offers an especially compelling case study. Hockey players have been moving across borders and oceans as long as the sport has existed. Before it was known as hockey, British soldiers and settlers played games with curved sticks on the ice of colonial Canada and New England. Eighty years before Wayne Gretzky was traded from Edmonton to Los Angeles, skaters crossed the border from Canada to the United States to play for money. And in the years between the world wars, teams of Germans, Czechs, Austrians, Swiss, Swedes, and Canadians traveled from city to city in Europe, playing before thousands.

Already in these early decades, there was resistance to the globalization of hockey. When the infant NHL admitted teams from Boston and New York in the 1920s, Canadian writers objected to the influence of big American audiences and big American money. The narrative began in Canada that professional hockey's greedy rulers emphasized fighting and scoring to appeal to ignorant Americans, diluting the game's original beauty. In fact, rough play was a distinctive feature of Canadian hockey. In postwar international tournaments, Europeans claimed that Canadians were thugs. Canadians countered that Europeans didn't know how to play "real hockey." Meanwhile, everybody said the Russians were robots. The recriminations continue to today. When teams in southern cities reach the Stanley Cup finals, journalists in the North disparage their fans' lack of knowledge. Canadian commentator Don Cherry ignited controversy for decades with his slurs against Europeans. Even the highest-scoring European player in NHL history has acknowledged the broad divide in the hockey world. "It's another sport,"

Jaromír Jágr said of North American hockey in his memoirs. "I think the hockey played in America and the European kind can't be compared."[25]

Ice hockey is now played in parts of the world that never see a snowflake, let alone a frozen pond. Before 1960, the IIHF had twenty-eight member countries, only three of which (Australia, Japan, and South Africa) were outside Europe and North America. In 2020, fifty-four men's national teams and forty women's teams competed in the federation's various tiers and divisions, with sanctioned tournaments played in such renowned hockey towns as Mexico City and Abu Dhabi. In the United States, the presence of NHL teams in Florida, Texas, and Arizona has spurred youth programs in those states. Over the past decade, California has added more than ten thousand new players.

As hockey expands on the map, it also expands on the calendar. No longer restricted to winter, tournaments fill the summer months. Specialized camps are available for players of all ages. There is a camp at Lake Placid where skaters meet members of the 1980 Olympic team and a camp in Toronto where young goaltenders can learn from Vladislav Tretiak. Camps in the Czech Republic have web pages in English, German, Swedish, Russian, and Chinese. Summer training has brought greater uniformity to how players are developed. "Kids in northern Minnesota are doing the same things as kids as in Phoenix or Dallas," says one American college coach. We can say the same about kids in Stockholm, Seoul, and Saskatoon.

With year-round training and competition, today's players are better coached and in better physical condition. Up and down the roster, around the world, the quality of players is more balanced. There are still standouts, like the Edmonton Oilers' young star Connor McDavid. But the "middle class" of hockey players, as one NHL veteran explained to me, is now larger, with greater parity of talent. When I asked John Harrington, a member of the 1980 Olympic Team, about the skill of today's players compared to his generation, he first looked around the restaurant as if preparing to speak blasphemy. "If you watch videos of NHL games from the 1970s and 1980s, it often looks like players are moving in slow motion compared to today," he said. On average, today's players are faster and stronger. A past great, like the Montreal Canadiens' Guy Lafleur, would certainly be great today, but not as dominant as he was in his playing days. "You watch a video from forty years ago of Lafleur coming down the wing, his hair flying," Harrington said. "He takes a shot from beyond the top of the face-off circle and beats the goaltender to the far side of the net. I'm not sure that happens in today's game.

Every goaltender in today's NHL seems to be 6'5", and he's just as skilled and athletic as any forward or defenseman."[26]

The improvement of hockey training has come at a cost. Other youth sports, from tennis to soccer, have become more expensive in recent years. But the fastest game in the world has become one of the most costly, across the globe. "Hockey is an expensive sport," acknowledged Vladimir Plyushchev, former coach of the Russian national team, "and it should not only be the children of wealthy families who participate."[27] Former NHL star Mats Sundin admitted the same in Sweden: "Hockey is expensive, it takes a lot of time, and it requires a lot of sacrifices."[28] In my conversations in Korea, I heard a similar charge—that hockey was a game for rich kids. And while just gaining access already has a steep price tag, the additional training needed to advance costs a king's ransom. An investigative report found that most young players who rise to Ontario's elite major junior league typically come from affluent suburban neighborhoods.[29] As one college coach observed, "Hockey is a blue-collar game being played by white-collar kids."

Overall, however, hockey gains more participants every year, around the world. It is a global game, with rising popularity. There are greater payoffs for players, both men and women, in the form of university scholarships and pro contracts. And the competition for those payoffs is fierce, as well-trained players travel the world in pursuit of opportunities. Yet many are uneasy at what they see in contemporary hockey. Players of past generations, who developed their skills during countless hours on iced-over backyards and frozen ponds, lament that players today are overcoached. In interviews with former players, a word I heard repeatedly was *robotic*. Current players are proficient in skills, these older players insist, but they are mechanical; they lack vision on the ice. Two of the sport's most celebrated stars, Bobby Orr and Wayne Gretzky, have even wondered whether players of their creativity would find a place in hockey today.[30]

Granted, every sport has its old-timers who complain about how the game has changed. There has been griping about hockey's decline throughout its history. But the debates in contemporary hockey point to deeper transformations in the sport. I heard similar concerns from hockey veterans who grew up in Canada, Switzerland, and the former Czechoslovakia and Yugoslavia, people who are still involved in the game today. They observe that the structures of the game, the ways in which it is taught and learned, have changed. They recognize that the sport is being shaped by forces larger than hockey. What they miss, however, as do past greats such as Orr and Gretzky, is that they were part of the transformation.

There are roughly 1.1 million children and teenagers around the world who play hockey today. More than a million families invest in sticks, pads, and skates, and then sit inside giant refrigerators cheering their children on the ice. Weekend after weekend, at summer camps and tournaments, it's the same around the globe—in Canada, Sweden, Russia, and every other hockey-playing country. Even the Hong Kong U8 team played a tournament last year in Beijing, over twelve hundred miles from home.

Here is the real-world effect of the globalization of hockey and other sports. When eager young players aspire to advance in the game, their families must dedicate treasure and time to the sport. Maybe it's your family, asking why hockey is so costly, why it takes up so much of your time. The answer is found in developments that go back decades, that arose in different countries for different reasons. These multiple currents from the sport's global history have merged to create today's hockey world.

ONE

Up from the Ice

THE SPORTS WE WATCH AND PLAY TODAY took shape in a world much different from our own. Hockey, baseball, football, soccer, rugby—all the games that fill our flat screens—emerged in an age of steam trains, gaslight lamps, and livery stables. Baseball's National League played its first season the same summer as the Battle of Little Big Horn. When England's Football Association was founded, Florence Nightingale was teaching her first class of nurses. In the 1890s, hockey was being played in the imperial capitals of London, Berlin, and Vienna, and in the frontier town of Edmonton, with plank sidewalks and dirt streets.

At the same time, there was much that is familiar in the world that gave birth to our games. Even though they wore top hats and ankle-length dresses, spectators cheered, groaned, and argued with as much passion as we do today. Media entrepreneurs and property developers found there was plenty of money to be made in sports, while civic leaders and business owners broke the bank and skirted rules to put together winning teams. Young men gained money and status for their athletic ability. Young women sought their own place on the field or rink.

We can see the links between our day and theirs in the photographs. Look past the uncomfortable uniforms and stiff poses and you find young people full of energy and ambition. One of my favorite photographs from this era shows a women's team from Edmonton, promoting a brand of skates. They pretend to tie their laces or study the blades. A few are caught in the moment, amid the scattered sticks and pucks. Rather than having the serious expressions people of the time wore for photographs, they are relaxed, with the hints of smiles on their faces. In this moment, they are freed from the restrictions of the age. They are teammates. They are hockey players.

The Edmonton Ladies' Team promoting Starr skates, 1899 (courtesy of Glenbow Museum).

We see similarities as well in the underlying foundations of our games. The basic structures of the sports club and commercial franchise took shape in this period. So did the idea that sport teaches virtues essential for moral character and productive citizenship. One of the most popular books in the English-speaking world at the time was the story of a boy who sets off to boarding school, where he meets new friends, has adventures, and learns moral lessons. The young hero, Tom Brown, shows his bravery not in battling evil wizards but in playing sports. There is a direct line from this novel, *Tom Brown's Schooldays*, to our own stories of how sport builds character, to movies like *Miracle* and *Remember the Titans*. Europe and North America of the late nineteenth century are foreign to us in many ways, but the strange world of the past gave shape to the beliefs and institutions that still guide our games today.

LANDS OF ICE AND SNOW

The world in which hockey emerged was different from ours in one other important respect—it was a lot colder. In general, temperatures have to be below 23°F (−5°C) over at least three days to freeze a surface of water strong enough to hold an adult. When hockey had its beginnings in the 1800s, this kind of sustained cold was more common across the Northern Hemisphere than it is today. During the nineteenth century, hundreds of New Yorkers would skate on the frozen Central Park lake. Outdoor natural rinks were common in Britain and Germany. Even as late as the 1920s, skaters took to the ice on the Reflecting Pool in Washington, DC.

The latter half of the nineteenth century was the closing stage of the climatic era known as the "Little Ice Age." Using a range of data, from tree rings to temperature recordings kept by monks, researchers have marked a period from the early 1400s to the late 1800s during which the Northern Hemisphere was approximately 1.4°F (0.78°C) cooler than it was in the late twentieth century.[1] There were numerous winters during these centuries when the Thames, the Danube, and even the Venice lagoon froze solid. The cold survives in Charles Dickens's story *A Christmas Carol*, when Ebenezer Scrooge throws open his window on Christmas morning to a snow-covered London. Dickens's childhood, from 1812 to 1820, corresponded with some of the coldest winters of the Little Ice Age, when a white Christmas was an annual occurrence in England.[2]

As we see with the trials of Scrooge's employee, Bob Cratchit, life during the Little Ice Age was a struggle. Some parishes in England and Scotland lost over a third of their population during the seventeenth century.[3] Yet even with the scarcity of food and fuel, people across Europe went outside. During the Little Ice Age winter became a time of play. Many of our winter sports had their origins during these cold centuries, as people invented outdoor entertainments to keep their blood moving. There is evidence of curling in Scotland and the Low Countries in the sixteenth century. A Scottish writer of the early 1700s praised the sport's benefits in the cold climate: "It clears the Brains, stirs up the Native Heat / And gives a gallant Appetite for Meat."[4] Other recreations had more practical origins. North American natives traveled the winter landscape with toboggans and snowshoes. As historian Gillian Poulter shows, British colonists in Montreal turned these Indigenous means of transport into the equipment of organized sports.[5] Skis were likewise used for transportation and hunting in Scandinavia. During the snowy winters of the late nineteenth century, Norwegian students brought along their skis to German, Austrian, and Swiss universities and adapted them to the descents of the Alps.[6]

Skating began in the Netherlands as both a means of transport and a leisure activity. Frozen canals served as thoroughfares for Dutch maids, as promenades for stately men and women, and as racetracks for children. While exiled in the Netherlands after the English Civil War, members of the House of Stuart learned to skate in the Dutch manner, with iron blades attached to their boots with leather straps. They brought back their skates when they returned to England in the late 1600s. Skating became popular among the British upper class in the eighteenth century, with the first skating club founded in Edinburgh in 1742. By the early nineteenth century, skating was regarded as a manly activity. Skating figures required discipline, strength, agility, and grace—attributes expected of a dignified man.[7]

Refinement also characterized social skating. Skating clubs in Europe and North America served members of high status. Prints from the nineteenth century show skaters dressed to the nines at festive balls and masquerades. In places like Montreal, Quebec City, New York, and Chicago, indoor rinks were built to protect skaters from the elements. By the second half of the century, enclosed rinks for skating or curling were common in Canada and the northern United States, varying from ornate halls in large cities to simple, barn-like buildings in smaller communities. Indoor rinks in English cities had artificial ice by the turn of the century. Already in 1876, British inventor John Gamgee developed the basic method of freezing an artificial rink still in use today—pumping refrigerated brine through a network of pipes, which then freezes a layer of water above the pipes.[8] Meanwhile, all Canadian rinks had naturally frozen surfaces until the early twentieth century. The walls and roof offered shelter from wind and snow, but the uninsulated interior was cold enough to keep ice frozen. Even in the 1920s, the Montreal Canadiens played on natural ice at their home arena.

According to Adam Gopnik's essays on the cultural history of winter, skating was one part of the season's transformation in the nineteenth century. People of the 1800s celebrated winter—with outdoor games and festivals, with poetry and painting, with Christmas shopping and gatherings. Coal-fired furnaces also helped. Rather than the bleak season of death, winter became a time of beauty and conviviality. Gopnik points out that we can draw a direct line from the German Romantics of the early 1800s, who wrote of winter's mystery, down to popular Christmas songs of today. The love of winter, he writes, "is part of the modern condition."[9] We should remember this when looking at prints of Victorian skaters, dressed in their colorful fashions, with brass and strings playing in the background and gaslight lamps shining overhead. Rather than seeing them as quaint, we should recognize them as similar to ourselves. Like those skaters, we look forward to the winter months, to putting on our brightly colored jerseys and venturing into the night, braving the cold and joining the crowd.

ROOTS OF A NORTHERN GAME

It was at one of these rinks, in Montreal, that the first indoor hockey game was held. According to newspaper reports, a large crowd turned out to the Victoria Skating Rink on March 3, 1875, even though temperatures outside were well below freezing. The young men who played did not invent hockey. The *Montreal Gazette* reported that the game was already "much in vogue on the ice in New England and other parts of the United States." The principal organizer, a young engineer named James Creighton, apparently adopted rules he knew from his hometown of Halifax.[10] The innovation that Creighton and his friends made was moving the game indoors, into an environment more hospitable for spectators. "It would be indoors where hockey became a sport," observes writer Michael McKinley, "gaining definition and character by the very fact of its physical confinement."[11]

Like baseball, another sport with European roots that gained its distinctive form in nineteenth-century North America, hockey's origins were varied.[12] One winter landscape from the early 1600s, by Dutch painter Hendrick Avercamp, shows a man with a crooked stick and a ball on a frozen canal crowded with skaters. When Europeans explored Canada and New England, they discovered Native Americans playing their own versions of hockey. There is debate as to whether the word itself is derived from the Iroquois *hoghee*, meaning tree branch, or the French *hoquet*, meaning shepherd's crook.[13] For much of the nineteenth century, there was no common name: the words *hockey*, *hurley*, *ricket*, *bandy*, *shinny*, and *shinty* were all used to describe the games played on frozen ponds and rivers. There were also no common rules. Some played on skates, some on boots. Games might have a hundred skaters or four a side. The common DNA had only a few essential features: goals, sticks, and some projectile, perhaps a rubber ball, a chunk of wood, or a frozen animal turd.

There was no clear evolutionary thread leading to the Victoria Skating Rink, nor did the match played by Creighton and his friends bring a sudden transformation to these varied ice games. Local versions continued to develop in Canada, the United States, and Europe. For example, the world's oldest existing hockey club kept playing according to their long-standing norms.

The Bury Fen Club dated its origins to the winter of 1813–14, when men of the village played on the flooded washes and meadows of the Fens, in eastern England. Bury Fen traveled up to sixty miles to face some opponents, with a leg of mutton going to the winner. The men of Bury Fen always took the spoils—the club did not suffer a loss until 1891.[14]

By that time, as interest in the sport grew throughout England, it was necessary to set uniform rules. The official name was established as *bandy*, the word for the sticks players used—roughly three feet long with a seven-inch, curved blade. Yet the game was also commonly called *hockey*. According to the rules, the sport was played on a frozen area larger than a football pitch, with eleven players on a side. In reading William Tebbutt's descriptions of matches and players from Bury, his hometown, one recognizes the common elements between bandy and the game played in Montreal. The necessary skills were the same: passing, stickhandling, and shooting—or "combinations," "dribbling," and "hitting power," as they were called. Of course, speed was essential. Tebbutt wrote of players with quickness and size, and of a brilliant stickhandler whose only fault was "that he kept the ball too long."[15]

As this ice game spread into continental Europe, it was welcomed as an English sport. In some places, the term *hockey* was used, in other places *bandy*. Some called it *bandyhockey*. Czech sportswriter Josef Laufer called the game hockey when he discovered it as a teenager, at the turn of the century. In his memoir, Laufer recalled first learning field hockey one autumn in Prague. After hearing that hockey could be played on ice as well, he and his friends tried it out that winter, on the frozen Vltava River. Along with their skates, they had a tennis ball and an assortment of sticks, including a cane belonging to someone's grandfather. They played into the night, chasing the ball over vast stretches of the river, with faint lighting from electric lamps on the embankments and gas candelabras on the bridge. As with many pickup games, the action ended when the ball was lost, disappearing between the docked barges.[16]

Like field hockey, soccer, and most other sports, the rules of hockey on ice were imported from England. Bandy had made its first appearance on the continent in 1891, when the Bury Fen Club played matches in Haarlem and Amsterdam against Dutch soccer teams. William Tebbutt was the initiator of these first international contests, and he went on to promote the sport in Scandinavia and Switzerland. The sport quickly gained popularity in Sweden: university students in Uppsala played, as did the elite classes of Stockholm, including both male and female members of the royal family.[17] Games with

Women and men playing bandy in St. Moritz, 1910 (courtesy of Swiss National Library).

mixed teams of men and women were also popular at Swiss mountain resorts, typically among English tourists.[18] By the turn of the century, the sport was being played in Germany, Austria-Hungary, and Russia.[19] The National Bandy Association in England was acknowledged as the game's authority, but few in Europe used its official name. Instead, it was known as hockey.

"Bandy," wrote William Tebbutt, "or, as it is often called, 'hockey on the ice,' is too good a game to have been always confined to one district of England."[20] People in Europe agreed. Match reports of English, Dutch, German, and Czech clubs highlighted the same features that thrill hockey fans today: end-to-end rushes, staunch defensive play, hard shots to the corner of the net, quick saves by goalies.[21] Observers remarked especially on the game's speed, how a skilled player could accelerate down the ice—"with a velocity of perhaps ten miles per hour or even more," a German writer exclaimed.[22] Owing to the pace and size of the rink, bandy did not lend itself to rough play, making it suitable for women. Yet female players were not immune to the game's knocks. The "hockey-girl," an English writer advised, "makes no worse a wife if she has learned by falling to take the hard bumps of life."[23]

"The Canadians are reputed to be the finest bandy players," remarked British figure skater Edgar Wood Syers in 1906, "but no team from the other side has yet visited Europe."[24] By that time, Canada had hundreds of organized hockey teams, representing athletic clubs, schools, universities, army garrisons, and churches. For close to two decades already, the best teams in the dominion had played for the silver cup donated by Lord Stanley of Preston, former governor general of Canada. The Canadian version of hockey had even displaced ice polo, the skate-stick-and-goal game popular in New England and the Midwest during the nineteenth century.[25] Yet Syers cannot be faulted for his confusion, calling Canadians bandy players instead of hockey players. The two organized sports—Canadian hockey and the English game of bandy, or hockey, or European hockey, as it was variously called—were two branches of a common family. One commentator compared the Canadian and European versions of hockey to the two football codes: soccer and rugby.[26] The analogy is appropriate. European hockey generally adopted the rules, terminology, and formations of soccer, while Canadian hockey drew largely from rugby. When Canadian hockey reached Europe, skaters in some places saw the similarities to bandy and took to it with enthusiasm. People elsewhere preferred the familiar game adopted from England. In neutral Switzerland, there were occasions when two clubs would play bandy and then make way for two clubs to play by Canadian rules.

The ultimate success of Canadian hockey was due to a variety of factors. First was that the sport had been devised for an indoor rink. Before March 3, 1875, the ice games played across North America looked more like bandy than contemporary hockey. But to play those traditional games required a lot of ice, and the weather was changing—at least in Europe. Already in the 1890s, William Tebbutt lamented that temperatures in England allowed only a few matches each winter.[27] Bandy never took hold in France, because of a lack of ice. "The strange winters we have been having for the last few years do not lend themselves to enough ice," noted a French sportswriter in 1902.[28] The strange winters would soon be the norm. The Little Ice Age was coming to an end. Of the two versions of hockey, the one able to survive the thaw would become the global game.

AN IMPERIAL GAME

What, then, distinguished Canadian hockey from other games on ice? Even the Canadians did not agree on that. In the years after the first indoor game in Montreal, hockey in Canada did not have a clear set of rules or a clear name—some called it "lacrosse on skates," "shinty on skates," or "curling hockey on ice." Observers and participants alike agreed that it was derived from other sports, but the exact formula was not certain. One veteran of the 1875 game recalled that James Creighton had devised rules from rugby and the layout of the rink and player formation from lacrosse.[29] Meanwhile, skaters in Creighton's hometown of Halifax were playing to different rules, allowing forward passing and offsides. "It appears to be a mixture of football, shinny, and lacrosse," wrote a Toronto journalist when the game arrived in that city.[30]

Like Canadian hockey at the turn of the century, Canada itself was a recent creation—and still a work in progress. Confederation in 1867 had unified separate colonies of British North America into a new state called the Dominion of Canada. Canadian history of the late nineteenth century is a tale of political, economic, and cultural nation building. At the same time, it is a history of empire. Public events opened with the singing of "God Save the Queen," "Rule Britannia," or "Maple Leaf Forever," with its evocation of the English flag planted "on Canada's fair domain." The flag that flew over the dominion was the Red Ensign, with the Union Jack in the upper-left canton. The young men who played hockey were subjects of Queen Victoria, and many early clubs were named in her honor. These first hockey players were students, soldiers, and engineers from the Anglo-Protestant communities of Montreal, Ottawa, Kingston, and Toronto. Within these communities, which included many immigrants from the mother country, the majority identified themselves as British. They shared outlooks and enthusiasms with people back home. Hockey would become a popular Canadian enthusiasm, indeed the quintessential Canadian game, but it was born out of the culture of the British Empire. Like most of our modern team sports, hockey began as an imperial game.[31]

In the decades before and after Confederation, Canadian sport developed on British foundations. Cricket, tennis, curling, and golf had been brought to North America by the English and Scottish. Boys in Canada grew up playing rugby or soccer at school. The ideals of "Muscular Christianity" had proponents in Victorian Canada, particularly at the elite boys' schools of Ontario, where the sons of the English-speaking elite were educated. Developed at English boarding schools, most notably Rugby School, Muscular Christianity taught that men of status were to lead lives of moral and physical fortitude, demonstrating self-control, purity, faith, courage, and a sense of patriotic duty. Sports were essential to this process of character formation. In schoolyard games, boys learned endurance, loyalty, and hardness; they put into practice the essential virtues of fair play and keeping a stiff upper lip.[32]

Like their counterparts in Britain, Canadian apostles of Muscular Christianity aimed to build more than bodies and souls. They were building the empire. George Parkin, headmaster of Toronto's Upper Canada College (UCC), the oldest of Ontario's elite boarding schools, was one of the strongest spokesmen of Canada's imperial mission. A devout Anglican who called himself "the wandering Evangelist of Empire," Parkin argued that Canada was an integral part of Britain's global realm.[33] Indeed, with its abundant minerals, coal, and wheat, with its natural harbors and the newly constructed Canadian Pacific Railway, Canada was the empire's linchpin. According to Parkin, British imperial rule was "the best guarantee of permanent peace that the world could have." To the Christian and moralist, Parkin wrote, no greater satisfaction could come than from seeing "the growing strength of the Empire," that its "immense energy might be turned in directions for the world's good."[34] Parkin was not alone in this belief. At the turn of the century, English Canadians saw themselves not as a subject people of distant Britain. They were British. The empire was theirs. Even more, they were its most dynamic part.

As shown by the example of Canadian soldiers who served in the Boer War (1899–1902), the empire needed young men of toughness and courage. In the view of Parkin and other imperialists, the best way to instill these virtues was through sports. As principal of UCC, Parkin was especially dedicated to cricket, which he saw as binding the empire's various lands to the mother country. When students asked permission to play the more popular game of baseball, administrators refused. In fact, cricket remained the school's only approved spring sport until the 1990s. But Parkin and headmasters at other schools did allow the new game of hockey. Already in the 1880s, boys were challenging each other to interhouse games. By the turn of the century, teams representing the elite schools competed in city and provincial leagues. In 1902 the UCC skaters won the provincial championship of Ontario. Parkin celebrated by giving students a day off.[35]

Why did the headmasters of Canada's elite schools embrace this new sport of hockey? First of all, organized hockey began as a sport of the elite class. The Montreal athletic clubs that gave birth to the first hockey teams were exclusive associations, their members coming from the ranks of Anglo-Protestant professionals and businessmen. Early teams also formed at the universities and military colleges of eastern Canada. The leaders of Canadian hockey's first institutions were from the same social circles as the leaders of educational, political, and cultural institutions. For example, the cofounders of the Ontario Hockey Association (OHA) were Arthur Stanley, son of the governor general, and John Augustus Barron, a member of Parliament and later a judge. The donor of the Ontario league's championship cup was J. Ross Robertson: politician, newspaper publisher, and alumnus of UCC.

Hockey was a game of the elite class, and it was a Canadian game. Imperialists like George Parkin spoke of world trade and Britain's benign rule, but at the root of their ideas was an ardent Canadian nationalism. Imperialism meant "the realization of a Greater Canada," wrote author Stephen Leacock.[36] This meant not only a prosperous, populous Canada that reached across the continent, but also a Canada of social order and good government. According to Parkin and other spokesmen of imperialism, Canadians were characterized by their strong moral sense, their endurance and energy, their self-reliance and clear thinking. They were a northern people, whose strength of character was bolstered in the challenging environment and purifying climate. Already in its first decades, the winter sport of hockey was touted as an expression of "Northern hardiness," ideally suited for "building up a race of men, hardy and self-sufficient."[37] Hockey was not yet the national game; but as a strenuous game played in the bracing winter air, it accorded with a developing notion of Canada's national character.[38]

Above all, hockey was a manly sport. "A manly nation is always fond of manly sports," declared J. Ross Robertson at the 1898 meeting of the OHA. "If we want our boys to be strong, vigorous and self-reliant, we must encourage athletics."[39] Hockey fit the bill—it was physically demanding, team-based, and competitive. And it was rough. In the culture of English school sports, the name of the game was violence. For example, a common defensive tactic in boarding-school football was "hacking"—kicking the ball-carrier's shins as hard as you could. At the founding meeting of England's Football Association, the practice was a subject of heated debate. One club leader warned that if hacking were outlawed, "I will be bound to bring over a lot of Frenchmen who would beat you with a week's practice."[40] Boys at Rugby School wore white pants when playing football to show they were impervious to hacking. The blood-stained cloth proved the wearer could play through pain.[41] The ability to take a hit, to get up after being knocked down, to soldier on through injury—these are the legacies of English boarding-school sports. We see this today on the rugby pitch of New Zealand, the footy oval of Australia, the American gridiron, and the hockey rink of Canada.

Among the various sources for early organized hockey, a key influence was rugby. James Creighton and his fellow players at the Victoria Skating Rink were members of the Montreal Football Club, and their winter game was intended as a way to keep fit for rugby. The onside rule and the ban against forward passing were both adopted from rugby. So was the violence. "Shins and heads were battered, benches smashed and the lady spectators fled in confusion," read one report of that first game in Montreal.[42] Slashing, "donnybrooks" (i.e., fights), and confrontations among fans, players, and referees were common in the early decades. The violence inherited from English boarding schools became a distinctive feature of Canadian hockey. "It was largely because of this excessive violence that hockey became a sport Canadians could call their own," writes hockey scholar Michael Robidoux.[43] As he shows, violence became the Canadians' calling card from their first international matchups. When teams traveled south in the 1890s, American newspapers highlighted the visitors' constant slashing and rough checking. Even before players from Canada crossed the Atlantic, they were known in Europe for their aggressive play.[44]

There were critics at the time. "We must call a halt to slashing and slugging, and insist upon clean hockey," declared J. Ross Robertson in 1904.[45] But Robertson was on slippery ground. How do you preserve the vigorous nature of the game while limiting its violence? As Alan Metcalfe pointed out in his study of Canadian sports, one man's slashing and slugging was another's manly play. "The line between acceptable and unacceptable behaviour was thin indeed."[46] Accepted by its elite-class founders, violence was present from the beginnings of Canadian hockey—it was not a later addition to the game made by working-class players, nor was it fomented by ignorant American spectators. The young English-speaking men who organized the sport in the late nineteenth century saw themselves as building the empire. They needed a sport equal to the task.

ACROSS THE DOMINION

Canadians did not take to organized hockey right away. Only in the 1890s did the sport expand out of elite Anglo-Protestant circles in Montreal, Ottawa, Kingston, and Toronto and gain broader popularity. Historian Michel Vigneault has calculated that there were fewer than two hundred players in the whole of Montreal in 1890, only five of whom were French. A decade later, there were 744 English and 148 French players.⁴⁷ In Toronto, the OHA played its first season in 1890–91 with nine clubs. In 1900, the OHA had a total of fifty-seven clubs in three divisions. In the last winter before the war, 107 teams were part of the Ontario association, and the league's championship drew over seven thousand spectators.⁴⁸

In the 1890s, the winter sport of the English elite in eastern Canada also reached the dominion's western lands. This advance was made possible by another national institution: the Canadian Pacific Railway. After its start in 1881, the railway reached Calgary within two years. The last spike was driven in November 1885 at a pass through British Columbia's Monashee Mountains. As prairie communities grew along the rail line, a distinct cultural and political environment developed. Yet despite the West's unique social and cultural fabric, it was still Canada. The businessmen, educators, and journalists who led these growing cities and towns were nearly all from Ontario, and they held to the same notions of imperialist mission as businessmen, educators, and journalists in Toronto, Kingston, and Ottawa.⁴⁹ They were at the front line of empire, bringing civilization to the prairies. Their games were an important mortar. As historian and former pro player Morris Mott states, these Anglo-Protestant men "were only slightly less anxious to reproduce their best sporting practices than they were to reinstitute their best political, economic, legal, educational and religious ones."⁵⁰ Hockey, rugby, cricket, and other sports reminded them of home. More importantly, the rules undergirding these games ensured that the prairies had the same moral and social structure as Upper Canada and Britain.

Sports were also an outlet for local pride. When Winnipeg's Victoria Hockey Club traveled to Montreal in 1897 and 1899 to challenge for the Stanley Cup, hundreds gathered at the city's hotels and theaters to hear telegraphed reports of the games read out loud. On their return with the cup, the Vics were hailed at the station and feted at banquets. City leaders and newspaper writers announced the club's victories as proof of the West's equal standing with the East, if not its superiority. When matches were heated, as they were in 1899, Winnipeggers proclaimed their team's superiority in sportsmanship and fair play. And newspaper writers jabbed that hardy Manitobans surpassed the easterners in manliness.⁵¹ Just as Canadian imperialists saw the dominion as the most dynamic part of the empire, people of the West saw themselves as the most dynamic part of Canada. And they were loyally British. In 1902, after the Winnipeg Vics defended the cup, the front page of the *Free Press* announced "The Stanley Cup Stays" with a large illustration under the headline: an English bulldog guarding Lord Stanley's silver punch bowl, atop a draped Union Jack.[52]

Since respectable English Protestant men viewed hockey as necessary to building the empire, they wrestled with how to integrate non-English Canadians. While English clubs in Montreal did allow a middle-class Irish team to compete in their league in the 1880s, they outright refused the French. In protest, a self-professed "admirer of fair play" wrote to the *Gazette* to chide established clubs for not playing French teams. He argued that admitting a French club to the league would end "the false impression [that] English athletic organizations in Montreal are prejudiced against anything French."[53] The Victorias and other Winnipeg clubs also closed their rinks to immigrant teams—in particular, teams comprised of Icelandic Canadians, whom the English derided as "Goolies." The Icelandic community responded by building their own rink and founding their own club, called the Falcons.

For immigrants, Irish Catholics, French Montréalais, and others excluded from elite Canadian society, there was still something compelling about the winter pastime of the Anglo-Protestant gentlemen. Of course, the game was fun. But they were also drawn to many of the same benefits that English men saw in their sports: social connections, organized leisure, and improvement of body and character. For example, the black clergy of Nova Scotia who started the Colored Hockey League in 1895 saw organized hockey as a means of spiritual formation for the young men of their community. They intended their league to be based on the Bible, doctrines of the Baptist church, and the teachings of Booker T. Washington. Excluded from white teams and leagues, these black Baptist ministers sought to create their own associations that would be models of organization and clean play. Players would also learn the virtues Washington urged for black advancement: self-discipline, determination, and hard work.[54]

The ideals of nineteenth-century English sports and Muscular Christianity have been widely criticized. Today's abusive coaching practices, such as those that brought the resignation of Calgary Flames coach Bill Peters in 2019, have their roots in the football grounds of English boarding schools, where boys were taught that emotional hardness was necessary to becoming men. As theologians point out, Muscular Christianity's linking of physical prowess and spiritual formation isn't all that Christian. But Muscular Christianity took on new guises as sports like hockey moved from elite clubs and boarding schools to other communities. Values-based sport inspired members of immigrant clubs, women's associations, and trade unions. Most leaders of early Canadian sport did not concern themselves with the rights of women or the trials of Indigenous, immigrant, and working-class communities. Yet, as Bruce Kidd points out, "with their strong belief in the educational benefits of athletic participation, they helped the public schools, YMCAs, colleges, universities and police athletic associations establish strong, broadly based programmes."[55]

JOIN THE CLUB

The sports of British boarding schools had influence well beyond the boundaries of the empire. When merchants, engineers, and students traveled the world, they often brought a football or cricket bat in their steamer trunks, or even a scull and oars. We do the same today. One year when my family lived abroad, we brought along four baseball gloves, three pairs of cleats, two scooters, a wiffle ball and bat, a soccer ball, and an American football. The skates didn't fit, so we had to rent those at the rink. All this equipment got us moving outside. It opened up social connections. And it helped create a sense of the familiar.

British expats of the Victorian age carried along their sporting equipment for similar reasons. Travelers wanted to satisfy their love of sports. People they encountered found their games intriguing, understandable, and fun—and they joined in.[56] To be sure, there were avid British sportsmen who believed the locals would benefit from their games. William Tebbutt was determined to introduce bandy in the Netherlands upon seeing its untouched frozen rivers. "These deserted areas of ice seemed to be 'sinful waste,'" he wrote.[57] Tebbutt and others of more evangelistic intent often found local sportsmen of equal or even greater enthusiasm. Young European men were drawn not only to the games themselves but to the whole apparatus of English sports. They tabulated records, diagrammed playing areas, translated rules, designed club shields, and connected with young men from other countries who shared their enthusiasm. British sports opened up a fascinating and interconnected world.[58]

Rowing, rugby, soccer, and hockey reached continental Europe in the last quarter of the nineteenth century. The first landing points were trading hubs, university towns, and capital cities. Embassy clerks in Vienna, merchants in Hamburg, and students in Zurich were all products of elite English schools, and they carried the games they had learned as students. They also carried the values of these schoolyard games. Some ideas found fertile ground. For middle-class German men, the concept of the sports record, a measured mark of achievement, was especially attractive. They had grown up with the *Turnen* movement, the dominant form of physical education in the German states since the early nineteenth century. In *Turnen*, boys and young men engaged in activities with military application: gymnastic exercises, fencing, horse riding. The aim was strengthening the body for service to the nation. But young Germans of the late nineteenth century had different motivations. With Germany's industrial economy surging, the idea of being a "self-made man" or "man of action" took hold within the rising middle class. The English emphasis on competition and measured achievement was more attractive to ambitious Germans than the gymnastic exercises they had repeated in their youth.[59]

Another aspect of British sports that was especially attractive was their basic organizational unit—the club. The first associations we recognize as clubs emerged in England in the early 1700s. Political and economic changes of the time made it possible for people of common interest to come together voluntarily—free from church, state, or guild—with the autonomy to administer their own affairs. This was not the case in continental Europe, where governments were wary of their subjects gathering without sanction. Only in the second half of the nineteenth century did subjects of the German, Austrian, and Russian monarchies gain the right to form associations.[60]

Once restrictions were loosened, English sports clubs appeared across continental Europe and in Russia, some founded by British expatriates, others by local enthusiasts. The first soccer clubs—in Copenhagen, Haarlem, Antwerp, and St. Gallen—date their origins to the late 1870s. The following decades brought an explosion of new clubs, for all varieties of sports. In Hamburg, fifty-eight rowing clubs were founded between 1880 and 1900. Seventeen new soccer clubs were founded in Hanover alone in the 1890s.[61] In St. Petersburg, there were clubs for eighteen different sports by 1900, including skiing, running, weightlifting, and tennis.

Although the activities, rules, terminology, and outfits were all borrowed from England, these first European clubs built upon local traditions. Sweden, Germany, and the Czech lands originally had mass organizations for gymnastics, with members taking part in different activities at community halls. The first sports clubs followed this pattern: being community-based and having sections for multiple sports. Clubs in Scandinavia and Central Europe were also open to members of all classes—in theory, at least. By contrast,

British clubs typically organized teams in only one sport and were segregated by class or religion—the upper-class alumni of a boarding school playing rugby in one club, factory workers playing soccer in another.[62]

In some cases, English-style clubs established rules and norms of competition for activities that had long been practiced for leisure. This was the case with skating. The ornate figures that gentlemen had traced in the ice to demonstrate their grace were now subject to a judge's scoring. Children's games of chase were channeled on oval courses, measured to the meter, and clocked by timekeepers. Across Europe, skating clubs organized competitions in figure skating and speed skating, sometimes with participants competing in both events. Competitive skating was especially popular in Central Europe, where the lingering frost of the Little Ice Age kept outdoor rinks frozen from December to February. Berlin had two skating clubs, Berliner Schlittschuhclub (Berlin SC) and Berlin Eislauf Verein. Hamburg was home to seven skating clubs. At the turn of the century, when the Vienna skating club moved to a massive outdoor rink in the city center, some four thousand people were members.[63]

Organized hockey in Europe developed within these sports clubs, adopted from England and altered to local contexts. In the winter of 1899–1900, skating clubs in Berlin, Prague, Vienna, and Budapest formed teams to play "English bandy or ice-hockey." The first team in Vienna included well-known players from the city's soccer and cricket clubs. The best player, reported the *Illustrated Sport Zeitung*, was well-known figure skater Gustav Euler, "who combines extraordinary assurance and speed on the ice with brilliant ball-handling technique."[64] Two mainstays of contemporary Czech hockey, the Prague clubs Slavia and Sparta, added the sport to soccer and cycling. Likewise, the Swedish soccer clubs Djurgårdens IF and IFK Stockholm launched bandy sections in the first decade of the new century.

From the start of hockey's emergence on the continent, clubs in different countries made connections across boundaries. International links typically built upon relationships that clubs had already established in skating or soccer. Hockey teams were traveling between Prague and Berlin already in 1899, immediately after they were formed. Berlin SC, one of the strongest early clubs in Europe, competed against teams of English tourists in Davos and St. Moritz at the turn of the century. In 1907, the St. Petersburg Skating Club made the long trip to Berlin for two matches against local clubs. The results foretold things to come: the Russians won by a combined score of 36–0.[65]

"The cultural transfer of the British sport model had a high impact on the creation of a European scene," writes German historian Christiane Eisenberg.⁶⁶ The first generation of Europe's sportsmen, as they called themselves, established international organizations and competitions as soon as they adopted the new disciplines. Federations for skating and cycling were founded in 1892, for soccer in 1904, and for weightlifting in 1905. Like these other organizations, the hockey federation formed in 1908 was intended to regularize international links and establish common rules. Contrary to the current image of world sports officials as jowly men enjoying the fruits of their corruption, the founders of the Ligue Internationale de Hockey sur Glace (LIHG) were young men who played for and managed club teams. The LIHG's first president was twenty-seven-year-old Louis Magnus, a champion figure skater, officer of the Paris Club des Patineurs, and eager convert to the new game. He and the other six men present at the founding meeting organized the LIHG like a club of clubs—members paid their dues, elected officers, wrote a constitution, and agreed to settle disputes democratically.⁶⁷ The language was French, but the template was English.

PLAY THE PUCK

When researchers find a reference to hockey in turn-of-the-century European sources, the first question is "Which hockey?" In most cases, it is the English version of the game, bandy-hockey. Only in the late 1890s do we see the telltale signs of Canadian hockey—the long, flat-bladed stick and, most importantly, the rubber puck.

The earliest pucks were flat pieces of wood or balls shaved flat. The Mi'kmaq Indians of Nova Scotia played with a wooden puck in the mid-nineteenth century.⁶⁸ Perhaps James Creighton had played with a puck himself while growing up in Halifax, since he used it for the indoor game he organized in Montreal. The object was so novel that the *Gazette* offered an explanation in its announcement of the scheduled game: a flat wooden disk was being used instead of a ball, the paper stated, owing to spectators' fears that "accidents were likely to occur through the ball flying about in too lively a manner."⁶⁹ As hockey moved indoors and became an entertainment, the puck was a necessary innovation.

The puck seems to have made its first appearance in Europe in 1895, on the frozen lake at Buckingham Palace. Lord Stanley's sons challenged a team from the palace, led by the Prince of Wales (later King Edward VII) and his brother, the Duke of York (later George V). The princes and lords used curved bandy sticks to hit the imported puck.[70]

The Stanley brothers were avid promoters of the game they had followed in Canada. After their father's arrival in Canada in 1888, they had played on their own outdoor rink at Rideau Hall in Ottawa. The Stanleys' sister Isobel, who was thirteen years old when the family moved to Canada, also took to hockey. In the one surviving photograph of Isobel on ice, we see the accomplished form of a seasoned player, cutting hard on her skates. The photograph also shows the women using short sticks, roughly the length of bandy sticks. Other illustrations from the 1880s and '90s likewise show male players using short sticks. A portrait of Isobel Stanley's brothers and their fellow players shows them brandishing their sticks: some about waist-high, another barely above the knee. The sticks already have the wide, flat blades characteristic of Canadian hockey, as opposed to the upturned blade of a bandy stick. These were sticks made by the Mi'kmaq. Shaped from a single piece of wood, Mi'kmaq sticks (or Mic-Mac, as they were called) were renowned for their lightness and durability. Sporting goods companies copied the design with factory-produced sticks. But, as Bruce Dowbiggin notes in his history of the hockey stick, original Mic-Mac sticks were the class of Canada until the 1920s.[71]

By the time Canadian players came to Europe in the first decade of the twentieth century, their sticks were measurably longer than those Europeans used. Bandy was a one-handed game, with players pushing the ball with their short sticks. The common technique for shooting was to hold the stick with both hands at the end of the handle and then take a whack. This did not work with a hard rubber puck. As Europeans discovered when the puck arrived, they also had to adopt the Canadians' equipment.[72]

When the founders of the LIHG met in 1908, they declared that their organization was concerned solely with "the ice hockey that is played with a puck and not bandy with a ball."[73] Yet one of the federation's first matters of business was figuring out how this game with the puck was played. The earliest documents of the LIHG include a set of tables handwritten on large sheets of paper cataloguing the various forms of the game. The different hockey-playing countries were named across the top, while down the left margin were listed different apsects of the sport. The table shows differences in goal sizes (two by two meters in Switzerland, four by four feet in England) and length of halves (thirty minutes in Canada, twenty in France). Canada and Switzerland had an offside rule, France did not. England's offside rule was the same as in soccer.

In nearly every area of the game, the table indicated the same standard for Germany: "indifferent." It's difficult to imagine Germans being indifferent about the rules of anything. Rather, what the designation indicated is that both versions of the game, European and Canadian, were being played in Germany. Hockey in Switzerland and elsewhere in Central Europe was likewise "indifferent." When Canadian sticks and pucks arrived, hockey players in these regions did not immediately toss away their bandy sticks and rubber balls. Clubs continued to play European-style hockey, and converts had to argue the benefits of the imported equipment. A writer for a Prague sports newspaper defended the new object of the game in 1908, shortly after players there began using the puck: "The puck seldom flies through the air, which is important in accurate handling. This is indispensable, since sophisticated passing is a potent weapon for teams and makes for greater enjoyment for spectators."[74]

MISSIONARIES OF THE CANADIAN GAME

The first time Josef Laufer saw Canadians play hockey in Prague, in 1911, he was amazed. The illustrations in his memoir depict the Canadians with chests like bears and forearms like tree trunks. These were giants from the north woods, towering over the Europeans. And they played like masters, like magicians. "They flew like a whirlwind," he recalled, and "the puck raced between them like zig-zags of lightning."[75]

As secretary of the Czech hockey association, Laufer had organized the visit. He was eager to see Canadian hockey played by its inventors, as it was meant to be played. But he was also nervous. These Canadians had defeated teams across Europe by dozens of goals. After the visitors trounced Slavia 15–0 in their first game in Prague, Laufer feared the worst for the national team, who took the ice against the Canadians the following day. He expected another 15–0 drubbing, maybe 18–0 at the worst. "They wouldn't get to twenty—or maybe they could?"[76] The founder of the Czech association sat next to Laufer, nervously twisting the ends of his handlebar mustache. As the Canadians scored their first goal and then their second, Laufer did the math and watched the clock. How badly would it turn out?

But then, midway through the first half, Czech defensemen started to keep pace, hounding the Canadians down the ice. The Czech goalie turned away blistering shots. At the break, the hosts were down only 4–0. Laufer was relieved: the Czechs could hold them to single digits. The second half, however, was stunning. The Canadians became increasingly frustrated as they tried to add to their tally. The Czech players were out of breath, chasing the Canadians across the rink, keeping them away from the goal. Laufer kept his eyes on his watch, counting down the thirty-minute half, not believing what was happening. At the end, the Czechs held the score to 4–0. Cheers from the home crowd swept over the rink. Laufer screamed himself hoarse. "Lord in heaven," he wrote decades later, "the second half without any goals and a final score of 4–0!! The world had never seen anything like it!"[77] It was a victory for all of Europe.

Not many Canadians were playing hockey in Europe at the turn of the century. The team that visited Prague in 1911 was made up of students from Oxford University. The Oxford Canadians, as they were called, traveled the continent during winter break in the years before the First World War, playing clubs and national teams. The scores were typically lopsided. Even though Europeans were no strangers to skating or hockey, the Canadian version of the game was unfamiliar.

The Canadians were compelling figures for a number of reasons. Coming from the New World, they were a subject of fascination for their hosts. At the same time, as students at Oxford, the Canadians represented one of Europe's most august universities. More importantly, they represented the power, wealth, and modernity of Britain. In visits to some European sites, local organizers stressed that the hockey players were coming from Oxford over the fact that they were Canadian.

The Oxford Canadians hockey team came into existence thanks to a bequest of Sir Cecil Rhodes. After Rhodes's death in 1902, the scholarships bearing his name were established to create an Anglo-American elite distinguished not merely by academic accomplishment but also by shared values of courage and duty. An essential part of this vision, as stated in Rhodes's will, was that young men selected as scholars must have a fondness for sports. Although he had spent only one year at the university, Rhodes sought to give Oxford the upper hand in its rivalry with Cambridge. After his death, the

Rhodes Trust brought athletic young men from Canada, the United States, South Africa, Australia, and New Zealand, all contributing their talent to Oxford's rugby, rowing, and hockey teams. Trustees of the Rhodes Scholarship took this athletic requirement seriously. In 1911 the program's administrator, former UCC principal George Parkin, advocated for a student from Dalhousie University who walked with crutches yet still played goalie in hockey. The trustees' response was direct: the "Dalhousie cripple" was "undesireable."[78]

The imperial direction of the Rhodes Scholarships fit Parkin's views of Canada. The Oxford Canadians, however, did not act as imperialists in bringing their version of hockey to Europe. To be sure, they ran up high scores against opponents (in one game in 1911, they crushed Belgium 26–0). But a number of games were competitive. The Paris Club des Patineurs and Prince's Skating Club of London were able to play even with the Canadians, earning the occasional win or draw.[79] Those were games played with a puck. In places where hockey with a ball was still the norm, the Canadians played along. Photographs from the January 1910 issue of *Sport im Bild* show the Oxford Canadians playing various styles of hockey at a tournament in St. Moritz. In one photo, they are playing the puck; in another, they are shown after a game holding short bandy sticks.

When playing European hockey—on a large rink, with large goals and a ball—the Canadians were evenly matched with their opponents. Still, spectators recognized that the visitors' speed and skill were beyond those of any European team. For example, the Oxford students visited Vienna in 1912 for a two-game set. In the first game, played with a ball, the hosts beat the Canadians 7–4. A Vienna sportswriter observed that the Canadians were not used to playing with a ball and had difficulty adjusting to the larger rink. The students showed their true abilities in the second game, "where they played the Vienna team into the ground." After the previous day's loss, the Canadians took the rematch 14–4.[80]

The Oxford University Ice Hockey Club sparked interest in the Canadian version of the game in Europe. After their tours in the winters of 1910, 1911, and 1912, the term "Canadian hockey" appeared in the German and Austrian press to denote a game distinct from bandy. Yet despite the talent of the Canadians, despite the allure of their Oxford status and their North American origins, their game did not fully displace Europe's version of hockey. Canadian hockey was promoted by the LIHG and national federations, but clubs in Vienna, Prague, Budapest, and Berlin still played with short sticks and a ball in the winter of 1914. And they still called the game hockey.[81]

FRANCHISE PLAYERS

By the start of the war in 1914, the foundations of two hockey cultures were already established. The pillars on which North American and European hockey would develop over the next century had both derived from English sources, yet they had clearly different features—the confined indoor rink as opposed to the broad spaces of bandy, the influence of rugby versus soccer, the cosmopolitan atmosphere of the continent compared to the parochialism of the Canadian game.

Perhaps the most significant difference came with the emergence of professional hockey in North America. The first openly professional league was founded in the United States in 1904, and over the next decade a number of pro circuits came and went. By 1914 there were two left standing: the National Hockey Association (NHA), with teams in Quebec and Ontario, and the Pacific Coast Hockey Association (PCHA), based in Vancouver and Victoria. That March, the champions of the two leagues met to determine the winner of the Stanley Cup.

Historians have described in detail the development of pro hockey in North America, particularly the process by which one circuit—the National Hockey League (NHL), successor to the NHA—came to dominate the sport.[82] The story is complex and colorful. Professional hockey was founded by small-town mill owners and big-city promoters looking to fill dates at the amphitheater when there was no boxing. They found that hockey could sell tickets. The elite guardians of amateur sport objected fervently. Nevertheless, club owners found plenty of young, working-class men willing to travel from city to city in search of another payday.

Openly professional sports were nothing new, nor were they unique to North America. Cricketers, jockeys, and boxers were being paid in England already in the eighteenth century. The Football Association had allowed soccer clubs to pay players since 1885, and professional cyclists and runners were competing on the continent at the turn of the century. By contrast, European hockey was still an amateur game played by sportsmen of respectable status, like Canadian hockey in its early decades.

In comparing top-level hockey in North America and Europe, and other team sports as well, the significant distinction was not whether players were paid. Rather, the more important contrast was how teams were organized. In the early decades of Canadian hockey, teams followed the English model: they were clubs, based in a community or connected to a school or workplace.

With the advent of professionalism, the basic unit followed the model of American baseball: the privately held franchise operating within a closed league, controlled by owners and directed toward profit. This was not an inevitable process. English soccer maintained the club structure after allowing players to be paid. FC Barcelona and Bayern Munich are still organized as clubs, with hundreds of thousands of members paying dues. In hockey, however, the structures in North America and Europe diverged. The sport's history would be shaped by both the franchise and the club.

The professional sports franchise was a distinctly American invention, devised in the nineteenth century by wealthy patrons of baseball clubs. In 1871 professional players in various cities organized their own league, open to any club willing to pay the ten-dollar fee. The ballplayers received the gate receipts, but they proved ill-equipped to run a league. Clubs regularly canceled games after players jumped to other teams. Such snafus were especially wearing for local backers who fronted money for club expenses and then took a cut of the gate.

Hit by losses from the unstructured league, these patrons staged a coup. In February 1876, backers in nine cities organized themselves into the National League of Professional Baseball Clubs. The backers now owned the clubs, and each had the exclusive right to operate a team in his city. Soon after the league's founding, owners also gained control over player movement: the reserve clause bound a player to his club even after his contract had expired. If players crossed league rules, they were expelled. If owners failed to meet their obligations, they were expelled. As its founding agreement stated, the National League was a "closed corporation."

The National League put the owners of franchises firmly in control, but it was not simply a power grab. Rather, it was aimed at minimizing risk: a well-conceived plan designed to protect those who put up the money to keep clubs operating. As economists Louis Cain and David Haddock have shown, a professional baseball club of the late nineteenth and early twentieth centuries had considerable expenses, much more than professional soccer clubs in England. Player salaries were higher because of the longer and more intensive schedule. And travel costs were steep. The longest trip in the Football League was between Plymouth and Newcastle, a distance of 410 miles—the same as between Boston and Baltimore, or Montreal and Hamilton. Teams in the National League, by contrast, were as far as one thousand miles apart.[83]

Owners of the first professional hockey teams likewise had to contend with high travel costs. The International Hockey League (IHL) was founded in 1904 in the mining towns of Michigan's Upper Peninsula. The only Canadian team was in nearby Sault Ste. Marie. The league was founded by local businessmen and rink owners to entertain miners in the booming region. They had grand plans for a larger association stretching from Minnesota to Montreal. Ultimately, however, the only big city in the league was Pittsburgh. Owners agreed to split receipts at Pittsburgh's five-thousand-seat Duquesne Gardens in order to mitigate the costs of traveling from northern Michigan.[84] Teams managed to earn small profits, yet pro leagues that emerged afterward steered clear of the IHL's geographic spread. Travel costs kept hockey leagues compact. Even in the 1950s and '60s, NHL owners were reluctant to expand to the West Coast because of the high cost of travel.

The larger expense for hockey's early professional teams was player salaries. In launching their pro circuit, owners in the IHL declared their intention to find the best hockey talent in Canada. But enticing talent to move to northern Michigan was expensive, as was convincing them to become openly professional and thus risk a ban from Canada's amateur leagues. Hod Stuart of Ottawa, considered the best player of the day, received $1,800 to play for the team in Calumet and manage its rink. A talented twenty-year-old named Fred Taylor signed with the club based in Houghton, earning $400 for twenty-four games. At the time, miners in the Upper Peninsula earned $500 for a year's labor.[85]

Although it lasted only from 1904 to 1907, the IHL transformed the sport. Professionalism was now in the open. A hodgepodge of leagues formed in the following years, and the high salaries of the IHL rose even higher, as players jumped from league to league. Owners sought to lure players who would help their teams win and draw spectators. To sell tickets they needed stars. From the start, the word *star* was a constant in press coverage of pro hockey. Then, as now, the measure of a sports star was not only athletic talent but also market value. Newspaper writers often made mention of players' pay, as confirmation of their star status. Unquestionably, the biggest star was Fred Taylor. After his early stint in Michigan, Taylor returned to his native Ontario and joined the Ottawa Senators, signing for $500 and a job in Canada's Immigration Department. When Taylor scored four goals in a game, the governor general at the time, Albert Grey (the fourth Earl Grey), dubbed him "a cyclone if ever I saw one." One of Cyclone Taylor's later teammates, Frank Patrick, coined another term to describe him—*superstar*.[86]

The early years of professional hockey were much like the unorganized first seasons of professional baseball. Early pro hockey teams were not run to make profits for their owners as North American franchises are today. As Dan Mason points out in his study of the IHL, the professional clubs in Michigan functioned more as community teams. Owners sought to provide entertainment to the towns' workers and boost civic pride. "As long as the owners could achieve limited financial rewards, or even bear a small loss, the teams continued to operate," Mason observes.[87] This was also the case with the Cobalt Silver Kings and the Kenora Thistles—teams in small, resource-producing towns in northern Ontario that stockpiled talent for one or two seasons in hope of winning the Stanley Cup. After their runs, the clubs parted with the high-priced players; the small towns did not have enough people to produce the necessary gate revenue. Like small-market teams that have had recent success in professional sports—for example, Leicester in English soccer or the Kansas City Royals in baseball—hockey teams in small towns could not keep spending year in and year out. In driving up salaries, they ended up driving themselves out of pro hockey.

In the process, these small-town teams drove the transformation of pro hockey's economic structure. In Montreal, Quebec City, and Ottawa, formerly amateur clubs decided to become openly professional. But managers recognized that to gain control of the player market, their teams could no longer function like clubs. They needed to make contracts, and they needed capital. Meanwhile, owners of the indoor rinks wanted to ensure that a quality entertainment product would be filling dates at their venues. In 1909, a director of the Wanderers club of Montreal bought out the financial stakes of his colleagues and sold the team to the owner of one of the city's rinks. The new owner then moved the team from their old home rink to his rink. Here was the first instance of the pattern we see in North American hockey and other pro sports down to today: a businessman buys a team and then moves it to a different place where presumably it will generate more profits. Critics objected to the move. "Does one man comprise a club?" asked a representative of Ottawa's club.[88] Properly, the answer was no. But the Wanderers were no longer a club.

AN EXCLUSIVE LEAGUE

The other professional clubs in Montreal, Quebec City, and Ottawa did not approve of the Wanderers' new owner, nor of the move to a new rink. With a smaller capacity than the team's old home, away games at the Wanderers' rink promised smaller gate shares. The other club directors took a step that was common in early hockey: to eliminate an undesirable member, they scuttled the entire league and formed a new one, the Canadian Hockey Association (CHA)—the same as before but with a different name and without the offending member.

The Wanderers were not lost for long. The Montreal team founded their own league, joining with the owner of the Cobalt Silver Kings, Ambrose O'Brien. The twenty-one-year-old O'Brien had also been spurned by the established clubs of the CHA. Bankrolled by the fortune his father had made in railroads, timber, and silver mining, O'Brien owned three teams in small towns of the Ottawa River valley: the Silver Kings, the Haileybury Comets, and the Renfrew Creamery Kings. He brought all three into the new league, the National Hockey Association, along with the Wanderers. O'Brien also paid for a fifth team in the league. With the Wanderers drawing English hockey fans of Montreal, O'Brien intended this new club to appeal to the French community, luring away a Québécois star from the rival league, Jack Laviolette. In January 1910, Laviolette and his teammates hosted the Silver Kings to launch the first season of the NHA. Their club, Les Canadiens, won in overtime before a near-capacity crowd. When the Montreal teams in the rival CHA played their first games across town, most seats were empty.[89]

The creation of the NHA was characteristic of the organized sport's beginnings in Canada. Despite the new league's name, there was no nationwide association in Canadian hockey. Instead, there was a constantly changing patchwork of regional leagues, both amateur and professional. Leaders of the amateur associations saw the upstart pro leagues as a threat: not only did they violate the tenets of sportsmanship, they also raided the amateur clubs of talent. The executives of the OHA were especially adamant about preserving amateurism in the ranks. In 1912, they banned a team representing Eaton's, Canada's leading department store, because of its association with a commercial enterprise.[90]

Within regional associations like the OHA, there was some movement of teams between senior and intermediate tiers. However, there was not a regular mechanism in Canadian hockey by which strong teams moved into elite circuits and weaker sides were culled. By 1899, the English Football League had formalized the system of promotion and relegation between its first and second divisions. As a means of ensuring competitive parity among clubs, this tiered league structure was later adopted by other European soccer federations and then by hockey federations. In North American hockey, however, a variety of factors kept this open structure from developing—travel distances between cities, lack of parity among teams, the need for indoor rinks with large capacity, and self-interest among team owners and league leaders. Owners of the first pro clubs simply chose to follow the model they knew best. The founders of the NHA agreed to limit expenses "by an introduction of the business principles applied to baseball."[91] Locked out of one closed league, Ambrose O'Brien founded another. Eight years later, O'Brien's successors did the same. To rid themselves of another troublesome owner, they shut down the NHA and created a new association, minus their nemesis. This was the NHL, an organization created to minimize risk by allowing in only reliable business partners—like all North American professional leagues.

The logic of the closed league reached its culmination with the creation of the Pacific Coast Hockey Association in 1911. Using their father's timber fortune, Frank and Lester Patrick founded the circuit in British Columbia. They owned all of the teams, built the arenas, wrote the rules, distributed the players, and played and coached. Constructed in Vancouver and Victoria, the Patricks' arenas were the first indoor rinks in Canada to have artificial ice, a necessity in the mild, wet winters of the Pacific Northwest. With no outdoor ice in coastal British Columbia, there had been no hockey. The Patricks thus had to build a hockey league in an area where the sport was completely new. Many of their savvy innovations, aimed at drawing spectators to the PCHA, remain features of contemporary hockey. Most influential was the brothers' solution to keeping fans interested and spurring ticket sales at the end of each season. While the English practice of promotion and relegation took hold in Europe, including in hockey, North American team sports adopted the Patricks' invention for their hockey league: postseason playoffs.[92]

The only thing holding these various Canadian leagues together, other than players jumping from one to another, was the Stanley Cup. Ambrose O'Brien had spent his father's money in hope of winning the Stanley Cup. After starting their league, the Patrick brothers applied right away to challenge for the trophy. In 1892, when Lord Stanley donated the silver cup that would later bear his name, he had stipulated that it be awarded to "the champion hockey team of the Dominion." The governor general left it to the cup's two trustees to determine how and when it would be contested, although he did set down some conditions—one being that the trustees "arrange means of making the cup open to all, and thus representative of the hockey championship as completely

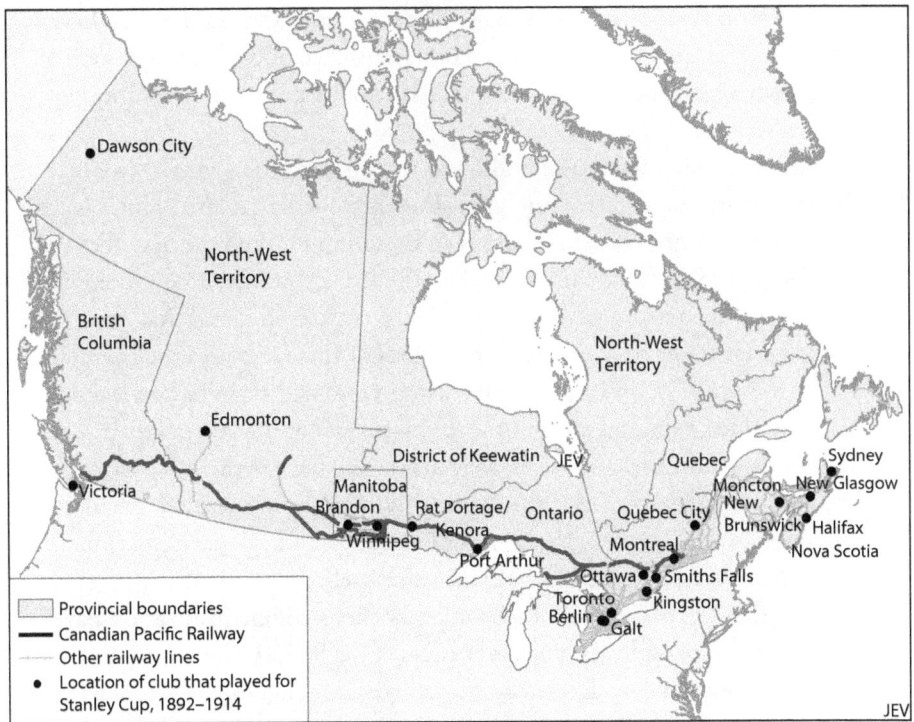

Canada in 1894 and locations of Stanley Cup challengers, 1892–1914. Data source for boundaries and rails: ESRI Canada, Education and Research Department, 2012.

as possible, rather than of any one association."[93] The trustees met this charge at first by allowing teams from western Canada to challenge Montreal and Ottawa clubs. After the Winnipeg Victorias claimed the trophy three times at the turn of the century, challenges came from Kenora, Ontario; Brandon, Manitoba; and even Dawson City, Yukon. Small towns in the East also played for the cup, such as New Glasgow, Nova Scotia, and Smiths Falls, Ontario. For these small-town clubs, competing for the Stanley Cup brought prestige and a boost in revenue, both from gate receipts and from gambling earnings.

Turn-of-the-century critics decried the commercialization of the Stanley Cup as well as the confusion of challengers. The trustees took occasional steps to establish order in how Canadian hockey determined its champion. They turned down some teams that were judged not strong enough to challenge for the cup, such as O'Brien's Cobalt Silver Kings. And they cracked down on the mercenary hiring of players at season's end for a run at the cup. Overall, however, the trustees took a hands-off approach to Canadian hockey's development. As they stated in 1908, "The trustees of the Stanley Cup have never before during the fifteen years of its existence offered any opinion of their own regarding the constitution, laws and proceedings of hockey leagues."[94]

That same year, the trustees allowed the openly professional Montreal Wanderers to compete for the cup. They reasoned that the trophy was intended to recognize the best hockey in the dominion, and the best hockey was being played by pros. In 1914, when the Patrick brothers moved one of their PCHA teams to Portland, Oregon, the trustees declared that the cup would no longer go to the hockey champions of Canada but to the champions of the world. Also in 1914, the trustees conceded that the pro leagues would decide among themselves the arrangements of the cup competition. There were a few instances when they demurred, but for the most part the trustees accepted whatever the leaders of professional hockey decided. Although invested with authority over Canadian hockey's greatest symbol, they did not exercise authority over the game itself.

Over the decades, critics of Canadian hockey's commercialization have pointed to various culprits. But the trustees of the Stanley Cup get a pass. In popular accounts of hockey history, the trustees are congratulated for staying above the fray of early hockey's feuds. Yet this view avoids acknowledging that the trustees, by acts of omission and commission, set Canadian hockey on the path to a single, closed corporation dominating the sport. As Bruce Kidd and John Macfarlane wrote in their 1972 analysis of the state of hockey, the death of the Canadian game began when "the Stanley Cup was turned over to the professionals."[95] When other pro leagues sought to compete for the cup, the NHL insisted that its teams alone were qualified. In 1947, the trustees sealed this arrangement, granting the NHL full authority over how the cup would be contested. There would be no nationwide competition for Canadian hockey's highest prize; community teams would be excluded in favor of privately owned franchises. Unlike cup competitions in European soccer, which have seen the likes of Guingamp and Wigan win trophies in recent years, the Stanley Cup no longer fulfills its namesake's charge, that it be "open to all."

When Justin Trudeau paid a visit to the White House in 2016, Barack Obama knew how to needle his visitor. "Where's the Stanley Cup right now?" Obama asked at the press conference. "I'm sorry. Is it in my hometown, with the Chicago Blackhawks?" Trudeau parried that Canadian players had been important contributors to the Blackhawks' win—which was true. The fact is, however, that while Lord Stanley's cup may be kept in

Toronto, guarded at the Hall of Fame by Canadian keepers, each spring it's more likely to be American fans in an American city cheering as their team circles the ice. Yes, Canadian players lift the cup, as do Russians, Czechs, Swedes, Swiss, Slovaks, Finns, and Americans. By that time, when the cup is awarded, many Canadian fans have quit watching. Even in the 1960s, television executives knew that if one of the league's Canadian teams, Montreal or Toronto, was not in the playoff finals, ratings in Canada dropped. Each spring today, when hockey arenas in Nashville or San Jose are full while viewers in Canada are tuning to the Blue Jays or Raptors, we have the Stanley Cup's Canadian trustees to thank.

The history of the Stanley Cup underscores a significant fact about Canadian hockey: it is not as purely Canadian as advertised. Contrary to the conventional picture of the sport as originating in Canada and then spreading to the United States and Europe, it is more accurate to describe the game with a puck as one version of a family of sports, many called hockey, that were played on both sides of the Atlantic. James Creighton and his Montreal friends were not inventors; they were innovators, who drew upon British and Indigenous source material. As their game and its later iterations went into the world, it was adopted as an improvement on skate-stick-and-goal sports that Europeans and Americans were already playing. Given that Canadians were extraordinarily skilled at any kind of hockey, their version was all the more compelling. But the fact that hockey was a global game from the start also influenced its development within Canada. The British-style club and association, which the Queen's representative recognized when he presented his cup, gave way to the American-style franchise and closed league. These imported institutions quickly took possession of the Canadian game's prized trophy—and ultimately the Canadian game itself.

TWO

Into the Arena

THE STREETS OUTSIDE ANTWERP'S PALAIS DE GLACE were crowded hours before game time. Men in top hats offered to carry the players' skates in order to gain entrance. Inside the rink, the house orchestra played while spectators made bets. Even before the game started, a lone fan stood on his seat and started yelling: "Canada, Canada, come on Canada!" Others in the crowd, from Britain and the United States, gasped "with astonishment." Apparently, they were not used to seeing exuberant Canadians.[1]

The crowd was there for the Olympic semifinal, between Canada and the United States. Hockey was making its debut at the 1920 Antwerp games—what we would call the Summer Olympics. Figure skating had been added to the program already at the 1908 games in London, on the initiative of Baron Pierre de Coubertin, founder of the Olympic movement. When preparations were under way in Antwerp, the owner of the Palais de Glace agreed to open his rink for figure skating only if hockey was added. As it was, maintaining the artificial ice would be costly. The skating competition was scheduled for April, four months ahead of the other events, so that cooler spring nights would keep the ice from melting. With the rink owner insisting on another revenue-generating event at his venue, and with the hockey-playing gentlemen of Europe lobbying for their sport, the International Olympic Committee (IOC) granted approval.

The inclusion of hockey in the Olympics was decisive for a number of reasons. First, it gave the Canadian version of the game leverage over bandy. In Nordic Europe, Russia, and pockets of Germany, hockey with a ball remained the more popular ice sport for decades, but it could not match the prestige that puck-hockey gained from the Olympics. Second, in becoming part of the Olympics, hockey had to adhere to the IOC's code of amateurism.

The semifinal in Antwerp showed that hockey had the potential to be a popular entertainment in Europe. Yet once people started buying tickets, commercialization and professionalism were steps away. As both a money-making entertainment and an Olympic event, with all the demands of amateurism, hockey would be a sport at war with itself.

The front line in this conflict was between the hockey-playing nations of Europe and Canada, already recognized as the sport's homeland. When the Canadians arrived in Antwerp, European teams watched their practices and then mimicked what they had seen. Following the Canadians' win over the Americans at the Palais de Glace, a Swedish journalist wrote that comparing North American hockey to European was like comparing "sparkling fresh champagne to stale cheap lager."[2] Although the US team kept it close, falling only 2–0, Canadian players were clearly the world's standard. The Americans had homegrown talent from Massachusetts and Minnesota, but their top scorer was Ontario-raised Herb Drury. Three other players on the American team were likewise imports, a fact that the Canadian press repeatedly mentioned.

Canada was a difficult fit within this emerging international sport. Toronto alone had more registered players than any European nation. At tournaments, Canadian amateur teams scored goals by the bushel. The two hockey cultures emerging before World War I became even more distinct during the interwar decades. In North America, professional hockey continued to grow, as the National Hockey League established franchises in major American cities and as its cultural influence extended across Canada. Meanwhile, European clubs and federations adhered to amateurism. Styles of play also varied, with corresponding differences in rules, rinks, and strategies.

There were, however, some common elements. Europeans welcomed visiting Canadian teams and sought instruction from Canadian players. In both North America and Europe, promoters seized upon the sport as a profitable winter attraction. Mass media pushed hockey as well. European newspaper reports were colored by the European emphasis on passing: the word *combination* appeared regularly in Austrian, Czech, German, and Swiss coverage. By contrast, American and Canadian writers highlighted power. Players were "sturdy," defenses "stalwart," and shots "pummeled" the goalie. The one thing that drew writers and fans in both places was speed. NHL skaters "raced" and "rushed." In Europe, the pace was "sharp" and "furious." In the 1927 Stanley Cup finals, Ottawa took down Boston in a "tornado attack." That same year, the Zurich newspaper *Sport* described German star Gustav Jaenecke as leading a "lightning" offense.[3] While these two sporting cultures had much to separate them during the interwar years, observers on both sides of the Atlantic agreed that hockey was the fastest game in the world.

A GAME FOR THE WORLD

When the Ligue Internationale de Hockey sur Glace met after the Olympic semifinal between Canada and the United States, European delegates welcomed the Americans and Canadians into the association and voted unanimously to adopt Canadian rules. Toronto sportswriter William A. Hewitt, known as Billy, spoke on behalf of the Canadian Amateur Hockey Association (CAHA) to welcome European interest in the game. Along with the American delegate, Hewitt proposed that the world championships "always be played in Europe, in order to promote the development of hockey."[4] Raoul Le Mat, representing Sweden, offered to hold the following year's tournament in Stockholm. The first meeting of North American and European hockey appeared to signal good things.

But forging unity in the sport would not be as easy as changing rules and scheduling tournaments. The planned championship in Stockholm was a bust. Raoul Le Mat had no authority to speak for Sweden; he wasn't even Swedish, but an American filmmaker working in Europe. A former hockey player and speed skater, Le Mat had been named coach because he knew the Canadian game. The Swedish team at Antwerp was something of an experiment, pushed by a few top officials in the soccer federation. The roster was made up of bandy players, along with a few who had experience playing puck-hockey in Germany and England. Even after the Olympics, bandy remained the ice game of Sweden. The following winter, only eleven hockey games took place in the country, all in Stockholm. One of these matches was the supposed world championship, a 7–4 win over Czechoslovakia. Canada and the United States did not send teams, however, and neither did any other country.[5]

Max Sellig, the new Swiss president of the LIHG, acknowledged that the postwar upheaval was not suitable for international hockey: "Economic and political complications persisting since the war have made things quite difficult."[6] In this unsettled environment, the sanctioned European championships of the 1920s were small affairs. A big problem was ice. Reliable skating seasons were already becoming a thing of the past. When Czechoslovakia hosted the 1925 tournament, organizers had to move games from Prague to a frozen lake in the Tatra Mountains of eastern Slovakia.[7] There were artificial rinks in Berlin, Munich, and Vienna. However, Germany and Austria were excluded from international sporting events over their presumed guilt for starting the war. Only in 1926 were the two countries reinstated to international competition.

Leaders of European hockey had discussed reinstating Austria and Germany earlier, but they were wary of crossing the IOC. The LIHG needed the status the Olympics provided. When the IOC began discussing a "winter sports week" to be held in 1924, officers of the LIHG enthusiastically took part in the planning, along with the international skiing and skating federations. The hockey federation offered to have its world championship decided as part of the Olympic program. LIHG delegates also accepted Olympic restrictions on amateurism, adopting the IOC's rules for its own tournaments. The Olympic definition of amateurism, affirmed by the LIHG, thus was woven into the fabric of European hockey. At the same time, the hockey federation's Olympic connections gave it an edge over bandy. In planning for winter sports week, one of the tasks assigned to the LIHG was determining bandy's status. Needless to say, proponents of hockey with a puck did not invite their cousins to the winter games.[8]

It soon became apparent that Olympic amateurism would be an obstacle to Canadian participation. Six years after the Antwerp games, the LIHG and the IOC looked into reports that the Winnipeg Falcons amateur club, which had represented Canada, had received a total of $2,500 from the provincial and city governments. Billy Hewitt, himself a firm defender of amateurism, assured the international bodies that there had been no hint of professionalism; the money simply covered the Falcons' expenses.[9] But suspicions about Olympic hockey's first champions foretold problems that international hockey would have with teams from Canada, where the pro game was to become dominant.

There were practical obstacles as well. The season for Canadian clubs typically lasted until March, whereas the LIHG tournament and the Olympics were scheduled in January or February. As shown with the NHL's decision to keep its players out of the 2018 Olympics, breaking a North American season for the sake of an international tournament remains a thorny problem. In the 1920s and '30s, travel to Europe meant a hiatus of a month or more. Canadian clubs that participated in the Olympics or in European tournaments had to recoup lost revenue at home. Consequently, Canada's representative team played exhibition games in various European cities for weeks in advance of the tournament. These barnstorming tours only stirred more suspicion about mercenary Canadians. European hockey leaders faced a dilemma: they wanted the world's best players to compete in their tournaments, but they also wanted hockey to have Olympic prestige, meaning it had to adhere to amateurism. For decades to come, world hockey would be unable to solve its Canada problem.

HOCKEY ON THE MAGIC MOUNTAIN

Banned from international competition, German and Austrian athletes had limited opportunities in the 1920s. In hockey, the one place where they could take the ice against skaters from other countries was Davos. Best known today for skiing as well as the annual economic forum that brings together heads of state and pop-star academics, Davos has been a hockey town since the sport's earliest days in Europe. In his novel *The Magic Mountain,* German author Thomas Mann made Davos the setting for an allegory of Europe's decline, with a cosmopolitan array of characters representing various schools of thought. After World War I, the "magic mountain" was the focal point of hockey's European development, with a similar mix of people and ideas stirring together in the brilliant Alpine winter.

European visitors began coming to the remote Davos plateau in the 1860s to seek treatment for tuberculosis. German physician Alexander Spengler was the first to experiment with treating patients in the high-altitude microclimate. He brought patients to Davos in 1866, when there was only one hotel among the farmhouses. The arrival of English patients—or, more accurately, the arrival of their family members, who searched for something to do—brought English sports culture to Davos. By the 1890s, British tourists were spending their winter holidays in the mountains, skating on natural rinks, riding bobsleds, and strapping on skis.[10] At this time, skiing was still a cross-country activity. Skiers trekked through the forests and foothills, using a long staff like a paddle to pull themselves along and as a balancing bar on descents. Arthur Conan Doyle became a proficient skier while his wife was being treated for tuberculosis. "The time will come," he predicted in 1894, "when hundreds of Englishmen will come to Switzerland for the 'ski'-ing season."[11]

British tourists came to Davos—as well as St. Moritz, Grindelwald, and other Alpine resorts—at a time when winters back home were becoming drearier. The Alps were an escape from England's winter fog, for those who could afford it. Then as now, Swiss resorts were a playground for the wealthy.

Skiing, skating, and tobogganing in the brisk Alpine air were billed as restorative for bankers and merchants: "the ideal spot for men beset with cares at home."[12] Sports were also social outlets. Alumni of English boarding schools started sports clubs in various Swiss towns. Unlike the schoolyard, however, winter games at the resorts generally brought women and men together. Illustrations from the time show women and men side-by-side on the skating rinks, bobsled runs, and skiing trails. In some mixed hockey matches, men were "handicapped" by wearing long skirts.[13]

Winter sports were also entertainment for guests at the resort hotels. Davos hosted international championships for both speed skating and figure skating. Swedish figure skater Ulrich Salchow defended his European title there in 1899, and Britain's Madge Syers won the first women's world championship at Davos in 1906. Hockey matches were a regular event. Both Davos and St. Moritz had large rinks suitable for bandy, and British hotel guests formed teams each winter (Arthur Conan Doyle took the ice for Davos).[14] Starting in the 1890s, these tourist teams hosted Dutch, German, and Czech clubs for weekend tournaments. The Oxford Canadians were invited regularly after the turn of the century. Their annual match with Cambridge was a high point of the winter social calendar, with alumni of both universities treating the students to banquets and dancing at the resort hotels.

After the war, hockey at Davos and other resorts was transformed. The British men and women who had once played now watched men from the Swiss towns. And the bandy ball was replaced by the puck. Davos dentist Paul Müller organized a puck-hockey club in late 1921, with a local physician playing goalie. But this was no beer-league diversion. As tourists returned to the hotels, Müller's club was slated to provide entertainment, and one of the teams on the schedule was the Oxford Canadians. When the Canadian students visited for the 1922 winter holidays, they put on a show, manhandling the dentist, the doctor, and their squad of locals, 22–0. Müller was not upset. "That was classic hockey!" he wrote decades later. "Davos was completely thrilled."[15]

Müller was an enthusiastic convert. He ordered equipment from Canada and kept contact with one of the Oxford players, who tutored him on strategy. Within five years, Hockey Club Davos had enough members for four senior teams and eight boys' teams. The club also had the financial strength to build a covered wooden grandstand with three hundred seats. Like today's franchises, HC Davos subsidized the project by selling two-year contracts for prime seats to hotel owners. The club also devised a means of making money that became common in European hockey long before it was adopted in North America: posting advertisements on the end boards.[16]

The partnership between the hockey club and Davos hoteliers brought other Anglo-Canadian and European teams to the mountain resort in the early 1920s. Most notably, Müller invited a team that had played frequently in Davos before the war: Berlin SC. The German team's visit in December 1922 went against the postwar ban instituted by the LIHG and IOC. Yet the perspective in Davos was much different. Close to Austria and Bavaria, Davos was a German-speaking community. Alexander Spengler himself had been an immigrant from Germany. During World War I, Germans and Austrians continued to visit the sanatoria, including soldiers suffering from trauma. Müller was eager to bring Berlin SC to Davos: "In my view, sport was especially needed to reestablish the international ties the war had torn apart."[17]

Alexander Spengler's son agreed. A physician like his father, Carl Spengler was well known for experimental treatments of tuberculosis and cancer at his Davos clinic. In 1923, he donated a cup for the cycle of matches Müller had scheduled for the upcoming January. The aim of the series was to bring together clubs from both sides of the conflict: along with HC Davos, the field included the Oxford Canadians and both Berlin SC and the Vienna Skating Club. The LIHG resisted this effort at hockey diplomacy. The organization's new Belgian president, Paul Loicq, refused to sanction the tournament. Officially, it was just a "friendly." Only in 1926, after Germany and Austria had been restored to international competition, did the hockey federation affirm the Spengler Cup as a legitimate competition.

From the start, the Spengler Cup was viewed in European hockey circles as more than a friendly. Austrian, German, and Swiss papers referred to the event as the Davos International Hockey Championship. When Berlin SC won the second tournament, German papers hailed the club as champions of Europe. Although it remained an invitational rather than a championship tournament, like the Stanley Cup playoffs or soccer's cup competitions, the Spengler Cup quickly became the most prestigious prize for European hockey clubs. German and Czech clubs regularly bested the field: Berlin SC won three times in the 1920s; LTC Prague lifted the cup four times in the 1930s.[18] English hotel guests cheered the Oxford Canadians each winter, while Cambridge also participated several times. Clubs from Milan and Paris competed, as did other Swiss teams, usually from Zurich.

A constant at the tournament was the host, HC Davos. After the first Spengler Cup, the Zurich newspaper *Sport* congratulated the club for organizing an event "on a neutral ground where former enemies can again have friendly contact." At the same time, the Zurich writer acknowledged, the international tournament allowed Davos "to improve its form against strong opponents."[19] Indeed, the Spengler Cup gave the Davos hockey team a yearly test against Europe's best clubs as well as visiting Canadians. The club steadily developed as one of the strongest in Switzerland. A key step was the hiring of a Canadian player-coach, Bobby Bell of Montreal. According to Paul Müller, Bell "made outstanding individual players" during his two seasons in Davos.[20] Building upon this Canadian instruction, international competition, and Müller's own emphasis on physical training, HC Davos was among Europe's top clubs by the 1930s. It helped that the team boasted a top line of talented local players: Bibi Torriani and brothers Ferdinand and Hans Cattini. Known as the *ni-Sturm* (because of the common ending of their last names), the trio were among Europe's first generation of hockey stars. Even among visiting patients at the sanatoria, they were celebrities.

Patients still came to Davos at the height of the Depression, as did wealthy tourists. By that time, they were using a recent invention, the t-bar, to ascend the mountains with their skis. At the center of town, however, the main attraction was still hockey. In the photography shops, alongside black-and-white postcards of snow-covered mountains, one could find photos of hockey players, skating under the brilliant Alpine sunlight.

Davos was an environment unlike any other. The same features Thomas Mann had observed—the wealth, the refined winter atmosphere, the stirring of people from many nations—all combined to make the mountain resort a hothouse of European hockey. The innovations of HC Davos and the international competition of the Spengler Cup had lasting influence on the sport, even beyond the interwar decades. During the 1920s and '30s, Davos was the pinnacle—a place where the rich and famous watched this new sport, giving their stamp of approval. The spectators were well heeled, but they did not lack in fervor. "In Davos," one Oxford Canadian wrote, "the people are real hockey fans."[21]

A GAME FOR THE NATION

When the Canadians played, there was no contest. At the 1920 Olympics, they surrendered one goal. Reportedly, the Swedish players thanked the Canadians for allowing them to score. Four years later, at the first Winter

Olympics, the Canadians outscored their opponents 132–3. The only people to score against them were Herb Drury of the United States and Colin Carruthers of Great Britain, who had both lived most of their lives in Canada. In 1928 at St. Moritz, officials allowed the Canadians to advance past the group stage. They tallied 38 goals in three medal-round games.

Canada's success in international hockey was a source of national pride, at a time when nationalism was surging. The war had brought spirited expressions of patriotism among English Canadians. Soldiers from Canada proved their mettle at Vimy Ridge and other battlefields of the Western Front, confirming the turn-of-the-century idea of the dominion as the integral part of the British Empire. Following the war, Prime Minister Robert Borden signed the treaties of the Paris Peace Conference, and the dominion gained a seat at the League of Nations. Although still part of the empire, Canada emerged from the war as a nation standing on its own in the world.[22]

But what exactly *was* this nation now represented at diplomatic conferences? Along with stoking Canadian pride, the war in Europe also opened deep clefts in society. The initial volunteers had been men largely of British background. French Canadians were less enthusiastic about the war. When Parliament passed a conscription bill in 1917, demonstrators rioted in Quebec City, and the provincial legislature debated secession. Meanwhile, hostility rose against recent immigrants, particularly those from Germany and Austria. After the armistice, social and economic unrest fueled strikes and demonstrations across the country, most notably in Winnipeg, where a three-week general strike brought the city to a standstill in 1919.

In the years following the war, the mythic vision of the Great War as a glorious moment was challenged by those who saw the conflict as a senseless waste. The disparate views of the war reflected the disparate views of the country. Was Canada still an integral part of the empire, or distinctly North American? Was it British, or a land of different peoples, faiths, and cultures? "Politically, the country is scarcely out of the colonial stage," wrote historian Gustave Lanctôt, a former player with the Oxford Canadians, "and a great number of its people have not yet acquired that national faith—of biblical mention—capable of moving mountains."[23]

Lanctôt recognized that a national faith was shaped by far more than political institutions. One thing that could lift Canadians out of their narrow allegiances was hockey. Victories at the Olympics or world championships were trumpeted in newspapers across the dominion. On their return, conquering teams were hailed from Halifax to Montreal, Toronto, and beyond. These victory celebrations were expressions of national, provincial, and local loyalties. Rather than selecting players from across the country for a national team, the CAHA sent the community club that had won the Allan Cup, Canada's amateur championship. In 1920 that team was the Winnipeg Falcons, the club formed by Icelandic immigrants at the turn of the century. Members of the Falcons had volunteered together for the army during the war. Yet even after serving overseas, they were still derided as "Goolies" and barred from the Winnipeg city league.[24] The reception was different when they returned as Olympic champions. Winnipeg's civic and business leaders pulled out all the stops to welcome the Falcons home from Antwerp. The sons of immigrants who had been snubbed for years were now heroes. The city that had been paralyzed by a massive strike a year earlier came together in celebration. All because of hockey.

Canadian wins in international tournaments confirmed hockey's standing as the national game. "It was in this country that the sport was born," declared the CAHA's annual report in 1924, "and it is here that the leading players have been, and will continue to be developed."[25] Writers had described hockey as Canada's winter game already before 1914, but social and economic changes after the war—a reduction of hours in the work week, rising wages, expansion of public education—increased participation and fan support. Amateur leagues were common in cities across the country in the 1920s, supported by municipal governments, local businesses, schools, and churches. For example, Peterborough, Ontario, had 115 amateur teams in various sports for adults and young people in 1929; over half of these teams played hockey. Conversely, the other claimant to the title of national sport, lacrosse, was being displaced by baseball and soccer. In 1925 there were amateur leagues for hockey, baseball, and soccer in Victoria, Regina, Quebec City, and Halifax. Only Victoria had a lacrosse league.[26]

Canadian proponents of hockey wrote of the sport's benefits in the modern age. The echoes of Muscular Christianity still sounded. Hockey instilled all the virtues of team sports: cooperation, obedience, loyalty. The sport's moral benefits were not only good for the Canadian nation; they were also key to individual success. "The game provides wholesome mental activity when played under proper conditions," wrote James Sutherland, purportedly one of hockey's founding fathers, "developing the individual's initiative, ambition, imagination, enthusiasm and self-confidence—all qualities that are essential to success in a business or profession."[27]

While hockey was touted as a school for preparing young Canadian men for "the stern responsibilities of business," the game also gained popularity among young women after the war. In the Maritimes, telephone companies organized teams for switchboard operators. The Ontario and Toronto amateur associations formed women's leagues. In Calgary, female employees of Imperial Oil and Canadian General Electric competed against church and school teams. Women's hockey was also popular with spectators from East to West. A crowd of more than twelve thousand watched a 1929 contest at the Montreal Forum between the champions of the Ontario and Quebec leagues. Each winter, the winners of the women's tournament at the Banff Winter Festival went on a tour of Alberta and British Columbia, drawing thousands. Lester Patrick, creator of the Pacific Coast Hockey Association, also got into the business of women's hockey. His team, the Vancouver Amazons, barnstormed throughout the Pacific Northwest during the 1920s.[28]

The surge in women's hockey came amid changes in gender roles brought by the war. When hundreds of thousands of soldiers left Canada for Europe, women took occupations formerly held by men. Although returning soldiers reclaimed most of these positions, young women continued moving to cities in the 1920s, prompting employers, universities, churches, and municipalities to organize activities for them. Across Canada, women joined clubs for basketball, softball, track, and hockey. The changing social and economic roles were reflected in the fashion of the times: corsets and petticoats gave way to rising hems and bobbed hair. On the hockey rink, women rid themselves of the ankle-length skirts they had worn before the war. By the mid-1920s, their uniforms were the same as the men's.

"We can no longer ask that old question, 'Are women interested in sport?'" wrote *Maclean's* sportswriter Henry Roxborough in 1929. "Undeniably, Miss Canada not only reads about athletic heroes and 'spectates' at important games, but definitely indulges in physical combat with a buoyant enthusiasm that is rarely surpassed by her national brother."[29] Roxborough was not alone among Canadian sportswriters in bringing positive attention to women's sports. Some male newspaper writers described women's hockey as *hockey*, recounting the action and evaluating passing, goaltending, and checking—part of the women's game in the 1920s. Nevertheless, even these reports included remarks on the players' "fairness." There were also newspaper accounts that sneered at the very idea of women on ice. For example, a cartoon from a 1925 edition of the *Toronto Evening Telegram* showed two players standing at center ice, wearing the fashions of the day. "Doris, is my nose shiny?" one asks. "Why, no dear," her teammate replies as the puck slides by, unnoticed. "You're stunning."[30]

Despite the slights to women players, Canadian hockey was different from other national games of the time. The masters of English soccer and American baseball explicitly banned women from their games. The Football Association forbade clubs from allowing women's games on their grounds in 1921. When seventeen-year-old Jackie Mitchell struck out Babe Ruth and Lou Gehrig in an exhibition game, baseball commissioner Kenesaw Mountain Landis voided her minor-league contract. By contrast, the male leaders of Canadian hockey associations didn't quite know what to do with women's hockey at first. Delegates to the CAHA's 1923 meeting voted down a resolution recognizing women in the sport. Yet two years later, Billy Hewitt, representing the CAHA, toasted the champions of the Ontario women's league at their postseason banquet.[31] By the decade's end, after women's hockey had grown in popularity, members of the Bruins and Canadiens were among the thousands at the Montreal Forum watching the women's champions of Ontario and Quebec. At a time when Canadian identity was forming, women in sports was further evidence of a strong, modern nation. Women's sports, wrote Roxborough, were helpful in "providing recreation for competitor and spectator in nearly every Canadian municipality; in emphasizing the freedom of women, and in advertising the Dominion."[32]

THE AMERICANIZATION OF HOCKEY

The New York Americans, the NHL's newest franchise, played their first game, against the Montreal Canadiens, on December 15, 1925, at the brand-new Madison Square Garden. The mayor was in attendance, along with the cream of New York society. Papers had been trumpeting pro hockey's arrival for weeks, but the sport's debut was lackluster. The Amerks, as they were soon called, fell 3–1 to the Canadiens, and the game's pace was noticeably sluggish. The Garden's "manufactured weather," as it was billed, was turned up too high. Players lost up to ten pounds per game because of the heat, and Amerks coach Tommy Gorman even sued rink managers to turn down the thermostat. But warm temperatures made for comfortable spectators. It was preferable to have the fashionable women of Manhattan watch the trendy new sport in their evening dresses "without even a wrap over their shoulders."[33]

New York's entry into professional hockey changed everything.[34] It wasn't the New York glitz, or publicity, or money, although there was plenty of that. It wasn't that the Americans were the first American team in the NHL—the

Boston Bruins had entered the league the year before. What made the Amerks' entry so significant was their arena. Boxing promoter Tex Rickard, the man behind Jack Dempsey's championship fights, had built the $4.75 million facility to replace the older Madison Square Garden (in declining condition, across town at Madison Square). Rickard saw pro hockey as a potential attraction to fill dates in his new building when there wasn't boxing, wrestling, or the circus. Although he did not own the team (the co-owners were Montreal promoter Tom Duggan and New York bootlegger Big Bill Dwyer), Rickard was its public face. He devised all manner of gimmicks to draw crowds, from having celebrities like Babe Ruth drop the puck to painting the brownish ice a brilliant white. In the first season, the promoter was so impressed with turnout that he decided to buy his own hockey franchise. His new team, dubbed Tex's Rangers, joined the NHL the following year and filled the remaining dates at the Garden.

Madison Square Garden embodied the modern arena, setting the template for iconic buildings that would be home to NHL teams for decades to come: Maple Leaf Gardens, Boston Garden, Chicago Stadium, the Detroit Olympia. Situated amid downtown department stores and transit lines, these arenas became civic landmarks: places for trade shows, entertainment events, and political rallies. "Hockey arenas served so many functions," writes architectural historian Howard Shubert, "that it might be more accurate to describe them as flexible containers for undefined mass spectacle."[35] They were also designed to better accommodate spectators, offering comforts that earlier rinks did not have—more washrooms, more concessions, and a heated environment. Owners of the new arenas aimed particularly for female spectators. Maple Leafs owner Conn Smythe, when planning a new arena for the team, insisted that it be a "place where people can go in evening clothes." Everything would be new and clean, he declared, in "a place that people can be proud to take their wives or girl friends to."[36]

For NHL owners, the new arenas' most important attribute was their size. With seats for nearly 15,500 people, Madison Square Garden was almost twice as large as the league's next biggest arena. In their first seasons, gate receipts for the two New York teams far surpassed those of other NHL franchises. For example, the Pittsburgh Pirates pulled in just under $55,000 for the 1926–27 season, playing in the five-thousand-seat Duquesne Gardens. By contrast, the Rangers' take was over $300,000. Other owners knew which model to follow. Between 1926 and 1931, teams in Montreal, Detroit, Boston, Chicago, and Toronto moved into larger new arenas and saw their revenues jump. In the Bruins' first season at Boston Garden, the team sold close to a half-million dollars' worth of tickets. The Black Hawks' gate receipts nearly tripled when they moved to Chicago Stadium. Meanwhile, the Pirates folded in 1928.[37]

Pittsburgh was not alone in being shut out as the NHL moved into larger, more lucrative digs. The Hamilton Tigers had been in the league since 1920, and in 1924–25 they finished atop the standings. But when the Tigers went on strike for more money before the playoffs, NHL president Frank Calder suspended the players. Hamilton fans lost the chance to watch their team play for the Stanley Cup. Soon after, they lost their team. With an arena that held only thirty-eight hundred spectators, the Tigers' owners were looking to sell. "The game was getting too big for Hamilton to handle," one later admitted.[38] Yet rather than selling the franchise, the owners sold the players. When the New York Americans first took the ice at Madison Square Garden, it was the same team that had skated in Hamilton nine months earlier. Big Bill Dwyer paid $75,000 for the entire Tigers roster. To prevent any more labor unrest, he doubled the players' salaries.

Hamilton fans saw the loss of their team as a blow to Canada's sport. "Our own Canadian national game has been, in a degree, prostituted for the monetary consideration of $75,000," wrote one to the Hamilton *Spectator*.[39] It would have been little consolation to know that the same process was happening in the United States, in another new pro sports league. In the first seasons after its founding in 1920, the National Football League had featured teams in smaller midwestern cities like Canton, Rock Island, and Racine. By the end of the 1920s these teams were history. Like the Tigers, the Saskatoon Sheiks, and the Regina Capitals of professional hockey, these early NFL franchises could not generate enough ticket sales to keep pace with Chicago and New York. In American pro football as in Canadian pro hockey, the business model of the commercial franchise operating in a closed league brought the concentration of teams in the largest markets.[40] Only the Green Bay Packers remained—a community-owned, small-market anomaly on the landscape of North American sports.

There would be no Packers in pro hockey. At the start of the 1920s, the three top-level pro leagues had teams in cities roughly the size of Green Bay— Hamilton with a population just over one hundred thousand, Saskatoon and Regina with fewer than fifty thousand. Of the eleven franchises in these leagues, only one—the Seattle Metropolitans of the Pacific Coast Hockey Association—was in the United States. In 1925 the Metropolitans folded, along with the entire PCHA. Frank and Lester Patrick merged their remaining teams, in Vancouver and Victoria, with the prairie clubs of the Western Canada Hockey League. But this league could not survive, either. Given "the desire of American financiers to get in on the ground floor," as Lester Patrick told a reporter, the NHL was an irresistible force.[41] The following season, he and other western owners sold their players to NHL franchises. For $100,000, Tex Rickard acquired Lester Patrick's services as coach of the Rangers, along with the entire roster of his team, the Victoria Cougars, winners of the 1925 Stanley Cup.

The 1926 season opened with the NHL as the only remaining association for major-league hockey. The league expanded to ten teams, but just four were in Canada: Toronto, Ottawa, and the Canadiens and Maroons in Montreal. The betrayal that Hamilton fans felt became a national concern. "Can the backers of professional hockey in Canada hold their own against the moneybags of rich United States promoters," asked *Maclean's* magazine, "or will Canadian hockey fans be forced year by year to see their stars disappear to shine in another firmament?"[42] The latter would prove to be the case.

Other Canadians saw a greater threat than American money. Hockey was being transformed to appeal to American audiences, they charged. Between 1925 and 1930, the league made a series of rule changes designed to generate more scoring. Most notably, the prohibition against forward passing, a legacy of the sport's roots in rugby, was rolled back. The new passing rules brought a doubling of goals in the NHL. For some, however, these changes degraded the game. A writer for *The Canadian Magazine* charged that the league's offensive turn had been done at Tex Rickard's insistence. Hockey had become a "spectacle," the journalist wrote. "Major hockey is no longer a sport, but an industry. In other words, it has been Americanized."[43]

Americanization was not limited to hockey. Canadian rugby teams imported American college football players, who brought along the forward pass. The athlete who was featured most often in Canadian sports pages was Babe Ruth.[44] In sports, radio, and movies, American popular culture dominated Canada. Meanwhile, Canada became a supplier of raw materials for the American economy. In the 1920s, output of Canadian newsprint more than doubled and metal production increased fourfold—much of it bound for the United States. It was likewise the case in entertainment. Whether a hockey player like Eddie Shore, an actor like Mary Pickford, or an artist like Joe Shuster, cocreator of Superman, talented young Canadians were well rewarded south of the border. Of course, the primary market for their products was the United States. Hollywood turned the Toronto-raised Pickford into "America's sweetheart," not Canada's.

During the interwar years, Canadian commentators lamented the Americanization of their economy, their culture, and their sports. Historians of hockey have looked to this period and asked: Was there a point when the national game could have been preserved? Could leaders of the NHL have made decisions to maintain community-based teams in a Canada-based league? Yet few of the NHL's Canadian owners were moved to protect the sport as a Canadian institution. In 1923, when Tom Duggan offered to buy two new franchises and place them in American cities, Frank Calder and the league's owners did not debate how the move would affect hockey in Canada. They were businessmen, challenged by two rival leagues. If they didn't bring pro hockey to America, someone else would.

NHL leaders applied the same logic a few years later, when the league's most storied team, the Ottawa Senators, was struggling to survive. One of the few figures to insist on keeping teams in Canada was Tex Rickard. Likewise, Black Hawks owner Frederic McLaughlin urged the creation of a revenue-sharing system to support the Senators. But Frank Calder would not have it. He dismissed the Senators' appeals for financial help in the same way an American millionaire dismissed welfare: clubs in similar straits, he argued, "might sit back and lose all initiative, knowing that it would be taken care of anyhow."[45] In 1934, the Senators left Ottawa for St. Louis. The following year, the franchise folded.

A decade earlier, when the Hamilton Tigers were up for sale, the *Spectator*'s sports editor made a canny prediction: "It will only be a matter of time until the largest cities will have the best teams, for with the greatest populations to draw from and great seating capacity of their arenas, they will be in a good position to pay top prices for players."[46] By 1935, this was precisely what happened: the NHL stood alone as the only major pro hockey league, with its franchises concentrated in big cities with big arenas. Canadian critics at the time decried the influence of American money in the game. But the difference was not money. It was markets. Surveys of Major League Baseball during this time showed that a team's place in attendance rankings nearly always matched its home city's national ranking in overall retail sales. The larger the urban market, the more fans at games. This did not bode well for Canadian cities. After the demise of the Senators, the only Canadian cities with NHL franchises were Toronto and Montreal, the only two cities in the country with more than a half-million people. It would be another forty-five years before the NHL returned to a smaller Canadian city.[47]

MAKING A EUROPEAN GAME

The setting for European hockey in the 1920s was much different than the steel-and-brick arenas of North American cities. Hockey games at the first Winter Olympics in Chamonix drew a few hundred spectators who sat on makeshift bleachers. Photographs of the 1925 European championship in Slovakia's Tatra Mountains show about fifty hardy souls standing in snowbanks around a frozen lake.[48] That was the same year Madison Square Garden opened.

In the 1920s, the closest thing Europe had to a North American arena was the Berlin Sportpalast. Opened in 1910 with capacity for over ten thousand spectators, the Sportpalast hosted all kinds of entertainment events—track meets, ice shows, film screenings, concerts, boxing matches.[49] Six-day bicycle races were a highlight on the Sportpalast calendar. Imported at the turn of the century from the United States, where they were popular at the original Madison Square Garden, six-day bicycle races at the Sportpalast were more than a sporting event. As cyclists pedaled around the velodrome, competing to see which two-man team could amass the most kilometers in 144 hours, Berliners of all backgrounds ate, drank, danced, smoked, and sang through the day and night. While the upper sets cavorted in boxes near the track, workers and students filled the cheap seats in the third balcony.[50]

There was also hockey in the Sportpalast. The annual tournament of Berlin clubs, known as the *Eishockey-Bezirk,* was held at the arena before the war. In the interwar years, the Sportpalast was the site of the German club championships and friendlies between the national squad and visiting teams. Gustav Jaenecke, leading scorer for the national team, was a star attraction at the arena. His club, Berlin SC, regularly hosted teams from Vienna, Prague, Paris, and Davos, with five to six thousand spectators in attendance.[51] By 1929, the press had dubbed hockey "the most popular sport in Berlin." Jaenecke himself recognized the game's attraction in the dynamic environment of 1920s Europe: "There is one thing that makes ice hockey better suited for us, for all modern young people, than any other sport—that makes it necessary for us. Speed!"[52]

Although the Sportpalast was an iconic center of Berlin's cultural life, the hall's finances were in constant turmoil. At the end of the decade the arena was on the verge of bankruptcy, and rumors circulated that it would be converted to a parking garage.[53] Other European sports halls were also unable to make a profit. The indoor rink at Berlin's Admiralspalast had been converted to a cinema after the war. In Paris, the ice was melting at the Palais de Glace

A game at the ice stadium in Davos, 1928. Note the square corners and the absence of boards along rinkside (photo by E. Meerkämper, courtesy of E. Meerkämper/ Dokumentationsbibliothek Davos).

on the Champs-Elysées. "Since winters are now much rainier, skating is relegated to the mountain resorts," noted *Le Miroir des Sports*. Meanwhile, the rink where Canadian hockey had first sparked excitement at the 1920 Olympics, Antwerp's Palais de Glace, was lost to fire in 1928.

In Central Europe, hockey drew consistent crowds during the 1920s. Matches in Vienna drew up to two thousand spectators to the massive rink near the Stadtpark in the city center.[54] Up to six thousand fans in Prague watched contests between local clubs and visitors from Berlin or Vienna. Of course, attendance at these matches—and the match itself—depended on the weather. Although not as warm as Paris, Central Europe experienced greater variation in winter temperatures than during the 1890s. By the late 1920s, Prague clubs were going to the mountains for training and often contended with choppy ice during the season.

Not only did fewer people attend European games, but the rinks looked different as well. Many hockey rinks on the continent were rectangles separated from a larger ice surface by a simple boundary. The rink at Davos was surrounded by a marker only a few inches high, with spectators standing on the other side. The Vienna Skating Club likewise marked out a section of its rink with a low boundary. Most rinks had boards behind the goals, but few were completely encircled. When Prague opened its new outdoor stadium in 1931, boards surrounded the entire rink. However, the barrier consisted of thick wooden slabs that fell over like dominos when players collided with them.

Without side boards and fencing behind the goals, European hockey of the interwar years was played largely down the center of the ice. Film from the period shows teams moving the puck down the rink with individual rushes or forward passes.[55] Even as full boards became common in the 1930s, European rinks retained their larger, rectangular shape. Corners were squared or only slightly rounded. The addition of side boards broadened the space, allowing for rushes up the sides and passing across the rink. Newsreel footage of the 1947 world championships shows the Czechoslovak team using the rink like a soccer pitch.[56] A wing might bring the puck across the blue line and then, rather than breaking for the net, stop to pass into the center or cut laterally through the slot, putting a forehand or backhand shot on goal.

At the same time, from the 1930s to the '40s, playing style also changed in North America.[57] The NHL's rule changes of the late 1920s were intended to generate goals by allowing for more passing. But the puck still had to be carried across the blue line, and this is where teams set their defense. Packed four or five across the rink, defenders turned the blue line into a fortified border. The lead attacker carried the puck through the neutral zone and was sent sprawling at the blue line. The defensive team then gathered the puck and began its own run, while the opposing forwards turned back to join the wall at their blue line—back and forth, like armies making futile charges at each other's trenches. There was an occasional breakthrough, a thrilling dash through the gauntlet. But as Ken Dryden lamented, "Few wondered what other possible changes were missed. This was the turning point. The limits of the forward pass were never explored. The limits to our game were set."[58]

An offensive breakthrough came not with passing but with power. Film of NHL games from the 1930s shows that players were already discovering a way to get past the line of defenders: a forward would cross the opponent's blue line and then flip the puck into the corner or take a long shot on goal. Rules at the time prevented the goalie from freezing the puck, so shots were swept to the corners. Forwards then pressed to win the loose puck. Coaches and players found forechecking to be a reliable offensive tactic, while the best way to get the puck into the opponent's end was simply to send it from the neutral zone. Unimaginative but effective, dump-and-chase became the defining feature of the North American game by the 1940s.

According to Dryden, Canadian hockey strategy reached a dead end at this time. "Without external competition, without incentive, there was no chance that this would change," he states in *The Game*. "So, locked in our rooms with nothing but our navels to look at, we saw nothing, and missed our chance."[59] However, it was not simply a lack of imagination or curiosity that led Canadian hockey to dump-and-chase. It was also the space in which they played. The new arenas of the 1920s followed the plan of the first building to be called an "arena": the Westmount Arena in Montreal, opened in 1898 as the first structure designed specifically for hockey games. The Latin name was apt—the building's interior resembled a Roman circus, with rounded corners. The rink was then designed to fit within this indoor stadium. Whereas earlier Canadian hockey rinks had the same rectangular shape as in Europe, arenas that followed the Westmount had curved ends.

Just as rectangular rinks influenced the style of play in Europe, so did curved rinks shape strategy in North America. Dump-and-chase became an essential part of the Canadian game because it was ideally suited for rinks with rounded ends. A puck fired into a rounded corner caroms behind the net, allowing forwards time to advance into the zone and challenge the defense for possession. More importantly, rounded corners allow room for players to maneuver. In soccer, an attacker steered into a squared corner has few options. But in hockey—North American hockey—playing out of the corner is an essential skill.

In the postwar decades, European rinks began to expand the curve of their corners, although they retained their broader, rectangular size. In watching footage of European teams from the 1930s to the '70s, one rarely sees players sending the puck into their opponent's corner and battling for control. For European coaches, dumping the puck meant giving it up. In soccer-playing countries, the idea was ridiculous—cross into the offensive zone and then give the ball away?[60] But in rugby, attacking kicks are a regular part of the game: one side punts the ball away and then crashes into their opponents to win possession. NHL arenas were well suited for this strategy. Above all, they were ideal for spectators. Like other features of the North American game, the very shape of the playing area was decided by arena owners. Curved corners allowed for continuous grandstands surrounding the ice. There were more seats, with better sight lines. Indeed, as many fans will attest, the best rinkside seats are in the corners.

ON THE RADIO

Listeners often asked the BBC's first hockey announcer, Bob Bowman, how he was able to keep up with the action. Bowman insisted that broadcasting hockey was not any more difficult than tennis or rugby.[61] It probably helped that he was Canadian. When the network's programming director decided to begin hockey broadcasts in 1935, Bowman was tapped largely because of his country of origin. "Bowman, you're a Canadian," the boss said to the young editor, "and I suppose you understand hockey?"

Bowman was worried that English listeners would have trouble following the unfamiliar game (and would bristle at his Canadian accent). But BBC broadcasts of the sport were surprisingly popular. After Bowman's first game on the air, seats at Wembley Arena sold out for the rest of the season. Listeners in East Asia wrote to ask for more matches on the Empire Service. Ironically, Bowman's best-known hockey broadcast was one the BBC pulled the plug on. Britain and the United States were in the second overtime of their medal-round game at the 1936 Winter Olympics when listeners heard Bowman's voice fade out. Yes, the gold medal may have been on the line, but the news was late. The broadcast had already run forty-five minutes over. To the surprise of Bowman and the BBC, people were furious. Hundreds of calls and telegrams came to Broadcasting House. Bob Bowman's career took off. The BBC meanwhile learned a fundamental lesson of broadcasting: beware cutting away from live sports to the regularly scheduled programming.

Hockey had already been on the radio on the continent since the early 1930s. Short reports were aired on Berlin and Frankfurt stations, while Finnish radio broadcast entire bandy matches with Sweden. In Czechoslovakia, the voice of hockey belonged to Josef Laufer, whose early athletic interests led to work as a sportswriter and radio announcer. Laufer had made the call for the first sporting event to be broadcast live in Europe: a 1926 soccer match between Slavia Prague and the Budapest club Hungaria. For all his love of hockey, he was wary of announcing the game on the radio. "Hockey moves at a much faster speed that any other sport," he wrote in his memoirs, "and it's not easy to capture all that happens in a match."[62]

A practical concern with early sports broadcasts was relaying the signal. In the first rounds of the 1931 world championships in Krynica, Poland, a small spa town in the Tatra Mountains, Laufer sent reports from a telephone booth at the rink. Things improved somewhat for the final round when organizers installed a broadcast box with microphone. But the box was sandwiched between the noise of the ticket booth and the clatter of the concession stand.[63] Managers of the new outdoor arena in Prague spared Laufer such indignities. At its opening that same winter, the Štvanice Winter Stadium had a booth for radio broadcasts. Unlike Foster Hewitt's famous gondola at Maple Leaf Gardens, suspended five stories above the rink at center ice, Laufer's vantage point was behind one of the goals. Close to the ice, Laufer recalled, the microphone captured "every sound, big and small" of the game: "the cutting of skates into the ice, the clashing of sticks, the boom of the puck into the boards, and the particular mood of the fans."[64]

In Canada as in Europe, the first radio broadcasts of hockey were rough experiments. Foster Hewitt also used a telephone to call his first game in 1923, from a stool inside a glass cube, next to the penalty box. As the glass fogged up, he could barely make out the players' numbers. An announcer for Toronto's first radio station, Hewitt initially wanted nothing to do with sports; he did not want to be known as the son of Billy Hewitt. But the day after his first hockey broadcast, letters began arriving to the station. Foster Hewitt was a hit. More games followed (with ventilation holes drilled into his glass box). By the early 1930s, Hewitt's voice was well known in Toronto and across Canada on the emerging national network.[65]

At that time, Hewitt entered the partnership that would make him one of the most famous Canadians of the century. In 1931, he began regular Saturday-night broadcasts from Maple Leaf Gardens. Conn Smythe was unusual at the time in recognizing the advantages of collaborating with radio. He sold rights for Leafs games to the Toronto-based MacLaren Advertising Company. MacLaren in turn found a sponsor, General Motors of Canada, to underwrite the production and distribution costs, in exchange for Hewitt promoting its automobiles during the game. After two successful seasons, the Saturday-night games from Maple Leaf Gardens went national. The Canadian Radio Broadcasting Commission, forerunner to the CBC, agreed to open ninety minutes of its schedule every Saturday night (9:00–10:30 Toronto time) to the hockey broadcasts. The following year, MacLaren and General Motors added French-language broadcasts of the Canadiens and English broadcasts of the Montreal Maroons. Listeners in Quebec heard the games of the two Montreal teams while the rest of the country received Hewitt's weekly greeting from Toronto: "Hello, Canada—and hockey fans in the United States and Newfoundland." Beginning in the 1930s, NHL hockey broadcasts became a staple of Saturday nights. As hockey scholars Richard Gruneau and David Whitson observe, "Never had so many

Canadians in all corners of the country regularly engaged in the same cultural experience at the same time."[66]

From the start, however, dominion-wide hockey broadcasts had their limits as a cultural institution. Without question, Saturday-night hockey was popular. As the percentage of Canadian households owning radio sets grew from 40 percent in 1930 to 90 percent in 1939, hockey's audience grew to an estimated two million listeners.[67] This popularity posed a problem. Getting a hockey game—or any other program—from one end of Canada to the other required sending the live transmission through telegraph lines. It was an additional expense to transmit the signal off the main line, to places like Prince Edward Island or the mountains of British Columbia. After the first season, General Motors decided it was no longer willing to pay for signals to remote communities. The radio commission likewise refused to pick up the costs, since hockey was a commercially sponsored program. Yet people in those communities wanted hockey.[68] Listeners appealed to local station managers, who in turn appealed to MacLaren, General Motors, and the broadcasting commission. A station manager in Trail, British Columbia, suggested that the commission "give the use of the lines."[69] But the three principals held firm. Nobody was willing to pay for Trail to get their hockey.

Throughout the history of the Saturday-night hockey program, first on radio and then, after 1952, on television, the partnership of producer, sponsors, and public broadcasting network had its tensions. General Motors dropped out after four seasons, unable to get increased car sales out of its advertising.[70] Imperial Oil took over as sponsor in 1936. To ensure the investment would be money well spent, the company's marketing department tutored gas-station managers on how to get "Canada's No. 1 radio programme to assist them in their selling efforts."[71] Foster Hewitt also chipped in. At the end of each game, he chose three stars as a promotional tie-in with Imperial's Three Star gasoline. Meanwhile, MacLaren continued to press broadcasting administrators to limit transmission costs, arguing the hockey program had become "very much of a national institution in Canada."[72]

Indeed, Saturday-night NHL hockey did become an institution. But Canadians also wanted other entertainment. When MacLaren asked the CBC to provide airtime for midweek playoff games or later appealed for the Saturday-night broadcast to start earlier than 9:00, network officials responded that not every Canadian wanted to listen to hockey. As a public broadcasting network, the CBC had to think of the whole listening public. Certainly, the hockey audience was engaged, demanding even. Sponsors of midweek radio programs surrendered their scheduled time during the playoffs, knowing that, in the words of an Imperial Oil newsletter, "they stood to lose a great deal of goodwill if they kept the hockey broadcast off the air." But hockey's audience was not as large as producers claimed. When the market research company Elliot-Hayes began compiling ratings in 1940, NHL hockey consistently placed among the top ten programs, but it wasn't close to number one. According to 1941 ratings surveys, just over a quarter of Canadian radios played hockey on Saturday nights while nearly 40 percent of all radios were tuned to American comedian Jack Benny on Sundays. Hockey was not even the most popular Canadian-produced program. That honor belonged to the quiz show *Treasure Trail*.[73]

The ratings remind us that sports are not as big as we often think. Economists point out that the cardboard box industry generates more revenue than professional sports. Yet there are no television networks dedicated to boxes, nor do cardboard factories occupy prime real estate in city centers. Likewise, not many Canadians look back nostalgically to evenings spent listening to *Treasure Trail*. Imperial Oil's savvy promotion of their broadcasts, the NHL's rise as the sport's premier circuit, and an emerging notion of hockey as the national game all combined to turn Saturday night in Canada into hockey night.

HAVE STICK, WILL TRAVEL

The Winnipeg Monarchs arrived in Europe in December 1934, seven weeks before they were to defend Canada's title at the world championships in Davos. They opened their exhibition tour with games in London. The *Times* described a 6–2 win over the Richmond Hawks as a "wonderful exhibition."[74] The Monarchs' third game in London drew eight thousand spectators to the new Wembley Arena. The Winnipeg players then set off across the continent. During their three months in Europe, the Monarchs visited ten different countries and played before close to a hundred thousand spectators. Like the Oxford teams of previous decades, they were welcomed as celebrities. "Everywhere we stay at the best hotels," wrote Monarchs goalie Arthur Rice-Jones to his parents. After games, there were autographs to sign at rinkside, followed by banquets and toasts with the host club, and drinks and dancing with young women of status. Rice-Jones was especially taken with Prague. "But holy smokes you can't read or talk to any lady," he wrote home, "their language is terrible."[75]

Even more impressive was Berlin. At their welcome, the Winnipeg players received gifts from Hitler, bestowed by one of the Führer's aides. In turn, the young Canadians were caught up by the enthusiasm of early Nazi Germany. The twenty-two-year-old Arthur Rice-Jones judged that the Nazis had made great strides in their first year in power. Germany's economic situation, he remarked to his parents, was even better than Canada's. A decade later, Rice-Jones would be wounded in combat against the Germans, but in 1934 the trappings of Nazism were novelties. Rice-Jones reported that the twelve thousand spectators at the Sportpalast "pretty near brought the house down when we gave them the Nazi salute."[76]

By the mid-1930s, Canadian hockey had taken hold across Europe. Fourteen European nations were represented at the 1935 world championships, along with the Canadians. "Stroll in winter through the business sections of these ancient cities," reported a *Maclean's* journalist, "and you will find store windows filled with Canadian-made hockey equipment, prominently displaying brightly colored group photographs of famous Canadian hockey teams."[77]

The Canadian team that had first visited Europe at the turn of the century was still touring the continent in the 1930s. From the start of their winter holiday in mid-December, the Oxford Canadians played exhibitions in France, Germany, and Central Europe before arriving in Switzerland for the Spengler Cup. Yet Canadian students were no longer able to dominate Europeans just by being Canadian. By the late 1920s, European clubs regularly defeated the Oxford students. The Rhodes Scholars found European players to be strong skaters and skilled stickhandlers.[78] Meanwhile, Canadian students of the interwar decades were more scholars than hockey players. When he first joined the Oxford team in November 1928, David Turnbull of Winnipeg acknowledged that there was only one real player on the team, a law student from Alberta named Clarence Campbell. The rest of the team was "pretty ghastly."[79] Canada's top amateur clubs were still in a different class, as the Monarchs showed on their tour. But a random team of Canadian students, even students selected for their fondness for sports, now faced steep odds against European skaters. Turnbull came to this conclusion that December, after an 8–1 loss in Vienna: "Hockey has made such strides in Europe that the big cities can provide all the competition necessary without importing a bunch of hams like ourselves."[80]

Turnbull was right: top European clubs did not want to beat up a bunch of Canadian hams. They wanted to get better. To do that, they needed to

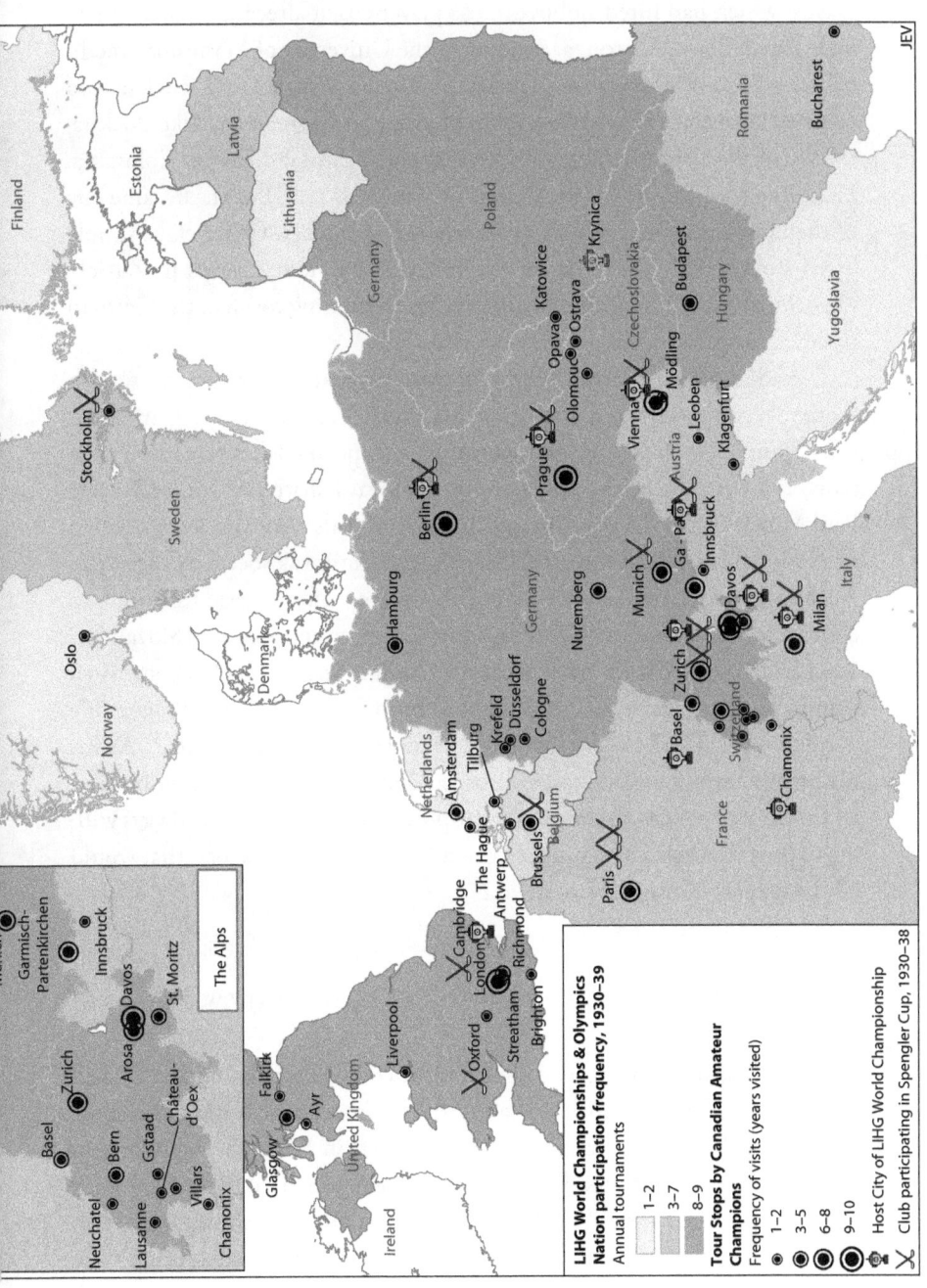

Hockey in 1930s Europe.

understand the Canadian way of playing. Clubs followed the model of HC Davos, which had hired Bobby Bell as player-coach after his amateur team had visited. Blake Watson, a graduate of the University of Manitoba's medical school, took hospital residencies in Vienna, Prague, and Zurich, and coached local clubs as a side job. LTC Prague gave the reins to Mike Buckna, the son of Slovak immigrants who grew up playing in Trail, British Columbia. Handling coaching duties for the national team as well, Buckna became one of the most influential figures in Czechoslovak hockey. Other clubs simply hired Bobby Bell. Over the course of the 1930s, he had stops in Zurich, Dusseldorf, Nuremberg, and Munich before becoming coach of the German national team.[81]

Canadian player-coaches were well compensated for their services, with money, accommodations, and other benefits.[82] Yet even as the Canadians went from one well-paying job to another, European hockey remained amateur. "For our players, the amateur question was a matter of course," wrote Paul Müller of HC Davos.[83] Prague hockey officials were also wary of open professionalism, which was established in Czechoslovak soccer by the 1930s. At the same time, they acknowledged that players often moved from club to club for material reasons.[84] In 1934, for instance, twenty-year-old Slovak forward Ladislav Troják was the object of a bidding war among his hometown club in Košice, nearby HC Poprad, and both Slavia and LTC Prague. He decided on LTC, the club that could arrange the best-paying job.[85] As his teammate Stanislav Konopásek discovered, money was never a problem at LTC. The manager, who owned a sugar-processing company, was always willing to provide a loan to help a player out. "Of course, it was a loan that would not be repaid," Konopásek recalled.[86]

HOCKEY STARS IN THE CITY OF LIGHTS

Despite declaring adherence to the amateur code, European hockey inched toward open professionalism in the 1930s. In France and Britain, the sport became a popular entertainment. Businessmen in England and Scotland replaced older skating rinks with new buildings configured for hockey, with grandstands to accommodate thousands of spectators. The showpiece of this boom was the Empire Pool and Sports Arena, a ten-thousand-seat multiuse facility adjacent to Wembley Stadium that opened in 1934. The stadium's owner, Arthur Elvin, decided to build the indoor arena after watching an exhibition hockey game between Canada and the United States. With two teams calling the arena home, like Madison Square Garden, Wembley was the center of a seven-team English league during the 1930s. By the end of the decade, there were player cards in cigarette packs, posters in Underground stations, dedicated hockey periodicals, and even hockey-themed films in British cinemas.[87] Elvin saw the sport as taking over Britain, envisioning "one hundred teams taking part in the game, rivalling football in importance."[88]

Whereas British hockey was promoted by a cadre of enthusiastic businessmen, the revival of the sport in Paris was due solely to one man: Jefferson Davis Dickson Jr. A proud son of Natchez, Mississippi, Jeff Dickson had gone to France with the American Expeditionary Force and then stayed in Paris after the war. In 1924 he bought a boxing hall with a bad reputation and lost six times what he had paid for it.[89] Five years later he was promoting fights at the Vélodrome d'Hiver in Paris and at London's Royal Albert Hall. Dickson split his time between both cities, yet he remained loyal to his home country. After the United States entered World War II he enlisted again in the army, at age forty-five.

The few times American newspapers took notice of Dickson, they dubbed him the "Tex Rickard of Europe." Like the New York promoter, Dickson moved from organizing bouts to owning the building where the fights were held, with an eye toward creating a modern entertainment center. Dickson found wealthy Parisian partners, most notably Charles Ritz, son of the famous hotelier, and Jacques Goddet, editor of the sports newspaper *L'Auto* (which had launched the Tour de France in 1903 to boost circulation). With their backing, he led the transformation of the Vélodrome d'Hiver into, as he called it, "a second Madison Square Garden." Dubbed the Palais des Sports, the arena on the Boulevard de Grenelle hosted boxing and cycling, as before, along with horse shows, theater performances, and the circus. The arena even staged chariot races, with a special hemp mat covering the floor. Compared to the forty events held each year at the old Vél' d'Hiv, Dickson planned for the new arena to offer sports and entertainment 260 days a year. Costing 7.5 million francs (over $290,000 at the time), the reconstruction turned the twenty-year-old velodrome into a state-of-the-art facility, with dozens of telephone lines for reporters, a health club, restaurants, and a retractable glass roof.[90]

Dickson expected hockey to be a key attraction at his Paris arena. He estimated that the sport would bring in 1.8 million of the planned 10 million francs in annual revenue, just below boxing's planned take of 2 million. The

Poster illustrated by Paul Ordner for the grand opening of the Palais des Sports, October 1931 (courtesy of Philippe Aurousseau/Philippe Ordner).

promoter convinced the leading Paris soccer clubs, Stade Français and Racing, to launch hockey teams, hoping their rivalry would draw fans. Their games against English teams were the featured event at the grand opening of the Palais des Sports in October 1931. To fill the rest of the schedule, Dickson arranged visits by other English teams, established European clubs, and touring Canadians. A following was slow to build; Dickson later recalled that he gave away a lot of free tickets. But by the time LTC Prague visited in 1935, with a standing-room crowd of sixteen thousand, hockey was a major attraction in the City of Lights. Beneath the steel and glass roof, with the Eiffel Tower rising only a few hundred meters away, thousands filled Dickson's Palais des Sports for twice-weekly games. "Boxing and cycle racing are the other attractions here," wrote an American visitor in Paris, "but ice hockey is easily first favorite."[91]

To sell tickets at their new arenas, Jeff Dickson and his English colleagues needed talent. Of course, the source of that talent was Canada. Along with coaches like Bobby Bell, Blake Watson, and Mike Buckna, Canadian players were scattered throughout Europe in the 1930s. "Davos is full of Canadians playing hockey," an Oxford student reported after the 1931 Spengler Cup.[92] While Czech, Swiss, and German clubs featured homegrown players who could skate with the Canadians—players like the *ni-Sturm* of Davos, Josef Maleček of LTC Prague, and Gustav Jaenecke of Berlin—English and French teams did not. Moreover, English and French teams were commercial operations first and foremost. Rather than adding one or two Canadians to strengthen their lineup, like Central European clubs, teams in Paris and London filled their rosters with imported players. The massive new sports halls of Europe, like the massive new sports halls of North America, became showcases for young Canadian skaters.

There was one skater who bridged these two hockey cultures, drawing sellout crowds to the arenas of New York and Berlin, Toronto and Paris—an athlete of extraordinary talent and charisma, whose wealthy father had imposed a strict diet and training regimen, with the aim of turning his child into a star.

This was Sonja Henie. During the years she rose to international fame, winning ten consecutive world championships and three Olympic gold medals, the Norwegian figure skater was a constant presence in hockey arenas. Already when she was thirteen years old, her ambitious father booked her between games at the Berlin Sportpalast. She later had a much-publicized romance with Gustav Jaenecke. Her father intervened, preferring that she accept the advances of Jeff Dickson, who gave her the spotlight at the Palais des Sports.[93] During her first professional tour of the United States, her promoter was Walter Brown, manager of Boston Garden and a leading figure in American amateur hockey. He booked her in arenas across the country, with Henie performing between periods of games. After she made her film debut in 1936, Chicago Black Hawks owner Arthur Wirtz gave the skater a stage of her own. His production, the Hollywood Ice Revue, starred Henie in storybook numbers, surrounded by dozens of skaters in full costume—many of whom were former hockey players. The ice show sold out its five performances at Madison Square Garden.[94]

The connection between figure skating and hockey was nothing new. Going back to the 1910s, hockey games in the United States regularly featured skaters between periods. In Europe, weekend ice-sport festivals had multiple hockey matches and figure-skating competitions. But Sonja Henie's popularity was astonishing—and transformative. Instead of adding skaters between periods to boost ticket sales, promoters discovered that shows like the Hollywood Ice Revue could fill arenas on their own. As hockey faced hard times during the Depression and war years, ice shows provided needed cash. Five nights of the Ice Follies at Maple Leaf Gardens grossed $110,000 in 1944—nearly a third of the Maple Leafs' season revenue. Henie's runs in New York and Chicago each brought in more than $600,000, far more than any NHL team earned. "The Ice shows have revolutionized the business of Arena management," observed Frank Selke, assistant manager of the Maple Leafs.[95] Even the most hard-nosed of Canadian players got in on the act. As owner of Springfield's minor-pro team, former Bruins defenseman Eddie Shore joined other arena managers to launch the Ice Capades in 1940.

Henie's star power also had a lasting effect on participation in skating. As the first female athlete to become an international celebrity, she sparked a boom in figure skating. Between 1935 and 1937, production of skates doubled in the United States. Frank Zamboni opened his Los Angeles–area rink at the height of the Sonja Henie craze (she was later one of the first owners of his new ice-surfacing machine). Figure skating became a widely popular activity, but this appeal was overwhelmingly with girls. As Mary Louise Adams shows in her history of figure skating, "what had once been a relatively gender-balanced sport practiced by privileged white adults was well on its way to becoming a sport of young middle-class white girls."[96]

Figure skating's emergence as a popular sport for girls corresponded with the decline of women's hockey. In the 1920s and '30s, women's teams in Canada played before thousands of spectators. When hockey grew in popularity in 1930s Europe, women's teams formed in London, Paris, and Vienna. Yet these teams did not survive the Depression. And after Sonja Henie, girls and their parents looked to figure skating as a more attractive winter activity. During the interwar years, when new venues and new media stoked hockey's popularity, the sport shared the ice with figure skating. But already by the war years, two paths diverged on the rinks: one for girls in their white figure skates, one for boys in their black hockey skates. "They seem to think figure skating is something for girls only and are ashamed even to put on a pair of figure skates," said Swedish skater Maj Britt of boys in his country. "For them exists only ice hockey."[97]

THREE

Out of the Storm

TEMPERATURES DROPPED IN NEW YORK on the evening of February 20, 1939, after a rainy day. The Rangers and Americans had the night off, but Madison Square Garden was full. More than twenty-two thousand packed the arena's floor and grandstands for the German-American Bund's "Americanism" rally. At one end, a thirty-foot portrait of George Washington towered over the stage. Flanking the first president were the stars and stripes, as well as flags bearing the swastika. "Wake Up America—Smash Jewish Communism," read a banner hanging from the balcony. "Stop Jewish Domination of Christian America," said another. Wearing a Nazi armband, Bund leader Fritz Kuhn praised the assembly for protecting "their children and their homes against those who would turn the United States into a bolshevik paradise."[1] After the speeches were over and the banners came down, the ice went back in. They played hockey at Madison Square Garden through the upheaval of the 1930s and '40s, just as they did at the Berlin Sportpalast.

Although we turn to sports as a haven from the cares of the world, arena gates cannot lock out forces of political and economic tumult. The Depression and World War II had lasting effects on hockey in North America and Europe. The sport's institutions were shaken, with some clubs and leagues brought to ruin. After the initial fanfare of Jeff Dickson's Paris arena, his debts mounted. The demise of the old Ottawa Senators was followed by that of the Montreal Maroons and the New York Americans, leaving only six NHL franchises standing. At one point, even the owners of the Montreal Canadiens considered selling out to Cleveland.

Out of the wreckage came rebuilding. The pruned NHL rebounded quickly after the war, becoming a multi-million-dollar business. The sport surged in North America, riding the economic and demographic wave of the postwar years. By contrast, European hockey could not regain the momentum of the early 1930s. Across the continent, the material base was tenuous after the war. As the climate continued to warm, hockey needed enclosed rinks, but steel and concrete were in short supply. Even in the early 1960s, when Canadian peewees were skating inside arenas, the world championships were held outdoors in Europe.

In this unsettled environment, a new power emerged. The rise of the Soviet Union in world hockey transformed the ways the sport was played, analyzed, and taught. Above all, the Soviets' entrance infused hockey with politics. Like all sports, hockey had long had political meanings—Canadian complaints about the game's Americanization were nothing if not statements about international political economy. But the Soviets launched their hockey program with an explicitly ideological aim. This political framework for sports, adopted as well by the other communist states, bent European amateurism in a new direction, weaponizing it for international competition. At the same time, NHL owners extended their reach deep into Canadian amateur hockey. The clash between these two powers would come decades later. But in the early years of the Cold War, these two structures—Soviet state-professionalism and the NHL's cartel-capitalism—fortified the boundaries of North America's and Europe's hockey cultures.

LIFE DURING WARTIME

In the first years of Nazi rule, the Führer took in the occasional hockey game. One photograph shows Hitler on his feet in the stands, saluting the crowd. Goebbels slouches in a seat next to him, apparently not happy to be there.[2]

Nazi leaders were not big fans, but they came to see the value of sports for building the German nation. When they took power in 1933, the party did not have its own sports policy. Instead, they adopted what Mussolini and the Fascists were doing in Italy.[3] The Fascists held that sports built strong bodies for the nation. Young people were involved in organized activities, and the nation was able to show its superiority in international competition, which Italy did by winning the 1934 and 1938 World Cups. Because sports were too serious a matter to be left to middle-class enthusiasts and their English-style clubs, the Fascists brought national federations under control of the party-state. When the Nazis put this model in place in Germany, they found willing collaborators.[4] The skating federation was on board from the beginning.

"We have no use for those who are only hockey players," wrote a federation official in 1935. "We want to train the player not only for sporting competition, but also for life, as a man. For us, sport is not an end in itself, but service to the Fatherland."[5]

Girls and women were also expected to participate in sports. According to Nazi ideology, the primary role of women was to serve as mothers, specifically as mothers of boys who would grow into soldiers. In preparation for that role, girls and young women were to be fit and strong. From age ten through their twenties, German girls were obliged to be part of youth, student, or worker organizations that emphasized exercise and recreational sports. Women also joined voluntarily; in the 1930s, female membership in sports clubs more than doubled.[6] In skating clubs and competitions, girls and women were prominent. Figure skating had the most attention, drawing more than ten thousand spectators to some competitions. But speed skating was also popular. Results show that female participants at races often outnumbered males, with up to five thousand spectators attending some events.[7]

Women of Nazi Germany were fit and strong, but they also knew their place. And their place was not on the hockey rink. As with organized German soccer, from which women were barred until 1970, women were excluded from hockey. German federation officials promoted hockey as a sport for men, although not for its roughness. Instead, hockey was a game of speed and teamwork. When Bobby Bell became coach of the German national team in the late 1930s, sports writers hailed his fast-paced, attacking style. Moreover, Bell emphasized that hockey was a game of vision and intellect—a principle that also resonated with the Germans. "It is essential to say that good hockey is less an exercise of strength than of the mind," Bell told a German interviewer. "Someone who lacks quick awareness will never become a good hockey player."[8]

After the start of the war in September 1939, the German skating federation turned up its message that hockey and skating were necessary for building the strength of the nation. "Do not rest!" wrote the editors of the federation's magazine in 1940, when the Battle of Britain was under way. Just as the German Luftwaffe did not waver, neither did sports organizations and German youth shrink from their commitment.[9] A sign of the nation's strength was that ice rinks were open during the war, that training went on without interruption. The skating federation proudly declared in January 1941 that skaters and hockey players continued to work at their skills. "They have not rested in this winter of war."[10]

Hockey went on throughout the Greater German Reich during the war. In the first years, crowds of more than ten thousand watched games in Munich, Mannheim, and Hamburg.[11] By the winter of 1943–44, as the army sought reinforcements for mounting losses, soccer and hockey clubs combined their remaining players into "war teams." The top hockey clubs in the capital, Berlin SC and SC Brandenburg, joined together to win the national title. As the war continued, hockey and other sports were less a means of strengthening the nation than of providing diversions. Newsreel film of the 1944 Reich championship showed the crowd at Garmisch-Partenkirchen's Olympic Stadium cheering the combined "war team" and their opponents, Berlin Red-White. For cinema audiences, the newsreel images of spectators in the grandstands— boys and girls, well-dressed young women, older men in overcoats and fedoras, soldiers in uniform—were proof that normal life continued.[12]

Hockey's value as a wartime entertainment is demonstrated in the fact that Germany's top players were excused from military service. Herbert Schibukat and Oskar Nowak, who had played against each other for Germany and Austria at the 1936 Olympics, were teammates for Berlin Red-White. Gustav Jaenecke was excused from military service, ostensibly because he owned a shoe factory. The rationale for keeping his teammate Rudi Ball was less clear. At the Winter Olympics in Garmisch-Partenkirchen, Ball had been the only Jewish athlete representing Germany. According to reports, Ball had been invited back from his exile in Milan on the invitation of the Reich's sport minister, Hans von Tschammer; other sources suggest that Jaenecke refused to play unless Ball was on the team.[13] Ball's background certainly was not hidden. At the Olympics, German spectators were eager to see the "Jewish hockey player" who had come back "like a king."[14] Whatever deal Ball made with authorities, whoever provided his protection, the arrangement was strong enough to last through the war. Ball survived in the heart of Hitler's Reich, scoring goals for Berlin SC and getting his name in newspapers across Germany.

In the end, the arenas were left in ruins. The Berlin Sportpalast, where Ball and Jaenecke played, where Hitler declared his thousand-year Reich and Goebbels called Germans to fight a "total war," was gutted by bombs. It was rebuilt only in the early 1950s, by a former hockey player turned banker.[15] By then, German hockey had shifted to Bavaria, with its colder winters. Already before the war, hockey officials recognized that the climate was changing and that more indoor rinks were needed to continue the sport's growth.[16] But with scarce resources to rebuild cities and infrastructure, hockey rinks were not a priority. Moreover, as the country was divided into East and West, rivalries that had once stirred fans were severed. Several thousand spectators still came to the Olympic Stadium in Garmisch-Partenkirchen in the late 1940s to watch Ball and Jaenecke. But their best years—and the best years of German hockey—had passed. "Iron Gustav" was in his forties. Rudi Ball left Germany for good in 1948.

In Paris and London, as in Berlin, the hockey boom of the 1930s did not survive. British hockey fared well during the war, but in the lean postwar years, rink owners like Arthur Elvin could not stave off losses. With food rationing still in place into the 1950s, even ice shows could not keep arenas in the black. By 1960, the British league had folded.[17] Jeff Dickson's scheme for hockey at the Vélodrome d'Hiver, his "second Madison Square Garden," did not last that long. During the Depression, he was unable to repay loans for the building's reconstruction. During the war, the once-spectacular Vél' d'Hiv became a place of infamy, when French police imprisoned over eight thousand Jews at the Paris arena before their deportation. At the time, Dickson was serving in the US Army Air Force. He was lost in action over Germany in 1943.

The period when hockey was a major attraction in Europe's largest cities was brief. "Hockey typified the manner in which new sports were able to expand and embed themselves," writes historian Daryl Leeworthy of the game's popularity in interwar Britain.[18] But this popular sport was quickly uprooted—by economic turmoil, by war and political division, and by the warming climate. In postwar Europe, without large crowds in the largest cities following the game, hockey gravitated toward the margins: to Czechoslovakia, to Sweden and Finland, and to the Soviet Union.

END OF THE HORSE-AND-BUGGY AGE

In winter 1934, Winnipeg goalie Arthur Rice-Jones spent the season in London playing for the Queen's Ice Club. Although he and his teammates enjoyed parties in Paris and Davos, he complained to his parents that the club's owners did not share the gate with players. His father sent a stern reprimand:

> You say the clubs are making money but never think of giving the players any. You don't want any. Whatever you do, don't take it if they offer it to you. . . . For it to come out that you had received money or to be branded as a pro

would kill you socially and injure you irretrievably. You will in the long run be much further ahead to be amateur.[19]

A British-born immigrant and respected member of Winnipeg's business class, Cecil Rice-Jones saw his son's hockey pursuits according to traditional ideals. In letters to London, he repeatedly urged "Art old boy" to keep his head, avoid enticements, and remain fixed on career prospects. He wrote of "the game" as a metaphor for life. His son needed to play fairly, mindful not to do anything that would bring shame. At the top of that list, for a man of Cecil Rice-Jones's station, was taking money. But Arthur Rice-Jones was of a different generation, and he did not hesitate to set his father straight:

> Again in reference to getting money for playing. Just to show you that you are wrong. All the members of the club and spectators and people who we come in contact with think we are well paid for playing hockey and are flabbergasted and sit with open mouths when we tell them we don't get a penny for playing.[20]

Five years after returning from London, when he was a married father of a newborn, driving a brewery truck and playing goalie for Calgary's senior club, Rice-Jones was glad to be paid. Although the Stampeders were an amateur club, he earned $20 a week plus a stipend for transportation and meals. The club also paid his wife $70 per month during the season, to make ends meet. The terms of his contract were stated on letterhead of the Canadian Amateur Hockey Association (CAHA).[21] Hockey in Canada had come a long way from the ideals of the empire.

The change in Canadian amateur hockey, from passing money under the table to openly paying contracted players, was spurred by people like Arthur Rice-Jones who had played in Europe. Before the war, the total number of Canadians playing in Europe each winter was only five or six dozen. But for the men who led the CAHA, they were a big problem. The organization was losing money during the Depression. Poor turnout for the two dominion-wide amateur tournaments, the Memorial Cup for junior teams and the Allan Cup for seniors, dropped CAHA reserves by more than 85 percent. During the war years, the senior tournament again sold tickets, as fans turned out to watch former NHL stars in the military who played as amateurs. Yet while the Allan Cup was revived, the Memorial Cup barely broke even, with some series ending deep in the red.[22]

CAHA vice president George Hardy understood that the losses spelled trouble for Canadian amateur hockey. It was expensive to operate an amateur club, with costs in equipment, travel, and rink maintenance. "All of these expenses have to come out of the money paid in by spectators," Hardy told an audience in 1939. "Well, you can't get the spectators unless you serve up a good brand of hockey."[23] A good brand of hockey required good players; Hardy recognized, however, that good players were leaving Canadian amateur clubs.

By the 1930s, competition for hockey talent was fierce. NHL franchises, minor-pro teams, and commercial amateur clubs were all searching for players. Scouts found a few in the United States, but the largest talent pool was the Canadian amateur ranks. Managers had no qualms about signing away multiple players from a successful senior team in Canada. They also nabbed players in the middle of the season, leaving a winning team without its best skater and biggest draw. Like the early days of professional hockey, when players jumped from league to league, the situation in the 1930s was becoming untenable.[24]

The popularity of hockey in Europe turned up the pressure even more. The problem was not the volume of Canadian players crossing the Atlantic. Rather, it was that many of them were being snapped up without the CAHA's permission. In 1935 the English teams started by Arthur Elvin and other arena owners sent recruiters to Canada with no limits on the number of players they could import. "It appeared as if all the senior players in the Dominion had been approached by these active agents," reported Billy Hewitt to the CAHA annual meeting.[25] Managers of American clubs followed suit. The CAHA responded by suspending forty-six Canadians on English and American teams. Included on the list were two Canadian players who joined the British national team for the 1936 Winter Olympics in Garmisch-Partenkirchen. Canada's loss to the British and second-place finish in the tournament—the first time the country had not won gold in Olympic hockey—only added insult to injury. CAHA leaders determined that the global movement of their players had to be brought under control.

George Hardy's day job was teaching classical literature at the University of Alberta. Yet he looked at the international migration of players from the pragmatic view of economics. Hockey was a market. As the sport gained popularity in Europe and the United States, Canada provided the bulk of the labor, and certainly the highest-quality labor. As the CAHA made clear to the Ligue Internationale de Hockey sur Glace in a 1939 memo, Canada was "the only territory from which hockey talent is available."[26] Hardy and other CAHA leaders did not object to Canadians playing in other countries, but this labor market needed to be regulated.

The first step was recognizing why players moved: they needed money. Hardy insisted that the strict definition of amateurism still binding Canadian hockey was framed in the nineteenth century, when only men of means were expected to take part in sports. "What suited the hockey of the horse-and-buggy era does not meet the needs and realities of this modern machine age," he wrote in *Maclean's*.[27] Mechanics and clerks who played hockey needed to be paid for their time. The clear-eyed classicist had little patience with appeals to the amateur tradition. If the International Olympic Committee believed that its definition of amateurism followed the ancient Olympics, Hardy jabbed, they needed to reread the classics. Cities of ancient Greece had showered Olympians with gifts, even direct payments of gold.[28]

In 1936 Hardy and his fellow CAHA leaders broke from the constraints of amateurism. The organization approved a proposal stating that if a player could get a job through his hockey talent, then he was free to do that. CAHA delegates also decided that neither players who tried out for pro teams nor those who played in games against pros would lose their amateur status. These were all violations of the traditional code, a "radical action" in the view of the Amateur Athletic Union of Canada. Nevertheless, the hockey association stuck to its reforms. The CAHA president declared that the step was necessary for "the best interests of hockey."[29]

After changing its rules, the CAHA turned to the leagues that had been siphoning off its players. In summer 1936 the association finalized an agreement with the NHL that set guidelines for when and how a pro team could sign a player. Agreements with the British and Americans followed. Yet even after coming to terms, CAHA officials knew that more had to be done on behalf of its members. Hardy was convinced that Canadian amateur teams had to be paid for supplying the world's hockey talent. "In spite of the work the CAHA clubs do in developing players," he argued, "the pros could sign them and not pay a cent to the CAHA club—at least, not officially." When the 1936 deal came up for renewal four years later, Hardy pressed NHL owners for compensation. They agreed to pay $500 for each player signed from an amateur club and $250 for each player signed to a minor-pro contract. When the agreement was renewed again in 1947, it set a flat annual payment rather than a per-player fee: every NHL team paid $2,000, every minor team $1,000, for a total of $30,000. By that time, the CAHA was sending sixty to eighty new players to pro teams every year. Compared to the earlier rate of $500 per player, the NHL was getting a deal.[30]

In the view of historians, the CAHA agreements with the NHL between 1936 and 1947 brought Canadian amateur hockey into a subordinate relationship to the pro league. Of course, CAHA leaders did not see it this way. "The CAHA believes," Hardy told an audience, "that its policy recognizes frankly, without humbug or hypocrisy, the realities of present-day hockey in modern Canada."[31] Hardy believed that by forwarding payments from the NHL to amateur clubs, the association was strengthening Canadian hockey.[32] Today, this principle of the top league compensating clubs for developing future players remains in place. Each year, the NHL pays development fees to European federations and the North American junior leagues. Payments reach tens of millions of dollars, yet it is still a bargain for the NHL compared to negotiating individual transfer fees, as in soccer. Leaders of European leagues know they are not getting fair market prices for their players. But like George Hardy decades ago, they recognize it's better to get something from the NHL than nothing at all.

THE NHL PREEMINENT

All intentions aside, Canadian amateur hockey did become subordinate to the NHL during the 1940s. Along with the league's annual payments to the CAHA, pro franchises contracted directly with amateur junior clubs to serve as development teams. Minor-pro teams sponsored their own junior clubs, and NHL-sponsored Junior A teams even made sponsorship deals with Junior B teams. By 1950, forty-two junior clubs were sponsored directly by NHL franchises or minor league teams. Franchises could secure the rights to players as young as sixteen (raised to eighteen in 1950) by signing them to one of three option forms. The CAHA approved this network of sponsorships in their 1947 agreement, even agreeing to stand aside when a franchise moved a teenage player from one club to another.[33] The yearly compensation of $30,000 was the pros' fee for burrowing deep into amateur hockey.

Just as CAHA leaders had sought to regulate the international movement of Canadian players, NHL owners looked to ensure their talent supply in difficult times. The Depression and early war years pushed the league to the brink. Reduced to six teams after the Amerks ceased operations in 1942, the pared-down league survived the rest of the war, despite losing players to military service. Like Major League Baseball, pro hockey was allowed to function as a useful entertainment. As historian Andrew Ross explains, both American and Canadian governments saw more value in keeping the league in operation than in conscripting its remaining players.[34] Hockey provided a welcome diversion: in the last three seasons of the war, all six teams saw increased attendance.[35]

Crowds grew even larger in the years after the war. The autumn of 1945 saw the return of popular players from the military. The league had a young star in Maurice "Rocket" Richard, who had scored a record fifty goals for the Canadiens in the last wartime season. The late 1940s also brought the emergence of Detroit's high-scoring linemates Ted Lindsay and Gordie Howe. This was the golden age of the so-called Original Six. And the gold came into the league's coffers. From 1946 to 1950, total attendance in the league was near 2.4 million. In 1949–50, total gate receipts topped $4 million for the first time.[36]

Already by that time, some twelve hundred hockey players were signed to NHL franchises, minor-pro teams, and sponsored junior clubs from Quebec City to Edmonton.[37] Of course, controlling the labor market from top to bottom had its advantages. The NHL kept player salaries in check and suppressed potential insurgencies, such as when players tried to form a union in 1957. Young players were also steeped in the NHL's style of play. Pro hockey demanded skill, toughness, and intuition. When *Sports Illustrated* sent William Faulkner to his first hockey game at Madison Square Garden, the author quickly recognized that there was an underlying sense to the dizzying movement of players. At first, the game seemed to him "discorded and inconsequent, bizarre and paradoxical." But then, Faulkner wrote, "it would break, coalesce through a kind of kaleidoscopic whirl like a child's toy, into a pattern, a design almost beautiful, as if an inspired choreographer had drilled a willing and patient and hard-working troupe of dancers."[38] The logic of that "kaleidoscopic whirl" was drilled into Canadian players from a young age. In the development system that emerged in the postwar years, boys learned hockey by playing hockey. The emphasis was on games rather than practice, because it was in a game that one learned "hockey sense"—how to move within and respond to the action on the ice. Over the decades, the season grew longer at all junior levels—all the better for young players to learn the NHL's style of play. "By the time a boy reaches the NHL," Ken Dryden observed in the early 1980s, "he is a veteran of close to 1,000 games."[39]

With full arenas and full control over player development, NHL owners were masters of a profitable operation. It was also a closed operation, allowing owners to better protect their assets. The six-team league was the same size it had been in 1924, when expansion first began into the United States. But whereas owners of the 1920s had been willing to take the risk of growing their fledgling league, owners in the postwar years were survivors—wealthy businessmen who had watched fellow members of their club go under. They turned down franchise bids from Cleveland in 1952 and from Los Angeles and San Francisco in 1960–61. Their logic was that new teams would have low-quality players, making games uncompetitive; turnout would be low, and teams would lose money.[40] By no means were owners willing to dip into their own stocks to help new franchises become competitive—after all, the league's haves, those with the largest networks of sponsored junior teams, did not even share talent with have-nots like the woeful Bruins and Black Hawks, who played to dwindling crowds in the 1950s. Despite pro hockey's resurgent popularity, owners were wary. It was a conservative cartel that ruled the NHL after World War II. And it was this cartel that gained control over Canadian amateur hockey.

THE BOYS' GAME

In winter 1943, author Morley Callaghan went to Maple Leaf Gardens for a game. Along the way, he stopped to watch a group of neighborhood kids playing boot hockey. With the streetlight illuminating their game, he noticed their faces—how, in his view, they represented a country of immigrants. "They were Anglo-Saxon faces and Scandinavian faces and Italian and Slavic faces," he wrote. "On the street that night, though, they were all one, they were just a collection of Canadian kids playing shinny. The game held them all together."[41] Coming from one of Canada's best-known writers, his words were an appeal for unity at a dark point of the war. They were also a declaration of hockey as the national glue. Indeed, as the title of Callaghan's essay stated, hockey was "the game that made a nation."[42]

Hockey emerged as a unifying symbol of the Canadian nation during the trials of the Depression and World War II. After the war, "hockey became the country's pride," in the words of Andrew Holman and Stephen Hardy.[43] In part, the sport's broader resonance was bolstered by the NHL's nationwide popularity. Saturday-night radio broadcasts from Maple Leaf Gardens were consistently among the highest-rated programs after the war. Ratings were especially high in the Maritimes and prairie provinces, with well over half the radio audience in those areas tuned to the game. Moreover, it was regularly the case that more women than men were listening.[44] When television broadcasts of *Hockey Night in Canada* began in 1952, the program claimed a similar spot near the top of the ratings.

But hockey was more than a popular entertainment. The sport also gained more participants after the war, as youth hockey programs swelled with baby boomers. Over 3.9 million children were born in Canada in the decade after the war. This rising demographic tide, along with changing ideas about child development, brought an expansion of organized activities for kids. Sunday-school enrollment at Protestant churches climbed by a third in the 1950s; membership in Brownies and Cubs doubled, to a quarter-million children.[45] Minor hockey experienced similar growth. In 1958, over 150,000 "youngsters" across the country were playing in CAHA-affiliated leagues; by 1962, that number was more than 200,000. The Toronto Hockey League alone had more than 25,000 players, ages eight to eighteen.[46]

The growth of youth hockey was characteristic of the times in several ways. First, playing had purpose. Proponents of minor hockey, like their predecessors going back to the nineteenth century, insisted that the sport built character and sportsmanship. Child-rearing experts of the postwar years also urged that guided, constructive activities were necessary for steering children away from immorality. Minor hockey fit the bill, claimed its organizers, "teaching co-operation and respect for authority." In the words of Jack Roxburgh, the CAHA's head of minor hockey, "To keep one lad out of trouble is worth the effort of all the managers of all the hockey teams of all the leagues in Canada."[47]

The guides for this character-building activity were usually volunteer dads. The baby boom brought a cultural shift in parenting, particularly in the role of fathers. Unlike previous generations, dads of the postwar years were more active in their children's play, whether leading a scout troop or organizing the family camping trip. Fathers "were supposed to be pals," Doug Owram remarks in his history of the baby boom. "Thousands of part-time hockey and baseball coaches around the nation testified to the power of this social role."[48]

Minor hockey was also accompanied by a lot of stuff. Owram notes that the expansion of children's activities fueled a growing corner of the postwar consumer economy: "The variety of playthings available was unprecedented."[49] In hockey, this meant sticks, skates, and equipment. At the time, the total cost of outfitting a young player was about $70 to $100, a considerable amount in the 1950s. Already there were concerns about the expense. But it was worth it, urged hockey advocates. Money spent on hockey was nothing compared to the amount needed to reform juvenile delinquents. "How do you wish your money spent?" asked the *Toronto Star*.[50]

Away from the ice, there were also products of all kinds promoting the NHL.[51] Posters and trading cards, team sweaters and tabletop hockey games—along with the Saturday-night broadcasts on TV—all reinforced the NHL as the object of dreams for Canadian boys. "There was nothing else I ever thought about," recalled goalie Glenn "Chico" Resch, who grew up in Regina in the 1950s. "I mean hockey was going to be my life."[52] The dream was not remote. Resch counted a number of boys from Regina's blue-collar north side who made the NHL, like him. Although NHL teams could not sign players to contracts until they were eighteen, they did sign boys as young as fourteen to option forms and assigned them to sponsored junior clubs. These clubs then had their own affiliated teams at younger age levels. Boys playing within these chains knew which pro team held their rights—a bantam in Winnipeg belonged to the Bruins, in Moose Jaw to the Black Hawks, in Humboldt to the Red Wings.[53]

Organized minor hockey in Canada was also characteristic of the times in that it was strictly for boys. The postwar years were a time when traditional gender roles were reinforced, and the division between supposedly male and female activities extended to Canadian rinks. Just as hockey grew with boy boomers, so did figure skating have a surge in popularity among girls, thanks to Barbara Ann Scott. Winner of Olympic gold in 1948, Scott became Canada's sweetheart—she was even immortalized with her own doll, complete with fur-trimmed costume and white figure skates. "Like millions of other young girls of my generation, I took up figure skating," recalls sociologist M. Ann Hall, "but secretly longed for black hockey skates."[54] Even those girls with hockey skates, however, had little chance to use them. When nine-year-old Abby Hoffman, an all-star defenseman on a Toronto peewee team, was revealed to be a girl in 1956, her story made national and international news. League administrators claimed to be surprised a girl even wanted to play. When more girls, by the dozen, said they wanted to play as well, officials promised to start a league of their own. Then they let it die quietly. In years that followed, minor hockey associations rewrote their bylaws to ban girl players.[55]

Canadian hockey of the postwar years was also white. Certainly, there were black, Indigenous, and Asian players. But these individuals had difficulty navigating the organized minor system, and they endured slurs from other players and spectators. Fred Sasakamoose remembered trying out for a junior team with 130 other boys: "All white. I was shamed—shamed at being Indian."[56] Recalled Willie O'Ree of his years in juniors: "I heard 'nigger' so much on the ice, I thought it was my name."[57] Today, the two men are hailed as pioneers for reaching the NHL in the 1950s. But they were solitary figures. With the closed amateur system providing a reliable supply of players, NHL owners were not looking to make bold experiments by promoting hockey for all.[58]

Youth hockey also grew in the United States after World War II, although on a far smaller scale than in Canada. Participation was largely limited to pockets in the Northeast and Great Lakes states—the same areas that had been hearths of American hockey since the early twentieth century. In the early 1950s, just over two hundred high schools nationwide had hockey teams; a third of these were in Massachusetts.[59] At the decade's end, the Amateur Hockey Association of the United States reported rapid growth in the number of youth teams, with most in Michigan. By 1963, there were 24,195 registered players nationwide at the youth levels.[60]

In cities with NHL teams, people involved with the pro game helped promote youth hockey. Lynn Patrick, coach of the New York Rangers, launched peewee programs at Madison Square Garden and the franchise's minor-league arena in New Haven.[61] Red Wings players raised money for youth teams in the Detroit area, and the sons of Gordie Howe, Alex Delvecchio, and Terry Sawchuk played in the city's parks league. The league was founded by the Red Wings' publicist, who was not necessarily looking to build local boys' skills: "I thought that if we could get the youngsters playing at the Olympia, there would be a greater chance of them becoming hockey fans and remaining fans in their adult years."[62]

In smaller communities, youth programs were based at community parks. During the Depression, the Works Progress Administration built warming houses in hundreds of cities and towns, which served as bases for house teams. From the beginning, all-star teams and travel tournaments were part of American youth hockey. We can also presume there were arguments about ice time, given that the Boston area association mandated equal time in its rules.[63] Yet with most programs based in public parks, early youth hockey allowed for broad access. In many communities, civic organizations or local businesses helped offset costs. The Cleveland Rotary Club paid for equipment in the 1950s. Teams in Detroit's parks league were sponsored by auto dealerships, small manufacturing companies, and labor unions. In towns on Minnesota's Iron Range, unions paid for equipment. Players would take helmets from a big cardboard box in the warming house and put them back after the game.

Like in Canada, youth hockey in the United States was limited to boys. The *Boston Globe* reported that women were essential to the success of local peewee leagues by allowing their husbands and sons to spend time at the rink. There was no such a thing as a hockey mom yet; instead, there were "hockey widows," who spent weekends "raking the leaves, cutting the grass, shoveling snow, hauling the barrels to the dump and hammering nails into a loose shingle."[64] American youth hockey was also largely restricted to white communities. One exception was Cleveland, where a peewee league operated by the parks commission involved a handful of black players. The newspaper of Cleveland's black community, the *Call and Post,* encouraged its readers to check out the sport. "Some day we may read about these youngsters performing in big time hockey," mused the reporter. "Who knows, it could be with the Cleveland Barons."[65]

The reality was that American boys—whether black or white—had little chance of playing professional hockey. With their control over Canadian amateur hockey, NHL scouts and general managers seldom looked beyond its confines. Prior to and during the war, pro teams included a handful of players from American colleges and amateur clubs. In 1938, ten Americans were regular players in the NHL. But in 1958, only one American-born player was on a roster—and he had been raised in Canada. Even minor-pro teams, like the Barons, were made up entirely of Canadians. By the 1950s, youth amateur hockey in Canada had become a reliable feeder system, with players under the watch of pro scouts by the time they reached their teens. As for American boys playing hockey, NHL President Clarence Campbell judged they would be lifelong fans of the game, although few would ever attain "professional standards."[66] Only those who climbed through the closed system controlled by the NHL could reach that level.

"IT SHOULD BE CALLED RUSSIAN HOCKEY"

On March 7, 1954, the hockey world was upended.

At the world championships in Sweden, the senior amateur team from East York, Ontario, took the ice for the tournament's final game. Wearing white sweaters with the red maple leaf, the Canadians looked to claim their country's sixteenth title. Like their predecessors, they had made easy work of the field, winning all six games by a combined score of 57–5. In the final game, the Canadians met a team new to the tournament. The Soviet Union had started playing hockey with a puck only six years earlier, yet they had already proven themselves equal to the Swiss, Czechoslovaks, and Swedes. However, few in the crowd at Stockholm's Olympic Stadium expected these recent converts to Canadian hockey to challenge the Canadians. Even Soviet officials were doubtful of their team's chances.[67]

It wasn't even close. At the end of the first period, the Soviets were ahead 4–0. Three more goals in the second gave them a commanding lead, while the Canadians could find the net only twice. According to the *Globe and Mail*, the Soviet team "simply skated the Canadians off their feet." Led by the tournament's top scorer, Vsevolod Bobrov, the Soviets moved the puck with unexpected speed. They also showed a toughness right out of the Canadian playbook. Soviet players won the puck with hard hitting and then controlled it in the offensive end, unhampered by Canadian checking.[68] "There's no doubt about it," acknowledged the East York manager. "The best team won."[69]

From the Soviets' first appearance on the world hockey stage, observers understood that they were doing something entirely new—something potentially menacing. Already in the 1950s, North American sports pages described Soviet players as being like robots. "The Russians are a machine," one hockey official told the *Globe and Mail* in 1955.[70] Today, Russians themselves proudly claim this Western characterization of Russian hockey. Fans tagged tweets with #redmachine after their team won gold at the 2018 Winter Olympics. During the Cold War, however, Canadians and Americans intended no compliments. The Russian machine was respected for its design and efficiency, but it was also inhuman, cold, and crushing.

Canadian hockey began in the Soviet Union soon after the war, when the country was both devastated and triumphant. World War II, known in Russia as the Great Patriotic War, brought the deaths of tens of millions of people. In the end, soldiers of the Red Army were in Berlin, standing on the rubble of the Nazi regime. The Soviet experiment, launched in the Bolshevik Revolution of 1917, entered a new phase. Its political and economic system had overcome the greatest invasion in history. Stalin sat in council with other world leaders. The Soviet Union was a world power.

In this new position of global prominence, leaders of the Communist Party determined that Soviet athletes would also compete on the world stage.

During the interwar years, the Soviets did not participate in "bourgeois" competitions like the Olympics or World Cup. Although its athletes were absent from major international events, a vibrant sporting culture developed in the world's first socialist state.[71] Boxing and wrestling filled theaters and circus halls, while soccer was widely popular. Against the backdrop of rapid industrialization and urbanization, the government promoted voluntary sports clubs as a means of building strong workers and providing entertainment. Clubs affiliated with factories or unions, such as Spartak or Lokomotiv, paid their athletes as employees. The club of the state police, Dynamo, and the club of the military, Central Army Sports Club (CSKA, or as it's known in the West, Red Army), lured talented athletes with rank and salary. Sports became part of the planned economy. Just as hero workers spurred greater productivity with their feats of labor, so did athletes inspire Soviet citizens to strive toward communism's promised future.[72]

When Soviet athletes began competing internationally after the war, it was under a clear imperative: You must win. After the war, the Communist Party's Central Committee called for greater emphasis on sports participation "so that Soviet sportsmen might win world supremacy."[73] Nikolai Romanov, head of the State Sports Committee, first had to send a note to Stalin guaranteeing victory in order to gain permission to enter international tournaments.[74] Soviet athletes were not simply representatives of a nation; they were the embodiment of humanity's future. Soviet communism was founded upon the scientifically correct understanding of history, sociology, and economics, which provided a clear knowledge of humanity's future development. Citizens of the Soviet Union believed this utopian ideology, with its mix of scientific certainty and religious eschatology. As historian Juliane Fürst observes, commitment to building socialism was deeply held among young people after the war.[75] In working toward this ideal future, ordinary Soviet citizens could accomplish the extraordinary. If the Soviet worker was capable of great deeds of production, if the Soviet soldier could defeat the greatest invasion in history, then great achievements were likewise expected of the Soviet athlete. Winning was a given.

The insistence on Soviet victories was also rooted in soil deeper than Marxist-Leninist ideology. For centuries, Russian leaders had been aware of the advances of the West and their own relative backwardness. If Russia was to be a great power, its material and technological development had to keep pace. But how to do this in a land as vast as Russia? Beginning with Peter the Great in the late seventeenth century, Russian rulers adopted the strategy of making spectacular leaps in order to prove Russia's standing with the West, if not its superiority. Soviet leaders adopted the same strategy. Behind the West in steel production, Stalin's government ordered construction of the world's largest steel plant at Magnitogorsk. Behind in aerospace technology, the Soviets built the largest airplane. These epic achievements were intended to demonstrate the superiority of Russian/Soviet technology, even though the country's overall level of development was far behind Western Europe and North America. As historian Scott Palmer explains, these projects were exercises in "compensatory symbolism" rather than lasting steps in technological or economic development.[76]

A similar motivation drove Soviet sports authorities' decision to adopt Canadian hockey. After the Communist Party leadership determined that the Soviet Union should enter international sports federations, particularly those sports included in the Olympics, the State Sports Committee had to determine how to implement this directive. Hockey posed a particular problem. During the interwar decades, Soviet clubs had teams of men and women playing bandy, which Russians called hockey. The sport had a significant following, with contests between rival clubs in Moscow and Leningrad drawing as many as thirty thousand fans. Canadian hockey, on the other hand, was played only at physical education institutes. The State Sports Committee recognized that building an Olympic team in this unknown sport would be long and costly. Perhaps, however, it would be possible to convert the country's best ball-hockey players into puck-hockey players, and then send those players to the Olympics. Instead of building an international-caliber team from the ground up, the Soviets would take a spectacular leap forward.[77]

Like other Russian monuments of compensatory symbolism, creating an Olympic hockey team first required the know-how of foreigners. Sergei Savin, head of the Department for Football and Hockey, went to the only people in the Soviet Union who had experience with Canadian hockey: the Latvians. Prior to the war, Latvia had been an independent state—like Estonia and Lithuania—with a distinct sporting culture shaped by links to Germany and Scandinavia. These European ties had brought puck-hockey to the country, and Latvia regularly competed in international tournaments. When the Soviet Union annexed Latvia at the start of the war, these sports connections were severed, yet Latvian clubs kept playing Canadian hockey. In spring 1946, at the close of the first postwar season, Savin visited Edgars Klāvs, captain of Dinamo Riga and veteran of the 1930s Latvian national teams. Klāvs gave Savin a stick, a puck, and a Latvian copy of the rules. Quickly translated into

Russian, this rulebook became the founding text of Soviet hockey. Savin gathered the captains of Moscow's hockey clubs and sent them to Archangel, with a cadre of Latvian tutors. Located near the Arctic Circle, the city had plenty of ice for a crash course in playing the puck.[78]

Held the following winter, 1946–47, the inaugural season of Canadian hockey was more a clunky experiment than an efficient implementation of a master plan. With factories still in ruins, players had to improvise for uniforms and equipment. Some wore cycling helmets and boxing headgear. One team received a bundle of sticks from a local factory, perfectly modeled on the stick Savin had received in Latvia, but they shattered at first use. When the long sticks did not break, players found them cumbersome. Red Army's goalie kept throwing his stick away in the middle of games and playing the puck with his hands. Yet despite the strange equipment, the Russians quickly took to the game. The more experienced Latvians could manage only fourth place that first season. As Canadians and others would later discover, long-held knowledge of the game was no match for Russian speed and endurance.[79]

Fans also took to the game. The championship of the inaugural season, between Dynamo Moscow and CSKA, drew ten thousand fans to Dynamo's soccer stadium.[80] "It should be called Russian hockey," said Politburo member Kliment Voroshilov at an early game, refuting critics who dubbed Canadian hockey a bourgeois sport. "It requires courage, split-second reactions, resourcefulness, and great endurance. And if necessary, you can fight."[81] But even though authorities—and fans—gave the stamp of approval, Savin and other officials were reluctant to compete against foreign teams. Even after the Soviets stunned LTC Prague with an exhibition victory in Moscow in 1948, officials were wary. Failure had consequences. Nikolai Romanov was sacked from the State Sports Committee after Soviet speed skaters lost at the 1948 world championships. Red Army's entire soccer team was disbanded after a loss to Yugoslavia in 1952.[82] Only six years after beating the Czechs, when officials judged that their team had a chance to win—and when the country's best athlete, Vsevelod Bobrov, was available to play—did the Soviets enter the world championships.

In that decade, from the end of the war to the Soviets' first hockey championship in 1954, the system that would dominate international sports was established. The government opened hundreds of sports schools for young athletes. Members of club teams started year-round training, at first because of the lack of facilities. Hockey players (many of whom also played soccer for their clubs) completed dry-land drills because there were not enough rinks.[83]

By the mid-1950s, the training schedule was more specialized. To allow athletes time for this regimen, they were paid—technically not as athletes, but as soldiers, students, or physical education instructors. Officials and journalists in international sports saw through this ruse of putting athletes on the payroll of a state-owned factory, the army, or the police. "They certainly are not amateurs," wrote IOC vice president Avery Brundage in 1950, after looking into the Soviets' request to join the Olympic movement.[84] Still, the IOC approved their application. The Soviet state-professional athlete entered the arena, and international sports would be transformed.

THE FATHER OF SOVIET HOCKEY

The Soviet Sports Committee's decision to create an Olympic-level hockey team proved to be one of the greatest feats of compensatory symbolism in the country's history. When the world's largest steel mill opened at Magnitogorsk, it was plagued with breakdowns. The world's largest airplane made only a handful of test flights before crashing. But the Soviets won the world championship and Olympic gold within a decade of adopting hockey, and then went on to dominate the sport internationally. By contrast, the Swedes and Finns also played bandy for decades before the war. Yet the development of puck-hockey in those countries came slowly, as clubs shifted to the new game, rinks were built, and children grew up with the sport. The Soviets, on the other hand, leaped past the Nordic countries, past the Czechoslovaks, Germans, and Swiss, and eventually past the Canadians.

A large part of Soviet hockey's early success was the conditioning of its players. Athletes in the Soviet Union trained far more than those of other countries. But this regimen was not simply an adaptation to a lack of resources; it also had an ideological foundation. A tenet of Soviet communism under Stalin was that workers could surpass the limits of strength and endurance, and that normal, long-term processes of development could be overcome through dedication and enthusiasm.[85] Anatoli Tarasov, co-coach of the national team, revealed this ideological basis to his intensive training system in a conversation with Czech coach Luděk Bukač in 1966.

"Luděk," Tarasov asked, "how many years have the Canadians played ice hockey?" Bukač guessed about seventy-five.

"And how many years have the Soviets played ice hockey?" Tarasov continued. About twenty-five years, Bukač answered.

"You're wrong," said Tarasov. "The Soviets work eleven months a year, the Canadians seven or eight. We work three or four hours a day, the Canadians two. We work with great intensity always. The Canadians do not. You see, Luděk. We've played for seventy-five years, too."[86]

Tarasov believed in the promises of communism. He believed in the great mission of the Soviet Union. In statements to the press and in his writings, Tarasov stressed the collective nature of Soviet hockey, its display of "team work and comradeship," as opposed to the Canadians' reliance on individual skill.[87] By the mid-1960s, when Bukač spent months with Tarasov's Red Army club, studying his training methods, Tarasov was widely respected for building a new approach to hockey based on this team-oriented principle. Today, he is revered on both sides of the Atlantic as the father of Russian hockey—a genius who transformed the sport and built one of the greatest teams of any age.

To be sure, Tarasov was a key figure in building the Soviet hockey dynasty, and his ideas on training and strategy reached far beyond Russia. However, Soviet hockey did not spring forth from the genius of Anatoli Tarasov, contrary to the conventional picture in North America and Russia. Other coaches had far greater influence on early Soviet hockey. Above all, the sport was shaped by the particular political and cultural environment in which it emerged. Tarasov was likewise a product of that environment. His success as a coach was due not only to his belief in Soviet ideology but also to his mastery of other skills essential in Stalin's Soviet Union: the ability to maneuver within the system, to cultivate allies and denounce rivals, to push beyond the system's boundaries, and to promote himself as an individual.[88]

In the first seasons of Canadian hockey in the Soviet Union, Anatoli Tarasov distinguished himself first on the ice. As player-coach of the air force team VVS, he was the league's top scorer in the inaugural season. Disagreements with the club's patron, Stalin's son Vasily, led to his firing, and he moved to Red Army. The conventional portrait highlights Tarasov's careful study of the sport and his strategic innovations as a coach in these early years. Not mentioned as often are his connections with the army and party, which secured his position and allowed him to draw on more resources. With support from the military, CSKA had better facilities than other clubs; it was the only hockey team with an indoor arena in the 1950s. Moreover, the club was able to secure talented young athletes by having them drafted into the army. In his decades-long tenure as Red Army coach, Tarasov used these two advantages to build the strongest club in the Soviet league.

In the early years of Soviet hockey, coaches at other clubs studied the new sport and experimented with strategy and training. Like Tarasov, these player-coaches came to Canadian hockey from ball-hockey and soccer. When the combined team of Moscow players shocked the visiting Czechs in 1948, the head of the coaching staff was Pavel Korotkov, who had won national cup tournaments in soccer and bandy as a defender for Dynamo Moscow. Korotkov's former teammate at Dynamo, Arkady Chernyshev, led the Soviet national team to its first world title in 1954 and to Olympic gold in 1956. Perhaps most innovative of all was Vladimir Yegorov, coach of Soviet Wings. Yegorov was the first to train his goalies by bouncing tennis balls off walls, the technique later used by Tarasov with young Vladislav Tretiak and now used by goalies everywhere. He developed new techniques for summer training, even setting down sheets of aircraft metal as a surface for shooting practice.[89] As a factory team, Soviet Wings did not have the resources of Red Army or Dynamo, nor did they have the same access to talent. Nevertheless, Yegorov's team won the first USSR Cup competition in 1951 and the league title in 1957, and he was behind the bench with Chernyshev in 1954 at Stockholm.

Tarasov's reputation was mixed at this time. His best player at CSKA, Vsevelod Bobrov, left for Vasily Stalin's air force team in 1950. Extraordinarily talented, Bobrov deserves a place among the best athletes of the century for his accomplishments in both soccer and hockey. He was not, however, extraordinarily disciplined. Tarasov, by contrast, was already putting in place an intensive training regimen. In the late 1950s, hockey officials recognized the value of this program and entrusted the Red Army coach with preparing the national team.[90] "You will sleep with your sticks," Tarasov warned one player. Some, however, were not enthused. Although commonly depicted today as a good-natured grandpa, his knit hat askew atop his head, Tarasov was abrasive, demanding, and dictatorial. In 1961, he was briefly ousted from CSKA when players mutinied against him. Alexander Yakushev, one of the best players of the 1960s, refused to play under the "despotic" Tarasov. He remained with Spartak through all the seasons he wore the national team colors.[91]

One area where Tarasov did surpass his fellow coaches was self-promotion. By the early 1960s, he was comfortable with American and Canadian newspaper writers. They cast him as a mix of folksy sage and back-slapping salesman. Taking them by the lapels or jabbing them with a forefinger, Tarasov was always good for a quote—when his interpreters could keep up. By contrast, other coaches rarely spoke to the press. Tarasov also wrote—"every year," journalist Stanislav Gridasov points out, he published "notes in newspapers, review articles, books and manuals." As he grew older, and former rivals and colleagues went silent, Tarasov wrote their contributions out of the history of Soviet hockey "and markedly exaggerated his own."[92]

In both North America and Russia, the standard account of Soviet hockey history has adopted these exaggerations. The story even goes that Stalin himself tasked Tarasov with launching Soviet hockey. The suggestion that the Great Leader would grant an audience to an undistinguished soccer player in his twenties is far-fetched. If anything, Soviet hockey had multiple founding fathers: for one, the official Sergei Savin, who pushed the sport's adoption; and then coaches Pavel Korotkov, Arkady Chernyshev, and Vladimir Yegorov, all of whom were older and more respected than Tarasov, with more successful careers as athletes. Tarasov's accomplishment was to navigate the cutthroat politics of Soviet sports and ultimately secure his role with the national team. This is not to deny his innovations as a coach. Looking at the day-by-day training schedule he devised at Red Army—a carefully structured regimen of strength and endurance work, skills development, and tactical preparation—we see the roots of today's programs for developing athletes, in hockey and other sports. Owing to the influence of those ideas, we can call Tarasov the most important figure in hockey history. But, as Stanislav Gridasov concludes, "Tarasov himself created his reputation as 'the father of Soviet hockey.'"[93]

THE LOST TEAM

At the end of the war, the dismembered country of Czechoslovakia returned to the map of Europe. The Communists drew the largest share of votes in the first postwar elections, and their leader, Klement Gottwald, became head of a coalition government. Politicians in Prague saw their country as a model for the postwar world, a place where the best of socialism and capitalism would combine to make a secure, prosperous state—a bridge between East and West.

A symbol of Czechoslovakia's dynamic revival was its hockey team. In December 1945, LTC Prague made its triumphant return to Davos, beginning a three-year hold on the Spengler Cup. Fans again filled the grandstands of Štvanice Stadium to watch visiting clubs from France, Sweden, and Canada. Prague hosted the first postwar world championship in February 1947; with the Canadians absent, Czechoslovakia took the title. Even greater victories followed. At the next year's Olympics, the Czechoslovaks skated to a scoreless tie with a team of Royal Canadian Air Force airmen and earned

Bohumil Modrý returning to Prague after winning the 1949 world championship (no. 28490, collection of National Museum, Prague, Czech Republic).

silver. They defeated the Canadians for the first time the following year, at the 1949 world championships in Stockholm. Thousands greeted the returning champions in Prague's Wenceslas Square.

By that time, Europe's political situation had darkened again. Despite talk of a bridge between East and West, Stalin wanted Czechoslovakia and the other states of Central and Eastern Europe firmly under his control. In February 1948, Prime Minister Gottwald and the Communists staged a bloodless coup and took full power. In the years that followed, Czechoslovakia's state police, known as the StB, arrested journalists, academics, and business owners. The archbishop of Prague was thrown in prison. Prominent noncommunist politicians were put on public trial and executed.

Even the world-champion hockey team did not escape the StB's reach. In March 1950, a year after their victory in Sweden, the Czechoslovak national team prepared to defend its title in London. One significant change to the roster was the loss of the team's goalie, Bohumil Modrý, regarded as the best netminder in Europe. Like many goalies, Modrý tended to be cerebral. Trained as an engineer, he had interests outside of hockey and had become dissatisfied with management of the national team. Yet even with Modrý's loss, the team was stocked with talented players, chief among them linemates Vladimir Zábrodský and Stanislav Konopásek.

Their story has become infamous.[94] When the team arrived at Prague's airport for the trip to London, they were informed that their plane had technical problems. After waiting for hours, players were told to return the next day. The following day they waited again, until StB agents announced that they would not be going to London at all. Because the British government had refused visas to two journalists accompanying the team, officials decided to withdraw from the tournament. Disappointed and angry, most of the players went to a pub. There they heard the report over the radio—that the team itself had decided not to attend the world championships, out of solidarity with the journalists.

"Liars!" one player shouted to the radio. "Why don't you tell the truth."

Others cursed into their beer: "To hell with communism. To hell with Gottwald. They've brought the country to shit."

The StB came for them at 9:00.

During their individual questioning at police headquarters, the eleven players who had been at the pub discovered that agents were concerned about more than their grumbling. "It was a terrible shock," recalled Konopásek, that "the charge was espionage and treason."[95] Officers asked in particular about former goalie Bohumil Modrý, who was arrested a few days later. The StB built their case over months of interrogations: Modrý had made plans with American agents to create a Czechoslovak hockey team in exile, and he recruited others on the national team to join. The outbursts in the pub simply gave further proof that the hockey players were enemies of the people. Modrý, Konopásek, and their teammates—a total of twelve defendants—were put on trial and convicted in October 1950. Modrý received the longest sentence, fifteen years, while Konopásek was sentenced to twelve years. The other players received sentences of eight months to fourteen years. With more than half its members in prison, the national hockey team was essentially dissolved. Czechoslovakia did not return to international competition until 1952.

Why did the Communists do this? Although the incident at the airport was clearly planned, historians have not found a direct order for the hockey team's arrest. What we do know is that the emigration of top athletes had become an embarrassment for the government. Tennis player Jaroslav Drobný, a finalist at the French Championships, defected in July 1949. Just a week before the hockey team's arrest, figure skater Alena Vrzáňová stayed in London after winning the world title. As the hockey players admitted, there had been talk of emigration for over a year. At the Spengler Cup in January

1949, LTC Prague players voted on whether to stay in Switzerland. While most players agreed to return home, two decided to remain behind.

In the months after the Spengler Cup and especially after their world championship in Sweden, emigration remained on players' minds. Most eager to leave was Modrý.[96] After the 1948 Olympics, the goalie had informed the Communist minister of sports of an opportunity to sign with an NHL team. He suggested that a Czech playing pro hockey in North America would be good for the country's image. The minister agreed and granted permission, but only after Modrý played for the national team in the following year's world championships. However, once Modrý returned from Sweden a national hero, he was disappointed to learn that the government had gone back on its promise.

Shortly afterward, in the spring of 1949, Modrý made the acquaintance of William Bowe, an American military officer with the Prague diplomatic corps. Bowe, a hockey fan, raised the idea of a Czechoslovak team in exile. Modrý introduced the officer to his teammates, who were growing more dissatisfied with their treatment by the government (one complaint was that the cars they had been promised if they won the championship never materialized). Meanwhile, Modrý himself reached the breaking point by the start of the season. When his Swiss wife learned that her father was seriously ill, Modrý applied for travel visas for his family. They were denied. In frustration, Modrý quit the national team. He was arrested before he could get his family out of the country.

When the twelve hockey players went on trial, prosecutors portrayed them as traitors to the working people of Czechoslovakia. They had been well compensated, yet they still plotted to emigrate. Socialist justice had to be carried out. After their convictions, Modrý, Konopásek, and others were sent to work in uranium mines. Five years later, following the deaths of both Gottwald and Stalin, the twelve were released. Although they were not allowed to play again on the national team, most returned to hockey. Konopásek played another eight seasons in the top division of the Czechoslovak league and then coached for a decade. One player who did not return to hockey was Modrý. After his release in 1955, his health steadily declined. In 1963 he died, at the age of forty-six.[97]

As the interrogation transcripts show, the charges against the players were not fabricated. They told police of plans to emigrate and contacts with Bowe.

In the first years of communist rule, the players believed they were still free to make such contacts. With each other, they discussed their anger toward the government and plans for emigration. In 1950, just two years after the communist takeover, they did not yet know what later generations in Czechoslovakia would—that the StB had informants everywhere.

Who informed on Bohumil Modrý and his teammates? The archives do not reveal the source, but in the decades since their arrest, suspicion has fallen on one man: team captain Vladimir Zábrodský. At the airport, Zábrodský had been the only player to agree that the team could not leave without the journalists. He had then excused himself from the group heading to the pub, saying he needed to go home with his pregnant wife. In their interrogations, players recalled that Zábrodský spent lavishly whenever the team was abroad, and they all wondered where he got the money. Zábrodský also met with Czech exiles when the team traveled. Indeed, his brother had been one of the LTC players who remained in Switzerland in January 1949. If anyone was a suspect to emigrate, it was Zábrodský. Yet state security gave him a pass.[98]

Zábrodský refuted the suggestion that he was the informant. Like the convicted players, he was banned from the national team. "Why would I turn in my own teammates?" he asked in his memoirs. "My livelihood was in hockey, my teammates were very important to me. You can't play hockey with only one person!"[99] But in the winter of 1949–50, Zábrodský was not so complimentary. Each of the arrested players spoke of Zábrodský's claim that he alone was the team. Resentment toward their captain was evident in the interrogation transcripts. Passing years did not heal the bitterness: after the revolution of 1989, when the episode could be discussed openly, a number of the players who had been imprisoned pointed to Zábrodský as their betrayer. However, if there is conclusive evidence that Zábrodský ratted on his teammates, researchers have not found it.

BEHIND THE CURTAIN

Stanislav Konopásek had his own idea of who had ordered the arrests: "The whole event was orchestrated from Moscow, so that we, the gold medal–winning Czechoslovak national team, would not stand in the way of any future success."[100] This charge is still heard today—that the Soviets eliminated the Czechoslovak team, perhaps to open the path for their own rise, perhaps to break Czechoslovakia's traditional sports structure. But the

Soviets did not need to press the Czechs and Slovaks to conform to their model. They were willing to yield the direction of their hockey program—and sports overall—to the Soviet Union.

When the Iron Curtain descended in the late 1940s, Stalinist models for political, economic, and social organization were put into place across Eastern Europe. Like other areas of social and cultural life, sports were organized under the authority of the single-party state. Formerly autonomous federations were now subject to government committees responsible for their respective sports. Independent clubs were attached to industrial enterprises, the military, or the state police. There were variations in policy from country to country. Rugby was eliminated in Poland but emphasized in Romania. Hockey received great attention in Czechoslovakia, but Hungarian authorities dismissed it as a "gentlemen's sport" and limited its funding.[101] East German Communists created hockey teams across the Soviet zone of occupation in the late 1940s, but in 1970 the government cut support for all but two clubs, both affiliated with the Stasi. In all cases, the Soviet model of state-professionalism was established. Athletes received a paycheck, an apartment, and other benefits from their employer, whether a factory or the army. There were bonuses for league titles, and even bigger bonuses for international victories and Olympic medals. On paper, they were amateurs. But their full-time job was sports.

As in other satellite states, the Committee for Sports and Physical Education in Czechoslovakia took authority over the various national federations and local clubs. The committee followed the Soviet model in emphasizing athletes' ideological education. During international trips, the national team received lectures from embassy officials on the political and economic structure in the host country. According to reports back to Prague, players were eager to discuss Marx and Lenin.[102] That may have been an exaggeration.

Hockey fans likewise used the language of Marxism-Leninism to complain about their team. Even in the Soviet Union under Stalin, citizens regularly sent letters to party committees, government ministries, or the media to express dissatisfaction. In Czechoslovakia of the early 1950s, when the Communists had been in power for less than a decade, angry hockey fans already knew how to craft their letters for maximum effect. After the national team finished fourth at the 1954 world championship, complaints to the state hockey committee came from across the country. Most letters closed with multiple signatures, to show collective disapproval. Even individual writers opened their letters with the statement that "everybody here agrees," to indicate they represented the will of the people. A number of writers identified themselves as factory workers, knowing that the people's democracy was supposed to serve their interests. They also incorporated the logic of socialist economic planning in their complaints. If the state is going to put so many resources into sport, they argued, then the people need to see better results.[103]

Hockey officials in communist Czechoslovakia found themselves in a bind, as did the country's political leaders. Prior to the war, Czechoslovakia had one of the most advanced industrial economies in Europe. When the Communists took power in 1948 and introduced the Stalinist model of economic planning, the country took a step backward. Yet, according to the new leaders, this was the truly modern path, the path leading to the socialist utopia. It was the same with hockey. In the brief window between the end of the war and the Communist takeover, the Czechoslovaks challenged Canada for the top spot in international competition. But after 1950, Czechoslovak hockey was broken. In meetings that went on for hours, the State Sports Committee debated how to fix the situation, without admitting that their own leaders had caused the problem. Some officials urged bringing back Zábrodský. Others countered that Zábrodský, like that whole generation of players, was corrupted. Instead, Czechoslovakia had to look to the one model of modern hockey, the Soviet Union. The Soviets were the teachers in all matters, they insisted. Czechoslovakia had to submit to their instruction.[104]

In his decades at the top of the International Olympic Committee, American Avery Brundage was well aware that athletes from the communist states were not amateurs. "From all reports the best Russian athletes are State proteges with all sorts of special concessions and rewards," he wrote in 1950.[105] Other IOC members, however, wanted the Olympic movement to be truly global. Some insisted that participation in the Olympics would have a positive effect on the Soviets, that they would learn to follow the rules and regulations of international sport. Others recognized that the IOC was backed into a corner: the Soviets would denounce any opposition as a violation of the committee's own principle of keeping politics out of sport.[106] Brundage did confront Soviet officials about their programs after becoming IOC president in 1952. They dodged and stonewalled; they complained the charges were politically motivated; and then they rolled out the red carpet when he visited in 1954. "I must admit," Brundage announced after his return, "Russian athletes are great!" Through the rest of his term, until 1972, the IOC president turned a blind eye to complaints about the state-run system in the Soviet bloc. "Sportsmen are presumed to be honest," he insisted.[107]

Unless, of course, they were Canadian hockey players. For Brundage, the root of all evil in sport was money, and he saw hockey in North America as rotten to the core. Already in the 1940s, he railed against the CAHA as "nothing more than a branch of the professional leagues."[108] Prior to the 1948 Winter Olympics, he sought to have the sport expelled entirely. Ironically, it was the Olympics' own commercial interests that kept hockey on the program—organizers in St. Moritz stressed that the sport was necessary for ticket sales.[109] Hockey remained, but Brundage's hostility hardened. Privately, he acknowledged that the winter games would be finished without hockey.[110] And that didn't bother him. With figure skaters cashing in medals for ice-show contracts and downhill skiers promoting branded equipment, Brundage saw the Winter Olympics as rife with commercialism. Only the intervention of other IOC members kept their president from putting an end to the winter games.[111]

If Brundage could not get hockey out, at least he could keep out the professionals. Even American college students were suspect. In 1964, the IOC questioned the US hockey team's two-month schedule of warm-up exhibitions before the winter games. National teams cannot spend this much time preparing, Olympic officials scolded.[112] By that time, Soviet hockey players were training throughout the summer. The core of the national team, as members of Tarasov's Red Army club, played a full season together before the Olympics. But the Soviets were allies in Brundage's fight against professionalism and commercialism. As the IOC president chased athletes in the West for receiving under-the-table payments or generous expense accounts, the countries of the Soviet bloc expanded their state-professional system.[113] Ultimately, this system would be just as destructive to the amateur ideal as the North American pros.

FOUR

Toward New Directions

IN MARCH 1961 THE HOCKEY WORLD APPEARED to be back in order. The Canadians claimed the world championship for the nineteenth time, closing with a 5–1 rout of the Soviets. Representing Canada that year were the Trail Smoke Eaters, from the small, mineral-smelting town of Trail, British Columbia. Like past Canadian teams, the Smokies toured Europe before the tournament, filling outdoor rinks in Sweden, Finland, Czechoslovakia, and Switzerland. Most popular was goalie Seth Martin, who was greeted with chants of "Marti! Marti!" at each stop. His attacking style of play and his skeletal face mask, made in the plastics shop at the Trail smelting plant, influenced European netminders for years to come.[1]

A decade later, the hockey world looked very different. The 1971 world championships returned to Switzerland, with all games now played inside arenas of steel, glass, and concrete. Plexiglass surrounded the rink, replacing the netting that had once protected spectators. All skaters as well as goalies wore helmets. Fans across the continent watched on color television as the Soviets won their ninth consecutive title. Czechoslovakia and Sweden earned silver and bronze, with Finland, a rising power in international hockey, finishing just off the podium.

The Canadians were not among the medalists because they were not at the tournament. For the second straight year, the Canadian Amateur Hockey Association refused to send a team, and word was that they would skip the 1972 Olympics as well. The Trail Smoke Eaters ended up being the last Canadian amateurs to win an international tournament. As competition stiffened during the 1960s, hockey officials in Canada insisted on sending their best players, those under professional contract. They pointed out the hypocrisy of amateur rules that allowed Soviet and Czechoslovak athletes to earn full salaries. Even the Swedes were cheating, they argued, as Tre Kronor players received handsome sponsorships from sporting-goods companies. But Avery Brundage remained firm. If the International Ice Hockey Federation (IIHF) allowed Canadian professionals to play in its world championships, then all other players would be ineligible for the Olympics. Amateurs who played against professionals were no longer amateurs, Brundage declared. Unwilling to pass up the Olympics, Europeans scuttled a deal that would have admitted pros to the world championships. So Canada walked out. Tensions that had been stirring since the Winnipeg Falcons went to Antwerp finally broke hockey apart.

But why did Canada even need international hockey? The standard take in Canadian circles was that the world championships were a lesser game. The world's best players were in the NHL. During the 1960s, the league was more popular than ever. Teams set attendance records, and *Hockey Night in Canada* was at the top of the ratings. And participation continued to grow. By the end of the decade, more than a half-million boys were playing organized hockey in Canada.[2]

Yet hockey in Canada also showed signs of being a cultural institution that was too secure, too powerful, and too satisfied with itself. Yes, the sport was immensely popular. But some prominent Canadians were concerned—people who professed to love hockey as the national game and at the same time were troubled by its corrupting influence.

Meanwhile, European hockey came into its own during this time. Following the postwar rebuilding, sustained economic growth improved standards of living, even in the socialist East. Junior hockey programs expanded to serve baby boomers, just like in North America. And as European hockey developed, enthusiasm for Canadian hockey diminished. When the Smoke Eaters returned in 1963, they were hounded by angry fans at their exhibitions. During the Belleville McFarlands' tour in 1959, Finnish spectators pelted the team with snowballs in response to their rough play; in Sweden, they needed a police escort. Before the war, Europeans had praised Canadians for their unmatched skill and speed. Now they were branded "a hooligan gang." Canadian hockey was no longer the model.[3] Instead, it was the Soviets who played the more compelling, dynamic game—fast, fluid, and organized.

In the Soviet Union, Czechoslovakia, and the Nordic countries of Sweden and Finland, officials, coaches, and players created new models of hockey during the 1960s. Just as in Canada, they saw the sport as an expression of national ideals and identity, and the models reflected their distinct political and social environments. As hockey in Europe developed, the decades-old bonds that had linked the hockey world—Canada's commanding performances in international tournaments, the amateur rules of world sport, the International Olympic Committee's authority—no longer fit. When Canada broke from international hockey, it was out of frustration with how the hockey world had changed. They were accustomed to being the best at their game, the game they had invented. But in the 1960s, the Europeans and Soviets took that game in new directions. They were able to let Canada go and play their own game.

OUR GAME

The 1960s were especially good for Canada's two NHL franchises. Montreal won the Stanley Cup five times during the decade, and the Leafs four (the Black Hawks took the cup in 1961, led by the phenomenal young scorer Bobby Hull). Both teams drew around a half-million fans per season, and they had a steady source of revenue from *Hockey Night in Canada*. The program's audience grew throughout the decade, reaching an average of four million viewers every Saturday night. In promotional materials, sponsor Imperial Oil presented the weekly games as a family event, with dad, mom, and kids all gathered around the TV on a winter's night.[4]

Hockey was king in a country that was undergoing far-reaching transformations. Cities grew. Industry grew. Under prime minister Lester Pearson (a former player with the Oxford Canadians), universal health care and pension systems were established, and English-French bilingualism and unrestricted immigration had their origins.[5] The visual symbol of this emerging Canada was its new flag, officially introduced in 1965.

Although Canadians now identify proudly with the red maple leaf, there was strong resistance to the flag when it was first introduced. One argument for the new standard was that it represented all Canadians.[6] The traditional Red Ensign, with the Union Jack in its canton, was a reminder of English dominance at a time when awareness of a distinctive Québécois identity was rising. Clarence Campbell's suspension of Maurice Richard in March 1955 and the subsequent riot in Montreal have long been seen as an influential spark in the political and cultural turn known as the Quiet Revolution.[7] Quebec author Roch Carrier argues that it was the Rocket himself who bolstered national pride among French Canadians. "Before he came along, our people had no one we could look up to with admiration," Carrier states in his

Hockey for everyone, including grandma upstairs with her radio. Schedule for the 1961–1962 season of *Hockey Night in Canada* (courtesy of Glenbow Museum).

biography of Richard.[8] But the importance of *le Club de hockey Canadien* goes beyond the Montreal riot and the iconic Richard. Television ratings show that the one institution binding most French Canadians together in the 1960s was Montreal's hockey team. At the start of the decade, nearly three-quarters of French households in the city tuned in to the games (by contrast, less than 40 percent of Toronto residents watched Leafs games).[9] In Quebec as a whole, which had fewer televisions per household, family and neighbors gathered around available sets for the Canadiens. The loyalty that bound Quebeckers in the 1960s was not a revolution led by writers and professors, or the Liberal Party, or the Catholic Church. It was the Montreal Canadiens.[10]

As Canada went through the changes of the 1960s, the question was raised: Is the national game changing, too? Figures like Richard and Gordie Howe were celebrated as respectable, hardworking men who represented the best of Canada. But different images began to emerge as well—the foul-mouthed juniors coach who berated boys on his team; parents who accepted thousands of dollars to allow their teenage sons to join a junior club in a distant town; the NHL executive, a Canadian by upbringing, who showed regard only for American dollars; the fans who cheered when blood was spilled on the ice.

In 1963, the *Globe & Mail* explored this darker side of the game in a ten-part series titled "What Happened to Hockey?" The author, a prize-winning journalist named George Mortimore, was appreciative of hockey's place in Canadian history. But the sport, he argued, had numerous problems—chief among them the NHL's dominance over amateur hockey. He wrote of Bobby Hull leaving home at age thirteen, drawn into a world in which he was prepared only for pro hockey. "The whole apparatus of hockey has been converted into a factory for making star professional players," Mortimore argued. The juniors network controlled by the NHL had grown fat, while the game at the community level had been left to starve. "Big hockey is often generous, often stingy, always autocratic," Mortimore wrote, and is "vengeful, jealous of its rights as a private business, suspicious of new ideas."[11]

The article series drew enough attention that NHL president Clarence Campbell felt obliged to respond. "They used to blame pool halls, now they blame hockey," Campbell said of the charge that the sport turned young men into uneducated bums.[12] He countered that NHL teams gave thousands of dollars in direct support to junior clubs each year, money for players' school fees. The league had a generous pension program for retired players. As for the charge that the NHL was somehow bad for Canadian hockey, Campbell pointed out that there had not been an unsold seat in Maple Leaf Gardens or the Montreal Forum in seventeen years. If NHL hockey was so bad, then why was it so popular?

Concerns about the NHL's influence over the game were not limited to crusading journalists. Prime Minister Pearson's offhand remark in Parliament that "practically every good player in Canada under the age of ten is on the negotiating list, at least, of some professional club" drew plenty of attention—and a firm rebuttal from Campbell.[13] Provincial governments in Quebec and Alberta took the matter more seriously, launching inquiries into junior hockey. The Canadian Amateur Hockey Association was feeling the heat. Leaders of the organization complained to their counterparts in the NHL that its public standing was suffering. Amateur officials proposed replacing NHL sponsorship of junior clubs with an open draft of all amateur players above a certain age. Campbell responded that NHL owners would be unwilling to give up control of their prospects, "who are, for all practical purposes, 'professionals.'"[14] When negotiations stalled, CAHA leaders joined critics of the pro league. At an amateur meeting in Calgary, CAHA secretary Gordon Juckes declared that the "money barons of the NHL" had reduced "Canada to the role of a gigantic hockey slave farm."[15] As always, Campbell was dismissive: "I don't know who the hell he's talking for."[16]

Yet criticism of the national game was gaining traction. In spring 1966, a branch of the Ministry of National Health and Welfare launched an investigation into amateur hockey. Unsurprisingly, news of the inquiry prompted the NHL to iron out a new agreement with amateur hockey. Franchises ended their direct sponsorship of junior clubs, and the league phased out the various negotiation lists that had been used to secure young talent. In their place, the NHL agreed to an open draft of amateurs. Soon after this new agreement was finalized, the ministry issued its report. While many recommendations were already included in the new CAHA-NHL pact, the investigation's judgment still made headlines: "What is good for the NHL is not necessarily good for hockey in general."[17]

A BANANA REPUBLIC

As with George Hardy's reforms of amateur hockey decades earlier, concerns about Canada's place in the hockey world were an important factor in the 1967 CAHA-NHL agreement. One issue was Canadian teams' declining fortunes in international tournaments. As the Soviets, Swedes, Czechoslovaks, and even Americans showed themselves equal to Canada's representative team, managers of Allan Cup–winning clubs scoured the amateur and minor-pro ranks in search of supplementary talent. Ringers were expensive. The 1959 world champions, the senior club from Belleville, Ontario, paid its players from the city budget. After an auditor revealed the scheme, Belleville citizens were left with a hefty tax bill—the equivalent of more than $2.3 million today.[18] Ringers were also getting harder to find. Lester Pearson's jibe about the NHL controlling every player under ten was in response to a question about Canada's fourth-place finish in the 1965 world championships. The implication was clear: there were few Canadian players who could qualify as amateurs and compete with international hockey's new powers.

A second concern was the international structure of the NHL. Complaints about American influence over Canada's game went back to the 1920s, when the Hamilton Tigers were sold to Big Bill Dwyer. These complaints ramped up in 1966, after the NHL announced six new franchises that would join the league the following year. The planned expansion had first been made public in March 1965, when Clarence Campbell invited investors in "major league" cities to submit proposals. At first, reactions to the planned expansion were positive. Montreal coach Toe Blake remarked that opportunities for Canadians to play pro hockey would double. Toronto sportswriter Scott Young quipped that the NHL was finally moving into the twentieth century.[19]

Pundits agreed that expansion would surely bring pro hockey to the West Coast. Between 1940 and 1960, California's population had more than doubled. Los Angeles had become the third-largest city in the United States, and another 2.7 million people lived in the San Francisco–Oakland metropolitan area. In all likelihood, both cities would gain franchises, as had been the case in 1958, when baseball's Brooklyn Dodgers and New York Giants moved to California at the same time. Eastern teams could then play two series on one West Coast trip, making travel costs more bearable.

Canadians expected another West Coast city to gain a franchise. With a population over four hundred thousand and a growing economy, Vancouver was the only Canadian city other than Toronto and Montreal that qualified as "major league." When the NHL announced plans to expand, the city's mayor immediately pushed for a franchise.[20] Campbell was encouraging. "It looks like Vancouver will go," he told reporters before bids were submitted. In the end, however, the city was shut out by simple math. From the start, the league's owners had planned to save on travel costs by placing two teams in the East, two teams in the Midwest, and two teams in the West—and the latter two were always going to be Los Angeles and San Francisco. According to the sports editor of the *Vancouver Sun,* the city "drew a blank card from a stacked deck." When the new franchises were announced—Pittsburgh, Philadelphia, Minneapolis–St. Paul, and St. Louis, along with LA and San Francisco—Campbell went back on his earlier remarks: "Vancouver was never in it."[21]

Vancouver's snub set off angry reactions across Canada. Members of Parliament raised the NHL's decision with Prime Minister Pearson during question time. "We would like to see Canada with larger representation in that league," opposition leader John Diefenbaker challenged, drawing a chorus of "Hear, hear."[22] A few days later, a Toronto MP called on Pearson to confront the league's leadership: "Would he point out to the directors of the NHL that the league was started as a Canadian league and the Canadians object strongly to it being turned into an organization which discriminates against first class Canadian teams for the benefit of owners in the United States?"[23]

Leaders of Canadian amateur hockey were even more incensed. They cast the struggle between the CAHA and NHL as a defense of the national game against a mercenary American operation. In his speech in Calgary, delivered the day after the NHL's expansion announcement, Gordon Juckes declared that the league's plans were "the final 'sell-out' of Canadian hockey." In their quest to grab as much money as possible, the league's owners were sowing seeds of the sport's destruction. "No longer can a few Canadian symbols (such as Maple Leafs) and Frenchified team names ('Canadiens') be used to fool the public that we should concede any of our principles for the NHL because it is Canadian," Juckes declared.[24] CAHA president Lionel Fleury was likewise blunt: "It won't be long before Canada becomes a 'banana republic' in the trade of hockey talents."[25]

Fleury's remark pointed to a larger concern about Canada's relationship with its imposing neighbor. To call Canada a "banana republic" was to equate the country with Latin American states that had fallen under the power of the United States. In the 1960s, Canadians across the political spectrum feared that their country was coming into a similar position. Oil from Alberta, uranium from Saskatchewan, and iron ore from Labrador were all shipped across the border to fuel the American economic and military expansion. For many Canadians, it appeared that not only the national game but also the national economy was being sold out. In the words of philosopher George Grant, Canada was becoming an "unimportant country."[26]

THE RED MACHINE IN HIGH GEAR

In April 1960 the Montreal Canadiens won the Stanley Cup for the fifth consecutive season—an unequaled run as NHL champions. The Canadiens dynasty would be revived later in the 1960s, claiming the cup another four times in five years.

During the same decade, in Europe, the Soviet hockey dynasty amassed an even longer string of titles in the IIHF world tournament and Winter Olympics. The national team's nine consecutive championships are unsurpassed as a record of sustained sporting excellence, outdoing the Boston Celtics' eight straight NBA titles and the seven consecutive national championships won by John Wooden's UCLA Bruins.[27]

Many fans, myself included, will say we don't like dynasties. We grumble, for example, about the Patriots in the Super Bowl or Golden State in the NBA finals—again. We insist that it's better to have parity within leagues, a more competitive mix of contenders. We're wrong. Economists have found that "outcome uncertainty" (i.e., parity) has little effect on attendance. Indeed, at the height of their dynasty, from the 1940s to the '60s, the New York Yankees had by far the largest road attendance in baseball. Bayern Munich wins the Bundesliga year after year, yet the German top division draws the largest crowds in European soccer. Dynasties drive attendance, they drive TV ratings, and they drive change in their sports—in coaching strategy, player development, and personnel management—as competitors work to keep pace.[28]

The Soviet hockey dynasty had this effect on international hockey. Their style of play offered a contrast to the rough Canadian game, building on the European preference for passing. Not only a model on the ice, the Soviets were respected, feared, and hated opponents. When the national team or clubs from the Soviet League toured the Eastern Bloc, they were met with hostile fans in packed arenas.[29] Crowds were just as large and vocal on the other side of the Iron Curtain. At the 1967 world championships in Vienna, over thirteen thousand spectators whistled the Soviets off the ice after their match with Czechoslovakia ended in a brawl. Games with the Soviets were must-see events—and must-see TV. When they played the Swedes in the 1970 world championships, up to 80 percent of Sweden's adult population tuned in to the game.[30]

Big television audiences and full arenas meant more revenue for hockey's governing body. Led by its president, London-based businessman John "Bunny" Ahearne, the IIHF was one of the first sports federations to negotiate a cut of Olympic television rights. The federation also handled all rights for the world championship, rather than entrusting contracts to local organizers. In 1967, for example, the tournament in Vienna brought in just under 350,000 Swiss francs for television and another 367,000 for publicity, including advertisements on the boards (a total equivalent to $1.3 million in 2020).[31] The federation used the money to fund further development of the sport: coaching clinics, tournaments for lower-tier national teams, and, beginning in 1967, a new competition for European junior squads, the forerunner to the World Junior Championships. While Ahearne was a savvy (and widely reviled) negotiator, he also had a product that audiences wanted to buy. Just as the Celtics and Bruins drove American basketball's rise in popularity in the 1960s, so did the growth of international hockey owe much to having a dynasty that stirred interest and fired passions.

The Soviet dynasty of the 1960s was built on the failures of the late 1950s. After winning the world championship in 1954 and Olympic gold in 1956, the Soviets stumbled in international play. When Moscow hosted the 1957 tournament, some fifty thousand spectators watched the final between the Soviets and Sweden at the outdoor Luzhniki Stadium—the largest hockey crowd ever, until teams began playing in football and baseball stadiums in the 2000s. The game ended in a tie, and Sweden finished one point ahead in the final standings. For Soviet sports officials, a silver medal on their home ice, in their colossal new stadium, was a failure.[32]

Over the next five years, as the Soviet team had a string of second- and third-place finishes, officials shuffled coaches. Chernyshev was sacked and Tarasov brought in. Then Tarasov was sacked and Chernyshev brought back.[33] Finally, in 1962, officials came upon the formula that would bring success—a team of rivals. Chernyshev was named senior coach and Tarasov second coach. The head of the Soviet Sports Committee told them to get the national team in shape. "This is not a request or a bit of advice," he added.[34]

During this transitional time, hockey officials built the structure that would bring Tarasov and Chernyshev success in the 1960s. In the wake of the 1957 defeat, the Hockey Department, under the authority of the State Sports Committee, set down a multipoint plan for improving the team's performance, an approach that followed the Soviet practice of economic planning. In the Soviet Union, economic development was guided by Gosplan, the State Planning Committee in Moscow, following a presumably rational, Marxist understanding of economics. Planners formulated broad five-year goals for national growth and specific, annual targets for all goods, from steel girders to children's shoes. Factories across the country then worked to fulfill Gosplan's mandated quotas. In the view of sports officials, planning was just as valid for producing athletes as it was for locomotive engines. As sociologist Hart Cantelon noted in his study of Soviet hockey, progress in sports was "equated with meeting and then surpassing objectively measurable standards; standards which have been developed through scientific innovation, improvement in technique or greater skill efficiency."[35] When the Hockey Department set out to resolve the national team's failings, it did so by setting strategic goals, determining specific targets, and drawing up week-by-week action plans.

The first goal was to develop ice hockey as a "mass sport." Canadian hockey had already shown rapid growth across the country by 1957. Yet, as with economic planning, the way to ensure continued growth was to set higher targets. In the city of Chelyabinsk, for example, the plan mandated an increase in the number of clubs from 100 to 150. Moscow was given an even higher target: from 200 to 350 clubs.³⁶ Overall, the committee aimed to double the number of hockey players across the country by 1960, up to 150,000.

In addition to expanding the base of hockey players across the country, the Hockey Department wanted to improve the skills of top-level players, the candidates for the national team. Their approach to player development likewise followed the principles of Soviet economy planning. Economic planners did not seek improvements in productivity through greater efficiency; rather, they held that increased production came from increased inputs. In the same way, hockey planners believed that more intensive training was needed to improve the national team's performance.

The Soviet team that competed in the 1957 world championships already dedicated more hours to training than any of its competitors. The following summer, when candidates assembled for two weeks, the regimen was even more intensive. Some days began at 7:45 A.M. and finished at 8:00 P.M., with a full schedule of skills work, individual fitness tests, on- and off-ice training, and scrimmages. When players returned to their clubs, they were to continue working toward fitness and strength benchmarks, with their coaches reporting back to officials.³⁷ This program, put in place during Tarasov's tenure as sole coach, became the hallmark of Soviet hockey. After Chernyshev returned as senior coach, Tarasov retained control over training. Their successor, Viktor Tikhonov, observed that Chernyshev was responsible for the team's head, its strategy, while Tarasov trained its body. "The national team had a strong body," he added.³⁸

In the Soviet Union, as in Canada and the United States, hockey participation rose with the demographic boom of the postwar years. Soviet boomers grew up with Canadian hockey, idolizing the stars of the Soviet Union's first championship teams and playing on neighborhood rinks. The Soviet equivalent of the North American backyard rink was the *korobka,* the box, a small rink built in the courtyard of an urban apartment complex. For millions of people in the Soviet Union, the courtyard was the center of daily life: there was space for a community garden, a playground, clotheslines, parking for those fortunate enough to have a car. "The courtyard was, for me, perhaps a second home, the primary school of life," recalled Boris Mikhailov, captain of the Soviet team in the 1970s. Growing up in Moscow's Khoroshevsky district, Mikhailov and his friends scavenged construction sites for planks to build their *korobka* and convinced maintenance workers to flood the makeshift rink.³⁹

Tabletop hockey for Soviet boomers (courtesy of Sokolniki Park Archive, Moscow).

The resourceful children of Mikhailov's day not only had to find their own boards, they also had to improvise for equipment. As in other areas of Soviet life, hockey was plagued with shortages. During the late 1950s, when Mikhailov and his friends played in their boots with a tin can for a puck, the Hockey Department was calling for construction of more rinks and setting production quotas for hockey sticks. Yet, as historian Paul Harder details in his study of Soviet hockey, the lack of basic equipment persisted.[40] With little gear available, authorities published instructions on how players could make their own. "We made sticks, pads, shovels to clean the rink," recalled national team player Viktor Kuzkin in a how-to article for the children's magazine *Young Technician*. "I shot the puck once with a simple stick with a board nailed on the end as a blade. But the blade immediately broke off. So I had to go back to the workshop to make a new one."[41]

Authorities also sought to structure the games of these *korobka* players. In 1964 the youth organization Komsomol launched the Golden Puck tournament for teams from apartment blocks and schools. In its first year, the

"The Goalie," 1961, photograph by Vladimir Lagrange (courtesy of Lumiere Brothers Gallery, Moscow, www.lumierephoto.ru).

competition drew fifty-seven teams of fourteen- to fifteen-year-olds. A decade later, the tournament had three age classes, several hundred teams, and—according to publicity—some four million players.[42] Anatoli Tarasov was credited as the tournament's founder and was a visible part of the event. He regularly attended games at the national level, telling the press that he was searching for boys to join the Red Army youth teams.

For a teenage boy playing in the Golden Puck, the sight of Tarasov in the stands was the stuff of dreams. In real life, however, earning a spot with Red Army or any other major club was something only the most talented young athletes could accomplish. When Vladislav Tretiak tried out with CSKA at age eleven, he was one of only four boys selected out of more than two hundred on the ice.[43] Those who reached the ice had already been screened for future athletic success. Team officials paid particular attention to the characteristics of a boy's parents: What was their physical stature? Had they been athletes? Those who passed the screening went through a series of off-ice drills to measure speed, strength, and agility. Finally, they completed skills tests on the ice. Competition was fierce. By the early 1970s, some one thousand boys responded to the annual announcement of CSKA tryouts. Fewer than a hundred were selected.[44]

Red Army had its pick of the best children starting out in the game. But Tarasov also recruited promising young talent from other Soviet teams. Players for other clubs knew that playing for Tarasov was the first step toward selection for the national team. If a player accepted the invitation, Tarasov arranged for the young man to be conscripted into the army.[45] Coaches of other club teams resented this sway over players, and the Hockey Department criticized the lack of parity in the domestic league. Nevertheless, other top teams followed suit. Moscow clubs Spartak and Dynamo both hoarded talent from the provinces, with offers of better pay and life in the capital. In the 1960s, these three Moscow clubs—Tarasov's CSKA, Chernyshev's Dynamo, and the trade-union club Spartak, coached by Vsevolod Bobrov—dominated the Soviet league, and the national team featured their best players.[46]

While Tarasov was notorious for working his players the hardest, all teams trained their players throughout the off-season. Soviet athletes made a full-time commitment, and they were paid well for their work. In the 1960s and '70s, a hockey player's stipend was two to three times an average worker's earnings (similarly, the average NHL salary in the mid-1960s was double the median salary in the United States or Canada). Each member of the national team also earned a 1,000-ruble bonus for winning the world championship, roughly equivalent to the annual average wage in the Soviet Union. Players pocketed even more money by bringing goods from abroad and selling them on the black market. "It was considered a decent trip if you could make three thousand rubles," recalled national team captain Boris Mayorov.[47]

In 1972, just a few months before the Soviet national team met Canadian NHL players for the first time, Avery Brundage forwarded a complaint about state payments for Soviet athletes. Moscow's response was terse: Our athletes are amateurs.[48] Although not as deceptive as the Soviets, the other hockey dynasty of the time, the Montreal Canadiens, likewise owed a good part of its success to gaming the system. The Canadiens had the NHL's most extensive network of sponsored feeder teams, giving the team control over hundreds of prospects. Of all NHL teams, Montreal had the most to lose when the sponsorship system was replaced by an amateur draft.

From their places at the pinnacle, the leading figures of the Soviet national team and the Montreal Canadiens recognized the limits of the hockey world's parallel structures. Anatoli Tarasov regularly reminded his players that the real measure of hockey talent was the NHL. Already in the mid-1960s, he was preparing for the Soviet team's ultimate test by diagramming defensive strategies to stop Bobby Hull.[49] During the same period, the Canadiens' new president, David Molson, likewise recognized that the NHL had to break out of its confines. A generation younger than Clarence Campbell, Conn Smythe, and the league's old guard, Molson was one of the strongest proponents for expansion. But expansion was only the beginning. In a 1965 interview with *Sports Illustrated*, Molson set out his vision for the NHL's future—and the future of the hockey world. The NHL would expand, as would the top minor-pro league. "I can see foreign leagues with Russian and Czech and Swedish teams," he said. Molson was aware of the reality in Europe and the Soviet Union, that players there dedicated more time to hockey than Canadian pros. He anticipated a time when these European professionals would compete directly with the NHL. "I can see eventually a world playoff for the Stanley Cup," he said, "with worldwide television." The NHL could not afford to remain static, Molson insisted, if it wanted to keep selling tickets and keep inspiring young players in the game. "Once you stop growing," he added, "you die."[50]

THE THIRD WAY

"I was thinking about when we played in Leksand," recalled a member of the 1963 Trail Smoke Eaters, more than a decade after the team's trip to Sweden for the world championships. "I think it must have been about 20 below zero. It was unbelievable how cold it was."

"Oh yeah, that game I wore earmuffs, a toque, and a helmet," a teammate added. "And we had to walk from that one dressing room to the outdoor rink in snowbanks."[51]

The former players were sitting for an interview with Scott Young, the dean of Canadian hockey writers.[52] In their interview, the old Smokies remembered a fight during a game in Gothenburg. One of the Canadian players went after a Swedish defenseman in the corner and started throwing punches. The Swede didn't fight back. But because he towered some six inches over the flailing Canadian, other Trail players went over the boards. Primed by previous episodes of Canadian assaults, the police were ready.

"Christ, they sent the dogs after us," one of the players remembered, "on the ice."

The Canadians fled from the rink to their dressing room.

"All I could see was the bloody dogs," recalled Norm Lenardon, who was knocked to the ground during the team's escape. "I'm saying, 'Somebody help me' ... I'm trying to get up and I'm saying, 'Holy Christ, the dogs are going to get me.'"

Lenardon made it safely to the locker room. The next morning, he was sitting in the hotel lobby when a seven-year-old boy walked by and thumbed his nose at him. "We were finished in Sweden after that game," he admitted. He was right: the Canadian Amateur Hockey Association ended the practice of sending the country's top senior club to the world championships. Nonetheless, the Smoke Eaters lived on in Sweden for years afterward. Historian Tobias Stark recalled that Swedish parents would keep their children in line with threats of the fearsome Canadians: "If you don't behave yourself, the Trail Smoke Eaters will come and get you!"[53]

Reading the interview transcript, one can almost hear the laughter among the old players as they recount their European adventures. The Swedes were the butt of the humor. In the view of players and pundits, Sweden was the foil—the inferior opposite of everything that was great about Canadian hockey, its players disparaged as "chicken Swedes." When Börje Salming joined the Toronto Maple Leafs in 1973, he was hailed for playing hard-nosed hockey, like a Canadian rather than a Swede. His Swedish teammate on the Leafs, Inge Hammarström, never earned the same respect. The team's owner at the time, Harold Ballard, scoffed that Hammarström "could go into the corner with a half a dozen eggs in his pocket and not break one of them."[54] Two decades later, Swedish players in the NHL were still charged with being soft. "I can play a tough game," Mats Sundin told the *Toronto Star* in 1994, when the Leafs acquired him.[55] Years later, after being named team captain, he was still making the case. Sundin's teammates came to his defense repeatedly, but the doubts were never silenced. "Maybe we weren't ready yet for a Swedish captain," said coach Pat Quinn, thirty years after Salming first joined the team.[56]

For the Swedes, Canadian hockey likewise provided a contrast. At first, it was a positive example. The Swedes initially played the game with a more rugged, individualistic approach, a style of play that supposedly evoked the "Viking spirit."[57] Canadians were respected for their skill and sportsmanship. But as the Smoke Eaters experienced, the admiration had dimmed by the early 1960s. The Swedes looked instead to the Soviets for an example of skilled, strategic hockey. Yet the Soviets also offered a contrast. Swedes saw themselves as having a disciplined, well-organized team structure, with the coach functioning as part of the team, as opposed to the mechanical Soviets, playing under a despot.[58]

Swedish hockey developed in the 1960s out of this intermediary position. Federation officials and coaches intentionally plotted a third way between the Canadians and Soviets, following upon Sweden's neutral position in the Cold War and its social democratic political system. The guiding ideal of postwar Sweden was *folkhemmet,* "the people's home": a modern society in which everyone's needs were met. Swedes took pride in an economic system that combined both capitalism and socialism, a social welfare system that provided for individual freedom and collective equality, and a political system that merged parliamentary democracy with centralized government planning. In the same way, many took pride in their hockey program as offering a better path than the Soviets or Canadians. Although they lost regularly to the Soviets in the 1960s, Swedes could content themselves with having a morally superior system. As Tobias Stark observes, hockey was intimately connected with the development of social democratic society. Indeed, more than any other area of culture, the sport dramatized postwar Swedish identity with a "particularly strong blue-and-yellow luminosity."[59]

Essential to the social democratic systems in Sweden and the Nordic countries was education: preparing young people to have a contributing role in modern society.[60] The Nordic model was built upon collaboration of individual citizens, social organizations, and the state. The basic aim of this arrangement, according to Danish historian Niels Keyser Nielsen, was "to establish a moral sense of belonging."[61] An individual's moral commitment required taking an active role within the community. Sports clubs had an important role in this process. As venues for young people to participate visibly in the community, clubs became vital parts of social democratic education in the postwar decades.

Sports clubs were also an instrument of state social policy. In Sweden, the national government provided funding to the Swedish Sport Federation, the governing body for all sports, while municipal governments partnered with local clubs in building and maintaining facilities. The partnership was effective. In Sweden between 1945 and 1970, membership in sports clubs nearly quadrupled, with soccer, gymnastics, and skiing having the most partici-

Fans at the 1963 world championship in Stockholm (photo by Lev Borodulin, courtesy of Lev Borodulin/Moscow House of Photography).

pants. Still today, in Sweden and other Nordic countries, the state works with sports associations to promote broad participation as well as the training of elite athletes. The result is that involvement in sports is greater in the Nordic countries than in other parts of Europe.[62]

The cooperation between the state and sports associations was key to the growth of hockey in Sweden. In the 1920s, Swedish skaters had played on German teams, and clubs like IK Göta had traveled to the continent in the 1930s. In Sweden itself, however, the more popular ice sport remained bandy. Promoters of Canadian hockey saw themselves in competition with ball-hockey, and they were eager to displace the more established game. At the international federation's first postwar meetings, Swedish delegates pleaded to host the world championships, seeing the tournament as a way to build hockey's popularity.[63] They were right. During the 1949 tournament in Stockholm, some ten thousand people forced their way into Stockholm's Olympic Stadium for the game between Sweden and Canada, tearing down fences and skirmishing with police.[64] Five years later, when the tournament returned to Stockholm, scalpers sold tickets for the Sweden-Canada game at four times their face value.[65]

International competition was a big part of hockey's draw in Sweden. Already in 1945, prominent sports commentator Sven Jerring sided with hockey over bandy as a game in which Swedes could compete on the world stage. Bandy was played in only a few countries, he stated in one of his radio commentaries. "Ice hockey, on the other hand, is international in its character."[66] As fan interest surged, the hockey federation also worked to increase participation. After taking the helm as federation chairman in 1948, Social Democratic technocrat Helge Berglund built ties with both the national government and municipalities. The federation was especially effective at convincing municipal officials to include hockey rinks in their building programs. By 1972, there were 190 artificial hockey rinks in the country, including fifty-five enclosed arenas—more than ten times the number of artificial bandy rinks.[67]

Once they had built the rinks, the players and spectators came. Puck-hockey soared past bandy in the mid-1950s in terms of overall participation and attendance. But the more established sport did not lose its audience. In fact, attendance at bandy matches grew by more than a third from 1953 to 1965, to just over three hundred thousand. Hockey, however, had more than twice as many spectators by that time. Some games between the Stockholm club Djurgårdens and Frölunda of Gothenburg drew over twenty thousand fans.[68] By the early 1970s, with more than nine thousand registered teams and total attendance in the top league of more than eight hundred thousand fans, Helge Berglund declared it no longer "an unrealistic dream" to expect hockey to "outflank soccer to become the biggest sport in the country."[69]

Hockey in Finland likewise had spectacular growth in the postwar decades. Prior to the war, the game with the puck had an even smaller following among Finns than among Swedes. Finnish officials had decided not to subject their bandy players to strange Canadian rules for the 1920 Antwerp Olympics.[70] In the 1920s and '30s, only a few clubs took up the sport. Bandy remained the popular winter game, and the annual match against Sweden was one of the biggest sporting events of the year. Finland was distinct from other Nordic countries, however, in that team sports in general were not that prominent. The population was largely rural and thinly dispersed. According to a Danish observer in the 1930s, Finnish athletes trained "not in a stadium, since the distances are too great, but outside the farm, where they have their daily work."[71] Paavo Nurmi and other Olympic medalists were celebrated for their success in what were regarded as the national sports: running, the javelin throw, and Nordic skiing. As historian Jouko Kokkonen points out, these individual disciplines were viewed "as more suited to Finns than team sports."[72]

At the end of the war, hockey was the smallest section in the Finnish Sports and Gymnastics Federation, with only twenty-three clubs and some twelve hundred members. Two decades later, there were 286 clubs and more than forty-four thousand registered players. One driver of this growth was the influence of Sweden. Although Finland was technically neutral in Cold War Europe, the country was firmly under Moscow's political influence. Sweden provided an outlet to the West. Hockey clubs in northern Finland competed in leagues across the border, and players and coaches visited Sweden for training. At the same time, social and economic developments within Finland fueled hockey's popularity. The postwar decades brought an expansion of Finnish industry, and the country had the fastest rate of urbanization in Europe. By 1970, a majority of Finns lived in urban areas. Hockey became the most popular winter sport in growing cities and suburbs.

Cooperation between state and sport contributed to hockey's growth in urban areas. The Finnish social democratic system had a later start than that in Sweden, but the model was similar in placing emphasis on youth development. As historian David Kirby states, the nation's economic development was due, above all, to "careful nurturing of Finland's most valuable asset, human capital."[73] For hockey, this meant that municipal councils in cities and suburbs invested in neighborhood rinks. Private businesses were also important partners. In the early 1960s, local companies contributed to the building of outdoor artificial rinks and established sponsoring relationships with clubs, complete with logos on jerseys.[74]

If there was a point when hockey became Finland's national game, it was 1965—the year Tampere hosted the world championships. The national team finished seventh in a field of eight teams, but a 2–2 tie with Sweden was cause for celebration. More significant was the tournament's setting: a state-of-the-

Opening of the 1965 world championship at Hakametsä Ice Hall in Tampere (courtesy of Finnish Hockey Hall of Fame).

art arena built in the style of contemporary Finnish architecture. As visitors to the tournament noted, the arena fit perfectly in the growing city, with its thriving industry, generous social welfare benefits, and inventive architecture.[75] Federation officials hailed the building as a model of the modern arena, while politicians in other cities realized they needed venues like it. New indoor rinks were built across Finland in the following years, with the justification that they were necessary for the social-democratic state. "These are better recreation centers," stated a sports official in Turku, "where a contemporary man spends his weekend and evenings."[76]

The arenas were also better for hockey. With access to year-round ice, the national team and top-division clubs intensified their training. The Finns looked to both the East and the West for expertise, importing coaches from Canada and Czechoslovakia. Like the Swedes, the Finns valued the Soviet emphasis on team strategy, and they were repelled by the brutish violence of the Canadians. At the same time, both Finns and Swedes held to the Western stereotype of Soviet players as machines, and they came to appreciate the usefulness of Canadian toughness. The Finns gained a lesson in hard-hitting hockey in 1968–69, when former Leafs defenseman Carl Brewer served as player-coach of Helsinki IFK. The Swedes overcame their aversion to rough play in 1972, when the NHL players of Team Canada stopped in Stockholm for exhibition games. Swedish players slugged out a 4–4 tie that left the ice stained with blood.

The Nordic countries' position between East and West was reflected in a playing style that combined power and passing. Their middle place in the hockey world also influenced the development of their institutional structures. The basic unit of Nordic hockey was the community sports club. Players were amateurs, holding jobs away from the rink. Yet a number still ended up on Avery Brundage's naughty list. The IOC Eligibility Committee investigated both the Swedish and Finnish hockey teams after getting reports of player bonuses. Brundage's file of suspicious athletes also included players paid to endorse products. Sven Tumba Johansson, Sweden's top player, reportedly earned as much as $50,000 per year in the mid-1960s for lending his name to hockey sticks and cartons of milk.[77]

Cooperation among private companies, community clubs, and the state were a distinct feature of Nordic social democracy. In the case of hockey, it was pressure from outside the region that drove this partnership toward greater commercialization—and ultimately professionalization. Faced with the challenge of Soviet and Czechoslovak state-professionals, federation officials in both countries recognized that their players had to dedicate more time to hockey in order to compete internationally. Added pressure came in the early 1970s, when the first Swedish and Finnish players signed with pro teams in North America. The Swedish federation sought to keep players at home by distributing bonus money to the clubs. In Finland, players were paid by companies that sponsored teams. By the mid-1970s, hockey officials in both countries saw the need for a different model. In 1975 the Swedish and Finnish federations created new top leagues—the Elitserien and SM-liiga, respectively—with corporate sponsorship and a mix of professional and semipro players.[78] At the same time that these top leagues moved in the direction of the NHL, the Nordic development programs resembled those in the Soviet Union and Czechoslovakia, with their grounding in sports science and emphasis on skills training.[79] Just as they did in politics and economics, the Nordic countries insisted on a "third way" in hockey. The aim was not mimicry, but to create something new, something better—to build players who could beat the Soviet machine and resist the riches of North America.

STATES OF HOCKEY

In the winter of 1960, hockey fever swept the United States. The Black Hawks' twenty-one-year-old sensation Bobby Hull was on his way to his first scoring title. Gordie Howe passed Maurice Richard for the record for most career points, while the Rocket himself was on the cover of *Sports Illustrated* in what would be his final season. Both major news magazines, *Time* and *Life,* did stories on Jacques Plante and his new piece of equipment—the goalie mask.

The big story was the Olympics. The winter games in Squaw Valley, California, were the first to be broadcast on American television. CBS news reporter Walter Cronkite hosted the network's fifteen hours of coverage, including the half-hour opening ceremony and the twenty-minute closing. One of the highlights was hockey. After the Americans upset the Canadians, CBS televised their medal-round games against the Soviet Union and Czechoslovakia. People across the country, many watching hockey for the first time, wired messages of support to the team. Their upset of the Soviets followed by a win over Czechoslovakia earned the US team its first gold medal in hockey and brought new attention to the sport.[80]

The star was goalie Jack McCartan. Less than two weeks after earning Olympic gold, he was on the ice at Madison Square Garden, making his debut with the Rangers. McCartan received a standing ovation after stopping thirty-three shots in a 3–1 win over the Red Wings.[81] Newspapers presented the goalie as an all-American hero: tall, modest, married, an all-around athlete at the University of Minnesota, an army private on furlough to compete in the Olympics. In the NHL season's remaining weeks, McCartan received nationwide media attention. Reports of his games were in newspapers across the country. He was featured in *Life, Newsweek,* and *Time* and interviewed on network news programs. As the league's media liaison observed, "No other hockey story in all history ever achieved such widespread acclaim before the American public."[82]

The media liaison, a veteran New York sportswriter named Herb Goren, also saw excitement over the Olympic team sparking broader involvement with the sport in the United States. "It would be impossible to calculate how many communities, inspired by the drama of the spectacle, wondered if they could build ice rinks," he reported to NHL owners.[83] Indeed, youth hockey in the United States continued to grow in the 1960s. From 1959 to 1967, the number of youth teams registered with the national amateur federation jumped from 720 to 3,626. Six years after that, there were more than ten thousand. "Hardly a day goes by that I don't hear of a new city or town starting a program," reported the director of a Boston-area program in 1965. "It's the fastest growing sport around."[84]

The biggest growth of youth hockey during the 1960s took place in Minnesota. As the number of amateur hockey teams increased nationwide, the state accounted for nearly a third of all registered players by the end of the decade.[85] The sport's growth in Minnesota was driven by demographic and economic changes that mirrored broader trends in postwar America. Hockey had first taken hold in small mining and milling towns in the North, and in the cities of St. Paul, Minneapolis, and Duluth. But in the decades after the war, the state's population shifted. In 1940, over half of Minnesotans lived in towns and small cities throughout the state's farming and mining regions. Thirty years later, the population had grown by a third, and a majority of residents lived in the metropolitan area of Minneapolis and St. Paul.[86] It was there, in the Twin Cities suburbs, that youth and high school hockey grew in the 1960s, setting the pattern for the sport's development in the United States.

Postwar Minnesota hockey and the broader changes in the state can best be explained as a tale of two cities. The first is Eveleth, a mining town of roughly seven thousand people on the Mesabi Iron Range. Eveleth had been the center of hockey on the Range already in the first decades of the century. In the 1920s the Eveleth Reds, an amateur team featuring well-paid Canadian imports, held their own against clubs from Cleveland and Pittsburgh. For home games, up to three thousand fans filled the Hippodrome, one of the state's first arenas with artificial ice. The town also produced its own talent. Among the few Americans to play in the NHL before the war were all-star goalie Frank Brimsek and Black Hawks captain John Mariucci, both from Eveleth.[87]

By the late 1940s and '50s, the town's big draw was the high school team. After the war, Eveleth High School had graduating classes of about a hundred students: children and grandchildren of immigrants from Yugoslavia, Finland, and Italy. Many of the boys played three sports, "just to keep busy," recalled Willard Ikola, a 1950 graduate. After the launch of the Minnesota high school hockey tournament in 1945, Eveleth's hockey team made twelve consecutive appearances and won five titles. For Ikola and his teammates, the six-hour bus ride to the state capital was like visiting a different world. "We got a thrill just to ride an elevator in a St. Paul hotel," he recalled. "We didn't have an elevator in Eveleth. We were a bunch of hicks."[88] Once on the ice, the hicks dominated. Between 1948 and 1951, the Eveleth Golden Bears did not lose a game. In his three appearances at the state tournament as a goalie, Ikola recorded five shutouts in nine games. His teammate John Mayasich set scoring records that still stand today.

At the same time that Eveleth was celebrating its hockey team's victories, economic forces that would undermine the town were stirring. From the turn of the century to World War II, the open-pit mines of northern Minnesota were the principal source of iron ore for America's steel industry. In the decades after the war, depletion of high-quality ore, imports from Canada and South America, and the overall downturn of the steel industry contributed to mining's decline. Meanwhile, technological advances had unintended, harmful effects. Processing of low-quality ore caused massive environmental damage, while automation made mining more efficient, thus requiring fewer workers. Thousands were still employed in the region's mines and processing mills in 1960, when Eveleth's hockey dynasty ended its run. But the migration was already under way.[89] By the time Eveleth returned to the state tournament in 1993, the town had lost a third of its population.

The second community that tells the story of Minnesota hockey is Edina, two hundred miles south of the Mesabi Iron Range on the western edge of Minneapolis. Edina had been a streetcar suburb before the war, a quaint town of fewer than ten thousand people. Between 1950 and 1970, the community's population more than quadrupled. The small town was transformed into a first-ring suburb within a booming metropolitan area. The Twin Cities' economy thrived in the postwar decades, as new technology companies emerged and long-established food-processing companies profited in the consumer economy. The metro area added more than seven hundred thousand people in the two decades before 1970, with all of the growth coming in the suburbs. Small towns like Edina filled with housing developments, commercial strip malls, and office parks. The streetcar lines that once linked these towns to the core cities were ripped up, and more than 150 miles of freeway were constructed in the metro area in the 1960s.[90]

In this time of dramatic growth, Edina gave the world that icon of suburban life, the shopping mall. Southdale Center, the first fully enclosed, climate-controlled shopping area, was planted just off the freeway, in the middle of a vast parking lot. The developer then sold more than two hundred acres for tracts of single-family homes—"ideal for modern living," said the advertisements.[91] Other residential projects in Edina were more exclusive in their promotions. A development of homes surrounding a country club was advertised as "a place where you can rear your children with the freedom of mind that comes with knowing they are more protected than would be possible in any 'hit or miss' city neighborhood." This appeal to "the better class" was backed by exclusions of black and Jewish property owners.[92] In 1970, Edina had only twenty-three black residents out of a population of forty-four thousand, fewer than any other Minneapolis suburb.[93]

Edina was white, and it was rich. Average household income was more than ten thousand dollars higher than the state average. The community had higher numbers of college graduates than any other suburb; it also had a higher percentage of residents who had moved there from outside the Twin Cities area and Minnesota. For example, Donald Nyrop brought his young family from Washington, DC, when he was named chairman of Northwest Orient Airlines. His son Bill was part of the first generation of successful Edina hockey players, eventually playing in the NHL in the 1970s. The social makeup of Edina hockey indicated the direction the sport would take in decades ahead. Unlike the sons of immigrant miners who had brought the state title back to Eveleth each winter, Edina's hockey players were the sons of executives.

Edina did have one important connection to Minnesota hockey's roots. After finishing his degree at Michigan and serving in the air force, Willard Ikola took a job in 1958 as the high school's hockey coach. Ikola worked with parents to develop community youth teams. Many of the volunteer coaches were fathers who had moved to Minnesota from the East Coast, where they had played high school and college hockey.[94] The hockey dads also lobbied the town council to build an enclosed rink. Opened in 1965 at a cost of $450,000 ($3.7 million in 2020), the new indoor arena gave Edina a boost over other suburbs. Edina's youth teams enrolled hundreds of boys, and the arena was booked twenty-two hours a day. When the high school team reached the state championship in 1969, Ikola paid tribute to the community feeder program—and to the new arena. "We didn't have to shovel any more snow off of the rink," he recalled.[95]

Edina's opponent in the 1969 championship was another team that embodied Minnesota hockey's rural, northern past. Warroad was a town of just over a thousand people on the southwest shore of Lake of the Woods, brushing up against the Canadian border. Their matchup had all the makings of a classic David-and-Goliath story: the school with a total enrollment of 175, whose team trekked from the very edge of the state, facing a wealthy suburban school that enrolled more than two thousand students. But Warroad had one player who could even the odds: Henry Boucha. In his senior year, Boucha averaged more than two goals a game and drew capacity crowds across northern Minnesota. "He can bring people into a hockey arena who have never thought of crossing the threshold before," said one Warroad businessman.[96] This was the case in the big city as well. The 1969 hockey tournament was the first to be played at the Metropolitan Sports Center, the suburban arena built for the Minnesota North Stars. Warroad's game with Edina filled all 14,400 seats, while people across the state tuned in to the game on radio and television.

Boucha and his teammates were clearly fan favorites.[97] Edina sports teams had already been cast as rich "cake eaters." When a hit by an Edina defenseman knocked Boucha from the game, the crowd became even more hostile, raining boos on the high schoolers. Jeers sounded again after Edina won the game in overtime and players skated forward to receive their trophy. In a contest between an affluent suburb and a northern, blue-collar "hockey town," the smaller school had the support of fans—even fans from the suburbs. Perhaps it was the American preference for the underdog, or nostalgia for Minnesota's traditional hockey-playing communities. Whatever the case, the 1969 state tournament set a pattern that would play out in decades to come. In Minnesota, as in other hockey-playing regions, there remains a tension between metropolitan areas and rural towns, with the underlying notion that the purer version of the game is played in places like Warroad and Eveleth.

A half-century after the Edina-Warroad final, the boys' state high school tournament remains the marquee event on Minnesota's sporting calendar. A 1983 feature article in *Sports Illustrated* called it "America's premier schoolboy event," topping the high school basketball tournament in Indiana and football in Texas.[98] Today, the Minnesota Wild vacate their home arena for a week every March to make room for the tournament. Games at Xcel Energy Center typically draw capacity crowds of more than twenty-one thousand fans.[99]

The 1969 final was a turning point for the tournament and for the broader history of Minnesota hockey. Over the next twelve years, the number of high schools with boys' hockey programs increased from 95 to 139, and nearly all of those new programs were in the suburbs. Prior to 1969, northern schools had won twenty of the twenty-four titles awarded to that point. But in the following decades, suburban schools were dominant. Between 1981 and 1989, no team from outside the suburbs even reached the title game. Shrinking schools in northern towns and in the urban centers of Minneapolis and St. Paul were unable to compete with the growing suburban districts.

The demographic transformation of Minnesota was duplicated across the United States. In 1950, a fifth of Americans lived in suburbs; by 1970, the number had grown to 37 percent. And just as the population shifted to the suburbs, so did American sport. From the 1940s through the early '60s, many of the country's most celebrated athletes came from small towns or working-class urban neighborhoods. By the 1980s, more top athletes were coming from the suburbs—in the case of hockey, from communities around Detroit, Chicago, and the Twin Cities. The suburbanization of American sports would produce highly skilled athletes, as affluent families and affluent communities were able to devote more resources to their children's athletic interests. At the same time, those who lived outside the suburbs, whether in urban neighborhoods or rural communities, would find a steeper path to sports success.

HOCKEY WITH A HUMAN FACE

In many ways, Europe of the 1960s looked similar on both sides of the Iron Curtain. Across the continent, there were concrete housing developments and expansive social benefits. There were more women in the workplace and more students in universities. There was rock music, and there were miniskirts.

With war, depression, and political tumult in the recent past, leaders in the East and West wanted stable societies and satiated citizens. Like politicians in Finland, France, Sweden, and West Germany, communist officials held that the path to these goals was through technocratic social engineering. Of course, policies in the East aimed toward an even brighter outcome—the state of full communism imagined by Marx and Engels. There were still believers in this utopian future. Yet, having survived the violent excesses of Stalinism in the 1950s, communist leaders of the '60s put greater faith in rational planning than in revolutionary upheaval.

Czechoslovakia in the 1960s was a technocratic socialist state, and one of the key figures in its technocratic hockey program was Luděk Bukač. As a player, Bukač spent 1965 in North America and followed that with a month-long stay in Moscow, where he took part in Red Army's preseason training.

Anatoli Tarasov picked Bukač's brain about the Canadians, while Bukač compiled a detailed record of Tarasov's program, which he then submitted to researchers back home.[100] After moving behind the bench, Bukač became Czechoslovakia's leading analyst of what was happening in the rest of the hockey world. His reports from the world championships detailed faceoff formations, shots and passes, offensive and defensive plays. His scouting team compiled page upon page of tables and diagrams, documenting each team's style of play.[101] Three decades before Arsène Wenger brought data to European football, before Billy Beane introduced "moneyball" to Major League Baseball, Bukač was doing the same kind of quantitative analysis. Where did Soviet forwards take their shots? How did the Swedes break out of their own end? Bukač's diagrams had the answer, like the iPads used by coaches today.

The architect of this analytical approach was Bukač's boss, Vladimir Kostka—senior coach of the national team, head of the Czechoslovak federation, and dean of Prague's faculty of physical education and sport. After Tarasov, Kostka was the most influential figure in European hockey. Tarasov claimed that the Czech stole his ideas: "He copied his book from me word for word," he said of his rival, "and he didn't even give me a bottle of vodka."[102] To be sure, Kostka did draw upon Tarasov's model. Like the Soviet coach, he believed in communism and held to the Marxist principle that theoretical knowledge is essential to practice. But in the view of Bukač, who worked with both coaches, Tarasov's approach was a "scientific illusion." Tarasov's method, Bukač judged, "like much in Russia, turned out to be only a novelty, not a fact-altering reality. Soviet hockey was not the product of a scientific understanding of people."[103]

By contrast, Kostka was first a teacher and academic, and his adaptations of Tarasov's model were drawn from pedagogical research. "The hockey coach is, first and foremost, an educator," he insisted.[104] This was the starting point of his lectures at international coaching clinics and his book *Modern Hockey*, which was translated into six languages. Kostka's approach to hockey reflected a broader current in Czechoslovakia's culture and politics. Czechs and Slovaks had to acknowledge the Soviet Union's place at the vanguard of history, but many also recognized the Soviets as being backward in comparison to their own country. Hockey player Jaroslav Holík, for example, recalled that visits to the Soviet Union meant terrible food, bedbug-infested hotels, and filthy arenas.[105]

In 1968 Czechoslovakia attempted to wrest itself from this ill-fitting Soviet model and plot a path to communism that better matched its own development. The slate of reforms that came to be known as the "Prague Spring" introduced market-style economic practices, an end to censorship, and limits to the StB's authority. According to Slovak politician Alexander Dubček, leader of the country's Communist Party, the aim of the reforms was not to end the party's authority but to introduce "socialism with a human face." Czechs and Slovaks embraced the new direction, which integrated the country's European identity with its place in the socialist camp. Others in the camp watched warily, however—especially Soviet leader Leonid Brezhnev and the Politburo in Moscow. They feared that reforms in one socialist country could get out of hand. By the summer of 1968 they had had enough.

On the night of August 20–21, the Soviet army moved across the border and occupied Czechoslovakia. Newspapers in the West showed photographs of young Czechs swarming around Soviet tanks parked on Prague squares, shouting insults at confused Russian soldiers perched atop the turrets. Meanwhile, Dubček was taken to Moscow and brought before Brezhnev in Moscow. He was allowed to remain party leader, but authority was no longer his. When he gave a radio address announcing that Czechoslovakia was correcting its erroneous path, he had to struggle through tears.

The weeks and months following the invasion were confusing. Soviet troops occupied cities and towns across Czechoslovakia, but Dubček stayed in office. Tens of thousands of people fled the country, while many who remained openly criticized the occupation. Sports figures were among those who spoke out. Emil Zátopek, winner of three gold medals at the 1952 Olympics, signed a protest. When gymnast Věra Čáslavská took the podium at the Mexico City Olympics, sharing the gold medal in floor exercise with Soviet gymnast Larisa Petrik, she looked away as the Soviet anthem played.[106]

As autumn turned to winter, tensions did not diminish. In January and February, two Czech students set themselves on fire on Prague's Wenceslas Square in protest against the occupation. Shortly afterward, the national hockey team left for the world championships in Sweden. Crowds in Stockholm cheered the Czechoslovaks at their games, while the Soviets were hounded with whistles. The two teams were scheduled to face each other twice in the round-robin competition. In the first match, on March 22, the Swedish crowd roared whenever a Czechoslovak player carried the puck past center ice. When Jan Suchý scored the game's first goal, Czechoslovak players mocked the Soviet goalie, batting the netting and pushing the posts off their moorings. In Prague, crowds celebrated in the streets after the team finished with a 2–0 win.

The rematch came a week later. A handful of Czech and Slovak players made their statement at the start of the game. The team's sweaters featured the state insignia on the front: the white Czech lion, a flame symbolizing the Slovak uprising in World War II, and the communist red star at the top. Before taking the ice, they blocked out the red star with black tape.

The game finished just before ten o'clock that night in a 4–3 win for Czechoslovakia. Immediately, people began pouring into Wenceslas Square in the center of Prague. Revelers drove their cars up and down the streets, honking their horns and flashing their headlights. Based on their experience the previous week, police had prepared for celebrations of "our team," as their report stated, but they did not anticipate that the crowd would keep growing. Within an hour, more than 150,000 people filled the square. Across the country the scene was the same; in the largest cities—Plzeň, Brno, Bratislava—tens of thousands took to the central squares. Their chants and songs expressed their true feelings toward the "friendly assistance" from the Soviet Union. "Fascists!" "Occupiers!" "Go home, Ivan!" "Brezhnev is an asshole!"[107]

In some cities, the jeers turned violent. In the small northern town of Jaroměř, roughly three thousand people marched to the nearby fortress where a Soviet detachment was housed. The crowd tipped over army vehicles and set fires. When Soviet soldiers rushed from their barracks to keep the vehicles from being ignited, demonstrators chased them back inside with rocks. Czech police units had to be called to protect the occupying army. In the Slovak cities of Bratislava and Košice, the crowds turned on police. A few dozen officers were injured by rocks in both cities before they used tear gas to clear the streets.[108]

Meanwhile, in Prague, some four thousand people converged at the offices of the Soviet airline Aeroflot on Wenceslas Square. "Czechoslovakia four," they chanted, "occupiers three." Then they smashed the windows. The overwhelmed police called for backup, but the mob fought off the reinforcements with paving stones. "Smash the Gestapo!" they shouted. People pushed into the Aeroflot office and started looting. They found bottles of vodka and cognac, tins of caviar, and cartons of Marlboros. The crowd smashed what they couldn't carry away or didn't want. They broke out the window frames and burned the carpets. By two in the morning the office was gutted and torched. Finally, police were able to clear the square.[109]

The Soviets were outraged. The following day, the Politburo condemned authorities in Prague for failing to stop the "rabid anti-socialist elements." They warned that future provocations would be met with "effective measures." The Soviet defense minister hand delivered the message from Moscow, ensuring that Czechoslovak officials understood just what was meant by effective measures.[110]

A cadre of opportunists in the Czechoslovak Communist Party welcomed the Soviet pressure. Most were former supporters of Dubček's reforms who saw their own path to power open before them. In the first meeting of party leaders in Prague after the riots, the turncoats went on the attack. Their leader, former Dubček ally Gustáv Husák, gained the support of Moscow and of antireform hardliners in Prague. Within weeks he was leader of the party. Under Husák's leadership, the Czechoslovak government imposed a rigid program known as "Normalization," restoring censorship and state control of the economy. The StB cracked down on vocal supporters of the reforms. Emil Zátopek was forced to renounce his statements. Věra Čáslavská disclaimed any political involvement. Dubček was sent to work as a mechanic in a Slovak lumber yard. Through it all, the Soviet regiments stayed in their barracks. Ivan did not go home for another twenty-two years.

The hockey riots in Czechoslovakia were unique—an episode when the connection between a sporting event, popular protests, and the actions of political authorities was direct. But the intermingling of politics and hockey was not unusual, especially in the 1960s. The more assertive Québécois identity that emerged during the Quiet Revolution was closely linked to support of the Montreal Canadiens, while resentment of American economic dominance stirred criticism of the NHL across Canada. The Swedes were explicit in linking their national team to the social democratic system. Even the construction of rinks in the suburbs of Minneapolis and Helsinki was the result of political decisions made by municipal councils.

Sports have long been a means of political expression. Already at the turn of the century, when the Czechs were still under the rule of the Austro-Hungarian Empire, hockey was a way to proclaim the nation's autonomy. Simply participating in an international tournament was an act of political defiance. Still today, sports teams allow people to assert their identity, whether as part of a nation, region, or community. Fredrik Backman explores this melding of sport and identity in his novels about Beartown, a small factory town in the Swedish forest. Whether contrasting themselves with the more affluent, neighboring town or with distant cities, the people of Beartown see their team as an expression of who they are. "We built a hockey team that was like us, that we could be proud of," declares Backman's narrator, "because we weren't like you."[111]

In the 1960s, as different groups expressed themselves through the game, the hockey world became more dynamic. The change was evident in the magazines and game programs of the time, their photos transforming from black and white to bright, vibrant color. In their history of global hockey, Stephen Hardy and Andrew Holman speak of this time as a period of divergence, characterized by different playing styles, different rules, different institutions.[112] We still see these disparate developments today—the hybrid style of the Nordic countries, Vladimir Kostka's analytical approach, Tarasov's training methods, the demographic shift of North America, the IIHF's fusion of television and international hockey. No longer confined to the corners where they emerged, these developments are now present throughout the hockey world. In order for this diffusion to happen, there had to be a catalyst. It would come with the clash of the hockey world's titans.

FIVE

On the Brink

THE 1972 SUMMIT SERIES BETWEEN THE SOVIET national team and a squad of NHL players representing Canada was an event unlike any other. In no other sport had there been a contest between opponents who represented such wholly separate worlds: hostile political systems, distinct approaches to their sport, professionals from a closed commercial league and Olympic champions. There was no template to work from. Pulling off the eight-game series—four games in Canada, four games in the Soviet Union—required years of negotiations among Canadian and Soviet hockey officials, diplomats in Moscow and Ottawa, the masters of the IIHF and IOC, NHL owners and players, television executives and corporate sponsors.[1]

Both sides needed to face each other. The Soviets wanted to maintain the crooked system that allowed them to win international tournaments as "amateurs." But they also needed to prove themselves against the world's best. The Canadians, meanwhile, could not break themselves off completely, even after storming out of international hockey. Their declining performance in the Olympics and world championships was a matter of such importance that the government created a new organization, Hockey Canada, to develop a competitive national team. "The Canadian public wants our best against the Russian best," said Charles Hay, the organization's chief.[2]

The Canadian public got more than it was expecting. Over sixteen million people watched the final minutes of the final game. They rejoiced in unison when Paul Henderson scored to complete the come-from-behind win. Today, this moment is enshrined in national memory. Every Canadian who had a pulse on September 28, 1972, remembers where he or she was when Foster Hewitt made his iconic call from Moscow: "Henderson has scored for Canada!"

Taking the deciding game in a deadlocked series appeared to confirm that Canadian hockey players were still the world's best. But Canada's footing on the pedestal was not secure. The Soviets were astonishingly good, and they proved that Canadian pros were mortal. Despite the series win, Canadian hockey took a hard lesson. "The Summit Series produced an almost unique result," Ken Dryden observed: "its winner was changed more than its loser."[3] Given the prominence of hockey in Canadian society and culture, the changes to the game would have far-reaching effects. The Summit Series became "a virulent national stomach virus from which we've never fully recovered," writes Stephen Smith in his examination of Canadian hockey culture.[4] In the years after 1972, this virus generated a fever as people across Canada rethought how they watched and played and raised up their sons in the national game.

THE MYTH EXPOSED

There was never any doubt how the series would turn out. Foster Hewitt, called out of retirement to announce the games, predicted a clean sweep. Canada was "two goals a game better," he judged. *Boston Globe* hockey writer Fran Rosa predicted a bigger spread: "8–0 Canada—and that's also the score of the first game."[5] A few experts granted the Soviets a win or two in Moscow, but the end result was assured. After years of beating Canadian students and journeymen, the Soviet team would see who really played the best hockey in the world.

With the result preordained, Team Canada did not devote much time to preparing. Shortly after Bruins coach Harry Sinden was tapped to head the team, he asked External Affairs officials in Ottawa if they had any films of the Soviets in action. There wasn't much available, just some poor footage from the 1969 world championships and three reels from the 1950s.[6] Writer Jack Ludwig visited the team's training camp and watched "that familiar kibitz-loaf-spurt style that goes with being an NHLer." The assumption held "that anybody good enough to make the NHL didn't need further coaching."[7] By contrast, Soviet players went through relentless ninety-minute workouts after their arrival in Montreal. What observers noticed, however, was their shoddy equipment. "You get better stuff at a garage sale in Flin Flon," jibed *Montreal Gazette* sportswriter Ted Blackman.[8]

The Soviets were aware that the Canadians had little regard for them. During practice, twenty-year-old goalie Vladislav Tretiak saw the NHL players lounging in the arena seats, laughing with each other. "They're sure they'll beat you on one skate" had been the scouting report before the team left Moscow. Coach Vsevolod Bobrov, who had replaced Chernyshev and Tarasov after their retirement as national team coaches, downplayed his side's chances. He repeated the standard line to the press: We are here to learn, not necessarily to win. While Bobrov was diplomatic, Soviet officials were genuinely worried. Before the first game, the head of the delegation came to the dressing room with instructions: "Guys, you need to lose with dignity."[9] The players had never heard anything like it. "We stood at the introductions, and I could feel a trickle of sweat rolling down my back right to my skates," Boris Mikhailov remembered. After Phil Esposito scored sixteen seconds into the game and then Paul Henderson made it 2–0 six minutes later, Mikhailov could see anxiety on his teammates' faces. Bobrov told them to calm down and play their game. "Easy for you to say!" Mikhailov thought to himself.[10]

"We saw a brutal, tough game, the kind we were not used to playing in Europe," Tretiak recalled. "The Canadians are big, bulky guys. It was very difficult to regroup, especially in the first period. But we made it through."[11] By the first intermission, the Soviets had found their game and evened the score. Bobrov changed his advice: "You know how to play. They don't. Teach them."[12] Watching from the seats, Jack Ludwig could see that the Soviets were the better team. They controlled the pace and withstood bodychecks like blocks of concrete. The Soviets "had more cool, better puck control, better recovery."[13] By the third period, the visitors were putting on a clinic while Team Canada descended to cheap shots. When the final horn sounded, Phil Esposito led the dash to the dressing room. The Soviets, winners by a 7–3 score, were left waiting for the postgame handshake.

A former colleague of mine, a theologian, once told me of his reaction to watching the game that Saturday night, when he was a thirteen-year-old in Kingston. Like others across the country, he expected a decisive victory, an irrefutable demonstration of Canada's supremacy in hockey. Instead, he recalled, it was like watching a funeral in slow motion. "I went to bed that night staring at the ceiling, wondering about the existence of God."

While at least one Canadian stared into the abyss of a universe without meaning, others made excuses. One was that Team Canada didn't include Canada's best, with Bobby Orr nursing a sore knee and Bobby Hull excluded for having signed with the NHL's rival, the World Hockey Association. Another was that Hockey Canada and the NHL had scheduled the games at the wrong time, when players were not yet in shape. If the teams had played in December, Esposito said after the game, the result would have been different.[14] Ted Blackman compiled all the dodges in his column for the *Gazette*, arguing that a team with Hull and Orr, playing at midseason form, would take four of five games from the Russians. Yet Blackman also acknowledged the deep wound: "Our national inferiority complex, defended only by our hockey, may now become terminal neurosis."[15]

The loss in Montreal set off a seismic shift. Despite Team Canada's 4–1 win in Toronto two nights later and then a tie in Winnipeg, tremors rippled across the country. They became audible in Vancouver on September 8, the final stop of the four-game leg in Canada. Fans sang "O, Canada" loudly before the game. But soon after the puck dropped, boos poured down. In the opening minutes, Bill Goldsworthy was sent to the penalty box twice, and Mikhailov scored on both power plays. The crowd howled when Goldsworthy skated to the bench after the second goal. They did not let up.

After the 5–3 loss, players bristled at the hostility of their home crowd. "I'll be glad to get out of Canada," said Brad Park. "I'm ashamed to be a Canadian," added Goldsworthy. In the postgame interview on national television, Esposito spoke for his teammates:

> For the people across Canada, we tried. We gave it our best. For the people who booed us—jeez—all of us guys are really disheartened and we're disillusioned and we're disappointed in some of the people. We cannot believe the bad press we've got, the booing we've gotten in our own buildings.[16]

Many Canadians were disillusioned as well. Their boos expressed a realization that this style of hockey, this game played by their countrymen, was woefully deficient. "The Vancouver crowd was booing a deteriorated brand of hockey," Ludwig wrote.[17] More than that, Ludwig and other critics pointed out, the disapproval of fans came from an awareness that the myth they had long believed—that Canadians in the NHL were incontestably the world's best hockey players—was false. The league peddled this myth, wrote a Vancouver sportswriter. "We in the media peddled it, you peddled it and we all swallowed it."[18] Puncturing this myth was painful. "Nobody likes to wake up to find his illusions are only illusions," Ludwig wrote, "or that his heroes are, in some measure, bushleaguers."[19]

To be called a "bush leaguer" is the lowest insult in North American sports. In its original meaning, dating back to early baseball, a bush leaguer was a player of low talent, someone with skills for small-town ball in some backwater league. Over decades, the term came to carry a moral judgment. A bush-league player was someone who showed no respect for opponents. Vancouver fans cast this judgment on Team Canada: they weren't just playing poorly, they were playing bush. Canadian players, in turn, sought to uphold their honor. "To be ridiculed like this blows my dignity. It blows our dignity," Phil Esposito said in the dressing room. Brad Park also felt obliged to defend the team's character: "Do these people think we're some kind of dishonourable men who just hit people for no reason?"[20] As the Summit Series closed its first leg, Canadian players found themselves fighting on two fronts, against an opponent far stronger than they had imagined and against their own fans.

Three years earlier, Carl Brewer had predicted the arc that the Summit Series would take. In a conversation in Helsinki, he and Tarasov had compared the strengths of Canadian and Soviet hockey. "If you came to Canada and played against the best pro teams," concluded the former Maple Leafs star, "first you would win and then you would lose." He went on to explain that the Soviets' unfamiliar tactics would be to their advantage, until the Canadians adapted.[21]

Observers who watched all eight games of the Summit Series saw the transformation. The Canadians put away habits they had picked up in years of playing in the NHL. Esposito, master of the garbage goal with the Bruins, played brilliantly at both ends of the ice. Paul Henderson, a solid forward with the Leafs, became Canada's clutch scorer. The Canadians still played a rough game—that was clear when Bobby Clarke broke Valeri Kharlamov's ankle with a vicious slash. Team Canada won the series by playing Canadian hockey—with violence, skill, and determination. As Tarasov had acknowledged to Brewer three years earlier, Canadians were ruthless competitors. "Canadians put winning first," the Soviet coach understood.[22]

In the end they won, and Canada celebrated. Henderson's goal with thirty-four seconds remaining in Game Eight was immortalized as the "Goal of the Century." Henderson himself was elevated to the pantheon of heroes. Today, commemoration of the Summit Series is an industry unto itself, with countless books, films, academic conferences, and anniversary events. Yet the dramatic series-clinching victory did not erase the humbling defeat in Montreal. As my former colleague puts it: "September 2, 1972 could never be undone—no matter how the rest of the series unfolded." Canadian hockey players showed their tenacity in coming back to beat the Soviets. But the Summit Series revealed they were no longer the world's best.

DOWN FROM THE SUMMIT

The final game of the Summit Series was a national television event. Work halted in offices, and teachers rolled televisions into classrooms for the Thursday afternoon broadcast. According to estimates, more than three-quarters of Canadians witnessed Henderson's goal. What made this touchstone moment all the more extraordinary was that it was "wholly Canadian," unlike other televised events such as the moon landing or Queen Elizabeth's coronation.[23] Team Canada's last-second win was cathartic. In the aftermath, however, came an emotional hangover. One effect was that Canadians could not watch hockey the same way again.

By 1972 the television program *Hockey Night in Canada* was a national institution. The Saturday-night games were consistently among the ten most popular programs in Canada. To meet demand, programmers added more hockey: Saturday-night games blanketed the country on both CBC and the independent CTV network, while CTV also showed games on Wednesday nights.[24] The addition of the Vancouver Canucks in 1970 gave ratings an additional boost. In 1970–71 the average audience of *Hockey Night in Canada* increased by 15 percent over the previous season. More than 3.7 million people watched the broadcasts on CBC; another 2.6 million watched on CTV and 1.6 million on CBC French.[25] The deciding game of that season's Stanley Cup final, between the Canadiens and Black Hawks, drew 11.7 million viewers—the largest television audience ever for a hockey game.[26] Until September 1972.

Immediately after the Summit Series, ratings began to slide. The average audience of the CBC's Saturday-night broadcast dropped to 3.1 million viewers during the 1972–73 season.[27] The bleeding continued the following year. Hockey on television was losing viewers. *Hockey Night in Canada*'s producers, MacLaren Advertising, needed to find out why.

In 1973 the company surveyed fans in Toronto to gauge their attitudes toward hockey on television and the sport in general.[28] This glimpse into Ontario living rooms showed that viewers were tiring of hockey. They said that the quality of the sport had declined after expansion, that talent in the league had become too "watered-down." The poorer quality was especially apparent when compared to the Summit Series. Fans saw the Canada-Soviet series as a more engaging and entertaining form of hockey: emotions were high, as was the standard of play. According to the research findings, the series was a "harsh awakening for many Canadian fans"; they realized that "NHL hockey was *not* the ultimate criterion for top quality play."[29]

Dissatisfaction with NHL hockey grew amid the transformation of North American television in the early 1970s. As with radio in the 1930s and '40s, the most popular programs on English Canadian television were imported from the United States.[30] In the 1960s, these were Westerns and variety shows; for much of the decade, *Hockey Night in Canada* competed with *The Ed Sullivan Show* for top spot in the ratings. But in 1971, television was forever transformed by the arrival of Archie Bunker. Beginning with the 1971–72 season, the sitcom *All in the Family* spent an unprecedented five consecutive years at the top of the ratings in the United States. It was no less popular in Canada: the Friday-night broadcast became Canada's highest-rated program in 1972. But viewers in most Canadian cities could also turn their antennas to American stations, and many preferred to watch new episodes of *All in the Family* when they first ran in the United States—on the preceding Saturday night. In Toronto alone, some four hundred thousand people watched *All in the Family* each Saturday on Channel 4 from Buffalo, a large block of viewers who were not watching hockey.[31]

The producers and sponsors of *Hockey Night in Canada* also had to contend with more sports on TV. As cable television emerged in the early 1970s, networks filled airtime with inexpensive programming: old movies, reruns of 1960s comedies, and sports. When Home Box Office launched in 1972, one of its first programs was a Rangers-Canucks game. Audience research found that more sports on television hurt *Hockey Night in Canada* by oversaturating the viewing market. Before cable, the Saturday-night broadcast had been an anticipated event. But already in the early 1970s, viewers were tiring of the din of televised sports. "There's far too much of it now," said a Toronto resident.[32]

Hockey Night in Canada not only faced the challenge of new and more content, it also had to contend with the problem of more televisions. As Japanese imports brought down prices, many households had two sets by the early 1970s. With multiple sets and multiple channels to choose from, the family—and the audience—splintered. When Canadians moved to different rooms to watch different programs, *Hockey Night in Canada* lost viewers—women in particular.

In its first years on television, NHL hockey typically drew just as many women viewers as men. Ratings reports from the late 1950s and early 1960s show that *Hockey Night in Canada* was unique among top-rated shows in this balanced audience. Among French families in Quebec, it was not unusual to have more women viewers for games, especially during the playoffs.[33]

By the end of the 1960s, this was no longer the case. Men over eighteen accounted for roughly half of the Saturday-night audience, while women were a third (children and teenagers made up the remaining 20 percent). The number of female viewers declined even more after the Summit Series. In spring 1973, when the Stanley Cup playoffs were on TV, only 920,000 women nationwide were watching Saturday-night hockey, down from more than 1.1 million in previous seasons.[34]

Initially, this was not a concern for the main sponsors of *Hockey Night in Canada*. Imperial Oil sold gasoline and tires. Molson Brewery, which sponsored Canadiens broadcasts in Quebec, sold beer. Their customers were men, and ratings showed that hockey remained the top-rated program for men—by far. Indeed, the sponsors cared little about women's interest in the program. When a market research firm surveyed NHL viewers in 1965, interviewers called phone numbers and asked if an adult male was home. If the answer was no, they ended the call.[35] In August 1972, as Imperial Oil executives were looking ahead to the upcoming season, a memo circulating in the marketing department asked about a new valuing system for viewers. Did a male viewer count as one person, an executive asked, "whereas a female is equal to 0.75 and a child 0.5?"[36] In terms of purchasing power, a woman was not fully human. The ad men chuckled that "Women's Lib would probably dispute this."[37]

By the mid-1970s, Imperial Oil came to the realization that it had better start paying attention to women. Market research showed that women were buying gasoline nearly as often as men. In addition, Imperial was looking to move into the heating oil market, where husbands and wives made decisions together. The company recognized that men were no longer its prime advertising target, yet the audience for *Hockey Night in Canada* was overwhelmingly male.[38] Marketing executives looked to shift advertising money elsewhere, but they feared the response to reducing Imperial Oil's association with hockey. The company had been the principal sponsor since the 1930s. *Hockey Night in Canada* schedules were fixtures at Esso gas stations. Furthermore, executives wanted to maintain the company's connection to an institution of Canadian culture. "In the ever-changing environment we are in today," the marketing director explained, "I believe it's important that we retain our association with something so closely linked with the company, something truly Canadian."[39]

But dollars and cents came to outweigh positive attitudes. The marketing department recognized that it had to reach a different customer base, especially more women and younger consumers. At the same time, the costs of sponsoring the program were increasing. The company judged that the $13 million directed to *Hockey Night in Canada* was not money well spent, in terms of reaching potential customers.[40] In February 1976, the Imperial Oil board of directors decided to end its forty-two-year sponsorship of the program. The marketing department prepared to answer every letter. But the expected backlash didn't come. A few Leafs fans swore they would never buy Esso gas again, but most people who wrote to the company offered congratulations. "You have made an important contribution to Canada and to professional hockey," one Mississauga resident wrote. "The game has deteriorated very badly," he added, "and I think you are right in reaching what must have been a painful decision."[41]

Even CBC executives agreed. During Imperial Oil's last season as sponsor, the head of program policy asked colleagues why the television network would sign another long-term contract to broadcast NHL games. Like all professional sports contracts, the responsibility to produce a high-quality program fell on the broadcaster rather than the athletes.

> They can play lousy hockey or baseball or whatever (and frequently do just that) and yet we're obliged to carry them year after year. Any other business would demand some kind of protection against a deterioration in the service it was purchasing but apparently no such thing has occurred to us. Are we bad businessmen or is it that we don't care enough to demand that standards should remain high? Surely, we would not commit ourselves to such a one-sided program purchase in any other program area. Why then should professional sports be an exception?[42]

The answer from the network's director was clear: despite falling ratings, CBC still made $8–10 million broadcasting hockey.[43]

Hockey Night in Canada remained among the top ten programs on Canadian television, although its following continued to shrink, reaching a low of two million viewers in 1978.[44] After 1972 the great hockey events were not Stanley Cup finals; instead, they were international showdowns. On December 31, 1975, 9.9 million viewers watched the Montreal Canadiens skate to a tie against Moscow's Red Army team. Eleven days later, the Sunday-afternoon game between Red Army and the Philadelphia Flyers drew an audience of 10.1 million. The National Hockey League was just another program. The international game—with its speed, skill, and patriotic emotions—became the best show on TV.

A GAME UNDER SCRUTINY

After the Summit Series, Canadians still insisted that hockey was "our game." The question was this: Why were Canadians no longer—unquestionably—the best? As they sought answers, people of various walks of life expressed dissatisfaction with organized hockey in Canada. They recognized that the embarrassment of Game One in Montreal and subsequent embarrassments in the 1970s were not necessarily the fault of the players, but rather were a reflection of Canadian hockey as a whole.

To understand the change in mindset, we need to look back, before the Summit Series. In 1971 Hockey Canada conducted a major study of attitudes toward the sport among players, parents, and people outside the game. In extensive surveys and interviews, researchers found that a large majority of Canadians viewed hockey favorably. Most saw hockey "as making a very wholesome contribution to the mood of home and culture of Canadians," the study concluded.[45] This was the case not only with minor hockey but also with the NHL. Pro hockey was seen as a prestigious occupation, and players were regarded as respectable people who modeled self-discipline, honesty, respect for authority, and tolerance of others.[46] The NHL, the study's authors concluded, "is seen as a positive attribute to the development of our way of life."[47]

But studies conducted after 1972 presented a different picture. A 1974 report by a Saskatchewan task force highlighted complaints about minor hockey. Parents were upset about expensive equipment and the lack of trained coaches. In turn, referees and coaches told of parents' abusive behavior toward themselves, other players, and the parents' own children. The final report urged parents to "do some soul-searching."[48] A committee set up by the Ontario provincial government recognized the same problem. Its 1976 guidebook for parents warned against swearing at referees and yelling from the stands.[49]

By the end of the decade, studies at the provincial and federal levels showed widespread dissatisfaction with organized hockey. The Ontario study had been based on questionnaire responses from over thirty thousand hockey parents. An overwhelming number of these parents (80–90 percent) found their children's skills development to be insufficient; there needed to be more practices instead of games, many said. A majority faulted coaches, who needed to be better trained. Parents were especially hard on other parents—some 80 percent of respondents saw parents' behavior at games as creating problems. In page after page of the report, comments from questionnaires and open meetings described a children's game that had been derailed by adults:

Is 65 games, plus one practice a week, too much hockey for a 7 year old?

My son's coach is on an ego trip. He yells, screams and belittles 9-year-old boys.

Parents should not be allowed to hit their child after games for poor performance.

To some parents, hockey is a matter of life and death. They turn into animals in the arena.[50]

A federal study looked at Canadian hockey in a different light, asking who played the sport. Researchers found that the national game wasn't all that national. During the winter of 1978–79, one million Canadian males played organized hockey, in a country of just under twenty-five million. Participation rates were equal among English and French households, although there were regional disparities: Ontario had the highest rate of participation, the Atlantic provinces the lowest. The bulk of these players—nearly six hundred thousand—were boys, ages five to fourteen. These minor hockey players were most likely to live in urban areas and to come from middle-class households.

Hockey was also a family sport, the study found: most boys in the sport had a father or older brother who had played. This was understandable, researchers acknowledged, but it meant that prospects were dim for the sport's growth. If a boy grew up in a family without a history of playing hockey, his chances of getting into the sport were less than two in ten. This was a problem. While Canada's population was growing, thanks to immigration, hockey registrations were declining. The study found that recent immigrants coming from Southern Europe, Asia, Latin America, and the Caribbean did not play hockey. Among households speaking languages other than French or English, there was virtually no participation in Canada's national game.[51]

The inquiry also pointed out that hockey endangered itself by excluding females. Researchers found that only 4 percent of Canadian women had played organized hockey. "This was the most contentious issue of all," the study's authors noted. On the question of whether to organize programs for girls, Canada's amateur organizations answered "with an unequivocal NO."[52] CAHA leaders claimed there was not enough ice available. As it was, local associations provided services to girls' and women's teams, if there was demand. But officials insisted there was no demand. Moreover, CAHA leaders argued, girls' hockey was a "threat to the future of the family and society." The inquiry committee conceded that the CAHA's position was secure from legal challenge, given that it was a private organization. But researchers argued that amateur hockey had better change for its own sake. "Unless modest-income and new Canadians as well as girls participate in hockey," their study concluded, "our national sport runs the risk of becoming classified as the prerogative of middle and upper-class, French and English-speaking male Canadians."[53]

THE GOONS TAKE OVER

The biggest problem was the violence. At the start of the 1970s, according to the Hockey Canada survey, over three-quarters of Canadians saw hockey as a "clean sport," a game of skill rather than toughness. Only a quarter of respondents thought the pro game was too violent.[54] By decade's end, that view had changed. According to the 1979 Ontario study, hockey parents saw violence as the main issue in the sport. When asked what needed to be improved in minor hockey, 84 percent pointed to the violence.[55]

Canadian hockey had always been a rough game, but in the 1970s the violence reached new depths. Violence became a key part of on-ice strategy. More than playing the body on defense or pressing opponents with forechecking, players used their sticks and fists to intimidate. The rationale was that if you knocked around the other team, then they would play hesitant, defensive hockey. Conn Smythe's old dictum was enshrined: "You can't beat 'em on the ice if you can't beat 'em in the alley." The "Big Bad Bruins" followed this strategy to Stanley Cup wins in 1970 and 1972. The Philadelphia Flyers played the bruising game to perfection in the middle of the decade, winning back-to-back titles in 1973 and 1974.

The Flyers' nickname, the Broad Street Bullies, was synonymous with a brutal brand of hockey. The fact that the team was based in the United States made a convenient excuse for Canadian writers. In the words of journalist and broadcaster Peter Gzowski, "the hordes in Philadelphia and all the other American cities" clamored for "blood and punishment in the place of grace and skill."[56] A *Toronto Star* columnist offered an anthropological explanation of American bloodlust: "Having an even more violent spirit than ours (or being more open about it), they've taken to the fighting and dirty play with so much enthusiasm they might be said to have restored these to respectability just at the moment when they had begun to lose favor here."[57] There was not much evidence to support this canard. Canadians had been pounding each other on the ice since the nineteenth century. If owners in the United States encouraged fighting to sell tickets in the 1970s, as was charged, they were only following the promotional strategy Conn Smythe had used decades earlier. After all, it was Smythe who uttered this famous bon mot after a Montreal-Toronto game featuring two fierce brawls: "We've got to stamp out this sort of thing, or people are going to keep on buying tickets."[58]

"Professional hockey is total war," Smythe said in his memoir. "On and off the ice."[59] In the 1970s the battles were carried out of the big arenas and into the youth rinks. Following a brawl-filled junior game in 1974, an Ontario government inquiry investigated the broader problem of hockey fighting. The committee chair, Toronto attorney Bill McMurtry, pointed to the NHL as the chief cause: "It is a natural phenomenon for any person to look up to what he has been told are the best, and to attempt to emulate them."[60] Academic researchers, however, found that the roots of the problem ran far deeper. According to a study involving more than seven hundred players, teenage boys felt that fighting earned them approval from coaches and fathers. Interviews with adults confirmed this. "This is a tough society we're in" said one dad, who served as president of his local association. "I put my own kid in hockey so he would learn to take his lumps." If his kid learned to fight back, all the better. "The day they turn hockey into a namby pamby game for sissies," he added, "is the day I get out."[61]

Players learned the strategy of intimidation early in minor hockey. University of Waterloo sociologist Edmund Vaz researched youth hockey throughout the 1970s, surveying thousands of boys, interviewing coaches and players, and sitting in dressing rooms for pregame talks. He found that players as young as nine and ten were taught that aggressive, physical hockey was the only way to win. The lessons took hold. Vaz asked a ten-year-old if his coach gave any special instruction on how to handle star players. "Yeah," the boy replied, "hit them real hard when you have a chance so they'll be scared of you."[62] Another researcher found that fighting likewise started early. Serious fights began with twelve-year-olds, yet even games among ten-year-olds had scraps involving multiple players.⁶³ As they advanced, boys learned that toughness, whether digging in the corners or dropping the gloves, was a way to get noticed. One Junior A player recounted how his dad told him at tryouts to go after the guy who was out for his position. "So I went out and picked on him and broke his leg, and I made the team."⁶⁴

The thuggery of Canadian hockey was starkly apparent in international play. A particular low point was the 1977 world championship in Vienna. The Canadians returned to the tournament for the first time in seven years after the IIHF allowed NHL players to compete. Hastily assembled with pros whose teams were out of the playoffs, Team Canada was twice embarrassed by the Soviets, by scores of 11–1 and 8–1. In both games, the Canadians resorted to cheap shots when it was clear they could not skate with the Soviets. In the first game, Wilf Paiement chopped opponents with vicious slashes. "I figured I could hurt somebody," he said afterward, to "make them think twice in the next game."⁶⁵ In their second meeting the Canadians were whistled for fourteen penalties, including two misconducts and a match penalty. Representing Hockey Canada, Alan Eagleson launched a profanity-laced outburst against the officials.⁶⁶ The Canadian press, however, would have none of their excuses. A "malicious buffoon," wrote one columnist of Paiement. "Savages," judged another.⁶⁷

Ordinary Canadians were likewise offended. Angry letters poured into the office of minister of sport Iona Campagnolo:

> Canada must decide whether or not they want their National Game to be played by Canadians as it should be played or be continually outclassed by European teams.
>
> Surely this proud and great land can find hockey players with intellect, with ingrained decency and sportsmanship to represent our country with honour.
>
> Please have someone look into this mess. Don't let them spoil the good image of Canada.⁶⁸

Responding to the outcry, Campagnolo launched an investigation into the embarrassment in Vienna. As with other investigations, this one included dozens of witnesses, hundreds of pages of briefs, and thousands of questionnaires. The conclusion? "Canadians must accept the somewhat shattering reality," began the final report, "that countries other than Canada can produce good players and teams."⁶⁹

LOOKING TO EUROPE FOR ANSWERS

In December 1973 the bantams of Sarnia went to Sweden. Featuring fourteen-year-old Dino Ciccarelli, a future NHL star, the visitors from Ontario coasted in the first three games of a junior tournament in Örnsköldsvik. In the semifinals, they met a team from Kiruna, a small mining town four hundred miles to the north. The Sarnia dads passed around cigars during warmups, but with the drop of the puck they saw that their sons were outclassed. Journalist Roy MacGregor was sitting nearby. He wrote of Kiruna's top forward as "beyond anything Sarnia had ever contended with." MacGregor watched one of the team's defensemen, a tiny boy, "poke-checking, intercepting passes, skating his check off the puck, cleaning scrambles out of the crease—he was, in a word, brilliant."[70] These two players, Mikael Andersson and Lars Karlsson, went on to careers in Sweden's Elitserien, a gold medal at the 1987 world championships, and bronze at the 1988 Calgary Olympics. In 1973 they showed a troop of Ontario teenagers and their parents that Europeans could play hockey, too.

The Summit Series and subsequent international defeats brought a reevaluation of how Canadians—especially Canadian children—played the game. The various inquiries conducted during the decade reached the same conclusion: coaches needed to be better trained, so that they could better train young players. The CAHA, Hockey Canada, and other organizations held clinics and published manuals introducing coaches to new methods. "Hockey is a game that many Canadians have taken for granted over the years," opened one manual. "The teaching of the game has been, by and large, a haphazard affair."[71] The traditional Canadian method of learning the game by playing games was no longer sufficient. Losses by NHL pros and Ontario bantams showed that hockey sense didn't do much good if you couldn't skate with your opponent. MacGregor saw this clearly in Sweden, when he watched one of Canada's top junior teams, the Regina Pats, get pummeled 15–2 by Djurgården. At one point, the Pats coach threw a stick at the referee. "If we're ever going to change this, we're going to have to send teams of equivalent calibre over," a Canadian embassy official later told MacGregor, "teams that can play up to the level of the Swedes."[72]

There were Canadians who knew of a better way, but they were outside the usual hockey circles. After the Summit Series, when the CAHA launched a coaching development program, it turned to coaches of university teams and professors of exercise science. They were well aware of the failings of Canadian player development. "There is sufficient evidence to conclude," reported one kinesiologist, "that the Canadian hockey player is not what one might call well trained." Their seminar presentations and manuals presented a new model of an effective hockey coach—someone who implements a program of dry-land exercise and skills development, drawing on his own training. As an example of this rational approach to hockey, the experts pointed to the Soviets. Their manuals included detailed summaries of Tarasov's training program.[73]

Not many people involved with the NHL took part in the coaching development programs. One active player who took a consistent role in the reform efforts was Ken Dryden. The Canadiens goalie spoke regularly to seminars and inquiry committees. Along with kinesiology professor Cecil Eaves, he wrote a development guide for young players, distributed by Hockey Canada and McDonald's. The glossy book included photographs of youth hockey in Sweden, Czechoslovakia, and the Soviet Union—boys on the ice, parents watching from the stands, just like in Canada. In his introduction, Dryden was blunt in telling young Canadians that their country did not have a monopoly on the game: "In the past we were, perhaps, a little too smug, thinking that because we invented hockey and gave it its early development, we knew all there was to know about the sport. As a result, we have not improved as much or as quickly as we should have."[74]

In contributing to the reform campaign, Dryden drew upon his own experience with Soviet and European hockey. In 1969, after finishing at Cornell University, he played for the Canadian national team in Moscow. Dryden realized, as he later wrote, "that the Canadian brand is not necessarily the best played."[75] The summer after the Summit Series, Hockey Canada sent him back to Europe on a fact-finding mission. In conversations with Russian players and coaches, Dryden gained an illuminating view of the Soviet hockey system. He discovered that the Western picture of Soviet hockey as a monolithic structure with Tarasov dictating from the top was wrong. There were different ideas of strategy and training among the clubs. Moreover, Soviet coaches and players had paid close attention to the Canadians during the Summit Series, and they were already adapting their way of playing. Nikolai Puchkov, coach of SKA Leningrad, compared this flexible approach to the Canadians' lack of creativity. "The Canadians just are not progressive," he told Dryden. "They're the same all the time."[76]

Dryden was not alone in looking to Europe for a way forward. National coaching clinics regularly featured guests such as Luděk Bukač and Swedish coach Tommy Sandlin. But Canadian hockey was slow to adapt. Swedes like

Mikael Andersson and Lars Karlsson could have their world championships. They were playing in a lesser league. A player like Dino Ciccarelli, able to score goals and go into corners, was the kind of gutsy player NHL scouts prized. Even after the Summit Series, when the well-conditioned Soviets outpaced the Canadians, pros were reluctant to change their ways. When Mike Eaves joined the Minnesota North Stars in 1979, he kept up with the strength and conditioning program he had learned from his father Cecil, the kinesiology professor. He once visited the team's weight room and found a couple of veterans there. They were lounging on the benches, using a ten-pound plate as their ash tray.[77]

One of the few pro players to incorporate new methods into his training was Dryden's older brother and fellow goalie, Dave. When the Dryden brothers faced each other in a 1971 game, weeks after Ken had been brought up by the Canadiens, Dave had already been in the league four seasons. At one point in his career, limited to a backup role for the Black Hawks, he had retired and gone back to teaching. A year later, he decided to take another shot. For help, he sought out Lloyd Percival, a pioneering figure in sports science. In 1951, Percival had published *The Hockey Handbook,* based on years of analyzing games. The book made recommendations on game strategy and player development, proposing similar advances as the Soviets and Europeans later made. Percival, however, was not a hockey man, so his suggestions had little influence in Canada.[78] Nevertheless, Dryden was looking to improve, at a time when coaching for goaltenders was nonexistent. He worked with Percival on strength, conditioning, nutrition, and psychology. Percival filmed the goalie performing rapid-response drills, which Dryden then analyzed— training that is common today, but remarkable a half-century ago. Dryden devised his own innovations as well. He created the first fiberglass mask with a cage—standard equipment for today's goalies. And he applied geometry to his positioning. With string and tape, he plotted radial grid lines on his basement's concrete floor, calculating how much net he covered when a shooter approached at a certain distance and angle. When Ken Dryden traveled to Europe in 1973, he found coaches using the same approach to train goalies.[79] Step by step, Canadian hockey was entering the age of science.

BREAKING THE MOLD

Dave Dryden's statistics improved after his return with the Buffalo Sabres. Yet following his most successful season as a pro, he chose to leave the NHL and join the rival World Hockey Association. Founded in 1972, the WHA is often described as a house of cards. Franchises started, changed names, changed cities, and folded—sometimes within the same year. At the time, when he joined the Chicago Cougars in 1974, Dryden saw a promising opportunity to be part of something new. Plus, the money was guaranteed—more than he could ever make in the NHL. Before the end of his first season, however, Dryden and three teammates had taken over the Cougars after the owner went bankrupt. The league promised to cover their expenses. Nevertheless, Dryden recalled, it was worrying when he and his co-owners went to the airport ticket desk and put the entire team's plane fares on their credit cards.[80]

Before we heap scorn on the WHA, keep in mind that the 1970s were not a banner time in professional sports management. The NHL's new teams in Oakland and Kansas City did little better than WHA teams in attendance and management. Even Major League Baseball had its share of dismal franchises, such as the ill-fated Seattle Pilots and the second iteration of the Washington Senators. Yet for all the empty seats and empty bank accounts, the WHA brought lasting changes to hockey. As Ed Willes writes in his rollicking history of the league, the WHA "revolutionized the game."[81]

One of the league's most important legacies was opening North American hockey to new sources of talent. In less than a decade, the number of major-league franchises grew from six to thirty-two (eighteen in the NHL, fourteen in the WHA). Teams needed players, and the traditional pipeline of the Canadian juniors could not meet demand. WHA teams in St. Paul and Hartford looked in their own neighborhoods, signing standouts from local colleges. Jack McCartan, hero of the 1960 Olympics, returned to major-league hockey with the Minnesota Fighting Saints. NHL general managers also signed a handful of American-raised players. Warroad's favorite son, Henry Boucha, joined the Red Wings. One of the few bright spots for the California Golden Seals was Bobby Sheehan, a legendary Boston-area rink rat. During the 1976–77 season, twenty American-born players who had played high school hockey in the United States were NHL regulars. A decade earlier, in the six-team league, there had been only two.

WHA teams cast their nets even wider in search of players. The Winnipeg Jets, in particular, needed talent to surround the league's marquee star, Bobby Hull. Signing the NHL's top scorer, with an unheard-of bonus of $1 million, had given the WHA a dose of legitimacy. But after two seasons of playing alongside no-names, Hull was considering retirement. Through connections in Sweden, the Jets front office found players who could skate with the

The Winnipeg Jets' high-scoring Swedish forwards, Anders Hedberg and Ulf Nilsson, celebrate winning the 1976 WHA championship (courtesy of Manitoba Sports Hall of Fame & Museum).

Golden Jet: two young forwards, Anders Hedberg and Ulf Nilsson, and veteran defenseman Lars-Erik Sjöberg, captain of the Swedish national team. From their first skate together, Hedberg, Nilsson, and Hull knew they had something special. "I was ready to call it quits," Hull told Ed Willes, "then I found a couple of kids who could play the game the way I wanted to play it."[82] The three forwards—with Sjöberg feeding them the puck—played a fast, improvisational style. In their first season together, the "Hot Line" averaged more than two goals per game. Hull alone scored 77—a pro hockey record. Attendance at Jets games soared. More importantly, coaches and general managers took notice that European-style hockey could pay off in North America. Two seasons later, ten Swedish players and six Finns were on WHA rosters.

The WHA's Toronto Toros also made big news with their European signing in 1974. For more than a decade, Václav Nedomanský had been a mainstay for the Czechoslovak team, scoring over 150 goals in international play. As early as 1968, he had asked for permission to play in North America. Of course, these requests were denied. Nedomanský had not wanted to defect because it would mean being separated from his parents. But when he learned in summer 1974, at age thirty, that he was being transferred to the army team and inducted into active service, he decided to make his move. Through connections, Nedomanský obtained tourist visas for himself, his wife, and their young son, and they drove off to Switzerland. A week later, they were in Toronto.[83]

Nedomanský's defection made headlines around the world. Czechoslovak authorities were furious. The StB sent an agent to Toronto to keep watch on him, while police back home recorded his parents' phone conversations and opened their mail. Hockey officials in Prague protested the theft of their player to the IIHF.[84] Their objections were somewhat disingenuous, given that both the Toros and the Atlanta Flames had sought approval for signing Nedomanský. But the unauthorized signing was a real concern. The Jets did not pay the Swedish federation for their players, either. The threat of North American money poaching European talent would only grow in years to come.

The escape of Nedomanský also posed a threat to the Soviet bloc. Just three weeks before his arrival, another prominent figure from the communist East left his touring group and asked for asylum in Toronto—ballet great Mikhail Baryshnikov. The two high-profile defections were an embarrassment. In Czechoslovakia, StB agents reported that citizens were talking about Nedomanský's departure. The following year brought more bad news when eighteen-year-old tennis sensation Martina Navrátilová defected. The StB turned up surveillance on other athletes who were a threat to run. One whom agents were especially concerned about was Slovak hockey player Peter Ihnačák. Prior to the 1980 Winter Olympics, the StB told national team coach Luděk Bukač to drop the talented forward from his roster.[85] But with their eyes on Ihnačák, state security missed two other Slovaks slipping away. In August 1980, Peter and Anton Šťastný made their escape from a tournament in Austria, along with Peter's pregnant wife. The following year, their older brother Marián and his family escaped through Yugoslavia and joined them in Quebec.

With its maverick owners and diverse mix of players, the WHA pushed the limits of North American hockey. The Jets began each season with exhibition games in Europe, to showcase their star Swedes. Other teams played in Europe and the Soviet Union, while Soviet and Czechoslovak squads made midseason tours of every city in the WHA, with their games counting in league standings. Veteran players noticed the effects of these outside influences. Bobby Hull told a coaches' seminar that he had started a conditioning program before preseason camp. "Never felt better," he reported. Hull noted that his Swedish teammates were better trained in fundamentals and more eager to learn. "They seem to get more out of the game because of their analytical approach," he said.[86]

Dave Dryden also saw changes in his five years in the league. After the shaky first season in Chicago, the league closed down the Cougars, paid off his credit card bills, and sent Dryden to Edmonton. The Oilers steadily improved after veteran forward Glen Sather took over as coach. Sather adopted the Jets' fast-moving offense and partnered with the University of Alberta's kinesiology faculty to develop training programs. As the Oilers' player rep, Dryden queried his teammates about possible changes to the game. Leaders of the WHA players' union wondered if it was possible to eliminate fighting, on the players' own initiative. Dryden sat down with Steve Carlson, already famous for playing one of the brawling Hanson brothers in the film *Slap Shot*. Dryden apprehensively raised the question—would it be possible for the players themselves to stop the fighting? "Oh yeah," Carlson replied. "We're so much better than that."[87]

The fights did not stop. Even the threat of legal action could not keep players from dropping gloves and swinging sticks, in either the WHA or NHL. In 1975 Bruins player Dave Forbes was charged with assault in Minneapolis after ramming the butt-end of his stick into Henry Boucha's eye socket. The jury did not reach a verdict, but NHL leaders were clear in their judgment. "This trial's a joke," said Flyers coach Fred Shero. "Courts are not the answer," added Clarence Campbell.[88] With league leaders uninterested in change, the number of fights continued to climb.[89] Newcomers were subjected to especially brutal treatment. "They took a shit-kicking that first year," Hull said of Nilsson, Hedberg, and Sjöberg.[90] Börje Salming withstood the same treatment in the NHL. Even though he showed his toughness from his first game, Salming was still a target of sticks and elbows, especially from the Flyers.[91]

In the 1970s, when he was one of the game's biggest stars, Bobby Hull recognized that Canadian hockey needed rejuvenation. Players like Hedberg, Nilsson, Sjöberg, and Salming brought a dose of fresh air. Yet Canadian players responded by chopping. Hull diagnosed the problem at a coaches' seminar: the violence wasn't a show for spectators; it was a way to protect the game. "Many Canadians appear to be saying 'these Europeans are coming over here and taking our jobs,'" said Hull.[92] Hockey reformers might have looked to Europe for new approaches, but the NHL's players, coaches, and general managers stuck with what they knew.

MAKING AMERICAN HOCKEY

"I'm not anti-Canadian, just Pro-American." Written in a 1973 memo, after his first season as coach at the University of Minnesota, Herb Brooks's statement was a declaration of hockey independence. At the same time that Canadians were struggling over how to reform their game, or whether to reform at all, Brooks and other coaches in the United States worked to build a distinct approach for developing American players. The challenge they faced was breaking free from Canadian dominance. After decades of players and coaches coming south, this would be a taller order than beating the Soviets.

Brooks inherited the fight for American hockey from the coach he had played under at Minnesota, John Mariucci. In the late 1950s and early '60s, Mariucci had been one of the most vocal critics of other college coaches importing players from Canada. "It's ridiculous," he said, "when we have a game for the college hockey championship of the United States and the Star Spangled Banner is played for the benefit of the referees."[93] Mariucci believed that American college hockey should be a place for American players to develop. He campaigned openly for fellow coaches to take a similar stand. The statement he made to the *Boston Globe,* similar to Brooks's memo, was one he shared with his players: "I'm not anti-Canadian. I'm pro-American."[94]

In Mariucci's view, the main culprit was the University of Denver. Unlike midwestern and eastern universities, where hockey had been played for decades, Denver's program began after the war. In 1949 the university erected a military-surplus drill hall on campus and rechristened it DU Arena. Nine years later the drill hall was holding more than five thousand spectators per night and the Pioneers were national champions. The success was due to coach Murray Armstrong. A Saskatchewan native, Armstrong had a journeyman career in the NHL before coaching his former junior team, the Regina Pats. After moving to Denver, Armstrong used his connections in western

Canada to fill his roster. Armstrong insisted that these recruits were looking to advance their education—and to be sure, most of his Canadian players majored in engineering and accounting. But they could also play. Denver won national titles in 1958, 1960, and 1961. The 1961 team, in particular, dominated opponents throughout the season, losing only one game. In the national tournament, the Pioneers outscored their opponents 18–3.

Denver's dominance split college hockey wide open. The controversy over Canadian recruits sparked at a time when American college sports was being transformed. University presidents, chancellors, and professors on faculty control boards exchanged long letters over the issue. In the background was the perennial question in American higher education: How does a school manage its sports teams? Athletics had been part of college life since the 1800s. When college football emerged as a mass spectator sport at the turn of the century, presidents at public universities like Michigan and Minnesota recognized the value of having tens of thousands of fans come to campus. After all, fans were also taxpayers, who funded the universities. Yet there were concerns about universities embracing commercial sport. As college football and men's basketball grew after the war, questions arose about the influence of sports in university life, about scholarships for students more interested in competing than studying, and about the rising power of pro leagues, which threatened to turn the college ranks into a farm system.[95]

These issues were present in the debate over Canadian players in college hockey. "It galls me to take scholarship money badly needed on many fronts in the college and give flat grants to students on the basis of physical prowess alone," wrote Colorado College president Louis Benezet.[96] Academic leaders were also concerned about the stain of professionalism. Many Canadian Junior A players were under contract with NHL teams. Bringing players from farm teams to college teams violated the nineteenth-century ideal of amateur sport, something in which many administrators, professors, and coaches still believed.

University leaders came to an agreement in the late 1950s. Teams were required to strictly follow rules of amateurism, and age limits were set for imported players. Yet Canadians remained prominent in American college hockey. Murray Armstrong continued to recruit players from the prairie provinces.[97] Michigan won its seventh national title in 1964 with a team of Canadian players coached by Toronto native Al Renfrew. Even Ivy League schools recognized the value of imported players. In 1967 Cornell University became the first eastern school in more than a decade to win the national championship, with a roster that featured skaters from British Columbia, Saskatchewan, Manitoba, and Ontario—including nineteen-year-old Ken Dryden.

Ken Dryden was not planning on a career in pro hockey when he left for college. He chose Cornell for its history program, with the idea of going on to law school.[98] In the 1960s and '70s, top-ranked Canadian juniors did not go to college in pursuit of the NHL. When forward Mike Eaves arrived at the University of Wisconsin from Ottawa, having been the top scorer for his Junior B team, it was due to the influence of his dad, Cecil, who had played for Murray Armstrong at Denver. There were few Canadian skaters as skilled as Eaves, who set a scoring record at Wisconsin that still stands. "I was the exception," he said, not as a boast but as a statement of fact.[99] Most talented Canadians did not see American college hockey as a place to develop.

With teams full of Canadian also-rans, college hockey of the 1970s was rough. In the 1970–71 season, each team in the Western Collegiate Hockey Association (WCHA) was whistled for more than six penalties per game. Forty-one players received ten-minute misconduct penalties during the season. Their offenses included

> shooting puck at official
> throwing glove at official
> spitting in player's face
> obscene language
> extremely obscene language
> very obscene language
> very, very obscene language[100]

Midway through the 1976–77 season, the league commissioner alerted coaches that there were already fifty-one misconducts and thirty-two game disqualifications.[101] The warning came after a Minnesota–Michigan Tech game that saw ten players ejected for fighting. Gopher defenseman Reed Larson received a year's suspension after pushing a referee. As it was, Minnesota was still under a cloud from the previous season, when a bench-clearing brawl erupted at the start of their national semifinal against Boston University. BU coach Jack Parker charged Herb Brooks with deliberately instigating the fight. "No question they came out with the intention of running at us," Parker said after his team's loss.[102]

Herb Brooks had become head coach at the University of Minnesota in 1972, only a year after hanging up his skates as an amateur player. It is well known that Brooks was the last man cut from the Olympic team that won gold in 1960, but he later made the 1964 and 1968 teams and played in five world championships. As a young player, Brooks was known for his intensity. He kept a rule book open on his desk, with passages underlined, to ensure he knew the rules better than the refs. In the off season, he pumped iron and ran with weights on his ankles.[103] He brought this dedication and attention to detail to his job selling insurance. When the coaching position at his alma mater opened, Brooks had to be convinced to give up a successful career in business.[104]

Brooks took over a losing team at Minnesota. The following season they were national champions. From the start, he set a goal of winning the title with players from the state, following Mariucci's idea that American college hockey should be for American players. Yet this goal of fostering homegrown talent could also produce an us-versus-them edge. According to Jack Parker's account of the 1976 brawl, Minnesota players had shouted anti-Canadian insults at his players. Terry Meagher, BU's top scorer, heard Minnesota players yelling "frog" at him. "My name's not French," he protested.[105] When the Gophers played for the national championship in 1979, their fans took up the crusade. "Minnesota, the homegrown team," read one banner hanging in the arena. "Look Ma, no Canadians," read another.[106] Brooks's critics saw him instilling a hostile form of tribalism. "It's Minnesota against the Canadians and the rest of the world," said Parker.[107]

Motivated by this mix of Minnesota loyalty and American patriotism, Brooks took on the role of enforcing NCAA recruiting rules. In memos to university administrators and the WCHA, Brooks reported supposed infractions by his coaching colleagues. He always claimed the high road. "The 'win at all cost' philosophy scares me to no end," he declared in one memo, adding that he questioned "some of the values of member institutions" in the WCHA. In particular, Brooks claimed to stand up for American players. Importing Canadians, he insisted, "will curtail the development of the American hockey player in the United States."[108]

In his self-appointed role as watchdog, Brooks kept a close eye on his rival at the University of Wisconsin, Bob Johnson. Brooks and Johnson had both grown up in the Twin Cities, and both had played under John Mariucci at Minnesota. But in the 1970s, Johnson was seen as a traitor at his old school.

Bob Johnson, coaching the University of Wisconsin Badgers (courtesy of UW-Madison Archives).

A good part of it was sour grapes. Since taking over as coach in 1966, Johnson had turned Wisconsin into the nation's top college program and made hockey the biggest show in Madison. More than eight thousand fans filled the city's new arena for each game. Campus radicals with long hair, middle-aged locals, and Johnson's wife, Martha, banging a cow bell—they were all part of a raucous atmosphere. "Where is the real action," asked one writer sent to investigate the madness, "on the ice or in the stands?"[109] Rubber chickens hung from the balcony, the band blasted riffs over the glass, and students made regular trips to the beer taps under the stands. Perhaps the refreshments inspired creativity, for Wisconsin fans invented the most effective jeer in hockey history: the "sieve" chant, which rained down whenever an opposing goalie gave up a goal. *Sports Illustrated* told of one goalie who gave up his post after hearing the chant too many times: "The goalie didn't bother with the bench. As sieve, sieve, sieve thundered throughout the coliseum, he skated directly to the locker room."[110]

With a modern arena filled to capacity and a devoted following of students and locals, the University of Wisconsin turned college hockey into an event. "Wisconsin's arena is the Montreal Forum of college hockey," said one referee. "Every referee wants to work there. Every coach wants to coach there.

Every team wants to play there."[111] At the center was Badger Bob. Like today's million-dollar coaches in college football and basketball, Johnson was more than a coach—he managed a brand. When he arrived in Madison, hockey was a novelty. He spoke to local organizations, imploring people to give it a try. When he couldn't make an appearance, Martha went in his place. Players as well were expected to promote the game, visiting the local mall to talk hockey with shoppers. By the mid-1970s, Johnson had his own local television show—something only a handful of football coaches had at the time. In the arena Badger Bob was always visible, wearing his bright red blazer.

Bob Johnson and Herb Brooks were like oil and water. "There are some people in life you just don't see eye to eye with," Brooks admitted after Johnson's sudden death from brain cancer. "Bob was that person for me, and I'm sure I was that person for Bob."[112] One example was recruiting. Johnson's teams included a number of Canadians, but he also nabbed talented high schoolers from Minnesota—sometimes, according to Brooks, in violation of NCAA rules. More broadly, the two men had fundamentally different personalities and approaches to coaching. Brooks was notoriously aloof and mercurial, while Johnson was gregarious and enthusiastic. Brooks had the detail-oriented approach of a businessman. He took an analytical view of the sport, seeking to understand what needed to be done to win; then, like a successful manager, he drove his players to implement the plan. Johnson, on the other hand, had started his career as a high school teacher. The rink was his classroom, and he filled practice time with devices aimed at engaging his players' attention. "For Herb, the game was a struggle. It was a fight every day," observes John Harrington, who played under both coaches. "For Bob, it was fun."[113]

Johnson and Brooks were similar in their single-minded dedication to the game. The enthusiastic Johnson could burn people out. "Bob Johnson just isn't aware that the players can't eat, sleep, and breathe hockey like he does," said an NHL veteran.[114] The enigmatic Brooks wore people down.[115] In their dedication, both men were avid students of hockey, particularly how it was played overseas. Brooks had encountered Soviet and European hockey as a player with the national team in the 1960s. Years later he told of how he would get on the Soviet team bus to go watch their practices. Tarasov would "give me a funny look," Brooks said, "but he'd let me come along."[116] Johnson watched the Soviets and Europeans practice when he coached the US national team in the 1970s, filling notebooks with diagrams of drills. A strength of his Wisconsin teams was their efficient power-play, which Johnson adopted wholesale from the Czechoslovaks.[117] On Sundays after a weekend series, Johnson himself skated in pickup games with his junior varsity players. His side would wear Soviet jerseys. "He was always Kharlamov," Mike Eaves recalled.[118]

Brooks and Johnson were not the only coaches who saw the limits of North American hockey. Brooks's former teammate Murray Williamson adopted Soviet drills as coach of the 1972 US Olympic team. The squad surprised the field by taking silver. Lou Vairo experimented with Soviet ideas as a coach in the Midwest Junior League. After his teams won titles and his players made college rosters, he was tapped by the US Amateur Hockey Association to lead the national junior squad. Contrary to Hollywood mythmaking, Brooks did not introduce European ideas to American hockey. As *New York Times* writer Gerald Eskenazi remarked, college hockey was more innovative than the NHL because American coaches, "unlike the Canadians," were not afraid to try something new.[119]

When Brooks took over as coach of the US Olympic team in the summer of 1979, he set out to instill what he called "American hockey": a mix of Soviet-style movement and Canadian-style hitting. According to players, particularly those who had been with him at the University of Minnesota, this was nothing new. One notable innovation Brooks did make was in the team's organization and planning, in which he applied his experience in business. Past Olympic teams had played a schedule of warm-ups against college teams. By contrast, Brooks put together a full sixty-game campaign against European national squads, minor-pro teams, and NHL clubs.[120] Even before the roster was set, the coach acted as a business manager—or a "technocrat," as *Sports Illustrated* called him. The first selections were made by a committee that included his fiercest rivals, Bob Johnson and Jack Parker. Ultimately, Johnson's son Mark would center the first line on Brooks's team and become its top scorer. Four of Parker's Boston University players would also make the final roster—Brooks chose one, Jim Craig, to be his goalie, and another, Mike Eruzione, to be his captain. Brooks was "extremely fair," Parker acknowledged. "I don't think anyone could have done a better, more rational job."[121]

In the 1970s, coaches in the United States and Canada searched for a more rational approach to hockey. The shock of 1972 revealed a game that had been stunted in its evolution. Hockey Canada, the organization formed in 1968 to oversee the sport's development, set plans for research projects and training programs. Their strategic plan looked much like what the Soviet Hockey

Department had produced in 1957, with an array of targets plotted on an expansive timeline.[122] The aims were ambitious, yet cultural inertia was difficult to overcome. When the two volunteer directors of a local association met with researchers, they were clear that "rules and regulations" were becoming too restrictive. "Pretty soon we are going to be relying on books instead of judgment if we are not careful," one said. "Like robots," the other added.[123]

At the same time, there were coaches eager for new ideas. And there were fans yearning for a new kind of game. Some already saw the seeds of change. When the producers of *Hockey Night in Canada* surveyed people in 1973 to find out why ratings were dropping, they heard plenty of complaints. But they also found fans who were hopeful for the future:

> The best NHL teams and the best WHA teams will amalgamate. It will be much better.

> The crowd's taken to those new Swedish players. This is a trend that will increase interest, more players from Europe.

> It'll pick up because of all the players coming out of the universities in the U.S.

> There are more youngsters playing hockey than there ever have been. The future looks great.[124]

SIX

In the Money

THE TORONTO FANS WHO HAD FORECAST hockey's future turned out to be prescient. In 1979, four teams from the WHA—the Edmonton Oilers, Winnipeg Jets, Quebec Nordiques, and Hartford Whalers—were admitted into the NHL. During the 1980s and '90s, some of the league's top players, both Canadian and American, came out of university programs in the United States. And NHL fans indeed took to European players. Among the league's biggest stars were the Šťastný brothers in Quebec City, Jari Kurri in Edmonton, Mats Näslund in Montreal, and Pelle Lindbergh in Philadelphia. An even greater dose of European talent came into the league with the fall of the Iron Curtain in 1989—something no one could have predicted in 1973.

The fan who expressed hope in all the "youngsters" playing hockey was also proved correct. But there were some twists. The number of Canadian boys in youth hockey continued climbing through the 1970s and early '80s, even as the overall cohort of children declined after the baby boom. Then, in the late '80s, the growth stopped. Registrations of Canadian boys stalled and even dipped. Still, the overall number of youngsters playing hockey across North America continued growing. The Americans' gold medal at Lake Placid spurred youth hockey in the United States. And in the early '90s, thousands of Canadian and American girls began playing organized hockey, bringing a new dynamism to the sport.

One other factor transformed North American hockey in the 1980s and '90s—and indeed, hockey around the world. Money. Lots of it. Pro hockey of the '70s had been a low-rent affair. The NHL's top players earned just over $100,000 per year, and owners barely broke even at the end of the eighty-game season. TV money was negligible, merchandising revenue a trickle. Five or six million could get you an NHL franchise, along with all its unpaid bills. By the early '90s, the picture had changed. Owners of new teams in San Jose, Ottawa, and Tampa paid $45–50 million for their expansion franchises.

The NHL was not alone in seeing its fortunes rise during this period. European leagues, the International Ice Hockey Federation, and even the tradition-bound International Olympic Committee cashed in on television deals and commercial sponsorships. ESPN grew from a cable curiosity to a media giant. Nike went from a running-shoe manufacturer to a multi-billion-dollar global brand. Sports had been big business before, but in the 1980s it became huge business, transforming the ways we watch and the ways we play. Still today, we live in the world the Eighties created.

WHY A MIRACLE MATTERS

What's so important about a hockey game?

Psychologist Thomas Joiner has found that major sporting events, whether a regularly occurring championship like the Super Bowl or a once-in-a-lifetime event like the final game of the Summit Series, create in us a sense of "pulling together." Whether we are in the stands or watching on TV, or even hearing about them secondhand, such episodes meet our individual need for social connectedness. For instance, Joiner's research team looked at health records across the United States on the date February 22, throughout the 1970s and '80s. They found that the number of suicides on that date was consistent over those two decades, except for one day, when the number went down—February 22, 1980, the day of the Miracle on Ice. In looking at suicide statistics on this date and the dates of other notable sports moments, Joiner concluded that these significant sporting events have a similar psychological effect as a moment of tragedy such as 9/11 or the Kennedy assassination. These episodes and their aftermath help fulfill our need to belong. People gain "an increased sense of positive identification with a valued group."[1] This sense of belonging, Joiner found, can prevent suicide.

What's so important about a hockey game? In this case, it saved lives.

The Miracle on Ice was a pivotal event for other reasons as well. One lasting legacy is that it changed the way American television networks broadcast the Olympics, particularly the winter games. Prior to 1980, ABC Sports had covered the Olympics as an expanded version of its program *Wide World of Sports,* the weekly show highlighting international sports such as weightlifting, downhill skiing, and soccer. American athletes were usually not competitive in winter events. The hockey team's success changed that. American viewers wanted to watch American athletes win, and American television networks were happy to oblige.[2] ABC had paid $15.5 million to broadcast the 1980 games. With the success of the hockey team and speed skater Eric Heiden, winner of five gold medals, the Lake Placid games had average nightly ratings of 23.6, more than any previous Winter Olympics. After the games, ABC Sports president Roone Arledge went back to the IOC, eager to secure an unbreakable hold on the winter games. He paid $91.5 million for the broadcast rights to the 1984 games in Sarajevo. Then, just before the Sarajevo games opened, Arledge signed the next contract, for the 1988 Calgary games. With a bid of $309 million, ABC paid more to televise the 1988 Winter Olympics than NBC did for the 1988 Summer Olympics. Arledge could not conjure another miracle, but he'd be damned if he missed one.[3]

With hundreds of millions in television money coming to the IOC, the Olympic movement and its affiliated federations were forever transformed. Television money allowed federations to expand their activities, with more clinics, more tournaments, and more support of developing programs—as well as more in-fighting and corruption.[4] Hockey's leaders recognized the value of their sport for the winter games, and they expected to be paid accordingly. For the Calgary games, the IIHF negotiated a cut of more than $3 million.[5] A decade later, for the Winter Olympics in Nagano, the federation's share of television money was over $11 million, more than the amounts either figure skating or skiing gained.[6] After Lake Placid, hockey was the must-see event of the Winter Olympics for the all-important American market, with millions in television rights and advertising on the line.

At the same time, the 1980 US Olympic hockey team represented the end of an age. The players were, in a real sense, amateurs. Nearly all had come directly from university teams. They did receive stipends for their year on the team, but not a lot, just enough that they didn't have to scrounge for beer money. These were also not year-round hockey players. Phil Verchota had been recruited to play college football; Buzz Schneider was a top baseball prospect. Only a couple had elite-level hockey in their bloodlines: Mark Johnson, of course; and Eric Strobel, whose father had played briefly with the Rangers.

Most of the players at Lake Placid came from working-class families. Their parents included a truck driver, an electrician, a carpenter, and an auto plant worker. Jim Craig sent money home to his dad, a widower who managed the cafeteria at a junior college. Mike Eruzione's father worked two jobs, as a maintenance worker at a sewage plant by day and a waiter by night. John Harrington's father held two jobs as well—on the railroad and at the post office. When Harrington left his hometown on Minnesota's Iron Range to play college hockey, his friends couldn't believe it. They were earning solid paychecks at the mines, enough to buy new pickup trucks and fishing boats. "College!" they kidded him. "Why would you want to go to college?"[7]

The 1980 Olympic hockey team was also the last of its kind in that they were underdogs. At the time, sportswriters compared the win over the Soviets to a high school football team beating the Pittsburgh Steelers, who had just won their fourth Super Bowl. One end of the analogy works: the Soviets were indeed like the Steelers, if the Steelers had been able to poach players from other NFL teams and then practice for eleven months. The Americans, however, were not akin to high school football players. Veterans of Herb Brooks's Minnesota teams had won two NCAA championships. Fifteen of the twenty players had been drafted by NHL clubs. They were underdogs, to be sure. But they were talented and well trained. At Lake Placid, they skated against future NHL stars Mats Näslund, Jari Kurri, and the Šťastný brothers, and they finished without a loss.

A year after the Olympics, Brooks described the meaning of the team: "The economy was screwed up. We were held hostage in Iran. The Russians were in Afghanistan. And then here we come, a real-life 'Rocky' story. We reflected the work ethic."[8] Today, American sporting success comes at a high price. More and more, professional and Olympic athletes are products of private coaching and specialized academies. Yet American popular culture still celebrates figures like Rocky Balboa—the athlete from a hardscrabble background who rises to the top. Perhaps even more telling than *Rocky* is *The Sandlot,* a 1993 film about a group of boys who play baseball each day on a rough patch of ground near a junkyard. At one point, the boys play a team of snotty rich kids, with clean uniforms, proper equipment, and shiny bikes. As the sandlot gang pounds the rich kids with hit after hit, the audience cheers. Americans identify with the kids from the sandlot. In fact, however, we're the rich kids. We're the Dream Team crushing opponents at the Barcelona games, and the US women's soccer team with its World Cup and Olympic titles. America's last true underdogs were the hockey players at Lake Placid. They were the underdogs Americans still imagine themselves to be.

AFTER LAKE PLACID

Setting aside all the underdog talk, this was a good team. Immediately after the Olympics, eight players signed with NHL clubs. Defenseman Ken Morrow won the Stanley Cup with the Islanders three months after winning Olympic gold. He and a handful of other players went on to long careers in the league. These players recognized, however, that even though they had NHL-level talent, their chances as Americans would have been slim if not for Lake Placid. Mark Johnson, who played eleven NHL seasons, acknowledged that the Olympics opened the door to his first contract with the Penguins. "Winning the gold medal helped make that a reality."[9]

The most publicized signing was goalie Jim Craig, who joined the Atlanta Flames just three days after the gold-medal game. With a three-year contract paying $85,000 per year and a signing bonus of $45,000, Craig nabbed a spectacular sum for an American rookie. There were also endorsement deals. Coca-Cola paid Craig $35,000 to film a commercial, while other Atlanta companies finally discovered the city had a hockey team. "They're knocking down our doors," said a team executive.[10] Even before his first game, Craig was hailed as the savior of the Flames, a money-losing franchise reportedly up for sale. When the goalie made his debut in Atlanta, the Flames had their first sellout of the season. Craig stopped twenty-four shots that night, leading the Flames to a win over the Colorado Rockies. But he could not save hockey in Atlanta. After the season the franchise moved to Calgary. Craig was traded to his hometown Bruins, yet he was never able to recapture the brilliance that had won Olympic gold.

Herb Brooks made a surprising career choice after the Olympics. In the weeks after Lake Placid, there were rumored offers from NHL teams but nothing definite. The only firm offer came from the lowly Rockies, after they fired coach Don Cherry. Rather than going to a losing NHL team, Brooks chose to sign with HC Davos. "Only four coaches in the NHL make more money than what I've been offered," Brooks said in explaining the unusual decision.[11] Davos signed the "star coach," as he was called in the papers, to a two-year deal, and there was a suggestion he would also lead the Swiss national team. Yet once the season began and Davos fell in the standings, it became clear the star coach was a difficult fit. Coaching methods that brought success at Minnesota and Lake Placid did not work with players who had jobs outside of hockey. Midway through the season, he returned home. A few months later, Brooks took the job he had been eyeing all along, with the New York Rangers.[12]

European clubs were also eager to sign Brooks's former players. "If the whole team would have come over they could have found a place for them," said Buzz Schneider, who played in Bern.[13] At every mention in the Swiss papers, Schneider and his former teammates were referred to as "Olympic champions." During his time with HC Lugano, John Harrington saw that fans regarded the gold medal as the pinnacle of achievement. Harrington signed with the Swiss club after making a run at the NHL. By contrast, Phil Verchota chose Europe right away. For the money he stood to make in the NHL, the grind of the long season and fending off goons was not worth it. He signed instead with Helsinki Jokerit and earned more than he would have in North America. Like the other Olympians, Verchota received plenty of attention in Europe, although he did not understand what the papers were saying about him. "Finnish has got to be one of the hardest languages in the world to learn," he told an interviewer during the season. "I know enough now to ask for a stick, tape, milk or beer."[14]

North American players had been going to Europe throughout the postwar decades. A few had been regular NHL players, such as Carl Brewer, who went to Finland during a contract fight with the Maple Leafs, and Jacques Lemaire, who finished his career in Switzerland after twelve seasons with the Canadiens. Typically, however, imported players were minor-league veterans or younger players who saw little chance in the NHL. The signings of Brooks and his players signaled a change. European clubs were selling stars, even a star coach, and they were willing to pay for them.

Meanwhile, European clubs began paying not only imports but also their own players. After the Swedish and Finnish leagues became professional in the mid-1970s, HC Lugano was the first Swiss club to pay Swiss players a decade later. With one of the country's richest men, Geo Mantegazza, as club president, Lugano paid its top Swiss forwards upward of 70,000 francs per season (equivalent of $65,000 today). Led by Swedish coach John Slettvoll, and with imported players from Sweden, Finland, Canada, and the United States, the Luganesi won four championships between 1985 and 1990.[15] With their success, the club pointed the way to the future of Swiss hockey: a core of homegrown talent, high-impact imports from Europe and North America, a successful foreign coach, and a wealthy president to pay for it all.

These changes in European leagues—like the growing numbers of Americans and Europeans in the NHL—had been developing before 1980. Yet the Miracle on Ice, like the Summit Series, was a catalyzing event. Publicity surrounding Brooks and his Olympians brought new attention to hockey in Europe. During the 1980s, the number of Canadians and Americans playing in Switzerland steadily climbed. Likewise, college hockey began to send more players to the NHL, both Americans and talented Canadian prospects. As was the case after the epic series of 1972, hockey's different cultures were further stirred together after the miraculous game in Lake Placid.

A HERO FOR CANADA

The winter of 1980 brought another momentous event in North American hockey: the emergence of Wayne Gretzky. At the start of the 1979–80 season, Gretzky's first in the NHL, the nineteen-year-old was commonly known as The Kid. As the season progressed and Gretzky held his own among the league's top scorers, some sportswriters called him the second coming of Bobby Orr. Others said he was a genius. By spring, he was The Great One. "I guess 'special' is the only word to describe Gretzky," said Ulf Nilsson. "The normal words don't really apply."[16]

Gretzky himself saw his success on the ice as the product not of some innate ability, but of hard work and experience. His endurance came from running cross-country, his elusiveness from lacrosse. His ability to anticipate other players' movements came from competing against older boys. He always paid tribute to the creative coaching of his father, Walter, on the rink behind their house. Gretzky was confident in his abilities, but he knew his limitations. "I can't do what other players do," he told an interviewer in 1985. Yet while he spoke humbly of his place in the league, he also recognized that he was in the spotlight. Walter Gretzky made the lesson clear when his son was making the papers already as a high-scoring peewee. Wayne Gretzky took it to heart. "I do have a bad habit of swearing on the ice," he admitted once. "I forget that there are people around the rink. It's a problem."[17]

Swearing on the ice a problem? Clearly, Gretzky was not your average hockey player. Writers and teammates noted that he was indefatigably polite. In interviews, he spoke of the game with a specificity few other players could match. With his long blond hair, blue eyes, and angular features, he had the appearance of a heartthrob. Yet he eschewed the temptation to be a sex symbol. "That's not a void I need to fill," he said.[18] He did, however, make himself available for endorsements—plenty of them. The various products featuring the Great One fill shelves in the Hockey Hall of Fame archive: lunch boxes, canned soup, pudding mix, breakfast cereal. Like Magic, Michael, and

Beckham, Gretzky became a brand. Hockey players had endorsed products before, but none before had been as talented, articulate, cooperative, and beautiful.

Part of Gretzky's greatness, demonstrated in his astonishing scoring records, was due to the fact that he played at the right time. Gretzky had teammates with the skill and speed to complement his game, starting with his Finnish linemate, Jari Kurri. More importantly, Gretzky had a coach who knew how to use him. When Glen Sather began coaching the Oilers in the WHA, he adopted the same fast-moving, creative offense he watched the Winnipeg Jets use. "I think the players should be like painters," he said.[19] He also continued the analytical methods he had initiated in the 1970s. "Glen is completely modern," remarked one of his veterans. "He is probably against all the principles of any coach in the NHL today."[20] By winning the Stanley Cup four times, Sather established new principles. A decade after the Summit Series, the Oilers confirmed that European-style hockey could work in the NHL.

"Gretzky's not Canadian," said Sergei Makarov, the top-scoring forward on Soviet teams of the 1980s, "he's a European player."[21] Makarov was not alone in recognizing Gretzky's European style of play. Yet while Gretzky and the Oilers drew from Europe, the Great One was a Canadian hero. Humble, polite, hardworking, uncontestably the greatest hockey player in the world—Gretzky was raised to the Canadian pantheon early in his career. "He'll be the greatest," said Maurice Richard as Gretzky approached his record of fifty goals in fifty games. Gretzky scored fifty goals in thirty-nine games, in his third season in the league. He finished that year with ninety-two goals—after only one player in league history, Phil Esposito, had ever scored more than seventy. His records were unimaginable: the once-in-forever statistical equivalents of Pelé in soccer and Don Bradman in cricket. Like those two athletes in their native Brazil and Australia, Gretzky became more than an icon in Canada—he was a treasure. "The joy of it all is that we have found him," wrote broadcaster and journalist Peter Gzowski, "that the game is so much a part of our lives that when a Wayne Gretzky is born we will find him."[22]

Gretzky became famous around the world, still the only hockey player to be widely recognized outside the sport. In the view of writers like Gzowski, Gretzky restored the Canadian game to Canada. After the Soviets had claimed supremacy, after the NHL had been watered down by expansion, after the Flyers had debased the sport, Gretzky reclaimed Canadian hockey's creativity. Plenty of people in Canada harbored resentment toward Gretzky: he didn't play defense, he didn't fight, he endorsed too many products, he made too much money. Still, as poet Doug Beardsley insisted, Gretzky was "the archetypal Canadian hero." Hockey was the fullest expression of the nation's identity, and Gretzky was the game's transcendent figure. "By finding greatness in him," wrote Beardsley, "we find it in ourselves."[23]

THE END OF THE WORLD AS WE KNOW IT

It was a rainy weekend in Edmonton, in those last days before everything changed. Unemployment was up—another sign that Alberta's oil-and-gas economy was slowing. There were fears that the province was becoming dependent on American markets, as the newly signed free-trade agreement tightened links with the United States and as energy companies secured subsidies to develop tar-sand deposits in the north. But baseball's Expos were on a winning streak, the Edmonton Eskimos were at the top of the CFL, and sprinter Ben Johnson was preparing for the Seoul Olympics. The sun came out in time for the last day of the Edmonton Folk Festival. Bob Dylan was scheduled to make his first visit to the city later in the month. And a rising band from Kingston, the Tragically Hip, played a local club on Monday night.[24]

The press conference was held the next afternoon: Tuesday, August 9, 1988. The morning's rumors were confirmed—Wayne Gretzky had been traded to the Los Angeles Kings. Speaking to the press, Gretzky admitted that he had initiated the trade, before breaking down in tears. Team owner Peter Pocklington said he agreed to the request, "despite a tremendous amount of trepidation."[25] By the afternoon, Gretzky was in LA. His wife of only three weeks, actress and dancer Janet Jones, was by his side as he donned his new sweater.

Gretzky left behind a city in shock. Callers clogged newspaper phone lines and radio talk shows. A few branded their hero a traitor. Mostly, however, their anger was heaped upon Pocklington and Jones. "Why couldn't he have married a nice Ukrainian girl and stayed in Edmonton?" asked one caller to the *Edmonton Sun*.[26] The city's daily tabloid stoked the anger. An editorial cartoon showed a dumbstruck Gretzky following behind Jones, holding her apron strings as she leads him away. "Why did Gretzky betray the values he claimed to believe in?" asked *Sun* columnist Graham Hicks. "It has to be Jezebel Janet."[27]

In the next two days the full story came out. Gretzky had not initiated the trade, Pocklington had. Local papers revealed that the owner's business dealings were stretched thin, and he needed the $15 million the Kings had sent in the deal. Jones broke her silence as well, telling an Edmonton sportswriter that Gretzky's tears were real. "Wayne speaks from the heart," she said. "People who aren't good at lying aren't good at lying."[28] Whereas there had been talk on Tuesday of burning Gretzky gear, by Thursday there was a run on number 99 jerseys, in both Oilers and Kings colors. In the pages of the *Sun,* Graham Hicks issued an apologetic retraction: "Gretzky is the honorable, trusting friend of this city we always thought he was."[29]

Still, the shock waves spread. There had been nothing like it in the history of North American sports. Gretzky was far and away the game's most dominant player and most popular attraction. At age twenty-eight, he was still in his prime, having just led the Oilers to their fourth Stanley Cup. More than that, he was going from hockey's homeland to California, a place where the sport struggled to draw attention. "They might as well send Wayne to the moon as to LA," said a member of Parliament. Once again, Canadians were reminded that no asset of theirs was too precious to be bought by the United States. One fan who called the *Globe and Mail* saw the trade as another step in Canada's economic dependence: "This is what happens with free-trade. We export a national hero to the United States." *Ottawa Citizen* columnist Earl McRae lamented that not only would the hero be owned by Americans, he would become one of them as well:

> His wife's American, the air he breathes will be American, the team he plays for will be American, the money he earns will be American, the money he spends will be American, his kids will be partly American, his kids will be schooled in American schools, pledge allegiance to the American flag, sing the American national anthem, pray for the American way.[30]

Los Angeles may not have been a hockey town, but it was a city of stars—and it knew a star when it saw one. In the years before the Great One arrived, the Kings had been near the bottom of the league in attendance. Losses ran from $3 million to $5 million a season. Immediately after the trade, ticket orders poured in. The team's new black-and-silver jerseys flew off the racks. In the next two seasons, the Kings' ticket revenue tripled and their television rights nearly quadrupled.[31]

LA was not alone in experiencing a hockey boom as the 1980s came to a close. After two decades in the league's basement, the Detroit Red Wings were winning again. Attendance also climbed in St. Louis, as a talented Blues team added young scorer Brett Hull, who had the cannon shot and rugged good looks of his father. The biggest turnaround came in Pittsburgh. In 1984 the Penguins were on the verge of bankruptcy when they drafted Mario Lemieux, a Montreal phenom touted as the next Gretzky. Lemieux proved the predictions correct. By 1988, he was challenging Gretzky for the league scoring title, the Pens were winning, and the Igloo was selling out. The NHL was on the rise. League president John Ziegler announced after the 1988–89 season that league revenue would be $350 million that year, compared with $82 million a decade earlier. Owners looked again to expand. In December 1989, they announced plans to add three new franchises, at a fee of $50 million each. The last franchise to change hands, the Flames, had sold for $16 million just nine years earlier.[32]

It was not only owners who were counting their cash. Average player salary climbed throughout the 1980s, eventually passing $200,000 in 1988, more than double what it had been a decade earlier. Following the Gretzky trade, player earnings shot even higher. Immediately after acquiring his new star, Kings owner Bruce McNall signed Gretzky to a contract paying $20 million over eight years—the biggest deal in league history. McNall insisted that a player of Gretzky's standing deserved to be paid more than $2 million a year. But what about Lemieux, who outscored Gretzky by thirty points that season? In summer 1989, the Penguins locked in their star to a five-year, $12 million contract. Not to be outdone, McNall added two years to Gretzky's contract, bringing the Great One's total haul to more than $30 million.

The massive contracts had a cascading effect. In 1989, only two NHL players earned more than $1 million per season: Gretzky and Lemieux. Three years later the league had more than two dozen millionaires. The pay scale in the NHL did not compare with other major sports leagues in North America, each of which reaped the benefits of enormous television contracts. Major League Baseball, for example, had 267 millionaires in 1992. Yet the salary boom following the Gretzky trade had a lasting impact on hockey. For one, rising salaries led to regular labor conflicts in the NHL, as owners insisted that revenue could not sustain their spending. Secondly, the boom separated the NHL from newly professional European leagues. When Jari Kurri joined Devils Milano in 1990, he was by far the highest-paid hockey player in Europe, making a base salary of $350,000. The next season, he was reunited with Gretzky in Los Angeles and making close to $1 million.[33] Managers of European clubs would find it difficult to keep their most talented players when the NHL offered riches.

Lastly, the rise in salaries changed the way North American players trained. With cash on the table and more competition coming from Europe, players recognized they had to commit themselves to the game in ways past players had not. "It is a 12-month-of-the-year commitment," said Bob Goodenow, head of the players association. Changes that were not accomplished by losses to the Soviets, or by coaching seminars and manuals, were finally brought about by money. "It's a reflection of the industry," Goodenow observed. "There's so much at stake, they have to take care of themselves."[34] The weight room was no longer a quiet place to have a smoke. With millions to be made, players stubbed out their cigarettes, hired personal trainers, and got themselves into shape.

MAKING FUTURE GRETZKYS

Since it began publication in 1954, *Sports Illustrated* has regularly devoted features to teenage athletes heralded as can't-miss stars of the future. Some of these predictions proved correct (e.g., LeBron James). A few did not. One the magazine got right was Pat LaFontaine. In 1983 *Sports Illustrated* profiled the eighteen-year-old Michigan native as one of the top prospects for the upcoming NHL draft.[35] LaFontaine ended up going third that year, to the New York Islanders. He went on to have a fifteen-year career in the NHL, leading ultimately to the Hockey Hall of Fame.

What made LaFontaine such a compelling prospect, one deserving a *Sports Illustrated* feature, was that he was an American playing major junior hockey in Canada. In fact, he was tearing up his league. As a member of the Verdun Juniors in Quebec, LaFontaine broke scoring records that had been sent by NHL greats Guy Lafleur and Mike Bossy. He finished the seventy-game season with 104 goals and 130 assists, giving him the third-highest point total in league history. LaFontaine's scoring feats gained attention across Canada—Prime Minister Pierre Trudeau even sent congratulations after he broke one of Lafleur's records. LaFontaine became a celebrity in Verdun, explained writer Jack Falla, despite his lack of skill in French.

Falla also devoted attention to LaFontaine's unusual path to professional hockey—unusual, that is, to American readers. Whereas in Canada it was customary for a teenage prospect to leave home and join a club in some distant town, in the United States it was not: most hockey players, like young athletes in other sports, developed their skills with their high school team or local club. LaFontaine had taken a bold step for an American teenager, saying goodbye to family and friends, moving by himself to a different country, and giving up his college eligibility. "If I wanted to progress, I had to come here," he explained to Falla. "Besides," LaFontaine added, "I've known since I was a kid that I wanted to play pro hockey."[36]

Pat LaFontaine's path to the NHL represented a significant shift in American sports. Rather than playing with a team in his community, he took an unexpected step to advance toward his career goal. His high school did not have a hockey team, and the Detroit-area league he had played in was not challenging enough (he amassed over three hundred points as a sixteen-year-old). LaFontaine also chose not to pursue a scholarship; college teams played only forty games, compared to seventy in Canadian major juniors. For an aspiring pro player, the move made sense. Talented American teenagers in other sports were making the same decision. The same year that LaFontaine was breaking records in Quebec, Andre Agassi moved across the country to train at Nick Bollettieri's tennis academy. Meanwhile, Mary Lou Retton was preparing for the 1984 Olympics at Béla and Márta Károlyi's new gymnastics school in Houston, over thirteen hundred miles from her family's home.

Then, as now, this kind of individualized, professional training required a considerable investment. Today, a year at the IMG Academy, successor to Bollettieri's tennis school, can cost more than $80,000, depending on which sport your fifth-grader plays. In the early 1980s, Mary Lou Retton's father calculated that her training cost $10,000 a year, roughly half of the median household income at the time. "I'll say this," he said. "A poor person couldn't afford it."[37] The Retton family could afford it, as could the LaFontaine family. John LaFontaine, Pat's father, was an auto company executive. According to reporters who visited the family, their lakeside home in a Detroit suburb was like a training facility. The elder LaFontaine spared no expense to develop the hockey talents of his two sons and the figure-skating career of his daughter.

Decades earlier, a successful business executive would not have sought a career in pro sports for his children. Recall the warning Arthur Rice-Jones received from his father: playing sports for money was beneath a man of his standing. Even reporters covering Pat LaFontaine's move to Quebec asked why his father went to such lengths. Jack Falla broached the question as to whether John LaFontaine, who had played hockey himself while growing up in Ontario, was "vicariously fulfilling his own admittedly frustrated hockey ambitions."[38] Pat LaFontaine's mastery of interviews gave another reporter the impression "that his fame was carefully programmed, step by step, by his dad."[39] Today, sportswriters no longer bat an eye at this kind of well-coached young athlete, with parents committing family resources to his or her development. When *Sports Illustrated* profiled Auston Matthews three decades later, the magazine did not question his parents' motives in sending him to Switzerland for a year.

To be sure, parents' dedication to their children's athletic success was nothing new. Brent Gretzky, Wayne's youngest brother, recalled occasions when their father was out of town and he could play ball-hockey with his friends on the backyard rink. He'd hear it when his dad came home: "What do you think I make the rink for, to fool around?" Sure enough, out would come the pylons and pucks for a few hours of drills.[40] For men like Walter Gretzky, a linesman for Bell Canada, sports offered an escape for their sons. But the children of business executives were not escaping a life of manual labor. Instead, elite sports were a path to greater wealth and celebrity. Stars of the early 1980s like Gretzky, Joe Montana, and Magic Johnson—and later Agassi, Mary Lou, and above all Michael Jordan—were a new type of athlete: well-spoken, attractive, and rich. What financially secure parents would not want that kind of status for their child?

Young athletes from affluent families were also part of a changing social and economic landscape in North America. In the 1950s more than half of Americans and over 40 percent of Canadians worked in either industry or agriculture; by 1991, less than a third of Americans and Canadians worked in those sectors. By contrast, the commercial, finance, and service sectors accounted for half the workforce.[41] The demographic shift to the suburbs continued, and birthrates declined. With greater household wealth and fewer children, parents could dedicate more resources to their children's pursuits. At the same time, youth programs that had expanded in the 1950s and '60s to accommodate the baby boomers became more entrepreneurial to attract participants from the smaller cohort of Generation X.

An example of these new youth sports programs was Compuware hockey in suburban Detroit. Founded in 1973 by Peter Karmanos, the son of Greek immigrants, Compuware was one of the largest software companies in the United States by the 1980s. Karmanos was also a Red Wings fan, and his sons played hockey. As business owners had done for decades, he sponsored teams in Detroit-area leagues. Then he saw opportunity. In the early 1980s, Compuware started new elite-level teams and took over management of its own suburban arena. By 1985, the company's hockey division was budgeting more than $600,000 per year. Families had to increase their budgets as well. "The parents have to spend a bit more," reasoned one Compuware team manager, "but if they truly want a chance at the NHL they have to get looked at."[42] Indeed, Compuware players did get looked at—ten reached the NHL in the 1980s. One NHL scout compared the Detroit-area program to the best in Canada: "They have good hockey organizations around Toronto and Montreal, but Compuware has to take the cake."[43]

Of course, a program with Compuware's success also had critics. Managers of rival organizations saw Karmanos's spending as creating an unfair advantage. "If I devoted 24 hours a day to hockey, I'd be a better coach," said the part-time coordinator of another Detroit-area program, "but I can't."[44] Some Compuware players and parents bristled at Karmanos's heavy-handed management style. "It became too much of a business," said the father of Jimmy Carson, who went on to play ten NHL seasons.[45] Too much travel, too many games, too expensive, too demanding, too focused on winning—elite programs like Compuware drew criticism for professionalizing youth sports. Even those involved in pro sports objected. In a 1981 interview, Sabres coach Scotty Bowman complained about the schedule his eight-year-old son endured. "They got him playing a 62-game schedule in Buffalo this year with road trips to Boston and Toronto." His son's coach wanted to add a four-hundred-mile trip to play a team in Montreal. "Eight years old," Bowman exclaimed. "I told him, 'Drive 'em across the bridge 12 miles to Fort Erie.'"[46]

Stanley Cup–winning coaches might object, but entrepreneurs like Karmanos knew their market. Boys came from both coasts to try out for Compuware teams, with parents willing to foot the bill. When one teenage player from Alaska made a Compuware team, his parents moved the whole family to the Detroit area. "That's what I love about Americans," said his Canadian coach. "They're so drastic."[47]

A GAME FOR ALL SEASONS

Karmanos found one area of particular customer demand: summer hockey. He launched Compuware's summer hockey schools in 1981. Within three years, they were grossing $400,000—equivalent to just over $1 million today.

Summer hockey was nothing new. Schools had been operating in Detroit and other cities since the 1950s, when NHL players offered lessons to local kids in order to supplement their salaries. By the 1980s, NHL players no longer needed the extra income, but rink owners did. As rinks stayed open year-round to provide ice for figure skaters, operators found that summer hockey helped boost revenue. "It is becoming more of an entrepreneur's operation," said a manager of summer programs in the Toronto area.⁴⁸ Organizers promoted their camps as an opportunity for younger players to improve their skills and for older players to perform in front of scouts and coaches. The organizer of one Detroit-area league—a competitor to Compuware's summer program—said the additional games gave players "hope for college scholarships."⁴⁹ By the late 1980s, summer tournaments in North America were drawing hundreds of teams. For many families in Canada and the United States, summer vacation meant a trip across the continent for hockey.⁵⁰

In becoming a year-round activity, hockey was similar to other youth sports in North America during the 1980s. At the same time, factors particular to hockey pushed the sport out of its traditional season. Reformers of the 1970s had emphasized off-season activity as part of a modern, European-style training program. The expanded calendar and increased specialization allowed for an even greater mix of international currents in the 1980s, especially in the United States. "I felt we had to borrow from other hockey cultures in order to become strong enough to play against Canada," said Lou Vairo, development director for USA Hockey. Long a proponent of Soviet methods, Vairo brought over Tarasov himself for summer clinics with players and coaches. He also launched summer development camps for boys from outside the traditional hockey-playing regions. "Coming from Brooklyn, I was sick of how everything was Minnesota, Massachusetts, Michigan," Vairo said. "Like hockey didn't exist anywhere else in the country."⁵¹ Players came from California, Texas, and Florida for the USA Hockey camps, and by the mid-1980s, teams were traveling to Phoenix and Dallas for tournaments. The seed planted by the Miracle on Ice began bearing fruit—boys across the country were choosing hockey.

Summer hockey was difficult for some to accept. "Hockey was the first sport to get a bad rap for playing year-round," a longtime NHL scout told me. The old guard might have objected, but parents and players believed the extra training gave them a needed edge in competing for the next level.⁵²

Ultimately, it was all about winning—beating out other kids for a spot on the team, moving to the next level. For those who kept on winning, there were prizes of real value: college scholarships, a shot at the pros. More valuable than money, for many parents, was the promise of status. The accomplishments of our children bring genuine joy, the undeniable biochemical surge that comes from seeing our offspring succeed. Even more than that, we want our children to win because it shows that we have won—that I am the better parent.⁵³

Why did parents need such validation? Fathers and mothers of baby boomers had been more involved than those of previous generations, and this trend accelerated in the 1980s. Families were smaller and more affluent. But this affluence was built atop anxiety. The baby boomers had been raised during two decades of uninterrupted economic growth. By contrast, Generation X came of age amid the transformation of the postwar industrial economy and regular cycles of expansion and recession. American and Canadian culture had long emphasized competition, but in the 1980s that competition became more intense. The spoils of getting ahead were great. The risks of falling behind were real.[54]

GIRLS TAKE THE ICE

Word traveled fast about the remarkable peewee player, as it always did in Ontario. By the end of the season, even the Toronto papers were paying attention. Top scorer for the league-leading team in Gravenhurst. Named MVP in five weekend tournaments. Good all-around athlete who plays lacrosse and basketball. Smart in school, too. Dad is a coach. Started all three kids on the backyard rink. Both the older and younger brothers are pretty good as well. This one, the twelve-year-old, wants to play for the Bruins. Hero is Bobby Orr. They say, though, that the family is moving to Peterborough for better opportunities. But the coach doesn't want to lose his best player. He's even offered a room with his family for next season.

Her name was Stephanie Boyd. She later played for the University of Toronto women's team, competed internationally for Team USA (thanks to her mother's American citizenship), and organized one of Canada's first summer hockey schools for girls. In 1985, when she was the best player on the Triton Engineering peewee team, Stephanie was at the center of the debate about girls' hockey. The Gravenhurst association had allowed her to play with boys because there was no girls' team nearby. The following year, however, the league administrator came on the ice during tryouts and told Stephanie she could not play.[55]

Stephanie's parents were not radicals. They ran small businesses and were reluctant to take legal action. Yet the Boyds saw no reason why their daughter should not have the same opportunities as their sons. "We are giving Stephanie the same chance we gave our boys," said Nancy Boyd, "to play better hockey and a chance at a scholarship." With Stephanie blocked from boys' teams, this meant driving her hundreds of miles to play with women's teams in Toronto. In response to a reporter's question about whether they were devoting too much attention to hockey, the Boyds stressed that they were instilling values that could be applied later in life. "You have to make your own opportunities," said Larry Boyd.[56]

Just as ambitious dads and moms drove the specialization of youth hockey in the 1980s, the increasing number of girls in the sport was brought by changes in parenting. When Abby Hoffman pretended to be a boy to join a team in 1956, reporters covering the story described her parents as unconventional. Three decades later, the idea that Hoffman's parents professed, that she should have the same opportunities as her brothers, had broader acceptance. Certainly, parents of the 1980s were wary when their daughters asked about playing hockey. Cammi Granato's mom bought her a figure-skating costume, hoping to draw her away from hockey. Granato refused. Like Stephanie Boyd, she wanted to play hockey with her brothers.[57] For Shannon Miller and Hayley Wickenheiser, the influence was their fathers, both coaches. These parents did not declare themselves as feminists or progressives. Yet they held the idea that their sons and daughters should be able to enjoy the same activities, that they should have the same opportunities. "He never made me feel like there wasn't anything I could do," said Miller of her father.[58]

Demand was always there, contrary to the claims of most men who ran amateur hockey associations. Detroit and other communities in eastern Michigan started teams for girls in the 1960s. A Boston-area league of girls' teams quickly grew to two thousand players in the early 1970s. Later that decade, universities in Canada and the northeast United States started club teams. Provincial organizations in Alberta, British Columbia, and Prince Edward Island added women's branches, and a wholly separate association was founded in Ontario in 1975. The launch of a Canadian national championship in 1981 stirred media attention and spurred registrations. As the number of players increased, sportswriters started describing women's hockey as a sport with a future, instead of a curiosity.[59]

As with the growth of specialized, high-stakes youth sports, the expansion of girls' hockey was fueled by broader social and economic changes. Along with fewer children, many households in the United States and Canada had two working parents, or, as was becoming increasingly common, a single working mother. Consequently, high school girls expected that they would have not simply a job but a career. By the 1980s, more women than men were enrolled at Canadian and American universities. Surveys of first-year students showed that young women now put equal weight on financial success and recognition from colleagues as factors in their self-fulfillment, along with family. As economic historian Claudia Goldin explains, young women at the time "had larger horizons than did previous generations."[60] Popular culture confirmed the shift: in the Keaton household on *Family Ties* and the Huxtable family on *The Cosby Show*, both parents were educated professionals who encouraged their daughters, as well as their sons, to pursue independent paths.

During the 1980s, girls' participation in school sports climbed in Canada and the United States. In its first decade, the 1972 Title IX legislation mandating equal educational opportunities at American schools had been hamstrung by legal challenges. By the 1980s, Title IX was affirmed, and school administrators added further programs for girls—some reluctantly, some enthusiastically. With these increased opportunities, there was increased demand. A 1988 study by the Women's Sports Foundation found that eight in ten American girls participated in sports and fitness activities and that 89 percent planned to make sports part of their adult lives. The study also showed that parents supported their daughters' athletic interests. Over 80 percent saw sports as equally important for boys and girls.[61]

Despite the apparent shift in attitudes, nagging obstacles remained. In the United States and Canada, the popular men's team sports had determined defenders. Leaders of Little League Baseball went to court to keep girls off the diamond, while powerful congressional allies of college football and men's basketball fought relentlessly against Title IX. Only in 1988, after further legislation and federal court decisions, was Title IX finally upheld. In Canada, Abby Hoffman promoted women's participation as head of the government agency responsible for sports policy and funding. The former peewee hockey pioneer had competed in four Olympics as a middle-distance runner. As director general of Sport Canada, she pushed for greater opportunity for women. Hoffman played a key role in launching the national tournament for women's hockey, and the championship cup was named in her honor.[62]

Hoffman knew that the Canadian hockey establishment would resist women players. Given the resources commanded by the minor hockey associations, she saw it as "virtually an impossibility" that a separate women's organization could gain equity "in respect of status and prestige and standing in the community."[63] The men who ruled minor hockey did take steps to support women's participation. The Canadian Amateur Hockey Association added two women to its board—joining forty-five men. In 1980, the Ontario Hockey Association (OHA) incorporated the formerly independent Ontario

Women's Hockey Association (OWHA). At the same time, the men who ran these organizations set boundaries on where females could play. The OHA argued that, as a private organization, it was free to limit membership to males. The courts agreed. The Ontario association and its subsidiaries allowed girls to play on boys' teams, up to age twelve. Teams that included older girls were threatened with suspension.[64] Coaches and administrators learned to keep quiet when a girl joined a boys' team. "Nobody wants to rock the boat," acknowledged a Toronto-area parks commissioner.[65]

THE TRAILBLAZER

It took a twelve-year-old to rock the boat. Justine Blainey had started figure skating before she was in school, while her brother played hockey. When she was eight, she told her mom she wanted to play hockey instead. "She insisted," her mother recalled, "for two years, she insisted."[66] Finally relenting, Caroline Blainey brought Justine to hockey school and signed her up for a girls' team. Justine knew right away she was getting short shrift. Her brother had more practices and more games. "My practices would be at 5:30 A.M., his would be at 11 A.M.," she recalled. "My tournaments would be a four-hour drive away, his would be close by."[67]

Justine was also disappointed with the level of training and competition. Practices were infrequent and attendance was sporadic. She dominated games. "I was like a one-man team," she said at the time.[68] In her second year in hockey, she tried out for a boys' peewee team in East York. Among the more than sixty players at tryouts, the coach judged Justine to be in the top five. She earned a place on the Young Bruins, beating out boys who had played on the team the previous season. But she was twelve years old, and she wasn't allowed to play.

Justine and her mother brought a complaint to the Ontario Human Rights Commission. The commission, however, affirmed previous rulings that hockey associations were private organizations and therefore able to define their own membership. The Blaineys appealed to the courts. Their argument was that both the hockey association's rule and the Human Rights Commission's decision were in violation of the Canadian Charter of Rights and Freedoms. With the charter having just been added to the federal constitution in 1982, the case was an important early test of its prohibition against gender discrimination. Looking back decades later, Justine Blainey acknowledged that she was

Justine Blainey at age twelve, taking her case to court (courtesy of Doug Griffin/Toronto Star/Getty Images).

unaware—as a twelve-year-old—of how important her challenge would be. "I had no conception of how far we'd go," she said in a 2017 interview, "how difficult it would be, that it would be a precedent—no clue."[69]

Blainey v. Ontario Hockey Association ultimately reached the Ontario Supreme Court in 1986. Case documents show that the OHA did not argue against girls playing hockey. On the contrary, president Brent Ladds insisted that his organization was working to promote hockey for girls and women. As a division of the OHA, the OWHA had support in securing sponsorships and organizing clinics. "Both the OHA and OWHA are dedicated to providing parallel opportunities for women hockey players which are equal to those opportunities provided to males," Ladds told the court.[70]

The head of the OWHA, Fran Rider, seconded this argument. A leader of women's hockey in Ontario since the 1970s, Rider testified that the OWHA had made great strides in its first decade. In 1986, the association had some thirty-five hundred registered players and more than two hundred teams. Rider acknowledged that the OWHA needed to draw more girls into the sport, since most female players participated at the senior level. Allowing girls to play on boys' teams threatened to undermine this effort, she argued. If the court forced Ontario boys' teams to integrate, the work of building an association for girls would be "irreparably damaged."[71]

In their testimony, Rider and Ladds only hinted at the real threat that girls posed to the minor-hockey establishment in Canada. Ladds told the court that the OHA needed a large base at younger age levels to ensure that enough players reached the top ranks. "Any impairment of interest at the junior level must be rigorously prevented," stated Ladds, "as it presents a threat to the whole structure."[72] The implication was that making room for girls on peewee teams would push boys out of the system and thus reduce the supply of players moving to the top. Fran Rider acknowledged what that top was: the OHA needed players for its major junior teams, "which then, in turn, 'feed' the professional ranks."[73]

Rider revealed a basic truth about the male-dominated youth hockey system in Canada. After all the inquiries, after all the research and reports, minor hockey was still integrally linked with the NHL. By the 1980s, major junior leagues were an autonomous branch of the CAHA, allowing them to operate as profit-making enterprises while remaining affiliated with the amateur body. In place of the old sponsorships, these teams received annual development fees from the NHL (up to $1.5 million in the mid-1980s), part of which they passed on to the CAHA to support lower-level minor hockey.[74]

Even stronger was the cultural hold that the NHL had in Canada. For boys in the minor ranks, as well as for their parents, playing pro hockey was the ultimate goal. For that reason, any roster spot taken by a girl was wasted, since a girl would never reach the NHL. Girls who dared play minor hockey, who knocked a boy off his path to major juniors and the pros, interfered in this Canadian dream. They paid a steep price. Justine Blainey was spat on and had coffee dumped on her.[75] Hayley Wickenheiser experienced the same abuse playing for boys' teams in Alberta. After one game, the mother of an opposing player followed Wickenheiser to her makeshift dressing room. "You little bitch! That's not the way to play hockey," the woman yelled, pounding on the door. "Get out of here and never come back!"[76]

Justine Blainey acknowledged that a future in men's hockey was unlikely, unless, as she said, "I turn into a six-foot giant."[77] Still, her mother argued in court that Justine's hockey career could have a practical end. "Justine needs the opportunity to progress and develop her hockey skills so as to be eligible for valuable post-secondary sports scholarships," she wrote to the court.[78] Already in the 1980s, American universities offered scholarships for women's hockey, and Canadian parents seized on this goal for their hockey-playing daughters. In her defense of the OWHA, Fran Rider cited recruiting visits by Ivy League coaches as proof of the association's success.[79]

However, the crux of the Blaineys' case was not lost benefits or access. It was equal conditions and opportunities. "Justine wants to play hockey as much as possible, at as high a level as possible," her mother told the court.[80] If a girls' team offered the same amount of ice time and quality of coaching as a boys' team, Justine would choose that. But even teams for older girls did not match what a boys' peewee team offered. In statements to the court, Caroline Blainey detailed the differences in her son's and daughter's hockey experiences. Having served in various roles for her son's teams, she knew minor hockey inside and out (she skewered an examining attorney who tried to mansplain the selection process of peewee teams). She pointed out that her son's game schedule and results were printed each week in the newspaper, and that Toronto media regularly did features on boys' hockey. "Girls' hockey is featured in none of the above publicity," Blainey told the court.[81] Most importantly, her son's team had more ice time and better coaching. Justine was talented, competitive, and determined. She wanted to improve. The best place for her daughter to do that, argued Caroline Blainey, was with a boys' team. Justine's peewee coach confirmed this point: "If she cannot play at the highest level of play at which she can compete, on a team for her age group for the coming hockey season, she will, at the end of that season, be at a serious competitive disadvantage."[82]

The court agreed. In April 1986, the Ontario Supreme Court struck down the law that had allowed the OHA to restrict team membership to boys. For Canadian jurisprudence, the decision established an important precedent: provincial laws have to accord with the guarantees in the Charter of Rights and Freedoms. For women's sports, Justice Charles Dubin's majority opinion set down a fundamental principle: equal opportunity must be guaranteed, because participation in sports is important to an individual's growth and fulfillment. "It is fundamental in a free and democratic society," Dubin wrote, "that all persons should be treated by the law on a footing of equality, with equal concern and equal respect, to ensure each individual the greatest opportunity for his or her enhancement." The justice went on: "Participation in athletics is important for the development of health, character and discipline."[83] The right to participate in such beneficial activity is guaranteed, Dubin asserted. According to the Canadian Charter, it cannot be subject to gender discrimination.

The Ontario court's decision did not erase the obstacles facing girls and women who wished to be part of the game. Still today, in hockey and other sports, women fight for equal conditions, for resources, for attention from media—the same areas of inequality that Caroline Blainey recognized in her court statements four decades ago. When women take action against discrimination—such as when the US women's hockey team threatened to boycott the 2017 world championships—their claims are based on the same principle that Justice Dubin expressed in his opinion. The value of sports is not found in ticket revenue or sponsorship contracts or television ratings. Instead, the value is found in what sports provide the individual participant.

CHOPPING AT THE BLOC

While big money transformed North American hockey in the 1980s, the lack of it caused even greater changes in the Soviet Union and Eastern Europe. Looking back at episodes of cooperation between East and West, we now see the signs of a system on the verge of collapse. Exhibition tours of the Soviet

Union by NHL teams brought in desperately needed hard currency. North American teams that traveled beyond the Iron Curtain, from juniors to pros, regularly reported stolen supplies, everything from hockey sticks to video equipment. In 1987 Czechoslovak sports authorities debated sending players and coaches overseas in exchange for cash. The Soviets were reluctant to give up their players, but they did send their old coach overseas—so that he could get medical treatment in the West. In 1987 Anatoli Tarasov led practices for the Vancouver Canucks; in return, the team paid for his surgery at a local hospital.

The sports system, the health system, distribution of goods to stores—it was all breaking down by the late 1980s. Despite the reform programs launched by Soviet leader Mikhail Gorbachev, *perestroika* (restructuring) and *glasnost* (openness), communism was failing. Not only were state treasuries nearly bankrupt, so were state propaganda departments. After 1968, there were few true believers. The invasion of Czechoslovakia had confirmed that the promised utopia was an empty illusion.

In the 1980s, several Czech and Slovak players followed the lead of Václav Nedomanský and the Šťastný brothers. Following a tournament in Munich in 1984, Petr Svoboda walked out of the arena. Months later, he appeared before twenty thousand fans at the Montreal Forum after the Canadiens introduced him as their first-round draft selection. "It was amazing," he wrote his parents. That first letter home also revealed the personal toll of Svoboda's decision: "I hope that you are not angry with me," he wrote.[84] For each one who left, there were many more who stayed. Three years later, at the world championships in Vienna, representatives of the Chicago Blackhawks offered Dominik Hašek a five-year, $1.2 million contract. The twenty-two-year-old Czech turned them down. "I am not the type like Petr Svoboda," he wrote in his memoir.[85] In our interview, I asked Hašek what he meant by that. For all the money the NHL offered, Hašek explained, "I could not imagine leaving behind my family."[86]

Players had to calculate the cost to their families if they left. Parents endured repeated interrogations, and security agents reviewed letters they received from their sons. Hašek was concerned that his father, a teacher, would lose his job. However, by the 1980s the crackdown on hockey was also falling apart. StB files show that defecting players were not as great a concern as they had been in the 1970s. Secret agents were no longer sent to shadow defectors. Likewise, the StB no longer blanketed Prague with officers when the Soviets came to town. When the city hosted the world championship in

1985, the only offender to socialist comradery was an old woman working in the arena cafeteria. She served the Soviet players cups of tea brewed with the water she had used to cook sausages.

Even though there were no longer mass protests in Czech and Slovak cities, animosity toward the Soviets had not abated. Hašek recalled that games against the Soviets had great political meaning. In his office outside Prague, he gave an animated account of how his teammates fired themselves up.

"We had to beat the Russians," he exclaimed, pointing angrily. "It was like, 'You fucking commies!'"

"But wait," he said, sitting back down. "We're commies, too."

Then he was back on his feet, pointing again at his old adversaries. "But we're the good guys. You're the bad guys. You're the bad commies, we're the good commies."

He sat down, laughing. "Now I'm friends with all those guys."

By the end of the 1980s, sports officials in Czechoslovakia recognized they could no longer keep players from leaving. Nor could they solve the structural problems in socialist sport. In need of money, federation officials raised ticket prices and looked for commercial sponsors. They also looked to sell their greatest assets: their players and coaches. Rather than watching top athletes sneak away, they allowed coaches and players to go abroad—for a fee.[87]

As Czech and Slovak officials tried to prop up their failing system, the neighboring Poles were preparing to vote. In May 1989, the victory of the Solidarity labor union in parliamentary elections brought a noncommunist premier to power and signaled the revolutionary changes to come. The Czechoslovak communist leadership, however, was reluctant to surrender their hold, even after the opening of the Berlin Wall on November 9. After the revolution finally sparked on November 17, Hašek and four teammates crammed into his old Škoda a few days later and drove to Prague. They joined hundreds of thousands of demonstrators on Wenceslas Square, demanding the government's resignation. When the party conceded power, sports officials promptly declared their commitment to democracy. Socialist language was scrubbed out, and the games went on.[88]

PERESTROIKA

Few things worked well in the Soviet Union during the 1980s. Yet as Soviet society and institutions declined, the national hockey team kept winning.

The loss at Lake Placid was only a momentary embarrassment. In the following years, the Soviets dominated international hockey, winning another six world championships and two Olympic gold medals. Under coach Victor Tikhonov, the team functioned as the Soviet Union was supposed to: rationally planned, efficiently productive, and internationally respected. But like the grand symbolic projects of Soviet and Russian history, the hockey team's success disguised deep structural problems. And like other masters of great Soviet undertakings, Tikhonov earned his victories by ruthlessly driving the people under his command.

Tikhonov was a Soviet man through and through. Having come of age in the Stalin years, his coaching philosophy reflected the basic principle of the age—that victory would come from unrelenting work, with individual interests subordinated to the good of the collective. Leading that collective was a coach with absolute authority, someone with a rational understanding of the team's path. "A great sports team is decisively influenced by the leadership approach of the man who stands at its head," he wrote.[89] This applied not only to his team, but to all of Soviet hockey. After becoming coach of both Red Army and the national team in 1977, Tikhonov adopted the practice of hoarding talent from other clubs, carrying it to an extreme that Tarasov could not have dared. Players like Igor Larionov and Sergei Makarov, who started with their hometown clubs in Voskresensk and Chelyabinsk, had no choice but to join CSKA when they became candidates for the national team. Tikhonov defended this strategy of concentrating all national team players on a single club, insisting that it was good for the Soviet domestic league. In his view, CSKA inspired other clubs "on the path to better results and improved performances," like a model worker of the Stalin age.[90]

Tikhonov also expanded the training program that Anatoli Tarasov had put in place. Like players of past generations, members of Red Army were together for ten months a year. But under Tikhonov, their training was more intensive, with players assigned to barracks at the club's facility outside of Moscow. Other than their weeks off, players were able to visit home only on Sundays. In 1984 Vladislav Tretiak asked if he could live with his family while continuing his training. "I have one discipline for everyone," Tikhonov replied. That discipline began with running at 7:30 A.M., followed by weight training, calisthenics, and two on-ice practice sessions. When practice finished at 7:00 P.M., players waited in line at a single telephone to talk with their families. With two children at home, Tretiak wondered what he had left to prove. He had won ten world championships. At the 1984 Olympics in

Sarajevo, he earned his third gold medal, posting shutouts in both games of the final round. Three years earlier, in the Canada Cup final, he faced a Canadian team featuring Gretzky and ten other future Hall of Famers. Tretiak gave up one goal. His teammates scored eight. "What else is there to win?" Tretiak asked himself in 1984. With no clear answer, he retired.[91]

When Tretiak retired, Igor Larionov was only twenty-three, a member of the national team and Red Army for only two years. As Larionov recalled in his 1990 memoir, the regimen Tikhonov imposed was bearable because he knew no different. Certainly, the military discipline was more restrictive. But all hockey clubs had their own year-round training centers. Members of the CSKA soccer team lived downstairs from the hockey players and went through their own regimen. Larionov's wife, a world-class ice dancer, began her training at age eleven. "We have known no other way," Larionov said. "The country cares for and feeds its athletes, and for this the athletes are expected to perform."[92]

Immediately after moving to Red Army from Khimik Voskresensk in 1981, Larionov centered Tikhonov's first line, the group known as the Greens for the color of their practice jerseys. In Soviet hockey, lines were complete five-player units, forwards and defense, who took the ice together in practice and games. Larionov's line, with Makarov and Vladimir Krutov on the wings and Slava Fetisov and Alexei Kasatonov on defense, became one of the most transcendent groupings in the sport's history. Larionov compared their dynamic style of play to Dutch "total football" of the early 1970s. "We had total hockey," he said.[93] The Greens' talents were so perfectly tuned they could play with a matchless creativity, able to intuit each other's moves on the ice. "Honestly, we probably could have played blind," Larionov recalled.[94] Fetisov compared their playing to jazz; Larionov likened it to a symphony. "We wanted to improvise and create and play the game in a beautiful way," he wrote, "that would make the crowd get up out of their seats and applaud."

Their brilliance was not applauded, however; it was expected—by their coach and spectators alike. Even in the Soviet Union, hockey fans regarded Red Army as a machine. As the club took the league title year after year, in some seasons amassing close to two hundred goals more than their opponents, the cheering they heard in Moscow was more out of habit. After a few seasons, Larionov recognized he had felt more joy playing for Khimik, where wins were hard-earned and enthusiastic fans filled the arena. This connection with spectators was missing in Moscow. Without that, he asked, "why play on the best squad in the world?"[95]

The Green line was together a long time—some 750 games over seven years. In 1988 they began to break apart. NHL general managers were already in talks with Soviet officials about signing members of the line. In the lead-up to the Winter Olympics in Calgary, Tikhonov promised his players that, after they won gold, there would be more time with families and a solution with the NHL. The following summer, New Jersey Devils general manager Lou Lamoriello flew to Moscow to finalize a contract with Fetisov and secure approval for his release. Officials had promised he would be the first Soviet player in the NHL. But come August, it was back to training. No NHL. No evenings at home. Perhaps later, the coach suggested, after the world championships in April.

When the 1988–89 season began, Larionov told Tikhonov it would be his last with CSKA. Then he burned the bridge. In October, Larionov published an open letter to the coach in the popular weekly magazine *Ogonyok,* one of the leading heralds of the glasnost reforms.[96] Larionov detailed the endless training, the humiliating insults, the isolation from family. "It's a wonder how our wives had children by us," he wrote. Tikhonov ruled as a "hockey monarch," or a dictator—as Larionov insinuated with references to that deviation of the Stalin era, the "cult of personality":

> The climate you created for the hockey players is reminiscent of the environment of a personality cult, only a bloodless, quiet cult, a cult in miniature, where "collectivist spirit" means a reign of terror imposed by a low-rank soldier, where democracy is replaced by unquestioning obedience, where our favorite game is placed in the service of you, our coach.

Not only was Tikhonov a dictator; he also was not the brilliant coach he claimed to be. The game was changing, Larionov noted, but Tikhonov did not recognize it. Relentless training no longer made the difference, when players of every nation were in top condition. Above all, the tightly controlled system of Soviet hockey had to allow for individual creativity. "The country is learning to think in a new way," he wrote. "It's time for athletes to do this as well!"

As a document in the annals of sports history, Larionov's letter is extraordinary. Yet he was not alone in taking advantage of the new openness under Gorbachev to criticize the Soviet sports establishment. In January 1987, figure skater Irina Rodnina, winner of three Olympic golds, told an interviewer that Soviet training turned athletes into "mechanical soliders."[97] Prominent figures like Valeriy Lobanovskyi, manager of the national soccer team, and world chess champion Gary Kasparov called for open professionalism. Tennis player Natalia Zvereva told officials they would no longer control her winnings. Meanwhile, journalists reported hooliganism at soccer stadiums, athletes smuggling goods when they traveled abroad, and declining participation and attendance. The youth magazine *Smena* caused a nationwide stir in 1989 with its investigation of widespread doping of young athletes. After the article's publication, dozens of parents wrote to the editors to say they were taking their children out of sports clubs.[98]

"The controversy inside the Soviet sports world is a microcosm of the battle over perestroika," reported historian Robert Edelman in the *New York Times*.[99] Athletes demanded reforms and journalists reported abuses, yet the officials who controlled the system held firmly to their power. Most resistant was Tikhonov, fortified by his victories and backed by the military's authority. Ultimately, however, even he could not withstand the currents of change.

At the 1989 world championship, the Soviets won their seventh title under Tikhonov. But the cost was steep. Twenty-year-old forward Alexander Mogilny, whom the coach expected to lead his first line in the future, slipped away from the hotel in Sweden and turned up two days later in Buffalo. Blame fell on the coach. At the annual meeting of Soviet coaches later that spring, delegates pushed for Tikhonov's removal.[100] He survived, but lost his stars. Larionov, Fetisov, Makarov, and Krutov were all released from the military that summer and allowed to sign with the NHL. Of the members of the Green unit, only Kasatonov remained, loyal to his coach, estranged from his friends. For his part, Tikhonov accepted no responsibility for the players' departure. They were traitors. "I do not like it when people use everything that the country provides when it is profitable," he said, "and then turn their backs when the country needs them."[101]

In October 1989, Mikhail Gorbachev went to East Berlin. The occasion was the fortieth anniversary of the German Democratic Republic, and the Soviet leader was joined by representatives of the other communist states. The main event was a grand parade, like those authorities had been staging for decades, with students and workers marching past the reviewing stand, singing socialist songs and waving banners emblazoned with Marx and Lenin. But this parade was different. The marchers hailed the reformer Gorbachev rather than their own hardline leader, Erich Honecker. Their makeshift banners called for perestroika in East Germany. The leader of the Polish Communist

Party leaned over to Gorbachev. "It means the end," he said. "I think you're right," Gorbachev replied. While they did not anticipate that the Berlin Wall would be open just a month later, the change in mindset was apparent. As historian Padraic Kenney explained, the people were no longer following the script.[102]

In the winter of 1990–91, Tod Hartje saw firsthand that hockey players in the Soviet Union were giving up on the script they had been forced to follow. Having signed with Winnipeg after finishing at Harvard, Hartje was sent overseas as part of the Jets' exchange program with the club Kiev Sokol. As the first North American ever to play in the Soviet league, he experienced a system in decline. Without question, Hartje's teammates could still play. When the Minnesota North Stars came to Kiev for an exhibition, Sokol won 5–0. "We couldn't keep up with them," Hartje overheard one of the North Stars say. But then, after the game, he watched the Sokol trainer scavenge the deserted dressing room, collecting used tape, paper cups, broken sticks—anything to supplement the club's meager supplies.[103]

Soviet hockey had been plagued by a lack of equipment throughout its history. Yet unlike previous generations of Soviet players, Hartje's teammates no longer believed things would improve. He learned of the enthusiasm of the 1950s and '60s, when Soviet players saw themselves as representing a dynamic new society. Now, his teammates looked defeated. Secluded from their families and training throughout the year, the young men of Sokol Kiev played without emotion. "They didn't look to life as offering possibility," Hartje observed. "They seemed caught up in a grim routine, wholly resigned to a script already written."[104]

At that same time, a new script was being written in North America. This one had familiar passages, reminiscent of the Soviet Union's script. Hockey, like all sports, demanded a full-time commitment. A player was expected to put in the work to become a peak athlete—weight training, running, agility drills—and to devote countless hours to mastering skills. But what was all this work for? Here was the difference. In the Soviet Union, even to its end, athletes were expected to dedicate themselves to the collective—to club and country. In North America, the goals were personal: a contract, a scholarship, the prize of wealth and status. Certainly, these athletes wanted their teams to win. But from peewees to the pros, young players—along with their parents or agents (sometimes the roles were combined)—became more calculating. Teams were judged by the opportunities they offered the individual player to improve, advance, and secure their future. This new script took hold in North America in the 1980s. It made inroads in Western and Northern Europe, as leagues became professional and more players signed with the NHL. With the fall of the Iron Curtain in 1989 and the dissolution of the Soviet Union in 1991, this script would also be adopted in the postcommunist East. Like top athletes in tennis and soccer, swimming and track, hockey players were about to become free agents in a global market.

SEVEN

Around the World

A NEW AGE DAWNED. The age of Jordan and Beckham, Serena and Roger. The age of Tiger and Lance. An age of international sports stars who were also international brands.

It was an age of 24/7 sports. A multitude of screens, a multitude of networks. A multitude of ways to engage the audience, to enhance the fan experience.

And it was an age of skills camps and travel tournaments. An age of international competitions for U12 players, and U10, and U8. An age of select teams and private coaches and parents willing to spend for their son's or daughter's athletic success.

Various currents came together to create this age: subscription sports networks, rising sums for broadcast rights, rising salaries for athletes, increased corporate sponsorship. The political transformations of the late 1980s and early '90s were decisive—the fall of communism in Europe and the Soviet Union, the transition from military dictatorships in Latin America, the end of apartheid in South Africa, reforms in China.

In hockey, this new age was heralded by figures like Teemu Selänne and Peter Forsberg, Jaromír Jágr and Sergei Fedorov—players from Europe and Russia who became stars in the NHL and icons back home. During the 1990s, the National Hockey League became a global league. At the start of the decade, less than 10 percent of players came from outside North America; in 1999, it was just under 30 percent. These new international players were not always welcomed. Part of the resistance came from fear that Europeans would change the North American game. Commentators observed that, in a new age of speed and passing, "bump-and-grind hockey won't get it done anymore."[1] Yet the power game was not discarded entirely. European skaters were valued for their speed and skill, but they were expected to hold their own in the corners. A new style of play was emerging, one that combined the world's fastest game with the roughest.

The new age also belonged to Gary Bettman, the former NBA executive who became NHL commissioner in 1993. During the 1980s, profits in pro basketball climbed far above those of hockey, as the NBA filled arenas, signed television deals, and sold merchandise. NHL owners wanted in on the action. With Bettman at the helm, the league expanded and revenue rose from the millions to billions. The age belongs to Bettman not simply for this success, or for his authority in world hockey—although that is vast—but for what he represents. Like other sports, NHL hockey under Bettman became a corporately managed, strategically marketed, highly lucrative global brand. Leaders of European hockey federations looked to the NHL and transformed their own top leagues according to this new model. Likewise, the IOC and IIHF saw it best to partner with this profitable brand rather than contest it. In the 1990s and 2000s, hockey's different cultures—once distinguished by amateurism and professionalism, by clubs and franchises, by speed and violence—became more interconnected. Money, talent, and ideas crossed oceans and borders, even those once marked by barbed wire and guard towers.

HOCKEY PLAYERS ON THE WORLD MARKET

Hockey players moved in both directions across the Atlantic during the 1990s. Russians, Swedes, Finns, Czechs, and Slovaks came to the NHL as well as to minor-pro leagues and Canadian major juniors. The main attraction of North American hockey was, of course, money. The NHL offered the most money, by far, of any professional league. It was also recognized as the world's premier league, in terms of the quality of players and the level of competition.[2]

At the same time, European professional leagues became a more common destination for Canadians and Americans. The number of imported players varied from league to league. The newly formed Deutsche Eishockey Liga (DEL) had an open import policy. During the 1997–98 season, the league's top ten scorers were all born and raised in Canada. Adler Mannheim, that season's champion, had only four German-born players who saw regular playing time.[3] By contrast, the Swiss, Swedish, and Finnish leagues set limits on North American imports. Roughly 80 percent of players in those leagues had their citizenship in the home country, while most foreign players came from elsewhere in Europe. In the 1997–98 season, the top scorer in the Swiss

National League A (NLA) was a Russian, in the Swedish Hockey League a Finn, and in the Finnish Liiga a Swede.[4]

Canadians and Americans typically set off for Europe after seeing their opportunities wane in North America. In most cases, imported players had spent years with farm teams, perhaps with one or two seasons in the NHL. Players who went overseas discovered that fans were no less passionate about hockey; in fact, bonds between teams and supporters were even more intense. "It was unbelievable," Mike DeAngelis recalled of the Italian league. Packed into small arenas, fans lit flares and threw coins. "Complete chaos. Police escorts to the rink. Police escorts from the rink. Fans fighting everywhere."[5] Dov Grumet-Morris experienced an atmosphere just as loud in Jesenice, a small industrial town in Slovenia: "It was deafening, with the drums and music and noise and flares. The rink would be filled with smoke, and you could hardly hear anything. It was some of the most fun I've ever had."[6]

European hockey was a well-paying opportunity for Canadians and Americans, a place to lengthen their careers, enjoy a good quality of life, and save money for post-hockey careers. DeAngelis lived the good life in Milan during his stint with the Devils in the early 1990s. The team was part of Silvio Berlusconi's entertainment empire, along with television networks and the soccer club A. C. Milan. Following the same strategy he used to take football's European Cup two years in a row, Berlusconi spent generously to build a winning hockey team. DeAngelis and his teammates celebrated at their boss's estate after winning the league title. They lifted champagne flutes when Berlusconi arrived in his helicopter.

The involvement of tycoons like Berlusconi in Milan signaled the new direction of European hockey. In Switzerland, entrepreneur Fred Bommes poured his wealth into reviving SC Bern. The president of HC Fribourg-Gottéron, Jean Martinet, pulled off a coup in 1990 by signing Soviet forwards Vyacheslav Bykov and Andrei Khomutov, who turned down million-dollar offers from the Quebec Nordiques to play in the NLA. Businessman Percy Nilsson funded the rise of Malmö from the lower divisions to two Swedish championships in the early 1990s. With deep-pocketed patrons and increased revenue from television rights, European leagues underwent restructuring in the 1990s. The Swedish and Finnish leagues moved to turn their top divisions into closed leagues, and clubs became privately owned companies.[7]

The most comprehensive reorganization came in Germany. In the early 1990s, after reunification of East and West, German hockey's top divisions were in disarray. Clubs were scraping to survive, with total debt exceeding

Total Player Migration, 2001, 2006, 2011

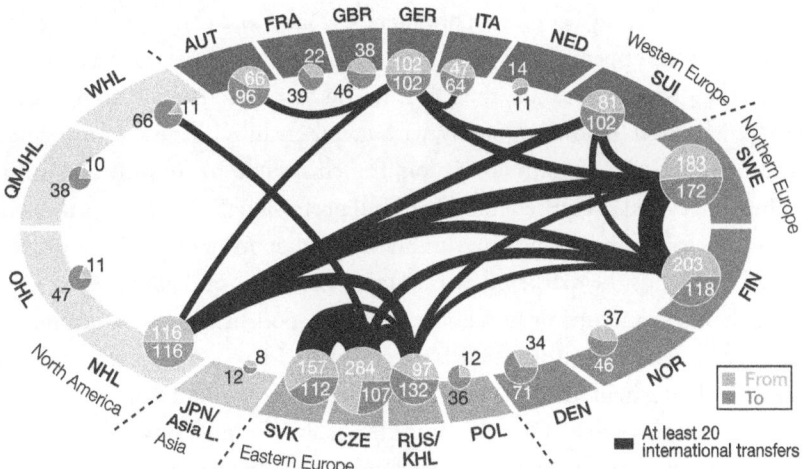

Balance of Imported and Exported Players, 2001–02
Positive balance of at least five player transfers

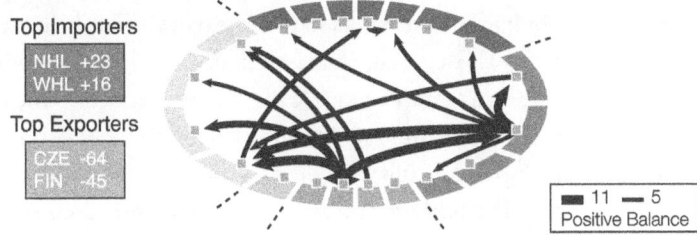

Balance of Imported and Exported Players, 2011–12
Positive balance of at least five player transfers

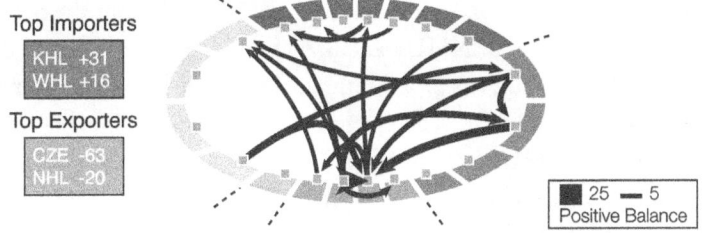

International migration of players during the 2000s (courtesy of CIES Observatory).

Abbreviations: WHL = Western Hockey League, QMJHL = Quebec Major Junior Hockey League, OHL = Ontario Hockey League, NHL = National Hockey League, KHL = Kontinental Hockey League, AUT = Austria, FRA = France, GBR = Great Britain, GER = Germany, ITA = Italy, NED = Netherlands, SUI = Switzerland, SWE = Sweden, FIN = Finland, NOR = Norway, DEN = Denmark, POL = Poland, RUS = Russia, CZE = Czech Republic, SVK = Slovakia, JPN = Japan.

50 million Deutsche marks (over $74 million in 2020 dollars). In 1994, German Ice Hockey Federation president Ulf Jäkel and club directors agreed to disband the upper two divisions and create a single league on the model of the NHL. This new league, the DEL, would be a closed association, organized as a limited liability company, with member clubs likewise transformed into corporations. To gain admission, franchises had to commit to a minimum budget and a required number of full professionals. The league, in turn, took control of merchandising, publicity, and sponsorships. "The professional clubs must be marketed as a common product," said Jäkel.[8] Across the DEL, helmets and uniforms all bore the same sponsorship logos, bringing a revenue increase of 1 million marks to each team. In a country where amateur ideals had long held firm, the new hockey league was a bold step.

The founding of the DEL did not fully resolve German hockey's financial problems. Of the eighteen teams that played in the inaugural season, only six remain today. Over the years, franchises in Munich, Frankfurt, Hannover, and Hamburg folded. Likewise, the organizational model of wealthy directors bankrolling clubs had mixed results in other leagues. Once he became Italy's prime minister in 1994, Berlusconi had less time for hockey. After winning the Italian league three seasons in a row, Devils Milano crashed to the bottom of the league and then folded in 1996. Malmö's patron Percy Nilsson was forced to give up leadership of his club when he was charged with tax fraud.

Even with wealthy backers and increased television revenue, European hockey still had fundamental structural differences from North American hockey. European arenas are typically much smaller than those in the NHL, and many teams are based in small communities. Without the ticket revenue or media contracts of NHL franchises, European teams have to depend on sponsorships—thus, the proliferation of corporate logos on player uniforms, arena boards, ice surfaces, even referees' striped shirts. There is also a fundamental difference in the driving motivation of teams. Like early pro teams in Canada and the United States, European clubs are community entertainments, with the added responsibility of training youth players. In Sweden, this connection to the community is mandated. In 1999, the national sports confederation ruled that a nonprofit club must own 51 percent of its affiliated professional teams. In Finland, there is no 51 percent rule, but sports clubs still own anywhere from a quarter to a full stake in Liiga teams.[9] The adoption of the North American model is a curious amalgamation, making professional hockey a unique part of European sports culture—a place where clubs act like franchises and franchises act like clubs.

THE NHL BECOMES COOL

On October 8, 1993, the National Hockey League saw one of the most extraordinary spectacles in its history. The league's twenty-sixth franchise, the Mighty Ducks of Anaheim, played its opening game at a new $123 million arena in the Los Angeles suburb. The team's owner, the Disney Corporation, pulled out all the stops for the pregame introduction. The twenty-minute, $500,000 show included Disney on Ice figure skaters, a guitar-wielding "Iceman," and a power-lifting duck mascot called Wild Wing who descended from the arena's rafters. After the players were introduced from clouds of dry-ice fog, more figure skaters danced to the team's hard-rock theme song while Wild Wing played guitar on a goalie stick and a giant model of the team's logo, the iconic duck-shaped goalie mask, flashed lights out of its eyes. "We overdid it a few times," one former Disney executive acknowledged.[10] "I don't know what he's referring to," responded Michael Eisner, the company's former CEO. "I thought we did really well."[11]

The Mighty Ducks' inaugural performance did not allay skeptics' concerns about Disney's entry into the NHL. First, there was that name. *The Mighty Ducks* is the title of a comedy film Disney had released the year before, about a ragtag team of kids playing hockey at a neighborhood park. Even fans in Southern California howled. "I live for cute," wrote a second-grade teacher to the *Orange County Register*. "But when I go to a hockey game, I don't want to see cute."[12] In Canada, the unveiling of the Ducks was something close to an abomination. "This is making a mockery of not only the game of hockey, but of all the great players who ever played, not to mention the NHL itself," wrote a St. Catharines woman to the *Hamilton Spectator*.[13] "The whir you hear is Lord Stanley," admonished the *Montreal Gazette*, "spinning in his grave."[14]

Other observers recognized that Disney's arrival was no laughing matter. Just as Tom Duggan and Tex Rickard remade hockey in the 1920s by putting a team in Madison Square Garden, the creation of a Disney-owned franchise in Southern California propelled hockey into a new age. "The new order is marketing, marketing, marketing," observed the *Hockey News*, "and it doesn't make much sense to sell the game in the mini-markets north of the border."[15]

When I mentioned these reactions to Eisner—the fear that the Mighty Ducks would Disneyfy the NHL—he was skeptical. Eisner saw Disney's entrance into the NHL as positive, yet he downplayed its long-term significance for the league. When I asked what he thought the company's influence had been on the league's development, his answer was direct: "None."

Despite his downplaying of Disney's impact, Eisner's involvement in the NHL corresponded with a major shift in how pro hockey was marketed. Many of the devices Disney introduced in the early 1990s are now standard. The Vegas Golden Knights' celebrated pregame shows are a direct descendant of the Mighty Ducks' opening. European clubs also adopted the spectacular introductions, as well as logos resembling Disney-style animated characters. The Mighty Ducks ushered in a new era in which sport, entertainment, media, and merchandise were wholly integrated. Michael Eisner and Disney stayed in the hockey business only thirteen years, but the sport bears the imprint of their innovations.

This new world of sports entertainment had a lot more stuff to buy. The Gretzky trade brought a spike in sales of hockey apparel. Featuring a new logo and colors, Kings gear became a fashion statement, with Queen Latifah and members of NWA donning the black-and-silver caps and jerseys. By the mid-1990s, hockey jerseys were standard attire among hip-hop artists.[16] Designers even introduced their own variations on the loose-fitting, oversized shirts. Jerseys had a great shape and appealing colors, observed Tommy Hilfiger. "And it's cool because hockey is kind of a rough sport."[17]

NHL franchises employed their own designers to craft logos and colors with greater market appeal. Management of the San Jose Sharks, who joined the league in 1992, put thirteen months of research into their stick-chomping shark logo and color combination. They discovered that teal was a color favored by both men and women, and then proceeded to buy an eighteen-month supply of material in the color. The investment paid off: in their first year, despite a woeful record, the Sharks sold $150 million worth of merchandise, more than any other NHL team—in fact, more than any sports team other than Michael Jordan's Chicago Bulls. Even young Prince William was photographed in a Sharks hat while skiing in the Swiss Alps.[18]

The Mighty Ducks topped that the following season. The team's goalie-mask logo and eggplant-and-jade color combination were hugely popular. On opening night at The Pond, the team sold $300,000 worth of merchandise. Shirts and caps flew off the racks at souvenir shops in Disney theme parks. The Mighty Ducks raced past the Sharks in sales in 1994, and then bested the Bulls. Taking their cue from the Sharks, Kings, and Ducks, franchises designed new logos and introduced third and fourth shirts (another Mighty Ducks innovation). Vintage jerseys were also popular, especially those of the

Original Six teams. By the mid-1990s, sales of NHL merchandise totaled $1 billion. When Gretzky first arrived in LA, it had been $100 million.[19]

European leagues took the same approach. When German federation officials and club directors launched the DEL, they looked to the NHL for marketing tips. Traditional club names and shields were replaced by North American–style mascots and stylized logos. EC Kassel and EC 80 Nuremberg became the Kassel Huskies and Nuremberg Ice Tigers. Swedish teams also adopted American-style names. Percy Nilsson unveiled IK Malmö's new moniker, the Redhawks, at a spectacular press conference resembling a Las Vegas production. "Americanization is the order of the day," observed a federation official.[20] The new logos were part of an explicit strategy to sell merchandise. As Jyri Backman shows in his study of Nordic hockey, the strategy worked. When Luleå HF introduced its new bear logo and opened a team store in the city center, sales increased by more than 1,700 percent. Total revenue for the league, with increased merchandising and television rights, more than doubled in the first five years of the new millennium.[21]

Royals and rap stars made licensed apparel a fashion statement in the early 1990s, but a shift in fan culture made team gear standard attire in the arena. This trend was first apparent in European soccer: by the early 1990s, most fans were wearing replica club shirts to the grounds.[22] By contrast, photos of the Stanley Cup finals at that time show spectators still dressed in their street clothes, as hockey fans had always done. By 2002, when the Detroit Red Wings took their third Stanley Cup in six seasons, Joe Louis Arena was awash in red and white jerseys.

Why this explosion in licensed gear? Of course, winning helps. The Calgary Flames leapt from twenty-sixth in sales to fifth in 2003, the year they reached the Stanley Cup finals. Dallas was third in sales in 1999–2000, the season after winning the cup; five years later, they were twentieth.[23] No matter the sport, wearing the team's colors indicates that the wearer is an authentic fan. As sociologist Richard Giulianotti explains in his study of English soccer fans, people identify with teams in different ways: there are committed supporters who identify strongly with the club, more casual fans, recent converts, and spectators who are interested in the game as a social or entertainment outing. For each type of fan, the team shirt justifies their presence in the arena. Their membership in the group is made legitimate by what they wear.[24]

With some teams, this social behavior is more pronounced, particularly older teams with long-established fan communities. The Sharks and Mighty Ducks started out with astronomical sales, but within a few years they were

How many differences can you find? Bobby Orr at Boston Garden, 1974 (photo by Nick DeWolf, courtesy of Nick DeWolf Foundation), and Tomáš Tatar at Joe Louis Arena, 2017 (photo by Amanda Bowen, www.akbmultimedia.com).

among the league's merchandising bottom-feeders. By contrast, teams that sold consistently well throughout the 2000s were the Original Six and three of the earliest expansion franchises: the Flyers, Penguins, and Canucks. For many fans of these teams, wearing a jersey expresses not only their current allegiance but also nostalgia. At a Red Wings–Canadiens game in Detroit, I noticed that most fans were wearing jerseys not of current players but of past icons: Gordie Howe and Steve Yzerman for the Red Wings, Maurice Richard and Guy Lafleur for Montreal. As the president of a leading manufacturer of licensed gear observed, "We're selling emotion, not just a product."[25]

THE ARENA AS EXPERIENCE

Hockey fans gained impressive venues to display their gear during the 1990s and 2000s. Across North America, teams in the NHL, the minor-pro leagues, and college hockey moved into new arenas. Venerated buildings from the 1920s made way for state-of-the-art facilities: Boston Garden closed in 1995, the Montreal Forum in 1996, and Maple Leaf Gardens in 1999. While traditionalists balked, the new arenas offered an improved environment for games. Restrooms were expanded, especially for women, and concourses were widened.[26] Seating capacity also increased: the Bruins and Leafs each gained space for over three thousand more fans, while the Canadiens' new home, the largest arena in the league, increased the capacity of the old Forum by more than five thousand.

The wave in arena and stadium building began in 1992, with the opening of Baltimore's Camden Yards. Whether designed with a retro aesthetic, like the Orioles' ballpark, or in a contemporary style, all new venues of the 1990s and 2000s incorporated features aimed at increasing revenue: more concessions, more space for advertising, and more opportunities for corporate sponsorship. Above all, the key to generating income was luxury seating. First introduced at the Houston Astrodome in 1965, luxury suites let affluent spectators enjoy events without sitting elbow-to-sweaty-elbow with other fans. The new arenas and stadiums saw the target market shift from wealthy individuals to businesses. By marketing their private boxes to local companies, some NHL franchises were able to bring in as much as $10 million annually in the mid-1990s. With over one hundred suites in most new hockey arenas, luxury boxes became a lucrative means for franchises to be subsidized by local businesses.[27]

The revenue streams promised by new arenas were desperately needed in the NHL in the 1990s. In the wake of Gretzky's and Lemieux's enormous contracts, average player salary quadrupled in the first half of the decade. But unlike other North American leagues, which saw player salaries rise in step with television revenues, the increase in NHL pay came without a boost in TV money. The NHL had no national contract with an American network, meaning that television revenues were limited to those from Canadian television and local media. Game-day receipts were essential. Just as with the first arena-building boom of the 1920s, NHL owners insisted that they needed new buildings to keep their franchises in business.

NHL owners and their supporters made the case that for a city to be on the map, it needed an up-to-date, multipurpose arena, one that could accommodate not only top-level sports but also concerts and conventions. By hosting these events, the new arena would spur business in the city, bringing customers into hotels, restaurants, and bars. Given all these benefits, franchise owners claimed, it only made sense that taxpayers help pay the cost of construction. So the argument went. Elected officials agreed. During the 1990s, eighteen new arenas were built for NHL teams, at an average cost (in 2020 dollars) of $300 million and an average public subsidy of $94 million. Overall, between 1990 and 2010, 104 new venues were built for North America's major sports leagues: the NHL, NBA, NFL, Major League Baseball, and Major League Soccer. For twenty-three of these facilities, public funding covered more than 80 percent of the cost.[28]

In negotiating for publicly financed facilities, an owner typically threatened to move his franchise to another city, one that would build a new arena. Civic and business leaders in the Twin Cities offered all manner of promises to the North Stars' capricious owner, Norm Green, but he decided anyway to move the franchise to Dallas in 1993.[29] When Peter Karmanos purchased the Hartford Whalers in 1994, fulfilling his long-standing wish to own an NHL franchise, the Compuware founder immediately looked to move the team. The recently deserted Twin Cities courted Karmanos, as did Nashville and Columbus, two cities eager for major-league status. Meanwhile, Karmanos baited Whalers fans with promises that the team would stay if they bought eleven thousand season tickets and the state built a new arena. Fans bought the tickets and the state offered a $150 million arena, but Karmanos still moved the team—to a $120 million arena in Raleigh. Like other officials who succumb to the lures of pro sports, North Carolina's governor touted the benefits of the new team. "It's going to mean millions of dollars invested," he told the press, "it's going to mean hundreds, maybe thousands of jobs. It's really going to do great things for this area—it puts us on the map."[30]

European clubs also got upscale new arenas. In the 1990s and 2000s, facilities seating more than thirteen thousand people were built in Helsinki, Malmö, Berlin, Cologne, Mannheim, Düsseldorf, Prague, and Minsk. The first in this wave of construction was Stockholm's Globe, a 280-foot-high spherical structure that opened in 1989. The Globe was designed to drive economic development in the capital's Johannesov district, functioning as

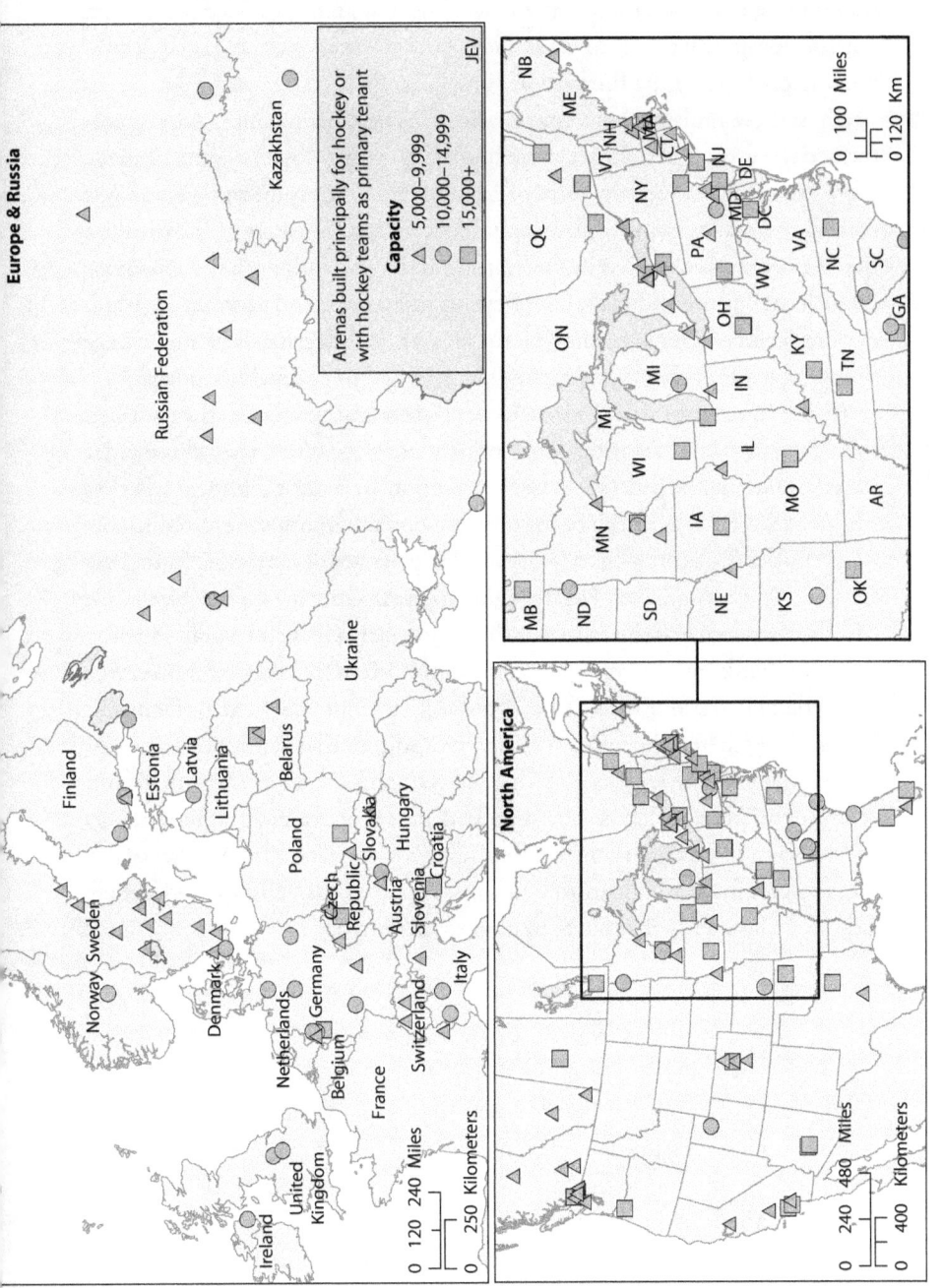

New hockey arenas in North America and Europe, 1990–2015.

the centerpiece of a $300 million complex that included a smaller rink, a shopping center, a hotel, and office space. The new arena provided Stockholm with a competitive site to host major events such as the IIHF World Championship and the Eurovision Song Contest.[31]

These new multipurpose sports and entertainment centers have transformed the way we participate as spectators. A live game is an event, one made more exclusive by the rising price of admission. We dress for the event in our team's colors. We choose from an abundance of food and drink. The items on the menu, the merchandise in the shops, and the decorations in the concourse evoke local culture and team lore. Beyond this local color, however, new arenas are largely indistinguishable. There is an architectural sameness. Like shopping malls or theme parks, they are designed to be reliably efficient.[32]

In my interviews with former players, men and women, I always asked them to name their favorite arenas to play in. Most often, they chose older rinks. Some mentioned the sense of tradition in older buildings, whether Maple Leaf Gardens or the barn in their hometown; others referred to distinct, quirky features, such as the clear plexiglass boards at the St. Paul Civic Center or the unwalled end of the Valascio in Ambrí, open to the Alpine air. Mostly, they spoke of the fans—of the atmosphere Cornell students created at Lynah Rink, or the way spectators at the Montreal Forum cheered for subtle demonstrations of skill, plays only expert fans could catch. Dominik Hašek remembered the noise of Chicago Stadium, that it was sometimes so fierce it felt as if the ice was quaking. Newer arenas don't produce that kind of noise, he noted. They're not supposed to—their spaces are designed to absorb sound, making them better suited for concerts. These new arenas provide comfort and amenities to fans. What is lost, Hašek and others judged, is the energy that older arenas provided to players.

HAVES AND HAVE-NOTS

All of this had happened before—new arenas going up in big cities, new media bringing the game to more fans, businessmen dropping bundles to buy a team, players moving to find more money. Hockey's boom of the 1990s and 2000s mirrored the boom of the interwar years. Of course, one important difference was the scale: whereas players had once counted their money in thousands and owners in hundreds of thousands, at the turn of the millennium their accounts were ringing with millions.

Just as in the earlier boom, some places were shut out as hockey became bigger business. The movement of people and money around the world created a global economy of haves and have-nots. Take Slovakia, for example. As soon as the country gained independence in 1993, Slovak hockey likewise broke away from the Czechs. The national team qualified for the Olympics and world championships, led by returning hero Peter Šťastný. The Slovaks medaled in three world championships in the early 2000s, including gold in 2002. But in hockey, as in other areas of its economy, the small country suffered from a talent drain.[33] Up to three dozen Slovaks played in North America each season; others were scattered in European leagues, in particular that of the Czech Republic, where pay was higher. With clubs back home depleted, attendance dropped. The Slovak Ice Hockey Federation privatized clubs in the late 1990s, but in a country dependent on foreign investment, there were few resources for professional hockey.[34] Today, Slovak players are on rosters in the NHL and major European leagues, but the domestic league is unable to gain solid footing. Slovakia's top league averages only sixteen hundred fans per game, ranking below the second divisions in German and Swiss hockey.[35]

In the economy of world hockey, Slovakia was not alone in its inability to compete with large, wealthy markets. Smaller cities in Canada couldn't either. In the 1990s, Saskatoon and Hamilton were repeatedly frustrated in their attempts to gain an NHL team. Quebec City lost its team to Denver, a city more than twice as large. Even though the Nordiques drew over fifteen thousand fans per night, the franchise could not keep up with rising salaries, especially as the value of the Canadian dollar dropped and players expected to be paid in American dollars. "There's just no money in Quebec," said one fan when the team announced its move.[36]

The struggles facing smaller Canadian markets mirrored the struggles facing Canada as a whole in an economic region dominated by the United States. We see this in the saga of the original Winnipeg Jets. By the early 1990s, the economy of Manitoba and the other prairie provinces had been transformed by free trade. Agricultural production shifted from wheat to crops for export and processing (e.g., potatoes for French fries, canola for cooking oil). American agribusinesses moved into the region, families left farming, and rural towns lost residents. While some moved to Winnipeg, an even greater number moved out. Rising crime and a lack of good-quality jobs spurred migration from the city, especially by educated young people. As Gerald Friesen notes in his history of the prairies, Winnipeg of the 1990s was "less prominent, less prosperous and less attractive to outsiders" than other western cities.[37]

The Jets were one source of civic pride, with attendance consistently above twelve thousand. But this was far below what other teams were drawing. An audit in 1991 projected that accumulated losses would be over $47 million in six years. Principal owner Barry Shenkarow appealed for a new arena to replace the forty-year-old Winnipeg Arena. At the same time, he started getting offers from potential buyers in Seattle, San Diego, and the Star-less Twin Cities.[38] Feasibility studies and talks for a new arena dragged on for four years. By spring 1995, Shenkarow wanted out. The question was whether someone else in Winnipeg could step in. Even with city, provincial, and federal officials all pledging money for a new arena, a group of investors could not get the numbers to work. If player salaries continued to climb, they would be losing millions.

When it appeared the franchise's departure was imminent, an extraordinary grassroots movement rose up. Stirred by local radio stations and the *Free Press* newspaper, the Save the Jets campaign rallied ordinary fans, small business owners, and corporate executives in May 1995. Winnipeg's business class promised millions, while Manitoba premier Gary Filmon pledged even more public money for a new arena. Some thirty-five thousand fans gathered one afternoon, wearing jerseys, holding signs, and donating their own money. An armored truck carried away over $100,000. "Helping the Jets is just one way to make Winnipeg a better place to live," said a neighborhood grocer who wrote a check for $1,500.[39]

The Save the Jets campaign was an admirable attempt to preserve a beloved team. The thousands carted away from the rally were real, but the tens of millions promised by businessmen and politicians were not. Negotiations stretched into summer and fall, but there would be no deal. The Jets opened the 1995–96 season still in Winnipeg. At year's end, Shenkarow sold the team to American buyers. The Winnipeg Jets became the Phoenix Coyotes.

Winnipeggers described their campaign as a David-and-Goliath struggle against the corporate rulers of the NHL. Some also expressed the view that the campaign to save the Jets was about more than Winnipeg—it was a fight for the national sport. "Will this be the end of Canada's hockey?" asked a headline in the *Free Press*.[40] Politicians and businessmen echoed the charge, accusing the NHL of not doing enough for Canadian teams. "This is our game," Premier Filmon declared. "For generations it has survived in the smallest of hamlets and villages throughout the country."⁴¹ The National Hockey League was leaving, but hockey would remain Canadian.

For all the declarations of "our game," hockey's hold on Canada was slipping. The absence of Canadian teams from the Stanley Cup finals dropped ratings for the NHL playoffs well below the Canadian Football League's Grey Cup. Viewers did watch the 1998 Olympics, when a team of all-stars were favorites for the first winter games to feature NHL players. But after that team failed to medal, losing to the Czechs and Finns, commentators raised the familiar question: What happened to Canadian hockey? The *Globe & Mail* published another investigative series. The culprits were the same: overzealous parents, win-at-all-costs coaches, a minor system that didn't develop players. A bigger problem was that fewer kids were signing up for hockey. From 1995 to 2009, the number of young players dropped by a third. Meanwhile, soccer registrations in Canada more than doubled over the same period. In the first decade of the new millennium, over twice as many children were playing the world's game as were playing Canada's game.⁴²

One notable commentator offered a different take. "We're still the best," said Don Cherry after the Nagano Olympics. If there was a problem, the former coach argued, it wasn't that the Canadians didn't play more like Europeans—it's that they didn't play like Canadians. "Hockey is not just getting points and skating like Sonja Henie," he said. "Hitting is a skill, body checking is a great skill, back checking is a great skill. And—I know people hate fighting—but fighting is a skill."⁴³

With his provocative commentary between periods on *Hockey Night in Canada,* Cherry was one of the most famous and controversial figures in Canada, regularly named the most popular man in sports media—and the most hated. Cherry was notorious for his rants against French Canadians, Europeans, and immigrants. "If you don't call yourself a Canadian, if you love your country and your language so much, go back wherever you came from," he told the *Toronto Star* in 1993, "and here's $10, take two more back with you."⁴⁴ As even his critics acknowledged, Cherry was a master showman. But there was no pretense in his act. Cherry identified proudly with white, English-speaking, small-town Canada, and saw himself as expressing the true values at the heart of the nation. "I'm trying to keep this country together," he said in a 1992 interview. "I'm the fucking *glue* that holds it together."⁴⁵ Of course, the national game was also necessary for holding the country together. All that was needed was to restore the game to its original toughness.

NASHA IGRA—OUR GAME

"When will we start winning?"

Vladimir Putin directed his question to the newly elected president of the Ice Hockey Federation of Russia, Vladislav Tretiak. It was May 2006. Weeks earlier, the Russian national team had finished fifth at the world championships in Riga. Three months before that, at the Winter Olympics in Turin, a team stocked with NHL players—including young stars Ilya Kovalchuk and Alexander Ovechkin—finished fourth after shutout losses to the Czechs and Finns. It had been over a decade since the Russians had won gold in an international tournament, and Moscow was due to host the world championships the following year. Tretiak spoke at length, telling Putin that a winning spirit was now taking hold. "It seems you have not played hockey for a long time, for how much you're going on," the president replied. "I am asking, when will we win?"[46]

At the time, midway through his second term, Putin enjoyed stratospheric approval ratings. When he first came to office in 1999, post-Soviet Russia was a failing state. Crime and corruption were constants, the oligarchs had grabbed millions in assets, and ordinary Russians had seen their own accounts gutted by the ruble's collapse. But whereas the 1990s had been a time of troubles, under Putin the Russian economy immediately took off. Exports of natural gas and oil, along with a global increase in oil prices, brought average GDP growth of 7 percent a year. The drivers of the economy became the large joint-stock companies Putin called "national champions." With the government holding majority ownership and Putin's friends and former colleagues in executive positions, these companies—notably Gazprom and Rosneft—gained control of resource production. Profits from gas and oil exports filled the Russian state treasury and enriched investors. The national champions brought home gold.[47]

"The collapse of the Soviet Union was the greatest geopolitical catastrophe of the century," Putin once declared. While he had no intention of restoring the Communist Party's authority, the president did want Russia to take up the Soviet Union's mantle as world power, to match the growing strength of its economy. International sports were to be one part of the new Russia's prestige. In 2007 Sochi was named host of the 2014 Winter Olympics. Three years later, FIFA awarded the 2018 World Cup to Russia. Of course, Putin not only wanted Russia to host tournaments, he wanted to win them. "Victories in sport," he said at the start of his presidency, "do more to cement the nation than a hundred political slogans."[48]

But reviving Russia as a power in world sports would prove more difficult than reviving the Russian economy. When the Soviet Union collapsed, sports infrastructure—like all infrastructure across Russia—was sparse and shoddy. In 1995 the country had only seventy-nine indoor rinks; Sweden had 255.[49] Starved of cash, the national hockey federation got into the import business. In 1995 it imported $25 million worth of cigarettes and alcohol, with government permission. The question of who had power over these funds, as well as the transfer fees for Russian players, was a subject of fierce rivalry. One morning in April 1997, while federation president Valentin Sych was on his way to work in Moscow, his chauffeur slowed for a vehicle parked on the roadside. Two men with Kalashnikov assault rifles raked the car with bullets. Sych was killed on the spot. "This is life in Russia right now," said Ducks goalie Mikhail Shtalenkov, one of fifty Russians playing in the NHL at the time.[50]

A decade later, there was an expectation that things would be different. Tretiak was federation president, and the national team featured a new generation of talented players. But after a disappointing third-place finish at the world championship in Moscow, Putin summoned Tretiak to the Kremlin, along with the minister of sport, Viacheslav Fetisov. The two former players were joined by a third man, a hockey fan: Alexander Medvedev, the head of exports at Gazprom. Putin tasked the three with reorganizing Russian hockey. The president was clear: it was time to start winning again.

From the start, the three men were divided in their strategy. Tretiak wanted to strengthen the traditional structure, with clubs in the domestic league serving as a training ground for the national team. Fetisov and Medvedev pushed a different idea: a closed league, separate from the federation, with franchises across the whole of Eurasia. This new league would be modeled on the NHL, and it would compete with the NHL for the best players in the world. If paid competitive salaries, Fetisov and Medvedev reasoned, the best Russian players would choose to stay home rather than play in North America.

Putin liked the idea of the new league, so much so that he later took credit for coming up with it. In fact, Fetisov had been raising the idea for years.[51] But to get off the ground, the new league needed Putin's political authority as well as his influence over the companies that had been built into Russia's national champions. Medvedev's involvement was key. When the Kontinental Hockey League (KHL) launched in 2008, Gazprom and other major corporations each made an initial investment of $10 million and then committed $5 million per year. Medvedev became the league's first president.

As Finnish historian Markku Jokisipilä shows, Putin's national champions had an integral role in the revival of Russian sports, most notably hockey.[52] Sponsorships by these major companies allowed teams to sign Russian players away from the NHL, such as former Islanders captain Alexei Yashin and rising star Alexander Radulov. But the new league's headline-grabbing signing was Jaromír Jágr. At age thirty-six, the Czech forward was still one of the sport's biggest stars, and Avangard Omsk was willing to pay $7 million per year—tax free—to lure him to Siberia. With the backing of Russia's richest corporations, the KHL served notice that it was going to pay big money for international talent.

In claiming to be the inventor of the KHL, Putin made clear that the league was part of his political program. Putin saw a strong, prosperous Russia as a counter to the United States in world affairs. Likewise, the KHL was to be an answer to the NHL, restoring the old competitive balance between Europe and North America. "It seemed to me," he explained in an interview,

> that after the confrontation—in a good sense of the word—between North American and Soviet hockey, a lot was lost. The sharpness disappeared. It seemed to me that if it was possible in the contemporary context to reestablish this struggle between European and North American hockey on a new basis, it would be very interesting. It will breathe new life into hockey.[53]

Along with breathing life into hockey, the KHL was intended to advance Russian political influence. Putin's foreign policy was rooted in the premise that Russia, not the United States, should have primacy in Europe and Central Asia. The name of the new league, "Kontinental," was significant. Putin envisioned the KHL incorporating European clubs and ultimately entire leagues. He posed this grand vision in positive terms: by expanding at the expense of the Swedish, Slovak, Czech, and Swiss leagues, the KHL would allow those nations' players to remain at home, playing within a broadly European association. Ultimately, a truly continental league would benefit hockey in its respective member countries and the sport as a whole. As Putin explained, if the NHL signed all the best players, "like a vacuum cleaner," then interest in the sport would diminish. "But we all want our clubs to be good in Russia, our own in Slovakia, our own in the Czech Republic, our own in Finland, our own in Sweden. This is the only way to raise the overall level of world hockey."[54]

At the start, only three of the KHL's twenty-four franchises were outside Russia—and they were all in post-Soviet states: Dinamo Minsk in Belarus,

Not your father's Red Army. Pregame introductions at the home arena of CSKA Moscow (photo by Aleksandr Mysyakin).

Barys Astana in Kazakhstan, and Dinamo Riga in Latvia. Of these three, Riga was most significant. Latvia had been among the first republics to break from the Soviet Union, and relations with Moscow remained tense afterward. The "hockey diplomacy" that brought Riga into the KHL was part of a broader improvement in ties. For the Russians, the inclusion of Latvia—a member of NATO and the European Union—provided the KHL with a needed opening to the West.[55]

Between 2011 and 2014, the league added more European franchises—in Bratislava, Prague, Zagreb, and Helsinki. Medvedev had plans for sixty teams, in a league stretching from Milan and Berlin to Tokyo and Seoul. Soon, Fetisov predicted, all of the best European players would be in the KHL, "and the NHL will be left with only the best players from North America."[56] Statistics appeared to back him up: in the 2003–04 season, 30 percent of players in the NHL were European; in 2011–12, only 22 percent. The number of Russians, Czechs, and Slovaks in the NHL fell by more than half after the founding of the KHL.

Russia also began to win again. After taking gold at the world championships in spring 2008, the national team defended its title the following year, with eighteen players coming from the KHL. Likewise, Russia's championship teams in 2012 and 2014 consisted mainly of KHL players, complemented by

NHL stars like Ovechkin, Evgeni Malkin, and Pavel Datsyuk. The teams they beat in the finals in those years, Slovakia and Finland, were also stocked with KHL players. Meanwhile, the Canadians and Americans, with rosters made up entirely of NHL players, didn't even make it out of the quarterfinals.

And yet, the same factors that undermined the revival of Putin's Russia also weakened his Eurasian hockey league. The KHL was launched at a time when the Russian economy was booming, thanks to resource exports and high global prices. Without the sponsorship of Russia's national-champion companies, franchises in Prague, Zagreb, and Bratislava could not survive in this league—just like small Canadian markets in the NHL. As of 2020, the only remaining KHL clubs within the European Union were Dinamo Riga and Helsinki Jokerit. The former was sponsored by the Russian energy company Areti, while the latter had been owned by three Russian oligarchs.[57]

Russian teams have also found the going rough. The economic expansion in Russia was vastly uneven, with the country having some of the highest inequality indices in the world. Like Russia as a whole, the KHL was an association of haves and have-nots. During its first decade, teams outside Moscow and St. Petersburg dropped to the lower league, merged, or folded. Even Spartak Moscow, one of Russian hockey's most storied teams, had to suspend operations for a year because of financial trouble.

Exacerbating these problems was the fact that the league's economic base, like that of Russia as a whole, was inextricably linked to the global energy market. When the league was founded, the price of oil was at $100 per barrel; in 2015, it was less than $40. As revenues for their corporate sponsors tightened, KHL teams were left on shaky footing. "The KHL is not a realistic business project," acknowledged the marketing manager of Metallurg Novokuznetsk, one of the league's Siberian have-nots.[58] Attendance and television revenue were a fraction of the NHL's. Even smaller European leagues had more reliable sources of revenue. The Swiss NLA and German DEL drew more fans, while television deals for the Swedish and Finnish leagues dwarfed the annual revenue of the KHL network.[59]

League president Alexander Medvedev insisted that the disparities needed to be put in perspective. "Are we the NHL?" he asked a *Toronto Star* correspondent. "No, but the NHL has been around for 100 years." Medvedev could point to restored enthusiasm in Russian hockey. New arenas were being built, and fans filled the seats—attired in team gear and encouraged by cheerleaders in the aisles. "We already have a great league and it's getting better," he told the visitor from Canada. Then he offered a reminder: "This is our game, too."[60]

PAST THE TIPPING POINT

It was only when I was writing this book that I thought to ask my sister the question: Did you and your friends want to play hockey?

"Omg yes!" she texted back. "Denied!"

Denied? By whom?

It was an unwritten rule, she explained. At our neighborhood rink in the 1980s, boys played hockey and girls played broomball, Minnesota's organized winter sport for girls. She remembered a couple of the broomball coaches talking with their players about playing hockey, but the idea did not go far.

Like my sister, other women who grew up in our neighborhood in the 1980s spoke of an "unwritten rule." No one stepped forward to challenge it, at least not at my rink. Not the girls. And not the boys. We never thought to tell a coach that the fastest, strongest athlete in the neighborhood was a girl, nor did we invite her to join the team. When I watched my sister and her friends play broomball, I never thought their ability to whistle a shot into the net made them just as suited for hockey as I was.

Then, less than a decade after leaving the rinks where I grew up, there were girls on them, playing hockey. In the 1990s the number of girls and women playing the sport skyrocketed. As often happens with cultural shifts, the turn was quick from skepticism to acceptance, or at least acknowledgment. When I first heard of girls' hockey in the early 1990s, I remember being surprised. I responded as one suddenly made aware of his ignorance. Why couldn't we have had girls playing all along?

Of course, there remained opponents. Lynn Olson, one of the founders of girls' and women's hockey in Minnesota in the 1990s, pointed to older men as the obstacle to girls' teams in northern communities: "As soon as that over-50 generation gets out of the picture and the new fathers come in, I don't think we'll have any problems getting programs started."[61] The women who organized girls' programs had to contend with limited resources and ice time. Nevertheless, they persisted. And they found allies in hockey-playing fathers who wanted their daughters to play the game. One British Columbia dad joined his players on a picket line outside the local rink when the association cut the team's ice time. "This isn't 1955 any more," he said.[62]

From British Columbia to Boston, newspapers reported on the surge in female participation. "Girls' hockey is here to stay," said the president of the Hamilton association in 1994, a year in which her organization tripled its registrations.[63] Ontario was the base of the sport in Canada, accounting for half of all registered female players in the country. Participation leaped after the Ontario Women's Hockey Association banned bodychecking in 1989. The first IIHF-sanctioned world championship, held the following year in Ottawa and broadcast nationwide on television, gave registrations a further boost.[64] In the decade after 1994, the number of registered players in Ontario grew more than 475 percent. Across Canada as a whole, there were just over 104,000 girls under age eighteen playing hockey by 2009; in the United States, there were more than 45,000.[65]

The rapid development of girls' and women's hockey in the United States and Canada was part of a larger surge in sports participation in the 1990s and 2000s. Title IX had spurred the historic increase in high school and college sports for women in the 1970s, while Abby Hoffman pressed for greater equality as director of Sport Canada in the '80s. The '90s saw an increase in young girls being involved in team sports. The main engine for this growth was soccer. Youth soccer exploded in both the United States and Canada in the '90s, with the larger share of increased participation being girls.[66] Other sports also experienced growth in the number of girls. At the end of the 2000s, studies showed that 69 percent of American girls and 70 percent of Canadian girls were participating in sports.[67]

The cultural marker of this surge was the 1996 Nike TV ad "If You Let Me Play Sports." The spot never showed Nike shoes; instead, it featured young girls on playground equipment speaking to the camera: "If you let me play, I will be 60 percent less likely to get breast cancer," says one. "If you let me play," another says, "I will be more likely to leave a man who beats me." Janet Champ, the ad's writer, recalled that the response was overwhelming. "It was like we had lit a fire."[68] At the same time, corresponding with the 1996 Atlanta Olympics, images of athletic, muscular women were appearing in North American advertising and popular media. Sprinter Marion Jones, volleyball player Gabrielle Reece, and other athletes were regularly featured in ads and cover photos.[69]

Coverage of international competitions also brought greater visibility to women athletes. The US women's hockey team earned that most American of honors—an appearance on the Wheaties box—after winning gold in the first Olympic tournament for women's hockey at the 1998 Nagano games. The following year, after their victory in the 1999 Women's World Cup, members of the US soccer team appeared simultaneously on the covers of *Time, Newsweek, Sports Illustrated,* and *People.* "Girls Rule!" announced

Newsweek over its iconic cover photo of Brandi Chastain, celebrating in her sports bra after scoring the cup-winning goal. Young girls joining sports teams at the turn of the millennium now had prominent heroes to look up to: women athletes who were models of strength, ability, and success.

TITLE IX AND WORLD HOCKEY

During the 1990s, as more American girls were kicking soccer balls and shooting pucks, Title IX gained new strength in promoting women's sports on college campuses. At the start of the decade, an NCAA survey found that virtually none of its member schools were in compliance. The problem was football. Division I schools offered eighty-five football scholarships, paid dozens of coaches, and spent millions on facilities. After a series of legal cases and further legislation added greater force to Title IX enforcement, schools had to balance the enormous resources dedicated to football—and other men's sports—with those for female athletes.[70] To meet federal requirements, administrators started programs for women in sports like soccer, rowing, and hockey. University of Minnesota athletics director McKinley Boston cited Title IX compliance as a prime reason for launching women's hockey. Boston pointed out that the program would "provide upwards of 30 additional opportunities for women to participate in intercollegiate sports."[71] When Ohio State added women's hockey in 1999, the twenty-five players on the team put the university over the threshold for Title IX compliance.[72]

In Canada, advocates of women's sports recognized that Title IX provided leverage they did not have. When members of the University of Saskatchewan women's hockey team brought a complaint in 2000 over the school's lack of support, they argued on the general principle of fairness and equity. Canadian Interuniversity Sport refused any jurisdiction, stating that each university was responsible for its own policies. Without a federal statute like Title IX holding the university accountable, the case dragged on for eight years before being settled.[73] The coach of the Canadian women's team at Nagano, Shannon Miller, referred specifically to Title IX as a main reason for her decision to lead the new program at the University of Minnesota-Duluth (UMD). "I believe in equality and I wanted to work in that type of environment," she told a Saskatoon reporter. Having gone unpaid for most of her seven-year tenure with Team Canada, Miller was eager to earn a living coaching.[74]

"They put a lot of resources behind their sports to be successful," Miller observed of American universities. The biggest difference was scholarships. UMD and other new women's hockey programs could offer up to ten athletic scholarships at first (later increased to eighteen). In Canada, meanwhile, athletic scholarships remained contentious. Many educators saw any kind of athletic scholarship as leading toward the win-at-all-costs mentality that marred American college sports. Coaches and athletic directors, however, complained that they were losing talented young Canadians. Women especially were targets of American recruiters.[75] To stem the migration, Canadian Interuniversity Sport loosened its scholarship rules in 2002, allowing schools to offer awards for full tuition. Still today, however, more than four thousand Canadians per year participate in college sports in the United States, including over seven hundred hockey players, women and men.[76]

Athletic scholarships also set apart the new hockey programs at midwestern universities from the established teams of the Ivy League. Schools like Harvard and Princeton had started women's varsity teams in the early 1970s, not long after the universities began admitting female students. Yet while other eastern schools, such as Providence College and the University of New Hampshire, offered scholarships for women's hockey, Ivy League programs did not. Like members of men's varsity teams, women athletes received need-based aid—and, of course, admission to the best universities in the world— but not athletic scholarships. When Minnesota, Wisconsin, and other midwestern universities started offering scholarships for women's hockey, they began to draw most of the talent. "I think the power base will shift to the Midwest," predicted Brown University coach Digit Murphy in 1999, "because that's where the money is, and money talks."[77] Indeed, after the NCAA women's hockey championship was established in 2001, teams from Minnesota and Wisconsin won the first thirteen titles in a row.

Five of those titles were won by Shannon Miller's teams at UMD. The Saskatchewan native had spent her life in coaching, following the example of her father. After moving to Calgary to become a police officer, she organized the city's first peewee team for girls. It was with this team that Miller first met Hayley Wickenheiser. "It's been like taming a wild horse," Miller said in 1996 of the prodigiously talented teenager. As a coach, Miller was every bit her match. "Sometimes it's just the look she gives you," Wickenheiser told an interviewer, after she and Miller had climbed to the national team. Miller's former players at UMD agreed. "She can walk in and change the whole room with just a few words," one recalled.

Like Murray Armstrong at Denver in the 1950s, Miller used connections back home to recruit players from Alberta and Saskatchewan. The trouble was getting Americans, who were not enticed to play in far-off Duluth. The lack of recruiting success prompted her to go to Europe, where her reputation as coach of the Canadian national team carried weight.[78] It probably helped that Europeans didn't know much about Duluth. Swiss goalie Patricia Sautter recalled her geography teacher mentioning the city when talking about iron ore mining, but that was all she knew when she accepted Miller's offer. "I pretty much flew into Duluth with my hockey bag and a few clothes," she recalled. "My only expectation was that I was going to be playing hockey, and I had to go to school a little bit. I had no clue what to expect."[79]

A number of the European players Miller recruited, like Sautter, had experience playing at the world championships and Olympics. Maria Rooth and Erika Holst of Sweden and Hanne Sikiö of Finland had all played internationally since their teens; they were UMD's top scorers when the team won the first of three consecutive titles in 2001. With success on the ice, Miller was able to recruit American and Canadian Olympians, such as Jenny Schmidgall and Caroline Ouellette. Yet her teams were distinguished by their international rosters. When UMD won the national championship in 2008, Miller's first-line forwards came from Sweden, Finland, and Russia, and her goalie was Kim Martin, who led Sweden to silver at the 2006 Olympics. Years earlier, the girls of my Duluth neighborhood had been steered away from hockey, like girls in other hockey neighborhoods. But now, at the start of the new millennium, my out-of-the-way hometown had become a global hub for women's hockey. The UMD women visited the White House so often that Miller was a familiar face to the president. "You'd better give her a raise," George W. Bush told the university chancellor.[80]

UMD did pay Miller more. Until they fired her. In 2014 Miller was the highest-paid coach in NCAA women's hockey when athletic director Josh Berlo decided the UMD program was spending more per win than its rivals. The decision to dismiss the coach and her staff was, in Berlo's words, "strictly financial."[81] Miller's firing showed that Title IX had its limits in mandating equity in college sports. "It would have never happened like this in men's sports," said Sautter. Indeed, the men's hockey coach was paid over $90,000 more per season despite having a lower winning percentage and only one national championship. Yet the law did provide a measure of accountability.

Miller filed suit against the university, citing its violations of Title IX and claiming that, as an older, gay woman, she faced discrimination within the athletic department. In 2018 a jury found in her favor and awarded $3.74 million in damages.

In winning championships with a roster of Americans, Canadians, and Europeans, Shannon Miller set a precedent for the rest of women's college hockey. When she began at UMD, less than 10 percent of players on all women's teams were from outside the United States. Other coaches followed her lead, going to Canada and Europe for recruits. By 2010, nearly half of all players in Division I women's programs were from Canada or Europe, compared to 38 percent of men's players.[82] At each Olympic tournament after 1998, roughly a quarter of Team Canada members were veterans of American college programs. Likewise, many top European players had experience at American universities.

Women's hockey was one of several sports to bring international athletes to American campuses in the 2000s. As we have seen with men's hockey, college coaches in the United States had been recruiting foreign athletes for decades. After the turn of the millennium, the number of international athletes at NCAA schools steadily climbed. In 1999, foreign students accounted for just under 2 percent of all Division I athletes; in 2009, they were 7.9 percent, with the increase of women athletes outpacing men. Today, dozens of Spanish tennis players, Kenyan runners, German soccer players, and Swedish golfers join women's teams at colleges across the country.[83]

For women hockey players from Europe, American college sports were an eye-opening experience. Most striking was the quality of facilities and support. Women who came to the United States had started playing on boys' teams at their local clubs. Many players, especially goalies like Sautter and Martin, had played with males through their teens, and they already had experience at international tournaments. But women's sports at an American university was a different world. "It was mind-blowing," recalled Swiss goalie Florence Schelling, who played at Northeastern University.[84] The facilities, equipment, and care available to women's college programs were far beyond what they had encountered in Europe, even in top-tier men's hockey. "I will honestly tell you, nothing equals NCAA hockey," said Alena Polenská, captain of the Czech national team, who played at Brown University. "I know it's amateur, but it's just as professional as I've seen hockey get."[85]

The verdict in Shannon Miller's trial confirmed the persistent inequality between men's and women's college sports in the United States. Yet as Miller herself acknowledged when she first took the coaching job at UMD, Title IX provided American women sports with institutional support that was lacking in other countries, even in Canada. European players returned home after experiencing a different model of organization in women's sports. "It was more professional," said former UMD goalie Kim Martin, "even though you don't get money."[86] When Martin later took over as general manager of the women's team at Linköping HC, she saw that level of organization as a model.

Title IX's boldest innovation, mandating equality in men's and women's sports, has also had global influence. Beginning in the 1990s, the International Olympic Committee took more assertive steps toward promoting women's sports, acknowledging the effect Title IX had in the United States. Following the 2018 recommendations of its Gender Equality Review, the IOC set the goal of full equality in the numbers of athletes and events for the 2024 Summer Games and the 2026 Winter Games.[87] A leading figure in that project was Angela Ruggiero, a college hockey player at Harvard and member of the gold medal–winning team at Nagano. Serving later as chair of the IOC's Athlete Commission, Ruggiero was a tireless proponent of sports for girls and women around the world. Speaking of her own experience playing hockey in Southern California, she acknowledged the hurdles. Yet she still holds to the game as having set her life's course, "simply having the opportunity as a seven-year-old to lace up my skates and get on the ice and fall in love with the sport that changed my life."[88] Every girl, she insists, should have the right to do the same.

BACK TO THE ICE

The headlines told the story: "Cost of hockey leaves kids on the sidelines," reported the *Toronto Star* in 1992. "In the high-cost world of junior hockey, parents' cold cash keeps their kids on ice," declared the *Colorado Springs Gazette* that same year. "You usually have to talk about children's hockey with a calculator in hand," reported a correspondent in Omsk in 2008. "To play football, you need a ball," remarked the *Neue Zürcher Zeitung* in 2013. "To play hockey, you need money."[89]

In nearly every interview I conducted for this book—in North America, Europe, and Asia, with elite-level coaches and junior club managers, with NHL scouts and federation officials, with former and current players, both women and men—the conversation turned to the increasing expense of youth hockey. They all recognized a growing problem. They all cast blame in different directions.

What drove the costs of hockey? First of all, the price is high for producing the game's basic ingredient: ice. When youth hockey expanded between the 1950s and 1970s, public funding had covered the cost of building and maintaining ice arenas. In North America, cuts in public support after the 1980s put greater responsibility on teams to meet the costs. Meanwhile, entrepreneurs built privately owned rinks, with new amenities like in-house eateries, workout facilities, and equipment shops. "We got away from communities owning rinks, and private companies now run them for a profit," said a New Brunswick hockey official in 2011.[90] Equipment costs rose as well, due to advances in design and materials. The $30 wooden stick I once used is now a relic, replaced by a $300 composite model.

Along with the built-in costs of ice and equipment, the rising expense was also due to market demand. The individualized development plans of the 1980s became more common in the 1990s and 2000s, as parents sought to advance their sons' and daughters' skills. Traveling teams, summer camps, and private coaching lifted annual costs well into the tens of thousands of dollars. Parents saw this extra training as necessary for their children to make the next step. At the same time, coaches and club managers were savvy marketers. Their appeals played upon all the aspirations and anxieties parents have for their children. One coach recruiting my eleven-year-old son to a travel club asked why I would not do everything to foster his talents. "He has a gift," the coach told me. "Why wouldn't you nurture that gift?" The coach knew his customers.

Why does this appeal work? What has caused parents' expectations of youth sports to change so much in the last twenty to thirty years? There are many currents, some of which we have seen rising in previous chapters. Ideas about player development that first took hold in North America in the 1970s led to increased specialization. Decades ago, parents wanted better-trained coaches and greater emphasis on learning skills, and that is what we have today—for a price. Popular media tells us of successful athletes who dedicated themselves from a young age to reaching their dreams, whose families supported them every step of the way. And above all, we still hold to the nineteenth-century belief that sports build character, that participating on a team instills in our daughters and sons the discipline and drive they need for adult life. Holding to this belief—that sport teaches us "valuable life lessons"—allows us to justify the commitment of money and time, no matter how steep.

The intensification of youth sports also corresponds to a recent development in child rearing. Connections to community have less weight; instead, parents themselves map the best route for advancement. A scout in Europe told me of parents who take their children from one club to another, buying coaches' promises of more playing time. "People weren't as concerned about having careers," Patricia Sautter said of playing for junior boys' teams in Switzerland during the early 1990s. "Now it's crazy."

This individualized, career-oriented approach to youth sports arose in part from the middle-class anxiety evident already in the 1980s. By the 2000s, the security of the middle class was made even more tenuous, especially in the wake of the 2008 global recession. In both North America and Europe, a university education no longer guaranteed a secure career. In this more competitive environment, parents saw the need for their children to distinguish themselves. Success in sports, music, or other activities confirmed a young person's giftedness and motivation, while at the same time building social competence—the "life lessons" needed to be successful adults. Sociologists have used the terms "concerted cultivation" and "orchestrated achievement" to describe this parenting strategy. Parents who engaged in these approaches saw sports and other activities as necessary preparation for admission to a distinguished university and then professional success. One American father stated it best: "You've got to have something that makes you stand out. That makes you unique. Otherwise you're going to fall short."[91]

At the same time, children's success in sports confirmed parents' success. The volunteer dads and supportive moms of the baby boomers set a model for later generations of parents. Research in both North America and Europe shows that parents commit themselves to their children's sports activities out of the sense that it is necessary to being a "good parent." Just as children will "fall short" in contemporary society if they do not distinguish themselves, so do middle-class parents believe they will not measure up in the estimation of their peers if they do not commit themselves to their children's success. Sociologist Jay Coakley, who conducted research on youth sports for more than three decades, sums this up:

> The achievements of children in an activity as visible and highly publicized as sports come to symbolize proof of one's moral worth as a parent. Talented child athletes, therefore, become valuable moral capital in neighborhoods, communities, and the subcultures associated with high-performance youth sport programmes. This leads many parents to feel obligated to "invest" in their child's sport participation. Not to make this investment would be taken by many people as a sign of a parent's moral failure.[92]

In hockey, the investment is huge. In 2017, *Time* magazine reported that the average annual cost for youth hockey in the United States was $7,013, nearly $5,000 more than what the average American family spends on youth sports in general. Recent investigative reports by Canadian newspapers show that private coaching, skills camps, and travel for tournaments can total more than $15,000. Hockey academies in Canada and the United States have fees ranging from $35,000 to more than $65,000. In Europe as well, the cost is climbing. In Sweden, for example, sports clubs remain community based, with significant public funding. Still, as parents aspire for their children's athletic success, they seek more training and more tournaments.

Hockey officials on both sides of the Atlantic have recognized that the sport's rising costs are pricing out families. The question observers raise is what that means for hockey's future. A young player from a family of lesser means might be able to start in the game. But they are less likely than a child from a high-income household to reach the game's elite levels. If their family does not have wealth, can they get the training to match their peers? If they are unable to travel to showcases, will they get the attention of coaches and scouts? As costs continue to rise, the days when someone of the working-class background of a Gordie Howe or Börje Salming reached the NHL might be over.[93] Instead, will hockey return to its earliest years, when the sport was the preserve of the affluent class?

As the sport becomes more expensive, as competition becomes more intense, many people who love hockey have sought to go back, to the game of memory. They have gone outside.

In 2002, the local association of Plaster Rock, New Brunswick, organized the first pond hockey tournament. Organizers groomed small rinks on Roulston Lake and the Tobique River, using snow plows and water pumps. The inaugural champions were the hometown Tobique Puckers, who bested a field of forty teams from the Maritimes and Maine. By the following year, word had spread. The field grew to sixty-four teams, with another twenty on the waiting list. More than four thousand people visited the remote logging village to watch hockey in the elements. The tournament reminded participants of what they understood as the traditional, Canadian roots of the game. As one organizer told a Toronto reporter, "This is Canada in a box, right here."[94]

Pond hockey's popularity is rooted in longing for a bygone form of the game. "We've touched a nostalgic nerve in people," a Plaster Rock organizer explained. "They want to play and they want to watch hockey in its natural form, the way it started."[95] Today, outdoor hockey—whether played on a frozen pond or inside a packed football stadium—is widely celebrated in the hockey world. A winter pond was depicted on the back of the Canadian five-dollar note, along with a passage from Roch Carrier's story "The Hockey Sweater"—"our real life was on the skating rink." Older players speak of hours spent on outdoor rinks as the time when their love for the game bloomed. "The sensation of the skate blades cutting into crisp outdoor ice, the crunching sounds of ice chips flying tidy arcs," recalled Bobby Orr in his memoir. "These are sights and sounds and feelings that are forever lodged deep in my mind."[96] At the close of his Beartown novels, some of Fredrik Backman's characters have a skate on the frozen lake. "As if it were all just a game and nothing else mattered."[97] We sift through such statements to find the essence of hockey, believing it lies in the thick, natural ice of some northern town. We want to return to that ice in part because of a sense of unease with the current sport, its expense, its hyper-organization. Pond hockey, billed as the true form of the sport, allows that return, or at least its semblance.

Yet the outdoor rink was not the haven some remember. As Mary Louise Adams points out, the Canadian culture of shinny, the pickup game played on neighborhood rinks, was largely male. "Among women my age and older, few have had any experience with shinny at all."[98] For male skaters as well, the outdoor rink could be an intimidating place. Peter Gzowski was one of the few to be honest, recalling "the way we looked on girls, with their white skates and their hours on the nearby—but separate—'pleasure rink,' or of those few of our own sex who chose not to play hockey at all, and were branded forever as outsiders."[99]

Like other sports, hockey has a tendency toward exclusivity. After all, it began as the pastime of young men of status, at a private club, in a wealthy city. Throughout the sport's history, it has been the object in a struggle for possession, like the puck in a game of keep-away. It belonged to the respectable Anglo-Protestant men of Montreal, as opposed to the French and Irish. It belonged to the NHL, as opposed to rival leagues. It belonged to boys, as opposed to girls. A good measure of the pride I felt in February 1980 arose from this sense of ownership—that my game was noticed by others, by people across the country celebrating the wins in Lake Placid. Yet at the same time, it remained *my* game, one I knew better than they did.

These struggles over the sport's ownership show that there is something universally appealing about the particular form of hockey devised at the

Victoria Skating Rink. Within a short time, this eastern Canadian game found new converts in New England and the Midwest, in Britain and Europe, because it resembled games already being played in those places. The essential skills were the same, yet skaters recognized the advantages of using a puck on a small rink, as opposed to chasing a ball over a field of ice. Resonating with people in these different regions, hockey became a world sport right away. In later decades, the sport gained further popularity—in the Soviet Union, in Sweden and Finland—not because it was a North American game, but because it was international. It was a way for these nations to compete on a world stage. A venue for national rivalries, an entertainment with broad appeal, a demanding game played in a confined space: these are the reasons hockey is a global sport today, rather than a regional curiosity.

We see something of the same process with pond hockey's recent boom. Immediately after the first tournaments in Plaster Rock, this celebration of local Canadian hockey was swept up by the same forces of globalization to which it had presumably provided an antidote. After being featured in international media, the tournament drew teams from far beyond the Maritimes: four-person squads brought their skates from Arizona, England, the Cayman Islands, even Singapore. And the idea of the tournament itself quickly spread. Today, there are more than a hundred tournaments in Canada and the United States, as well as events in Europe. Like the first tournament in Plaster Rock, these competitions are billed as bringing hockey back to its roots. Repeated on the websites of several tournaments is the phrase "the way the game is meant to be played." At the same time, tournaments have corporate backers, and many teams' jerseys bear the logos of their sponsors. The action on the natural ice might mimic the way hockey was traditionally played, but the tournaments are an example of the globalized, commercial entertainment hockey has become. Both aspects are at the core of the game, the root of its success. Hockey is a gripping spectacle, truly the world's fastest game. At the same time, it is a reminder of a different world, one covered in snow and ice.

Epilogue

EVEN AS THE COST OF THE SPORT RISES, the hockey world continues to grow. According to the IIHF, the number of players worldwide grew by more than 18 percent between 2010 and 2018.[1] In Britain, Hungary, and Latvia, where the sport was popular in the early twentieth century, participation is reviving. Addressing the high costs of participation, federations have implemented programs to expand access. Girls in Europe and North America continue to take up hockey, and the sport has grown further in the southern United States. The sport of sledge hockey is now played by athletes with disabilities in eighteen countries, and it is one of the most popular events at the Winter Paralympic Games.

One area of growth that has drawn considerable attention is China.[2] After the 2022 Winter Olympics were awarded to Beijing, Chinese sports officials began promoting the development of winter sports, including hockey. In preparing the men's and women's national teams for the Olympics, China has sent players to the United States, Canada, Finland, and the Czech Republic. Authorities also established professional teams in China. Kunlun Red Star, based in Beijing, joined the Kontinental Hockey League in 2016 with a roster of North Americans and Europeans, including a few of Chinese ancestry. The Shenzhen KRS Vanke Rays play in the Russian Women's Hockey League; the team is made up of players from Canada, the United States, and Finland, along with nine Chinese women. Shenzhen, Shanghai, and Beijing have also hosted NHL exhibitions. While the league's leaders were unwilling to send players to the Olympics in Korea, reports indicate they are taking a different approach for the Beijing games. The NHL cannot pass up the prize all Western professional sports leagues covet—the Chinese market.

The decade since 2010 has also brought tragedy to the hockey world. The 2011 plane crash that killed nearly every member of the team Lokomotiv Yaroslavl sent shock waves across Russia, Europe, and North America. Lokomotiv had one of the most dedicated fan communities in the KHL, and nine players on the team came from the city. At the same time, it was an international team. Canadian Brad McCrimmon was making his head coaching debut. The team's newly signed star, longtime NHL player Pavol Demitra, was revered in his home country of Slovakia.

Like the crash in Yaroslavl, an accident in rural Saskatchewan in April 2018 cast a pall over the hockey world. Sixteen people were killed and thirteen injured when a semitrailer truck smashed into the bus carrying the Humboldt Broncos junior team. In Canada and Russia, the devastating losses of entire teams stirred a broadly felt, profound grief. For people far from Humboldt and Yaroslavl, there was a sense of connection, an understanding that their own experiences were the same as those in the small Saskatchewan town and the central Russian city. They followed their teams, they knew the players, they sent them to faraway places. They comprehended the loss because it could have happened to them. The depth of grief in both countries confirmed that hockey was a common experience. It was indeed their national game.

The 2011 crash in Yaroslavl came at the end of a summer of harrowing events. The sudden deaths of three NHL players—Derek Boogaard, Rick Rypien, and Wade Belak—brought attention to the toll that pro hockey takes. Rypien and Belak both took their own lives; after their deaths, family and friends revealed that they had suffered depression for years. Boogaard's death was ruled an accidental overdose of painkillers and alcohol. Six months after his passing, the *New York Times* published an investigative series by reporter John Branch on the player's life and the circumstances of his death. Boogaard, one of the league's most feared enforcers, had become addicted to painkillers. The pills numbed the cumulative effects of years of fighting: constant headaches and chronic pain in his hands, shoulder, and back. "He would fight and his knuckles would be pushed back into the wrist," Boogaard's father said.[3] Encouraged by coaches, Boogaard had turned himself into a fighter to make it to the NHL. He achieved his dream, and it ruined him.

An autopsy revealed that the twenty-eight-year-old Boogaard had advanced symptoms of the brain disease chronic traumatic encephalopathy (CTE). An examination of former player Steve Montador's brain after his death in 2015 revealed the same—the most extensive case of CTE he had ever seen, reported the examiner. In his book *Game Change*, Ken Dryden argues that Montador's death is a warning that NHL hockey is hazardous to players' health. Although fighting is part of the problem, Dryden sees the danger as being intrinsic to the game itself. "Speed is hockey's most defining element," Dryden wrote. "It is also hockey's greatest vulnerability."[4] Over the decades, the pace of the game has accelerated—passing and offside rules have been loosened, training has become more intensive, players are larger and faster. Skaters of today collide with far greater force than those in Dryden's day. "This is a faster, more exciting, more dangerous game," he observed. "The evidence is found not in our memories, it's in the injuries we see around us."[5] Writing at the one-hundredth anniversary of the NHL, Dryden saw player concussions and brain injuries as the greatest threat to the game, one that has to be resolved to secure its future.

For his part, Gary Bettman insists that the NHL is addressing the problem of concussions. In testimony to a Canadian parliamentary committee in 2019, the commissioner detailed ways in which the league educates players, monitors injuries, and regulates hits to the head. At the same time, however, Bettman dismissed research on concussions and CTE. "Other than some anecdotal evidence, there has not been that conclusive link," he said. The commissioner deflected the suggestion of a complete ban on hits to the head and the elimination of fighting. When asked what changes he would make to reduce the risk of head injuries, Bettman stated that he likes the way the game is played: "Right now, I don't believe there is much we can do."[6]

Physics and physiology pose the most serious challenge to contemporary hockey. Other tensions in the sport today are fueled by economic, political, and cultural factors. Some of these were evident at the 2018 Olympics in Korea.

One concern is the future of international women's hockey. The thrilling final between the United States and Canada marked the fifth time that the two countries had faced each other for the Olympic title. In only one Olympic tournament has a team other than these two played for gold; likewise, in only one of the nineteen women's world championships has a team from outside North America reached the final. The dominance of the Americans and Canadians is not surprising. Each country alone has more female hockey players—Canada nearly ninety thousand, the United States nearly eighty thousand—than all other nations combined. Women's hockey in North America still does not receive anywhere near the resources and media attention that the men's game does, yet compared to programs in Europe and Asia, there is a vast difference. This gap in support has grown even larger since 2017. That year, after threatening to boycott the world championships, the US national team negotiated increased player compensation and development funding from USA Hockey. European players saluted the Americans' protest but privately scoffed at the extent of their demands, given how much better funded they already were. "My teammates would say, 'They should see what we get,'" a European player told me. "They would probably quit playing hockey."

One European player who has been open in her criticism is Finnish goalie Noora Räty. After her team lost to Canada 5–0 in the Olympic semifinals, Räty spoke to the *Washington Post* about the gap in support between North America and Europe. Yet Räty did not begrudge the Americans and Canadians. After all, she personally benefited from the funding of women's college sports as a student at the University of Minnesota. Instead, she criticized the neglect of women's hockey in her own country: "In Finland, you say you're a hockey player, [it's] like, 'Get a real job.'"[7] I heard similar complaints from other European women about the lack of support back home. Florence Schelling, for instance, told me how she organized a successful hockey day for girls in Switzerland after her team won bronze at the Sochi Olympics. But the Swiss federation didn't seem to care much. Asked if she wanted the remark to go on the record, Schelling dismissively waved her hand. "They know how I feel."

The national federations are key for building women's hockey. But federations follow hard economic logic: men's clubs generate revenue from ticket sales, television rights, and transfer fees; women's leagues do not. Räty described the mentality she sees in Finland: "If you're not making money out of sports, then [people believe] you should do something else."[8] I encountered the same attitude elsewhere in Europe: because parents do not see a payoff for their daughters' hockey interests, why invest time and money in the sport? Räty has insisted that the best solution to this dilemma is a professional league in North America that will provide a goal for women around the world. After the Canadian Women's Hockey League folded in 2019, she joined more than two hundred players in calling for the creation of a viable women's league.[9] Many players pointed to the Women's Professional Basketball Association, which has gained stability with support from the NBA. Critics counter that professional women's hockey first requires paying spectators, something even women's soccer leagues have had difficulty maintaining.

The struggle over women's hockey ultimately gets at the core value of sports. Are our games subject only to what sells in the marketplace, or is there something more fundamental at stake? Räty and other proponents of a women's league take a position similar to Judge Charles Dubin's finding in the case of Justine Blainey—that participation in sports "is important for the development of health, character and discipline." Therefore, opportunities in sport must be equal.

International politics also continues to entangle world hockey, particularly Russia's relations with the West. The Russian team won the men's tournament at the 2018 winter games. Except that it didn't. Russian athletes in Korea were forbidden from competing under their country's name and flag; they were instead called "Olympic Athletes from Russia." The designation was part of the IOC's ruling on the extensive doping program uncovered in multiple investigations; the Russian Olympic Committee was banned from the games, but athletes verified as clean were permitted to participate. Russian fans who made the trip to Korea disregarded the ban—they waved their country's flag and wore the national team's jerseys. After the hockey team defeated Germany for the gold medal, fans joined players in singing the Russian national anthem, drowning out the Olympic anthem playing on the loudspeakers. According to Ilya Kovalchuk, he and his teammates had planned all along to sing the anthem, in defiance of the IOC. "Yes, the flag and anthem were taken away from us, but not honor and conscience! We know that we are Russians, that we represent the best country in the world."[10]

To be sure, Russians do not have a monopoly on claiming national greatness. However, a distinct aspect of current Russian nationalism is its linking of nation and state, specifically the state led by Vladimir Putin. In presiding over Russia's post-Soviet recovery, Putin has become more than the country's leader; he is a symbol of Russia itself. At the Olympic arenas, Russians unfurled banners with Putin's face and wore jerseys with Putin's name. Russian players in the NHL, notably Alexander Ovechkin, have declared their support for the president. This connection of Russian sports and Russia's leader is problematic. After Russia's annexation of Crimea and invasion of Ukraine in 2014, the United States, Canada, the European Union, and other countries levied sanctions against officials in Putin's government and leading oligarchs. Consequently, Putin's foreign policy has been combative. According to the government and press, the doping ban was devised by a hostile alliance, orchestrated by the United States.[11] Reactions to the hockey team's win reflected this stance. A number of postgame tweets celebrated the

A Russian fan at the 2018 Winter Olympics, wearing a jersey with Putin's name (photo by Jenny Scrivens).

gold medal not just as a win for Russian hockey, but as a victory over Russia's enemies. Memes evoked the defeat of Nazi Germany in World War II and the Cold War conflict with the United States.

Putin's rehabilitation of the Soviet era also colored the online celebrations. The Russian double-headed eagle, tricolor flag, and pictures of Putin were common memes, as were the Soviet hammer and sickle and pictures of Stalin. Analysts of contemporary Russia assert that the Putin government has celebrated Soviet accomplishments in order to legitimize its increasingly authoritarian turn. Hockey has been a key component of this political strategy. Each year in charity games, the president takes the ice with government officials and past greats of Soviet hockey such as Slava Fetisov. The multiple goals Putin scores bolster his image as a vigorous leader. More importantly, these games are an occasion for Putin to associate himself with one of the few Soviet institutions that were an unqualified success, the national hockey team.

While Russia won gold, the 2018 Olympics showed that the real power in men's hockey belonged to the NHL. The Russian team was made up entirely of current KHL players. However, international sanctions and a drop in oil prices had brought an end to Putin's dream of the KHL as a counter to the NHL. By contrast, the NHL had the financial might to stand up to the IOC and IIHF, and the Olympics took the hit: without NHL players, attendance and television ratings sagged. The NHL also kept its players in line. Although some players, such as Ovechkin, wished to defy the league's decision and play for their national teams, none dared jeopardize their NHL contracts. Likewise, no national federation jeopardized its relationship with the NHL by encouraging players to leave. Even Vladislav Tretiak advised Ovechkin to stay.[12]

The NHL is now an irresistible force. "Of course, the NHL is by far the most powerful hockey league in the world," says Szymon Szemberg, managing director of the Alliance of European Hockey Clubs. "Powerful in terms that all players with NHL potential want to play there, for the prestige and money."[13] As the director of one European junior club told me, the ambitions of teenage players and their parents are fixed on the NHL. They see their own domestic league only as a fallback in the event they do not make it in North America.

Yet for all its wealth and power, the NHL's supremacy has some cracks. Each year the league reports growth in revenue. Expansion franchises generate surges in ticket and merchandise sales—and, of course, hundreds of millions in expansion fees. But fan surveys and television ratings show that the NHL has not gained a national audience in the United States. It is the same in Canada, where television viewers do not want to watch Canadians playing Canada's game for teams in the United States; instead, they want to watch teams from Canada. This was seen in spring 2019. After the Flames, Jets, and Leafs were knocked out in the first round of the playoffs, viewers turned off hockey and turned on basketball. The entire country was electrified as a team of West African, Spanish, and American players brought the NBA championship to Toronto.

"NHL hockey is an attendance business," observed a 2011 economic analysis of the league.[14] The model established in the 1920s remains the basic model today: build a big arena and fill it with fans night after night. As an attendance-based entertainment, NHL hockey is intensely local. Since Gretzky's retirement, there has not been a star player who attracts broad attention outside the existing fan base. Neither does the NHL have a singular, made-for-TV event that draws viewers who do not usually follow the sport. In Canada, the Super Bowl earns far higher ratings each year than the NHL playoffs. In the United States, game seven of the 2019 Stanley Cup finals between St. Louis and Boston drew 8.7 million viewers, one of the largest audiences for NHL hockey in recent years. In comparison, 11.8 million Americans watched the 2018 World Cup final between France and Croatia.[15]

There have been hockey games with large nationwide audiences in North America. Since 1972 in Canada and 1980 in the United States, international contests have been the sport's biggest television draw. For example, more Americans watched the 2010 Olympic men's final than the deciding game of the World Series, the NCAA basketball championship, or the NBA finals. In Europe, high ratings for hockey are an annual occurrence. Games of the IIHF world championship regularly rank among the most-watched programs of the year in Finland, Sweden, the Czech Republic, and Russia, with some semifinal and final matches drawing over 60 percent of viewers. In Germany as well, the national team's recent success has made hockey popular viewing.[16] Like soccer, the world's fastest game is a popular outlet for national passions. However, hockey's premier professional league has been unable to tap this interest in a way that brings it the lion's share of profits.

Certainly, the NHL's hybrid of speed and power is exciting. Yet history shows that when a single league dominates a sport, the result can be stasis. We see this with the NHL of the 1960s: a profitable organization that did not anticipate the creation of a rival league or the dynamic challenge of the

Soviets. Today, the NHL's dominance threatens to turn other leagues into feeders, as a Swedish federation official acknowledges: "We can't ever keep [the best players] in our league."[17] In their history of world hockey, Stephen Hardy and Andrew Holman identify cycles of divergence and convergence in the sport's development. The current stage of convergence, however, threatens to stifle any creative divergence. Men's hockey has one major league and one style of play. If the characteristics of globalization include the worldwide reach of powerful institutions and the diffusion of their norms and practices, then contemporary hockey is a textbook case.

We can see the effects of the present convergence in the saga of the South Korean men's team. The Korean federation's determined campaign to build an Olympic-quality team ended in disappointment at the 2018 games. When the Koreans took an early lead against the Czechs in the tournament's first game, it was clear they could skate with the world's best. Yet while the Koreans had speed, they did not have power. The average Korean player, not including the naturalized North Americans, measured 5′10″ and 181 pounds. In comparison, the Czechs averaged 6′1″ and 195 pounds; they controlled the corners and the front of the net. Korea lost narrowly to the Czechs and went on to finish in last place, without a win. As sociologist and former player Doo Jae Park points out, Koreans have resigned themselves to the idea of Europeans and North Americans as superior in hockey not because of a difference in skills but because of the difference in size. Today's hybrid game, as played in international tournaments and the NHL, favors the size and strength of big white men.[18] A Korean sportswriter put it to me directly: "There is a Korean way in taekwondo. There is not a Korean way in hockey."

Perhaps there will be a Chinese way that will transform international hockey at the 2022 Winter Olympics. Maybe hockey in East Asia will develop like baseball, with popular domestic leagues offering a distinct brand of the game. Then again, maybe the convergence of power in the NHL's hands will remain uncontested. If that's the case, then the hockey world will look less like baseball or world football, with its multiple leagues and varied styles of play, and more like American football, a sport dominated by a hugely profitable cartel that presides over a vast feeder system. It goes without saying, that would be to the NHL's liking.

At a young age, players begin moving through the hockey world's leagues, tournaments, and development camps. The top event in youth hockey, the

Quebec International Pee-Wee Tournament, draws teams of eleven- and twelve-year-olds from Australia and Japan. Across North America, Europe, and now Asia, tournaments for boys and girls as young as U8 run year-round. These events are part of a rapidly expanding global industry. According to a 2018 report, youth sports generated $22 billion worldwide—a sum that includes team memberships, travel, and equipment.[19] In comparison, the NFL brought in $16 billion that year; the top five European soccer leagues, a total of $17 billion. Although young athletes are not paid, they generate more revenue than the biggest pro stars.

From revenue-generating youth tournaments to the pro leagues, the hockey world is large enough to be self-contained and self-perpetuating. Men can live their entire working lives within this world. As players, they move from league to league, from continent to continent, and then they become coaches, scouts, and administrators, again moving from continent to continent. The globalization of hockey has created professional opportunities for former players. In general, these opportunities are not open to women, despite the growth in female participation. For instance, only 25 percent of the head coaching positions in NCAA women's hockey are held by women. In the European women's leagues, the percentage is even smaller. Research shows that even girls in hockey see male coaches as more competent. The consequence is that few female hockey players grow up with a sense of coaching as an option. "Most women don't see the sport as a viable career path," Randi Griffin told me.[20]

Of course, there are cultural differences among the various lands of the hockey world. Griffin and other North Americans who played in Korea encountered Confucian social rules off and on the ice. Younger players were required to carry older teammates' equipment bags, and they were expected to feed the puck to their elders. Czech captain Alena Polenská told me of the difference between coaches of her youth teams, who told her everything she did was wrong, and those she had in the United States, who told her everything she did was great. Overall, however, players who navigate the hockey world find more commonalities than differences. I asked one well-traveled player what set the tone in a particular arena. Were there differences from country to country, or perhaps among the cultures of North America, Europe, and Asia? "It's usually the guy who drives the Zamboni," she answered.

If there is one common thread among the different cultures of the hockey world, it is nostalgia. Certainly, hockey is not unique in constantly looking back to the past. All sports have their traditionalists who revere the way the game used to be played. It's often the case, however, that hockey nostalgia is more a lament than a celebration. "The books of hockey are filled with sighs for the good old days, the steady plainchant of regret, a chorus of loss," writes Stephen Smith.[21] In my interviews with hockey men and women, from North America and Europe, I heard this regret. They were concerned about changes to the game and changes to the players. Coaches and scouts spoke to me of broader developments affecting the sport: the lure of technology, goal-oriented parenting, greater specialization in society, global migration. Even though many of them have benefited from these changes, even though they continue to work within hockey, they fear for the game's future—at least for the game as they learned it.

One source of this nostalgia coursing through the hockey world stems from our recognition that winter is ending. Throughout the sport's history, even in the age of bandy, hockey enthusiasts have been aware that winter is not the same as it used to be. Today, that change is undeniable. Even in Canada, the ice is melting. In Brantford, Ontario, where young Wayne Gretzky learned to skate on his backyard rink, the average temperature in January has risen from 22°F (−5.8°C) in the mid-1960s to 30°F (−1.2°C) today. "You get one day cold, next day warm," said Walter Gretzky in a 2007 interview. "You can't get a rink going."[22] According to environmental scientists at Wilfrid Laurier University who track outdoor skating seasons using data from people who build backyard rinks, Toronto has lost a quarter of its skating days in recent years. They expect the number to fall by another third by century's end.[23]

Among our sports, hockey is unique in facing this dislocation. Baseball players still dig their spikes into the dirt and shield their eyes from the sun, like they did in the nineteenth century. The world's soccer grounds are outfitted with pitchside advertising and goal-line technology, but the game is still played on grass, in the elements. These games are not in danger of being removed from their original environments, at least not immediately. But this is the future of hockey, that it will be played only in a climate-controlled box, on a surface created by machines and chemicals.

What will be lost when that happens? Will something intrinsic to the game disappear when winter brings only longer shadows, when stories of Gretzky on his backyard rink are as distant as myth? "Without our memory of winter," Adam Gopnik writes, "the North, the snow, the seasonal cycle, something will be lost to our civilization too."[24] Perhaps a future historian of hockey will discern what this something is. Then again, maybe that historian will see things differently. Perhaps that historian, who grew up playing the game in Dallas or Dubai, rather than Duluth, will not be blinkered by the questions that perplex us, by the game's connection to winter, or its contested origins, or to whom it really belongs. That historian will surely see things we miss. After all, even the best fans sometimes lose sight of the puck.

ACKNOWLEDGMENTS

This book has allowed me to travel the world, make new friends, and rekindle my fascination with the game I first loved as a child. All of this would not have been possible without the help of a lot of people.

First of all, I owe a profound debt to those who were there at the very beginning: to my sister, Collette, who watched more boys' hockey games than she likely cared to; to my mom, Pat, who cheered from rinkside and warmed cold toes; and to the man who taught me how to play the game, how to follow the game, and how to ref the game. Thanks, Dad.

Chris Young, Will Katerberg, and Tobias Stark were essential partners at the start of this project, and they have been constant supporters throughout. I am grateful for their encouragement, advice, and friendship.

This book first took shape when I was a member of the history department at Calvin College. My colleagues there created a wonderful environment for research. Student research assistants Janaya Crevier, Chad Westra, and Kelly Looman made important contributions in the project's early stages.

This book would not have been possible without the support of a Fulbright Global Scholar grant, which allowed me to travel the hockey world in the winter and spring of 2018. Thanks to Cara Doble from the Institute of International Education, for managing the practical aspects of the grant; Leighanne Yuh and Jim Paek, who made possible my trip to Korea; Yoolim Song, who provided needed help in Seoul; Jan Lomíček, my academic sponsor in the Czech Republic; the family Špačkovi, my dear friends and hosts in Prague; and Matt Hoven and Peter Donnelly, who welcomed me to Canada.

Among the many archivists and librarians who aided in my research, a few deserve special tribute: Kateřina Procházková at the National Museum in Prague, Jitka Bílková and her terrific staff at the Security Services Archive; Timothy Nelson at the Dokumentationsbibliothek in Davos; Samantha Chianta and Miragh Bitove at the Hockey Hall of Fame; Elena Misalandi at the Moscow House of Photography;

and Kathleen Struck, Kaitlyn Van Kampen, and Sonja Timmerman, interlibrary loan librarians at Calvin College and Gustavus Adolphus College.

Along the way, several other people aided my research, by pointing me to sources, sharing their research, or engaging in great conversation: Roger Godin in St. Paul; Kim Jung-min and Kim Jin-hyouk in Korea; Blanka Elekes Szentágotai and Adam Steiss at IIHF; Daniel Derungs in Switzerland; Agnes Meisinger in Austria; René Feldvoß in Germany; Jouko Kokkonen, Kalle Rantala, and Vesa Tikander in Finland; Ján Holko in Slovakia; Robert Sovík, Zdeněk Janda, Ethan Schreiner, and Vojtěch Kučera in Prague; Stanislav Gridasov in Moscow; Paul Harder and Howard Shubert in Toronto; Marc Norman in Hamilton; Dan Mason in Edmonton; Andrew Ross in Ottawa; and Jason Blake in Slovenia.

The interviews listed in the bibliography are just a few of the formal conversations I conducted for this research. Unfortunately, there was not enough space to relay stories and insights from all of these people, but our conversations indelibly shaped this book. Thanks to Frank Serratore, Rick Plantinga, Noah Welch, Patrik Martinec, Kim Chang-bum, Gary Harker, Corey Millen, František Suchan, Diko Stevic, Olga Votolovskaya, Yuri Karmanov, Yuri Korolev, Lara Stalder, Emi Okayasu, Jenny Potter, Zsuzsanna Kolbenheyer, Emma Terho, and Deidre Honner. Above all, thanks to my old friend from West Duluth, Mike Vukonich, who gave the first interview for this book and then connected me with his contacts in the hockey world.

This project has had terrific support all along from the University of California Press. I'm grateful for the good work of Niels Hooper, Robin Manley, Peter Perez, and Kate Hoffman; copyeditor Richard Earles; and the editors of the Sport in World History series—Chris Young, Bob Edelman, Susan Brownell, and Wayne Wilson. My writing students at the Loft Literary Center provided welcome criticism on the book's early chapters. Megan Berglund read the first complete draft, and John Parker-DerBoghossian read the final version. Their comments, coming from avowed non–hockey fans, were essential to honing the text. My thanks go to Andrew, Jason, and Tobias for valuable critique, corrections, and follow-up comments. Jason VanHorn designed the maps. Raffaele Poli and Roger Besson of CIES Observatory provided the infographic, with additional design work by Jennifer Kurth. Alan Holiman and Ken Zurcher helped with translations from vernacular Russian.

A special shout-out goes to the men and women of "Noon Puck," at Gustavus Adolphus College. I am reminded every week why people are drawn to this fast, fun, and demanding game.

To friends in Minnesota, Michigan, Kansas, Prague, and points in-between; to the extended Berglund, Lenarz, and Blonigan families; to old colleagues at KU and Calvin, and new colleagues at Gustavus—thank you all for asking, "When is your book coming out? I'm looking forward to reading it." You have been a great encouragement.

Lastly, and most importantly, thanks go to my family. Will, Marta, Nils, and Vera have suffered through the quirks and annoyances of having a historian as a dad. Vera and Nils, in particular, endured my long absences during this project. But the greatest burden was borne by my wife, Megan. Just before this book went into production, Megan passed away from cancer. She didn't like my research trips or the long hours at the computer. Yet she supported me, she believed in me, and she cheered for me. She was just as excited as I was to see the book's cover design, and she told everybody how much she enjoyed the manuscript—always adding that she didn't even like hockey. "It's a hockey book, but it's not about hockey," she would say. "It's about everything." There could be no greater compliment.

Megan, I can never thank you enough—for everything.

NOTES

ABBREVIATIONS USED IN NOTES

AO	Archives of Ontario
AO Elliott	Archives of Ontario, Elliott Research Corporation fonds
AO Smythe	Archives of Ontario, Conn Smythe fonds
AO Young	Archives of Ontario, Scott Young fonds
G&M	*The Globe and Mail*
Glenbow ARJ	Glenbow Museum Archive, Arthur Rice-Jones fonds
Glenbow IO	Glenbow Museum Archive, Imperial Oil Limited fonds
HHOF Clippings	Hockey Hall of Fame, Clippings Files
IIHF Minutes	International Ice Hockey Federation, Collected Minutes
IOC HA	International Olympic Committee, Historical Archives, Olympic Studies Centre
LAC	Library and Archives Canada
LAC CAHA	Library and Archives Canada, Canadian Amateur Hockey Association fonds
LAC CBC	Library and Archives Canada, Canadian Broadcasting Corporation fonds
LAC CHR	Library and Archives Canada, Canadian Hockey Review fonds
LAC ExtRel	Library and Archives Canada, External Relations fonds
LAC HC	Library and Archives Canada, Hockey Canada fonds
MNHS	Minnesota State Historical Society

NACZ SVTVS	National Archive of the Czech Republic, Státní výbor pro tělesnou výchovu a sport, 1949–1956
NMCZ	National Museum of the Czech Republic, Archive of Physical Education and Sport
NYT	*The New York Times*
OSA RFE	Open Society Archives, Records of Radio Free Europe/Radio Liberty Research Institute
SI	*Sports Illustrated*
StBA	Security Services Archive, Czech Republic
UABA Hardy	University of Alberta Archive, W. G. Hardy fonds
UABA Sov	University of Alberta Archives, Archival Material, Centre for Research on Canadian-Russian Relations
UILA Brundage	University of Illinois Archive, Avery Brundage Collection
UMBA	University of Manitoba Archive
UMNA Ath	University of Minnesota Archive, Athletics Department Records

INTRODUCTION

1. The Friday broadcast of the hockey game and other Olympic events earned a rating of 23.9, barely topping that night's episode of *Dukes of Hazzard* on CBS, which drew a 23.6 rating. ABC's Olympic programming on Tuesday, Wednesday, Thursday, and Saturday all finished in the top ten of the ratings. See Nielsen ratings for the week ending February 24, 1989, *NYT,* 27 February 1980.

2. Douglas Coupland, *Souvenir of Canada* (Vancouver: Douglas & McIntyre, 2002), 51.

3. *Star Tribune* (Minneapolis), 25 February 1980.

4. *Pioneer Press* (St. Paul), 27 February 1980.

5. Dave Bidini, *The Tropic of Hockey: My Search for the Game in Unlikely Places* (Toronto: McClelland & Stewart, 2000), xvii.

6. Yoon Min-sik, "Shooting for the Future," *The Korea Herald,* 9 June 2019, www.koreaherald.com/view.php?ud=20170608000942; Andrew Jeong, "Stanley Cup Champion Goes Back to His Roots," *The Wall Street Journal,* 17 February 2018, www.wsj.com/articles/a-stanley-cup-champion-goes-back-to-his-roots-to-help-korean-hockey-1518927001; and Jim Paek, interview, 13 February 2018.

7. Peter Rutherford, "Olympics: Ice Hockey without Borders, Canada Gives Korea an Assist," *Reuters,* 29 December 2017, www.reuters.com/article/us-olympics-2018-naturalisation/olympics-ice-hockey-without-borders-canada-gives-korea-an-assist-id USKBN1EN0S9.

8. "Should Foreign Athletes Get Special Naturalization?," *The Korea Herald*, 4 June 2012, www.koreaherald.com/view.php?ud=20120604001275.

9. Matt Dalton, interview, 26 January 2018.

10. Marissa Brandt, interview, 22 January 2018; Randi Griffin, interview, 22 January 2018; and Caroline Park, interview, 27 January 2018. On the 2018 Korean women's team, see Seth Berkman, *A Team of Their Own: How an International Sisterhood Made Olympic History* (Toronto: Hanover Square, 2019).

11. "Moon's Approval Rating Plunges," *Yonhap News Agency*, 25 January 2018, https://en.yna.co.kr/view/AEN20180125001700315; "S. Koreans View N.K. Participation in Olympics with Mixed Feelings," *Yonhap News Agency*, 24 January 2018, https://en.yna.co.kr/view/AEN20180124005300315; Berkman, *A Team of Their Own*, 185–197; and Zsuzsanna Kolbenheyer, interview, 13 February 2018.

12. "Koreas' Combined Women's Hockey Team Debuts in Friendly," *NBCSports.com*, 4 February 2018, https://olympics.nbcsports.com/2018/02/04/koreas-combined-womens-hockey-team-debuts-in-friendly. See also Jonathan Cheng's coverage of the unified team for the *Wall Street Journal*.

13. Marissa Brandt, email, 10 July 2019.

14. Randi Griffin, email, 12 July 2019.

15. Popular histories on these topics include Michael McKinley, *Putting a Roof on Winter: Hockey's Rise from Sport to Spectacle* (Vancouver: Greystone, 2002); D'Arcy Jenish, *The NHL—A Centennial History: 100 Years of On-Ice Action and Boardroom Battles* (Toronto: Doubleday Canada, 2013); and Todd Denault, *The Greatest Game: The Montreal Canadiens, the Red Army, and the Night That Saved Hockey* (Toronto: McClelland & Stewart, 2014). Among academic histories, see Andrew Holman, ed., *Canada's Game: Hockey and Identity* (Montreal: McGill-Queen's University Press, 2009); J. Andrew Ross, *Joining the Clubs: The Business of the National Hockey League* (Syracuse, NY: Syracuse University Press, 2015); Michel Vigneault, "La naissance d'un sport organisé au Canada: le hockey à Montréal, 1875–1917" (PhD diss., Université Laval, 2001); and John Chi-Kit Wong, *Lords of the Rinks: The Emergence of the National Hockey League, 1875–1936* (Toronto: University of Toronto Press, 2005). An expert overview is Andrew Holman, "A Flag of Tendons: Hockey and Canadian History," in *Hockey: Challenging Canada's Game/Au-delà du sport national*, eds. Jenny Ellison and Jennifer Anderson (Ottawa: Canadian Museum of History/University of Ottawa Press, 2018), 25–44.

16. On the Canada-centric field of hockey scholarship, see Jean Lévesque, "Hockey et politique: jalons pour une historiographie raisonnée," *Bulletin d'histoire politique* 22, no. 2 (2014): 33–52. The best popular work on Canadian hockey is Michael McKinley, *Hockey: A People's History* (Toronto: McClelland & Stewart, 2009). At the forefront of the scholarly literature are Richard S. Gruneau and David Whitson's two books: *Hockey Night in Canada: Sport, Identities, and Cultural Politics* (Toronto: Garamond Press, 1993) and *Artificial Ice: Hockey, Culture and Commerce* (Peterborough, ON: Broadview Press, 2006). See also Jason Blake, *Canadian Hockey Literature: A Thematic Survey* (Toronto: University of Toronto Press, 2010); Michael Buma, *Refereeing Identity: The Cultural Work of Canadian Hockey Novels*

(Montreal: McGill-Queen's University Press, 2012); and Michael A. Robidoux, *Men at Play: A Working Understanding of Professional Hockey* (Montreal: McGill-Queen's University Press, 2001). The literature also includes important articles in social science and sports studies journals by Carly Adams, Kristi Allain, Anouk Bélanger, Hart Cantelon, Emmanuel Lapierre, Stacy L. Lorenz, and Nancy Theberge. A current barometer of Canadian hockey scholarship is the multiauthor blog *Hockey in Society* (https://hockeyinsociety.com).

17. Ken Dryden and Roy MacGregor, *Home Game: Hockey and Life in Canada* (Toronto: McClelland & Stewart, 1989), 101.

18. Ken Dryden, *The Game,* 30th anniversary edition (Chicago: Triumph, 2013), 262.

19. Stephen Hardy and Andrew C. Holman, *Hockey: A Global History* (Champaign: University of Illinois Press, 2018), 15. Useful references on world hockey include Andrew Podnieks et al., *Kings of the Ice: A History of World Hockey* (Richmond Hill, ON: NDE, 2002); Szymon Szemberg and Andrew Podnieks, eds., *World of Hockey: Celebrating a Century of the IIHF* (Bolton, ON: Fenn, 2007); and Dan Diamond, ed., *Total Hockey: The Official Encyclopedia of the National Hockey League* (New York: Total Sports, 1998).

20. Michael Robidoux uses the term "hockey world" to describe North American professional hockey, an enclosed culture in which players are immersed in "a collective whole with a belief system, world view, and values" (*Men at Play,* 126). Stacy Lorenz uses the term to describe an "'information system' that links people together in a broad-based community of interest," in Lorenz, "National Media Coverage and the Creation of a Canadian 'Hockey World': The Winnipeg-Montreal Stanley Cup Hockey Challenges, 1899–1903," *The International Journal of the History of Sport* 32 (2015): 2012–2043. This book takes both views into account: the hockey world as a cultural space encompassing players and coaches as well as fans and commentators.

21. Barbara J. Keys, *Globalizing Sport: National Rivalry and International Community in the 1930s* (Cambridge, MA: Harvard University Press, 2006), 2. With the concept of an "imagined world," Keys draws from Arjun Appadurai, "Disjuncture and Difference in the Global Capital Economy," *Theory, Culture & Society* 7 (1990): 295–310.

22. Lynn Hunt, *Writing History in the Global Era* (New York: Norton, 2014), 60.

23. Bruce Kidd, *The Struggle for Canadian Sport* (Toronto: University of Toronto Press, 1996), 5.

24. See Manfred B. Steger, *Globalization: A Very Short Introduction,* 2nd ed. (New York: Oxford University Press, 2011) and *The Rise of the Global Imaginary: Political Ideologies from the French Revolution to the Global War on Terror* (New York: Oxford University Press, 2008); Anthony Giddens, *Runaway World: How Globalization Is Reshaping Our Lives* (London: Profile, 1999); Jan Nederveen Pieterse, *Globalization and Culture: Global Mélange* (Lanham, MD: Rowman & Littlefield, 2004); Mauro F. Guillen, "Is Globalization Civilizing, Destructive or Feeble? A Critique of Five Key Debates in the Social Science Literature," *Annual Review of Sociology* 27 (2001): 235–260; and Keys, *Globalizing Sport,* 2.

25. Jaromír Jágr with Tomáš Šmid, *Z Kladna do Ameriky: Vlastní životopis* (Prague: Gutenberg, 2011), 275–276.
26. John Harrington, interview, 4 August 2017.
27. "Vladimir Plyushchev: 'Khokkei—dorogoi vid sporta,'" *Sports.ru*, 18 August 2010, www.sports.ru/hockey/72433653.html.
28. "Švédská legenda Sundin: Hokej je nejkrásnější sport, ale taky drahý," *iDnes.cz*, 20 May 2013, http://hokej.idnes.cz/mats-sundin-byl-uveden-do-sine-slavy-d7l-/ms-hokej-2013.
29. Teri Pecoskie, "Pay to Play: Odds Stacked against Many Young Hockey Players," *The Hamilton Spectator*, 28 October 2016, www.thespec.com/news-story/6933956-pay-to-play-odds-stacked-against-many-young-hockey-players/.
30. Ken MacQueen, "Bobby Orr: How We're Killing Hockey," *Maclean's*, 17 October 2013, www.macleans.ca/politics/on-being-left-broke-and-betrayed-pushy-rinkside-parents-and-the-future-of-the-game/; and "Gretzky Doubts He Could Play in Today's 'Systematic' Game" (video), interview of Wayne Gretzky by Peter Mansbridge, *CBC Sports*, 11 October 2016, www.cbc.ca/sports/hockey/nhl/wayne-gretzky-interview-national-1.3800604.

CHAPTER ONE. UP FROM THE ICE

1. H. H. Lamb, *Climate, History, and the Modern World* (York, UK: Methuen, 1982), 192 and 195; and Brian M. Fagan, *The Little Ice Age: How Climate Made History* (New York: Perseus, 2000), 50–55.
2. Lamb, *Climate, History, and the Modern World*, 228–229.
3. Ibid., 202–203 and 225.
4. Rev. John Kerk, "Curling," in *Skating* (Longmans, Green, 1892), 327.
5. Gillian Poulter, *Becoming Native in a Foreign Land: Sport, Visual Culture and Identity in Montreal, 1840–85* (Vancouver: UBC Press, 2009), 21–37 and 165–174.
6. Andrew Denning, *Skiing into Modernity: A Cultural and Environmental History* (Berkeley: University of California Press, 2014), 30–35.
7. On the early history of skating, see Mary Louise Adams, *Artistic Impressions: Figure Skating, Masculinity, and the Limits of Sport* (Toronto: University of Toronto Press, 2011), chap. 4.
8. On nineteenth-century indoor rinks, see Howard Shubert, *Architecture on Ice: A History of the Hockey Arena* (Montreal and Kingston: McGill-Queen's University Press, 2016), 25–38 and 78–80.
9. Adam Gopnik, "Romantic Winter," in *Winter: Five Windows on the Season* (Toronto: Anansi, 2011), 3.
10. J. W. Fitsell, *Hockey's Captains, Colonels & Kings* (Erin, ON: Boston Mills Press, 1987), 31–34.
11. Michael McKinley, *Putting a Roof on Winter: Hockey's Rise from Sport to Spectacle* (Vancouver: Greystone, 2000), 12.

12. See Carl Gidén, Patrick Houda, and Jean-Patrice Martel, *On the Origin of Hockey* (Stockholm: Hockey Origin Publishing, 2014).

13. McKinley, *Putting a Roof on Winter*, 13–14. See the table summarizing the various early names for hockey in Gidén, Houda, and Martel, *On the Origin of Hockey*, 24–25.

14. C. G. Tebbutt, "Bandy," in *Skating and Figure Skating* (London: Longmans, Green, 1892), 435.

15. Ibid., 432.

16. Josef Laufer, *Hokej—můj osud* (Prague: Mladá fronta, 1960), 8–11.

17. Torbjörn Andersson, "Bandy v. Ice Hockey in Sweden," *Sport in Society* 23 (2020): 3–4; and Bill Sund, "The Origins of Bandy and Hockey in Sweden," in *Putting It on Ice: Internationalizing 'Canada's Game,'* ed. Colin D. Howell (Halifax: Gorsebrook Research Institute, Saint Mary's University, 2002), 16–17.

18. E.K.R., "Hockey on the Ice," *Country Life Illustrated*, 23 February 1901, 246–248.

19. "Eishockey: Ein neuer Sport," *Prager Tagblatt*, 23 December 1900.

20. Tebbutt, "Bandy," 435. On bandy in England and Europe, see Karel Gut and Gustav Vlk, *Světový hokej* (Prague: Olympia, 1990), 45–47.

21. Laufer recounts early matches of bandyhockey, as he called it, in *Hokej—můj osud*, 14–19. See also match reports in *The Courier* (Davos) from 18 January 1895, 11 January 1900, and 15 January 1904.

22. "Eishockey: Ein neuer Sport."

23. "Hockey on the Ice."

24. Edgar Wood Syers, "Skating and Skating Resorts," *The Winter Sports Annual, 1906–7* (London: Horace Cox, 1906), 20.

25. Hardy and Holman, *Hockey: A Global History*, 92–98.

26. Captain E. G. Wynyard, "Bandy," *The Courier* (Davos), 23 December 1904, 6.

27. Tebbutt, "Bandy," 433–437.

28. F. Fos, "Le Hockey sur Glace," *La Vie au grand air: Revue illustrée de tous les sports*, 27 December 1902, 872.

29. Fitsell, *Hockey's Captains, Colonels & Kings*, 33.

30. Ibid., 74. On the early rules of hockey, see also 33–50 and 65–67.

31. On British elements in nineteenth-century and early twentieth-century Canadian culture, see the essays in Phillip Buckner and R. Douglas Francis, eds., *Canada and the British World: Culture, Migration, and Identity* (Vancouver: UBC Press, 2006).

32. Paul W. Bennett, "Training 'Blue-Blooded' Canadian Boys: Athleticism, Muscular Christianity, and Sports in Ontario's 'Little Big Four' Schools, 1829–1930," *Journal of Sport History* 43, no. 3 (2016): 256–257.

33. Carl Berger, *The Sense of Power: Studies in the Ideas of Canadian Imperialism, 1867–1914*, 2nd ed. (Toronto: University of Toronto Press, 2013), 36.

34. Parkin, "The Forces of Union," in *Imperialism and Nationalism, 1884–1914: A Conflict in Canadian Thought*, ed. Carl Berger (Toronto: Copp Clark, 1969), 29.

35. Bennett, "Training 'Blue-Blooded' Canadian Boys," 262.

36. Stephen Leacock, "Greater Canada: An Appeal" (1907), quoted in Berger, *Imperialism and Nationalism, 1884–1914*, 6.

37. R. Tait McKenzie, "Hockey in Eastern Canada," *The Dominion Illustrated Monthly*, February 1893, 64.

38. Richard Gruneau and David Whitson, *Hockey Night in Canada: Sport, Identities and Cultural Politics* (Toronto: Garamond, 1993), 41.

39. "A History of the Ontario Hockey Association," in *Hockey Pictorial—History of Canada's Great National Winter Sport* (Canada Amateur Hockey Association, 1924), LAC CAHA, G28 I151, vol. 1.

40. David Goldblatt, *The Ball Is Round: A Global History of Soccer* (New York: Riverhead, 2008), 31.

41. Tony Collins, *The Oval World: A Global History of Rugby* (London: Bloomsbury, 2015), 20.

42. Fitsell, *Hockey's Captains, Colonels & Kings*, 36.

43. Michael A. Robidoux, "Imagining a Canadian Identity through Sport: A Historical Interpretation of Lacrosse and Hockey," *Journal of American Folklore* 115, no. 456 (Spring 2002): 220.

44. Fos, "Le Hockey sur Glace."

45. Stacy L. Lorenz and Geraint B. Osbourne, "'Talk about Strenuous Hockey': Violence, Manhood, and the 1907 Ottawa Silver Seven-Montreal Wanderer Rivalry," *Journal of Canadian Studies/Revue d'études canadiennes* 40, no. 1 (2006): 126.

46. Alan Metcalfe, *Canada Learns to Play: The Emergence of Organized Sport, 1807–1914* (Toronto: McClelland and Stewart, 1987), 69.

47. Michel Vigneault, "Montreal's Francophone Hockey Beginnings, 1895–1910," in *The Same but Different: Hockey in Quebec*, eds. Jason Blake and Andrew C. Holman (Montreal: McGill-Queen's University Press, 2017), 39.

48. "A History of the OHA," in *Hockey Pictorial—History of Canada's Great National Winter Sport* (1924), LAC CAHA, G28 I151.

49. "The Old Century and New," *Manitoba Free Press*, 1 January 1901; and Marvin McInnis, "Migration," in *Historical Atlas of Canada, vol. 3: Addressing the Twentieth Century, 1891–1961*, eds. Donald Kerr and Deryck W. Holdsworth (Toronto: University of Toronto Press), plate 27.

50. Morris Mott, "One Solution to the Urban Crisis: Manly Sports and Winnipeggers, 1900–1914," *Urban History Review* 12, no. 2 (1983): 57.

51. Morris Mott, "'An Immense Hold in the Public Estimation': The First Quarter Century of Hockey in Manitoba, 1886–1911," *Manitoba History* 43, no. 2 (2002): 9; and "Brutality on the Ice," *Winnipeg Daily Tribune*, 20 February 1899.

52. *Winnipeg Free Press*, 24 January 1902.

53. Vigneault, "Montreal's Francophone Hockey Beginnings," 43–44.

54. George and Darril Fosty, *Black Ice: The Lost History of the Colored Hockey League of the Maritimes, 1895–1925* (New York: Stryker-Indigo, 2004), 50–51.

55. Bruce Kidd, "Muscular Christianity and Value-Centred Sport: The Legacy of Tom Brown in Canada," *Sport in Society* 16, no. 4 (2013): 410.

56. Christiane Eisenberg, "'Not Cricket!' Sport in Germany, or How the British Model Fell into Oblivion," *Britain as a Model of Modern Society? German Views,* eds. Arnd Bauerkämper and Christiane Eisenberg (Augsburg, Germany: Wissner, 2006), 243.

57. Tebbutt, "Bandy," 434.

58. See the collected papers of Josef Grüss and Josef Rössler-Ořovský, NMCZ.

59. Eisenberg, *"English Sports" und deutsche Bürger: Eine Gesellschaftsgeschichte* (Paderborn, Germany: Ferdinand Schöningh, 1999), chap. IV.1. On conflict between German advocates of English sports and defenders of *Turnen,* see Gertrud Pfister, "Cultural Confrontations: German *Turnen,* Swedish Gymnastics and English Sport—European Diversity in Physical Activities from a Historical Perspective," *Culture, Sport, Society* 6, no. 1 (2003): 82–86.

60. On clubs and the development of modern sports, see the forum "Associativity and Modern Sport," with contributions by Stefan Szymanski, Steven A. Riess, Arnd Krüger, and Malcolm MacLean, in *Journal of Sport History* 35, no. 1 (2008): 1–64.

61. Stefan Nielsen, *Sport und Großstadt 1870 bis 1930: Komparative Studien zur Entstehung bürglicher Freizeitkultur* (Frankfurt am Main: Peter Lang, 2002), 288–289 and 262–265.

62. Klaus Nathaus, "Between Club and Commerce: Comparing the Organisation of Sports in Britain and Germany from the Late Nineteenth to the Early Twentieth Century," in *Cultural Industries in Britain and Germany: Sport, Music and Entertainment from the Eighteenth to the Twentieth Century,* Christiane Eisenberg and Andreas Gestrich, eds. (Augsburg, Germany: Wissner, 2012), 84 and 87.

63. Agnes Meisinger, 150 Jahre Eiszeit: Die Grosse Geschichte Des Wiener Eislauf-Vereins (Vienna: Bohlau, 2017), 46.

64. "Eissport," *Illustrirte Sport Zeitung* (Vienna), 14 January 1900.

65. *Allgemeine Sport-Zeitung,* 10 February 1907.

66. Christiane Eisenberg, "Towards a New History of European Sport?," *European Review* 19, no. 4 (2011): 619–620.

67. Les Statuts de la Ligue Internationale de Hockey sur Glace, 15–16 May 1908, IIHF Minutes.

68. Fitsell, *Hockey's Captains, Colonels & Kings,* 25.

69. *Montreal Gazette,* March 3, 1875.

70. B. M. Patton, *Ice-Hockey* (London: Routledge, 1936).

71. Bruce Dowbiggin, *The Stick: A History, a Celebration, an Elegy* (Toronto: Macfarlane, Walter & Ross, 2011), 13–17.

72. Lední hokey a jeho počátky v Čechách, manuscript, Svaz kanadského (ledního) hockeye, NMCZ.

73. Les Statuts de Ligue Internationale de Hockey sur Glace, 15–16 May 1908, IIHF Minutes.

74. *Sport a hry,* 7 December 1908. Clippings book, vol. 1. Svaz kanadského (ledního) hockeye, NMCZ.

75. Laufer, *Hokej—můj osud,* 34.

76. Ibid., 33

77. Ibid., 35.

78. David E. Torrance, "Instructor to Empire: Canada and the Rhodes Scholarship, 1902–39," in *Canada and the British World: Culture, Migration, and Identity*, 261.

79. *Le Journal*, 22 December 1912. On the Canadians' games against the Prince's Skating Club, see Patton, *Ice-Hockey*, 30–34.

80. *Illustriertes (Österreichisches) Sportblatt*, 6 January 1912.

81. *Illustriertes (Österreichisches) Sportblatt*, 3 January, 17 January, and 31 January 1914.

82. The most thorough academic studies are Wong, *Lords of the Rinks;* and Ross, *Joining the Clubs*. See also McKinley, *Putting a Roof on Winter*, chap. 3; and Jenish, *The NHL—A Centennial History*, part 1.

83. Louis P. Cain and David D. Haddock, "Similar Economic Histories, Different Industrial Structures: Transatlantic Contrasts in the Evolution of Professional Sports Leagues," *The Journal of Economic History* 65, no. 4 (2005): 1129.

84. Daniel S. Mason, "The International Hockey League and the Professionalization of Ice Hockey, 1904–1907," *Journal of Sport History* 25, no. 1 (1998): 5.

85. US Department of Commerce, "Average Annual Earnings in All Industries and in Selected Industries and Occupations 1890–1926," in *Historical Statistics of the United States, 1789–1946*, Series D 603–617, issued in 1949. Miners in the Upper Peninsula earned, on average, $2.80 per day; $500 was the average annual earning for coal miners in the United States in 1905.

86. McKinley, *Putting a Roof on Winter*, 67.

87. Mason, "The International Hockey League," 7.

88. Wong, *Lords of the Rinks*, 50. See also Ross, *Joining the Clubs*, 36–39.

89. Wong, *Lords of the Rinks*, 51–54.

90. See the summaries of early OHA council meetings in "A History of the OHA." See also Alan Metcalfe, "Power: A Case Study of the Ontario Hockey Association, 1890–1936," *Journal of Sport History* 19, no. 1 (1992): 5–25.

91. Wong, *Lords of the Rinks*, 52.

92. Ibid., 64–69.

93. Stanley Cup Regulations, Appendix B in Wong, *Lords of the Rinks*, 159.

94. *G&M*, 2 March 1908.

95. Bruce Kidd and John Macfarlane, *The Death of Hockey* (Toronto: New Press, 1972), 18.

CHAPTER TWO. INTO THE ARENA

1. W. A. Hewitt, "How Winnipeg Falcons Beat Yankees in Semi Final," *Winnipeg Free Press*, 26 April 1920, www.winnipegfalcons.com/clippings/games_olympics/howwinnipegfalconsbeatyankees.jpg.

2. Kenth Hansen, "The Birth of Swedish Hockey: Antwerp 1920," *Citius, Altius, fortius* 4, no. 2 (1996): 10.

3. "Ottawa Ends Series by Beating Boston," *The Globe* (Toronto), 14 April 1927; and "Der Davoser Hockey-Club in Berlin," *Sport* (Zurich), 14 December 1927.

4. Minutes du Congress d'Anvers de la L.I.H.G., Antwerp, 26 April 1920, IIHF Minutes.

5. Tobias Stark, *Folkhemmet på is: Ishockey, modernisering och nationell identitet i Sverige 1920–1972* (Malmö: idrottsforum.org, 2010), 118–132 and 158.

6. Rapport du President sur l'activite de la la L.I.H.G. en 1920 et 1921, IIHF Minutes.

7. Gut and Vlk, *Světový hokej*, 85–86.

8. Minutes, Congres des Sports d'Hiver, Paris, 12 June 1923, IIHF Minutes.

9. Henri de Baillet-Latour to Paul Loicq, 26 July 1926; and Loicq to Baillet-Latour, 28 October 1926, IOC HA, IIHF Correspondence, 1926–1948.

10. H. Lunn, "Winter Sport in Switzerland," in Reginald Cleaver, *A Winter-Sport Book* (London: Adam and Charles Black, 1911), 28–36; and Max Triet, "Davos als Zentrum des Sports," in *Davos: Profil eines Phänomens,* ed. Ernst Halter (Offizin), 61–67.

11. Denning, *Skiing into Modernity*, 24.

12. Edward Lyttelton, Introduction to Cleaver, *A Winter-Sport Book,* 13.

13. Ibid., plate 11.

14. *The Courier* (Davos), 12 January 1895.

15. Paul Müller, "Die Entwicklung des Eishockeys in Davos (I)," *Davoser revue* 15 (February 1940): 79.

16. Müller, "Die Entwicklung des Eishockeys in Davos (I)," 100–102.

17. Müller, "Die Entwicklung des Eishockeys in Davos (II)," *Davoser revue* 15 (March 1940): 80.

18. LTC Prague (Lawn Tennis Club Praha) was founded in 1903 by members of the sports club Slavia who were interested in both tennis and track and field. The following year, the club created a bandy section. In the late 1920s, LTC Prague emerged as the strongest club in Czech hockey and provided most of the players on the Czechoslovak national team.

19. "Eishockey in Davos," *Sport* (Zurich), 4 January 1924.

20. Müller, "Die Entwicklung des Eishockeys in Davos (I)," 102.

21. Dave Turnbull, diary entry, 4 January 1930, UMBA.

22. Jonathan F. W. Vance, *Death So Noble: Memory, Meaning, and the First World War* (Vancouver: UBC Press, 1997), 6–10.

23. Gustave Lanctôt, "Past Historians and Present History in Canada," *The Canadian Historical Review* 22, no. 3 (September 1941): 253. On changing views among historians of the Canadian nation, its constituent regions, and its neighbor, see Elizabeth Jameson and Jeremy Mouat, "Telling Differences: The Forty-Ninth Parallel and Historiographies of the West and Nation," *Pacific Historical Review* 75, no. 2 (May 2006): 183–230.

24. Fred Thordarson, "The Romance of the Falcons," 1932 manuscript, published in *The Icelandic Canadian* (Fall 1996): 5–19 and 32–35.

25. "Hockey Pictorial—History of Canada's Great National Winter Sport" (1924), LAC CAHA, G28 I151, vol. 1.

26. "Organized Sport," in *Historical Atlas of Canada, vol. 3: Addressing the Twentieth Century, 1891–1961,* plate 35. See also Carly Adams and Jason Laurendeau, "'Here They Come! Look Them Over!' Youth, Citizenship, and the Emergence of Minor Hockey in Canada," in *Hockey: Challenging Canada's Game/Au-delà du sport national,* eds. Jenny Ellison and Jennifer Anderson, 111–124 (Ottawa: Canadian Museum of History/University of Ottawa Press, 2018).

27. "Hockey Pictorial—History of Canada's Great National Winter Sport."

28. On the Banff Festival and the Vancouver Amazons, see Wayne Norton, *Women on Ice: The Early Years of Women's Hockey in Western Canada* (Vancouver: Ronsdale Press, 2009); and Carly Adams, "Troubling Bodies: 'The Canadian Girl,' the Ice Rink, and the Banff Winter Carnival," *Journal of Canadian Studies/Revue d'études canadiennes* 48, no. 3 (2014): 200–220. For the broader history of Canadian women's hockey in the interwar years, see Brian MacFarlane, *Proud Past, Bright Future: 100 Years of Canadian Women's Hockey,* chaps. 2–3; Joanna Avery and Julie Stevens, *Too Many Men on the Ice: Women's Hockey in North America* (Victoria, BC: Polestar, 1997), 63–75; and Elizabeth Etue and Megan K. Williams, *On the Edge: Women Making Hockey History* (Toronto: Second Story Press, 1996), 37–41.

29. Henry Roxborough, "Give the Girls a Hand," *Maclean's,* 15 February 1929, 48.

30. *Toronto Evening Telegram,* 30 March 1925, clipping in Thora McIlroy fonds, University of Toronto Archive.

31. Banquet program, Ladies Ontario Hockey Association, 12 December 1925, Thora McIlroy fonds, University of Toronto Archive. On the CAHA's rejection of women's hockey, see Carly Adams, "Organizing Hockey for Women: The Ladies Ontario Hockey Association and the Fight for Legitimacy, 1922–1940," in *Coast to Coast: Hockey in Canada to the Second World War,* ed. John Chi-Kit Wong (Toronto: University of Toronto Press, 2009), 138–139.

32. Roxborough, "Give the Girls a Hand," 48.

33. J. Andrew Ross, "Hockey Capital: Commerce, Culture, and the National Hockey League, 1917–1967" (PhD diss., University of Western Ontario, 2008), 125; Shubert, *Architecture on Ice,* 88; and Kidd, *The Struggle for Canadian Sport,* 199–200.

34. Ross, *Joining the Clubs,* 129; Shubert, *Architecture on Ice,* 136–137; and Russell Field, "A Night at the Garden(s): A History of Professional Hockey Spectatorship in the 1920s and 1930s" (PhD diss., University of Toronto, 2008), 35–55.

35. Shubert, *Architecture on Ice,* 92.

36. Quoted in Field, "A Night at the Garden(s)," 111.

37. Gate receipts and attendance totals are taken from Ross, *Joining the Clubs,* appendix.

38. Ross, "Hockey Capital," 112, fn 201.

39. Jenish, *The NHL—A Centennial History,* 37.

40. David Surdam, *The Age of Ruth and Landis: The Economics of Baseball during the Roaring Twenties* (Lincoln: University of Nebraska Press, 2018), 96.

41. Ross, *Joining the Clubs,* 134.

42. Charles H. Good, "Will U.S. Cash Cripple Our Hockey?," *Maclean's*, 1 March 1926.

43. Leslie Roberts, "'Americanizing' Canadian Sport," *The Canadian Magazine*, November 1931, 8.

44. Kidd, *The Struggle for Canadian Sport*, 229–230; and Stacy L. Lorenz, "'Bowing Down to Babe Ruth': Major League Baseball and Canadian Popular Culture, 1920–1929," *Canadian Journal of the History of Sport* 26, no. 1 (1995): 22–39. On American trends in Canadian football, see Ronald S. Lappage, "Selected Sports and Canadian Society, 1921–1939" (PhD diss., University of Alberta, 1974), 40–44.

45. Wong, *Lords of the Rinks*, 124.

46. Quoted in Kidd, *The Struggle for Canadian Sport*, 204–205.

47. In 1931 Montreal had a population of 818,577, while Toronto's population was 631,207. In 1930 the smallest US city in the NHL was Boston (781,188). In 1979 the Edmonton Oilers, Winnipeg Jets, and Quebec Nordiques were the only Canadian teams of the World Hockey Association to join the NHL. According to the 1981 census, the Edmonton metropolitan area had a population of 740,882, Winnipeg 592,061, and Québec 583,820. In comparison, the smallest US metropolitan area represented in the NHL was Hartford, with a 1980 population of 726,114. Of those four small-market franchises, only the Oilers survived.

48. Gut and Vlk, *Světový hokej*, 85–86.

49. On sports culture in interwar Germany, see Erik N. Jensen, *Body by Weimar: Athletes, Gender, and German Modernity* (Oxford: Oxford University Press, 2010), 78–83.

50. The most famous literary descriptions of the six-day races come from journalist Egon Erwin Kisch's essay "Elliptische Tretmühle" (1919) and Georg Kaiser's play *Von morgens bis mitternachts* (written 1912, performed 1917). On these and other works, see Wolfgang Rothe, "When Sports Conquered the Republic: A Forgotten Chapter From the 'Roaring Twenties,'" *Studies in 20th Century Literature* 4, no. 1 (1979): 1–27; and Jon Hughes, "'Im Sport ist der Nerv der Zeit selber zu spüren': Sport and Cultural Debate in the Weimar Republic," *German as a Foreign Language (GFL)* (2007): 28–45.

51. Assorted clippings, 13–15 February 1926. Clippings book, vol. 2. Svaz kanadského (ledního) hockeye, NMCZ.

52. Sven Crefeld, *Gustav Jaenecke: Idol auf dem Eis* (Erfurt: Sutton, 2008), 46–47; and Steffan Karas, *100 Jahre Eishockey in Berlin: Faszination durch Tradition* (Berlin: Jeske/Mader, 2008), 53–71.

53. *Deutsche Allgemeine Zeitung*, 12 March 1929, ZEFYS, Staatsbibliothek zu Berlin; and "Sportpalast: Leidenschaft bedenklich," *Der Spiegel*, 5 December 1951, www.spiegel.de/spiegel/print/d-20833260.html.

54. Attendance figures taken from *Sport* (Zurich), 2 January 1928 and 22 February 1928.

55. See, for example, the Reuters Empire Newsreel of a 1929 game between clubs from Prague and Berlin, Reuters–British Pathé Historical Collection, www.britishpathe.com/video/VLVAEILX00H52YA9GKCF40WQ4ZGIX-CZECHOSLOVAKIA-ICE-HOCKEY-PRAGUE-VS-BERLIN/.

56. Czechoslovakia–Switzerland Ice Hockey, 1947, British Pathé Newsreel, Reuters–British Pathé Historical Collection, www.britishpathe.com/video/ice-hockey-4.

57. Ken Dryden looks at the development of the modern Canadian style of play in *The Game*, 241–249. Hardy and Holman offer a more thorough investigation of competing styles during the 1930s and '40s in *Hockey: A Global History*, 244–249.

58. Dryden, *The Game*, 245.

59. Ibid., 246.

60. See Vladimír Kostka, *Utok v ledním hokeji* (Prague: Sportovní a turistické naklad, 1963), 9–13.

61. Bob Bowman, *On the Ice* (London: Arthur Baker, 1937), 10.

62. Laufer, *Hokej—můj osud*, 69.

63. Ibid., 72.

64. Ibid., 69–70.

65. Scott Young, *Hello Canada! The Life and Times of Foster Hewitt* (Toronto: Seal Books, 1985), 29–35.

66. Gruneau and Whitson, *Hockey Night in Canada*, 101. On the beginnings of the Saturday-night broadcasts, see Young, *Hello Canada!*, 45–53.

67. Gruneau and Whitson, *Hockey Night in Canada*, 101.

68. C.M. Passmore to Hector Charlesworth, 1 November 1935, LAC CBC, RG 41, vol. 219.

69. T.G. Robinson to W. Arthur Steel, 5 November 1935, LAC CBC, RG 41, vol. 219.

70. In a newsletter about the broadcasts, GM asked its dealers: "Are General Motors Hockey Broadcasts useful in assisting you to sell motor cars?" The fact that the advertising department had to ask the question, and that GM ended its sponsorship after the season, suggests that the dealers' answer was no. *General Motors Hockey Broadcast News*, May 1934, Glenbow IO, vertical box 1a. IM-20-1a.

71. "Imperial Oil Hockey Broadcast on the Air Again," *The Salesmotor*, November 1938, 6–7. Glenbow IO, vertical box 1a. IM-20-1a.

72. C.M. Passmore to W.E. Gladstone Murray, 28 October 1936, LAC CBC, RG 41, vol. 219.

73. Elliott-Hayes Research Corporation, National Radio Ratings Reports, January–April 1941, AO Elliott, F-245-1-0-83.

74. *The Times* (London), 14 December 1934.

75. Arthur Rice-Jones to parents, 21 December 1934, Glenbow ARJ, box 6.

76. Ibid.

77. Frederick Edwards, "Envoys on Ice," *Maclean's*, 15 October 1934, 8.

78. Dave Turnbull, diary entry, 20 December 1930, UMBA.

79. Dave Turnbull, diary entry, 5 November 1928, UMBA.

80. Dave Turnbull, diary entry, 20 December 1928, UMBA.

81. "U.S. Hockey Squad Won't Finish Second Say These Canadians," *The Globe*, 4 February 1936.

82. Dave Turnbull, diary entry, 19 December 1930, UMBA.
83. Müller, "Die Entwicklung des Eishockeys in Davos (I)," 79.
84. Správa náčelníka A. Porgesa za rok 1933-34, Vyroční zpráva Pražské župy Čs.S.K.H, 8 October 1935, Československý svaz ledního hokeje, NMCZ, box 1.
85. Milan Čupka et al., *80 rokov slovenského hokeja* (Bratislava: Slovenský sväz ľadového hokeja, 2009), 36.
86. David Lukšů and Aleš Palán, *Stanislav Konopásek: Hráč, který přežil* (Prague: Edice ČT, 2007), 62–63.
87. Daryl Leeworthy, "Skating on the Border: Hockey, Class, and Commercialism in Interwar Britain," *Histoire sociale/Social History* 48 (2015): 208–209.
88. Bowman, *On the Ice*, 38–39.
89. "Down the Line: A Modern Promoter," *The Atlanta Constitution*, 27 April 1930.
90. "Creation du Palais des sports á Paris," *Paris-soir*, 18 April 1931.
91. "A Letter from Paris," *The Boston Globe*, 27 February 1933. On Dickson and the Palais des Sports, see Robert W. Lewis, *The Stadium Century: Sport, Spectatorship and Mass Society in France* (Manchester: Manchester University Press, 2017), 91–92.
92. Hugh Whitney Morrison to mother, 2 January 1932, LAC, Hugh Whitney Morrison fonds, MG 30, E 408, vol. 2.
93. Crefeld, *Gustav Jaenecke*, 53–58.
94. "Capacity Crowd to See Five Performances of Ice Show," *NYT*, 23 January 1938; "Miss Henie Skates in Garden Tonight," *NYT*, 15 February 1937; and Bryan Smith, *The Breakaway: The Inside Story of the Wirtz Family Business and the Chicago Blackhawks* (Evanston, IL: Northwestern University Press, 2018), 38–41.
95. Frank Selke to Conn Smythe, 27 January and 13 January 1944, AO Smythe, F223-3-1-102.
96. Adams, *Artistic Impressions*, 156.
97. Quoted in ibid., 157.

CHAPTER THREE. OUT OF THE STORM

1. "22,000 Nazis Hold Rally in Garden; Police Check Foes," *NYT*, 21 February 1939.
2. *Der Eissport* 44/1 (December 1933).
3. See Alessio Ponzio, *Shaping the New Man: Youth Training Regimes in Fascist Italy and Nazi Germany* (Madison: University of Wisconsin Press, 2017).
4. Arnd Krüger, "The Role of Sport in German International Politics, 1918–1945," in *Sport and International Politics: Impact of Fascism and Communism on Sport*, eds. Pierre Arnaud and Jim Riordan (London: Routledge, 1999), 85–86.
5. Alfred Steinke, "Von der Entwicklung des Europäischen Eishockey," *Der Eissport* 45/2 (1 December 1935), 13.

6. Michelle Mouton, "Sports, Song, and Socialization: Women's Memories of Youthful Activity and Political Indoctrination in the BDM," *Journal of Women's History* 17, no. 2 (2005): 67–68.

7. "Eissport—Volldampf voraus!" *Eis- und Rollsport*, 20 December 1940, 3–4.

8. "So spielen wir Eishockey! Bobby Bell über Eishockeytechnik und -taktik," *Eis- und Rollsport*, 15 June 1939, 7.

9. "Nicht ruhen und nicht rasten," *Eis- und Rollsport*, 20 November 1940, 2.

10. "Vor den Meisterschaften," *Eis- und Rollsport*, 27 January 1941, 2.

11. "Eissport—Volldampf voraus!" *Eis- und Rollsport*, 20 December 1940, 5.

12. Deutsche Wochenschau (20 January 1944), https://archive.org/details/1944-01-20-Die-Deutsche-Wochenschau-Nr.698.

13. "Ball Invited to Return," *NYT*, 19 January 1936; and Karas, *100 Jahre Eishockey in Berlin*, 84–89.

14. "Rudi Ball on Hockey Team," *Jewish Exponent*, 14 February 1936. See also "Olympia-Juden," *Der Morgen* (Vienna), 24 February 1936.

15. "Sportpalast," *Der Spiegel*, 5 December 1951, www.spiegel.de/spiegel/print/d-20833260.html; and Bernd Matthies, "Nicht nur zumVergnügen," *Der Tagesspiegel*, 13 November 2003, www.tagesspiegel.de/berlin/nicht-nur-zumvergnuegen/464926.html.

16. Alfred Steinke, "Von der Entwicklung des Europäischen Eishockey," *Der Eissport* (1 December 1935), 13.

17. Hardy and Holman, *Hockey: A Global History*, 319–321.

18. Leeworthy, "Skating on the Border," 213.

19. Cecil Rice-Jones to Arthur Rice-Jones, 10 February 1934, Glenbow ARJ, box 5.

20. Arthur Rice-Jones to Cecil Rice-Jones, 7 March 1934, Glenbow ARJ, box 5.

21. Canadian Amateur Hockey Association to Arthur Rice-Jones, 12 June 1939, Glenbow ARJ, box 2.

22. See George Hardy's comments on the organization's expenses in a 1939 speech, "Hockey and Amateur Sport," 12 March 1939. During the war years, the deficits for some Memorial Cup series exceeded $3,000. Summary of Receipts from Allan and Memorial Playdowns, 1929–1951. Schedule of 1939 Playdowns as Reported to Treasurer, CAHA Financial Statements, 29 February 1940, UABA Hardy, box 20.

23. George Hardy, "Hockey and Amateur Sport," 12 March 1939, UABA Hardy, box 20.

24. Ross, *Joining the Clubs*, 244.

25. Ibid., 247.

26. CAHA Memorandum to Paul Loicq, Ligue Internationale de Hockey Sur Glace (undated, 1939?), UABA Hardy, box 19.

27. W. G. Hardy, "Should We Revise Our Amateur Laws? Yes," *Maclean's*, 1 November 1936.

28. Hardy, "Hockey and the 1948 Olympics," not dated, UABA Hardy, box 20.

29. Wong, *Lords of the Rinks*, 150. See also Ross, *Joining the Clubs*, 246–251.

30. Hardy, "Canada Exports Hockey Players," undated, UABA Hardy, box 20.
31. "Hockey and Amateur Sport," 12 March 1939, UABA Hardy, box 19.
32. "Hockey Is My Hobby" (1941), UABA Hardy, box 19.
33. NHL Reserve List, 31 December 1949, UABA Hardy, box 19. On the different option forms, player lists, and sponsorship arrangements, see Ross, "Hockey Capital," 328–329 and 372–376.
34. Ross, *Joining the Clubs,* 311
35. Table I.1 NHL Club Gate Receipts, 1912–13 to 1968–69, in Ross, "Hockey Capital," appendix I.
36. Ibid.; and Table II.1 NHL Club Attendance 1924–25 to 1968–69, in ibid., appendix II.
37. NHL Reserve List, 31 December 1949, UABA Hardy, box 19.
38. William Faulker, "An Innocent at Rinkside," *SI,* 24 January 1955.
39. Dryden, *The Game,* 153.
40. On the failed bids for NHL franchises, see Ross, Hockey Capital," 366–369 and 493–498.
41. Morley Callaghan, "The Game That Makes a Nation," in *Words on Ice: A Collection of Hockey Prose,* ed. Michael P.J. Kennedy (Toronto: Key Porter, 2003), 25.
42. Blake discusses Callaghan's essay and its vision of Canadian nationhood in *Canadian Hockey Literature,* 30–32.
43. Holman and Hardy, *Hockey: A Global History,* 305.
44. Elliott-Hayes Research Corporation, National Radio Ratings Reports, 1946 and 1947, AO, F-245-1-0-167 and 168.
45. Doug Owram, *Born at the Right Time: A History of the Baby Boom Generation* (Toronto: University of Toronto Press, 1996), 4–5, 31, and 102–107.
46. "Dollar-Wise, Minor Hockey Is Bargain," *Toronto Star,* 28 January 1958; "Minor League Hockey Booming," *Toronto Star,* 6 November 1962.
47. "Dollar-Wise, Minor Hockey Is Bargain."
48. Owram, *Born at the Right Time,* 86. See also Robert Rutherdale, "Fatherhood, Masculinity, and the Good Life during Canada's Baby Boom, 1945–1965," *Journal of Family History* 24, no. 3 (1999): 351–373; and Jessica Weiss, "Making Room for Fathers: Men, Women, and Parenting in the United States, 1945–1980," in *A Shared Experience: Men, Women, and the History of Gender,* eds. Laura McCall and Donald Yacovone (New York: New York University Press, 1998).
49. Owram, *Born at the Right Time,* 84.
50. "Dollar-Wise, Minor Hockey Is Bargain" and "Minor League Hockey Booming."
51. Kidd and Macfarlane, *The Death of Hockey,* 111.
52. Glenn Resch, oral history interview by Andrea Kaminsky, February 1976, Columbia University.
53. Kidd and Macfarlane, *The Death of Hockey,* 55–57; Gruneau and Whitson, *Hockey Night in Canada,* 136–137; Holman and Hardy, *Hockey: A Global History,* 300–304.

54. M. Ann Hall, *The Girl and the Game: A History of Women's Sport in Canada* (Toronto: University of Toronto Press, 2002), 105–106. See also Adams, *Artistic Impressions*, 158–159.

55. Kevin Plummer, "Historicist: 'She Certainly Doesn't Play Like a Girl,'" *Torontoist*, 18 October 2014, https://torontoist.com/2014/10/historicist-she-certainly-doesnt-play-like-a-girl; Interview with Abby Hoffman, 20 December 1956, CBC Digital Archives, www.cbc.ca/archives/entry/ab-hoffman-turns-out-to-be-a-girl

56. "The Story of Fred Sasakamoose, An Indigenous Hockey Pioneer," *Only a Game*, 14 September 2018, www.wbur.org/onlyagame.

57. Cecil Harris, *Breaking the Ice: The Black Experience in Professional Hockey* (Toronto: Insomniac Press, 2003), 82.

58. Ibid., 48–49.

59. National Collegiate Athletic Association, "Scholastic Reviews," in *Official Ice Hockey Guide* (New York: National Collegiate Athletic Bureau, 1953).

60. Amateur Hockey Association of the United States, Bulletin 158, 20 August 1960, and Bulletin 185, 10 June 1963, MNHS, Benjamin Berger Papers, box 20.

61. "Pee-Wee Hockey," *NYT*, 5 February 1950.

62. "Shinny Grows Up in Michigan," *Detroit Free Press*, 21 January 1962.

63. "Pee Wee Hockey Is Big," *The Boston Globe*, 19 March 1960.

64. Ibid.

65. "Negro Youths Like Tough Hockey Game," *Cleveland Call and Post*, 2 April 1960.

66. President's Report, NHL Meeting, 19 September 1958, AO Smythe, F 223-3-1-70.

67. Prior to their final game, Soviet officials visited the Czechoslovak coaches to encourage them to defeat the Swedes. A Swedish win and the expected Soviet loss to Canada would have left the two teams tied in the standings, leading to a one-game playoff for the silver medal. Report on 1954 world championships in Stockholm, Předsednictví sekce ledního hokeje, March 1954, NACZ SVTVS, box 53.

68. "Russia Defeats Canada 7-2 to Win World Hockey Title," *G&M*, 8 March 1954.

69. "Russia Proves So-Called Canadian Senior B's Not Good Enough," *Toronto Daily Star*, 8 March 1954.

70. "Russians Are Thorough: Soviet Hockey Leaders Stress Training," *G&M*, 28 February 1955. Americans who played against the Soviets at the 1957 world championships described them as doing "everything automatically." Undated clipping (March 1957?), "Russians Change Hockey," clipping book, Wendell Anderson collection, MNHS.

71. See James Riordan, *Sport in Soviet Society: Development of Sport and Physical Education in Russia and the USSR* (Cambridge: Cambridge University Press, 1977), chap. 5; and Robert Edelman, *Serious Fun: A History of Spectator Sport in the USSR* (Oxford: Oxford University Press, 1993), chaps. 2 and 3. On the Soviets' entry to the

Olympics, see Jennifer Parks, *The Olympic Games, the Soviet Sports Bureaucracy, and the Cold War: Red Sport, Red Tape* (Lanham, MD: Lexington, 2017), chap. 1.

72. Riordan, *Sport in Soviet Society*, 150–151. On Soviet sport and the hero-worker ideal, see Hart Cantelon, "The Social Reproduction of Sport: A Weberian Analysis of the Rational Development of Ice Hockey under Scientific Socialism in the Soviet Union" (PhD diss., University of Birmingham, 1981).

73. Riordan, *Sport in Soviet Society*, 165.

74. Victor Peppard and James Riordan, *Playing Politics: Soviet Sport Diplomacy to 1992* (Greenwich, CT: JAI Press, 1993), 63.

75. Juliane Fürst. *Stalin's Last Generation: Soviet Post-war Youth and the Emergence of Mature Socialism* (Oxford: Oxford University Press, 2010).

76. Scott W. Palmer, *Dictatorship of the Air: Aviation Culture and the Fate of Modern Russia* (Cambridge: Cambridge University Press, 2006).

77. On early Soviet hockey, see Lawrence Martin, *The Red Machine: The Soviet Quest to Dominate Canada's Game* (Toronto: Doubleday, 1980), chap. 4. For accounts based on Russian archival sources and memoirs, see Mathieu Boivin-Chouinard, "Le hockey bourgeois est-il compatible avec la morale prolétarienne ? La naissance du hockey soviétique dans la complexité politique du stalinisme d'après-guerre," *Bulletin d'histoire politique* 22, no. 2 (2014): 53–76; Boivin-Chouinard, *Chaïbou! Histoire du hockey russe, vol. 1: Des origines à la série du siècle* (Longueuil, QC: Kéruss, 2011), 25–42; Hart Cantelon, "Revisiting the Introduction of Ice Hockey into the Former Soviet Union," in *Putting It on Ice, vol. 2: Internationalizing "Canada's Game,"* ed. Colin D. Howell, 29–38 (Halifax, NS: Saint Mary's University, 2011); Paul Harder, "Developing World Championship Hockey in the USSR: The Inside Story, 1946–1972" (MA thesis, Carleton University, 2004), chap. 1; and Konstantin Fuks, "The Rebirth of *Dinamo Riga*: From the Glorious Soviet Past to the Kontinental Hockey League" (MA thesis, University of Turku, 2013), 34–41.

78. Fuks, "The Rebirth of *Dinamo Riga*," 38–39.

79. Ibid., 39–40; "Nasha istoriya. Chast 1: 1946–1947," *Championat.ru*, 6 July 2010, www.championat.com/hockey/article-3103459-nasha-istorija-chast-1-1946-1947.html; Sergei Glukhov, "Pervoprokhodtsy," *Krasnaya mashina*, 9 February 2019, http://km1954.ru/moscowltc/pervye.php; and Martin, *The Red Machine*, 24–30.

80. Edelman, *Serious Fun*, 112.

81. Harder, "Developing World Championship Hockey in the USSR," 10.

82. Riordan, *Sport in Soviet Society*, 249–250; and Edelman, *Serious Fun*, 102–105.

83. Edelman, *Serious Fun*, 94; and Riordan, *Sport in Soviet Society*, 178–179.

84. Avery Brundage to Sigfrid Edström, 7 December 1950, UILA Brundage.

85. See Stephen E. Hanson, *Time and Revolution: Marxism and the Design of Soviet Institutions* (Chapel Hill: University of North Carolina Press, 1997).

86. This version of the story is adapted from Ken Dryden's article "To Russia with Love," *Maclean's*, 1 April 1974. Dryden heard the story during his fact-finding

mission to the Soviet Union and Czechoslovakia in summer 1973. Bukač told me the same story during our 2018 interview in Prague.

87. Anatoli Tarasov, *Road to Olympus* (Richmond Hill, ON: Simon & Schuster of Canada, 1972), 19.

88. Harder discusses writing by and about Tarasov, compared to what is revealed in Russian archives and memoirs by other figures in Soviet hockey, in chapter 5 of "Developing World Championship Hockey in the USSR." Stanislav Gridasov discusses Tarasov's historical role in the building of Soviet hockey and his own version of that role in his book *Kristal'nyye lyudi* (Moscow: Pyatyy Rim, 2018) and his various online essays.

89. Gridasov, *Kristal'nyye lyudi*, 262–269; and "Kak Tarasov perepisyval istoriyu sovetskogo khokkeya," *johndonne.ru*, 27 April 2018, johndonne.ru/kak-tarasov-perepisyval-istoriyu-sovetskogo-khokkeya/.

90. The records of the State Hockey Committee from this transitional period of the late 1950s have been copied from the Russian State Archive in Moscow and deposited in the University of Alberta Archives. See, in particular, Plan for Preparation for the National Team for 1958 World Championships, Fonds 7576, Opis 16, delo 312, UABA Sov.

91. "Aleksandr Yakushev: 'Kogda kanadskiy zhurnalist yel gazetu so svoyey statyey, my aplodirovali i krichali: "Molodets!",'" *Sport Ekspress*, 2 January 2017, www.sport-express.ru/hockey/russia/reviews/aleksandr-yakushev-kogda-kanadskiy-zhurnalist-el-gazetu-so-svoey-statey-my-aplodirovali-i-krichali-molodec-1082601/.

92. Stanislav Gridasov, "Kak Tarasov perepisyval istoriyu sovetskogo khokkeya," *Krasnaya mashina*, 27 April 2018, km1954.ru/hall/tarasov_4.php.

93. Ibid. See also Harder, "Developing World Championship Hockey in the USSR," 119–125.

94. The narrative draws from Konopásek's memoir, *Stanislav Konopásek: Hráč, který přežil*, and from the protocol of the state security agency, dated 20 July 1950, in the StBA, Proces Bohumil Modrý a spol., file v-2654 MV. Among the books and articles on the hockey players' arrests are Vladimír Škutina and Robert Bakalář, *Ztracená léta: Příběh hokejového zločinu* (Prague: Helios, 1990); and Jan Kalous, "Hokej jako politikum: Komunistický režim a hokej 1948–1989," in *Sport v komunistkém Československu 1945–1989*, eds. Jan Kalous and František Kolář (Prague: Ustav pro studium totalitních režimů, 2015).

95. Lukšů and Palán, *Stanislav Konopásek: Hráč, který přežil*, 153.

96. Bouhmil Modrý, interrogation transcript, 5 April 1950, StBA, Proces Bohumil Modrý a spol., file v-2654 MV.

97. Modrý's story is told in fictional form, on interviews with Modrý's daughter, in Josef Haslinger's novel, *Jáchymov* (Berlin: S. Fischer, 2011).

98. The most damning case against Zábrodský is made by Jiří Macků in his book *Kauza Zábrodský* (Prague: TYPO IP, 2005). The book's subtitle indicates the author's view: *Hokejový génius, ale jinak lotr*—A hockey genius, but otherwise a swine.

99. David Lukšů and Aleš Palán, *Vladimír Zábrodský: Skutečný příběh hokejové legendy* (Prague: Edice ČT, 2010), 225.

100. Lukšů and Palán, *Stanislav Konopásek: Hráč, který přežil*, 161.

101. "Hockey Is Considered a 'Bourgeois' Sport in Communist Hungary," 18 July 1953, OSA RFE 300-1-2-36973, General Records: Information Items, Open Society Archives, electronic record.

102. Secret report, Czechoslovak consulate, Zurich, to Ministry of Foreign Affairs, 21 March 1953, Lední hokej—zprávy 1952–56, NACZ SVTVS, file no. 123, box 53.

103. Viktor Veverka and coworkers at the Zbirovia factory, Zbiroh, to State Committee on Physical Education and Sport, 20 January 1954, Lední hokej—disiplinarní 1953-1954, NACZ SVTVS, file no. 154, box 53.

104. Minutes, Executive of State Committee on Physical Education and Sport, 14 February 1956, Předsednictvo 1953–1956, NACZ SVTVS, box 16.

105. Brundage to Sigfrid Edström, 7 December 1950, UILA Brundage.

106. Brundage, Private and Confidential Memo (undated, after May 1951), UILA Brundage

107. Parks, *The Olympic Games, the Soviet Sports Bureaucracy, and the Cold War*, 4–6 and 12–13; and Matthew P. Llewellyn and John Gleaves, *The Rise and Fall of Olympic Amateurism* (Urbana: University of Illinois Press, 2016), 116–118.

108. Brundage to Joe Forshaw, 24 June 1946, UILA Brundage, box 263.

109. Otto Mayer to J. S. Edström, 11 August 1947, copy, IIHF Correspondence 1929–1964, IOC HA, D-RM02-HOCKE/003. See also UILA Brundage, box 107, folder 5, and box 168, folder 15. On the disagreement, see Hardy and Holman, *Hockey: A Global History*, 308–309.

110. Brundage to James Groves, Toronto, 22 June 1965, UILA Brundage.

111. Brundage, "Problem of the Winter Olympics" (undated memo), Report of the Commission of Inquiry into the Olympic Games, submitted 6 August 1968, UILA Brundage.

112. Walter Brown to US Olympic Association, 13 March 1964, UILA Brundage.

113. Llewellyn and Gleaves, *The Rise and Fall of Olympic Amateurism*, 118–120.

CHAPTER FOUR. TOWARD NEW DIRECTIONS

1. "The Boys of Winters," *Maclean's*, 1 April 1975, 66.

2. Hardy and Holman, *Hockey: A Global History*, 305.

3. Ibid., 195; Markku Jokisipilä, "Maple Leaf, Hammer, and Sickle: International Ice Hockey during the Cold War," *Sport History Review* 37 (2006): 46–47; and Tobias Stark, "O Canada, We Stand on Guard for Thee: Representations of Canadian Hockey Players in the Swedish Press, 1920–2016," in *Hockey: Challenging Canada's Game/Au-delà du sport national*, 190–192.

4. CBC-TV Promotion Report: NHL Hockey, 12 July 1968, H.N.I.C. CBC Promotion, Glenbow IO, Series IM-13, box 10. On the cultural influence of televised

hockey in Canada during the 1950s and '60s, see Gruneau and Whitson, *Hockey Night in Canada*, 103–107; and Paul Rutherford, *When Television Was Young: Primetime Canada 1952–1967* (Toronto: University of Toronto Press, 1990), 268–274.

5. Andrew Cohen argues for Pearson's importance in the making of contemporary Canada, in *Lester B. Pearson* (Toronto: Penguin Canada, 2008).

6. On the debate surrounding the proposed new Canadian flag, see José Eduardo Igartua, *The Other Quiet Revolution: National Identities in English Canada, 1945–71* (Vancouver: UBC Press, 2006), chap. 7.

7. Benoît Melançon, *The Rocket: A Cultural History*, trans. Fred A. Reed (Vancouver: Greystone, 2009), 170–176; and Terry Gitersos, "'Ça devient une question d'être maîtres chez nous': The Canadiens, Nordiques, and the Politics of Québécois Nationalism, 1979–1984" (PhD diss., University of Western Ontario, 2011), 64–65.

8. Roch Carrier, *Our Life with the Rocket: The Maurice Richard Story*, trans. Sheila Fischman (Toronto: Viking, 2001), 210. On the 1955 riot, see Benoît Melançon, *The Rocket: A Cultural History*, trans. Fred A. Reed (Vancouver: Greystone, 2009), part II.

9. Elliott Research Corporation teleratings reports, January–March 1960, AO Elliott, F 245-6-0-1.

10. As Terry Gitersos points out, however, the leaders of the Quiet Revolution paid little attention to Canadiens hockey, except in the aftermath of the Richard riot. See "Ça devient une question d'être maîtres chez nous," 60–62.

11. G.E. Mortimore, "What Happened to Hockey? Polite Revolt against the Tycoons," *G&M*, 15 March 1963.

12. "Czar Spears Critics," *G&M*, 22 March 1963.

13. *House of Commons Debates, 26th Parliament, 2nd Session*: vol. 12, 12336, 15 March 1965, http://parl.canadiana.ca/view/oop.debates_HOC2602.

14. Quoted in Ross, "Hockey Capital," 541.

15. Ibid., 535.

16. "Statement by Juckes 'Ludicrous': Campbell," *G&M*, 15 February 1966.

17. "Fitness Council Asks for Bill to Protect CAHA from NHL," *G&M*, 26 January 1967.

18. Frank Lowe, "The City That Went on a Hockey Jag," *Weekend*, 9 January 1960, 2–5, 19.

19. On the NHL's expansion plans in the 1960s, see Jenish, *The NHL—A Centennial History*, chap. 7. Andrew Ross provides the most detailed account of expansion, based on archival records of NHL meetings, in the unpublished second part of his dissertation, "Hockey Capital," chap. 11.

20. "NHL Fever Soaring," *The Sun* (Vancouver), 12 March 1965.

21. "Canucks Tied to NHL Loss," *The Sun* (Vancouver), 10 February 1966.

22. Session of 10 February 1966, *House of Commons Debates, 27th Parliament, 1st Session*, II: 995. http://parl.canadiana.ca/view/oop.debates_HOC2701.

23. Ibid.

24. Ross, "Hockey Capital," 535.

25. Ibid., 553.

26. George Grant, *Lament for a Nation: The Defeat of Canadian Nationalism*, 40th anniversary edition (Montreal and Kingston: McGill University–Queen's University Press, 2005), 5, 9.

27. Other nine-year dynasties include Rangers FC in the Scottish Football League (1988–97), the Tokyo Giants in the Japan Series (1965–73), the University of North Carolina in women's soccer (1986–94), and the University of Iowa in wrestling (1978–86).

28. On dynasties in European soccer leagues, see Stefan Szymanski, *Money and Soccer: A Soccernomics Guide* (New York: Nation Books, 2015), chap. 1. On outcome uncertainty, see Brian Mills and Rodney Fort, "League-Level Attendance and Outcome Uncertainty in U.S. Pro Sports Leagues," *Economic Inquiry* 52, no. 1 (2014): 205–218. For praise of dynasties, see Mike Woodward, "Do Dynasties Kill Sports?" *Medium.com*, 2 February 2019, https://medium.com/@mikeaw/do-dynasties-kill-sports-7b418385b4c.

29. Mikhail Prozumenshchikov, "Sports as a Mirror of Eastern Europe's Crises," *Russian Studies in History* 49, no. 2 (2010): 51–93.

30. Stark, *Folkhemmet på is*, 281.

31. Minutes, 51st Annual Congress of the IIHF, Vienna, 18–29 March 1967, IIHF Minutes.

32. On debates within the Soviet hockey section during this transitional period after the Moscow world championships, see Harder, "Developing World Championship Hockey in the USSR," 50–56.

33. Gridasov, *Kristal'nyye lyudi*, 274–276.

34. Tarasov, *Road to Olympus*, 108.

35. Cantelon, "The Social Reproduction of Sport," 221.

36. "O rabote po khokkeyu v fizkul'turnykh organizatsiyakh SSSR: otchetnyy doklad Prezidiuma VKHS na plenume sektsii 1957," f. 7576, o. 16, d. 311, pp. 30–31, UABA Sov.

37. Plan podgoteki svornom komandy sssr po chokkeyu k pervenstvu mira 1958 goda, f. 7576, o. 16, d. 311, pp. 119–121. UABA Sov.

38. Valerii Vasiliev, "Moi krestnyi otets," in *Trenery sedeyot rano*, ed. L. V. Rossoshik (Moscow: Terra-Sport, 2001), 28.

39. Boris Mikhailov, *Takova khokkeynaya zhizn* (Moscow: Eksmo, 2008), 5.

40. Harder, "Developing World Championship Hockey in the USSR," 80–86.

41. "Slovo masteram khokkeya," *Yunyi tekhnik*, 1/1966, 45.

42. "Otkuda poshla 'Zolotaya shayba,'" *Zolotaya shayba*, https://zshr.ru/redaction/1/page/view; and Harder, "Developing World Championship Hockey in the USSR," 91.

43. Vladislav Tretiak, with V. Snegirev, *The Hockey I Love*, trans. Anatole Konstantin (Toronto: Fitzhenry & Whiteside, 1977), 16; and Andrew Podnieks and John Sanful, "The Essential Tretiak," in Szemberg and Podnieks, *World of Hockey*, 88.

44. George Edward Kingston, "The Organisation and Development of Ice Hockey During Childhood in the Soviet Union, Czechoslovakia, Sweden and Canada" (PhD diss., University of Alberta, 1977), 117–121.

45. Mikhailov, *Takova khokkeynaya zhizn*, 17. On Red Army's resources and its leverage with young athletes, see Robert F. Baumann, "The Central Army Sports Club (TsSKA): Forging a Military Tradition in Soviet Ice Hockey," *Journal of Sport History*, 15, no. 2 (1988): 160–161.

46. According to archival sources, Tarasov and Chernyshev were the main drivers of concentrating talent in Moscow, whereas the state hockey officials wished to have more competitive parity in the domestic league. See Harder, "Developing World Championship Hockey in the USSR," chap. 4.

47. Evgenii Rubin, *Pan ili propal! Zhizneopisanie* (Moscow: Zakharov, 2000), 309–310.

48. N. Kurdjukov and K. Romenski, Soviet Olympic Committee, to Artur Takac, IOC, 28 June 1972, UILA Brundage, file 14, box 161.

49. "Aleksandr Yakushev: 'Ves mir byl uveren, chto russkim v Kanade delat nechego,'" *Argumenty i Fakty*, 2 September 2017, www.aif.ru/sport/hockey/aleksandr_yakushev_ves_mir_byl_uveren_chto_russkim_v_kanade_delat_nechego.

50. "Private Game—No Admittance," *SI*, 12 April 1965. On David Molson's role in NHL expansion, see Ross, "Hockey Capital," chap. 11, especially 507–513.

51. Norm Lenardon, Ugo DeBiasio, Dave Rusnell, and Ad Tambellini, interview with Scott Young, undated, Notes—Hockey, AO Young, F 1134-6-0-48.

52. The interviews were part of Young's research for his book, *War on Ice: Canada in International Hockey* (Toronto: McClelland and Stewart, 1976).

53. Tobias Stark, "O Canada, We Stand on Guard for Thee: Representations of Canadian Hockey Players in the Swedish Press, 1920–2016," in *Hockey: Challenging Canada's Game/Au-delà du sport national* (Ottawa, ON: Canadian Museum of History/University of Ottawa Press, 2018), 190.

54. Tobias Stark, "'How Swede It Is': Börje Salming and the Migration of Swedish Ice Hockey Players to the NHL, 1957–2012," in *Constructing the Hockey Family: Home, Community, Bureaucracy and Marketplace*, eds. Lori Dithurbide and Colin Howell (Halifax, NS: Saint Mary's University, 2012), 364–393 and 376.

55. *Toronto Star*, 3 July 1994, HHOF Clippings.

56. *The Hamilton Spectator*, 31 March 2003, HHOF Clippings. See also *Toronto Star*, 22 April 2000; and *National Post*, 17 April 2001, HHOF Clippings.

57. Stark, "The Pioneer, the Pal and the Poet: Masculinities and National Identities in Canadian, Swedish, and Soviet-Russian Hockey during the Cold War," in *Putting It on Ice, vol. 2: Internationalizing "Canada's Game,"* ed. Colin D. Howell (Halifax, NS: Saint Mary's University, 2011), 39–40.

58. Ibid. See also Stark, "O Canada, We Stand on Guard for Thee," 185–194.

59. Stark, *Folkhemmet på is*, 40.

60. See Sejerstad, *The Age of Social Democracy*, chap. 9; and Niels Keyser Nielsen, *Body, Sport, and Society in Norden: Essays in Cultural History* (Aarhus, Denmark: University of Aarhus Press, 2005), 160–168.

61. Keyser Nielsen, *Body, Sport, and Society in Norden*, 168.

62. Stark, *Folkhemmet på is*, 229–230; Eivind Å Skille, "Sport for All in Scandinavia: Sport Policy and Participation in Norway, Sweden and Denmark,"

International Journal of Sport Policy and Politics 3, no. 3 (November 2011): 327–339; Johan R. Norberg, "A Mutual Dependency: Nordic Sports Organizations and the State," *The International Journal of the History of Sport* 14, no. 3 (1997): 115–135.

63. Minutes, 31st Congress of the LIHG, St. Moritz, 28 January–8 February 1948; and Minutes, European Executive Committee, Zurich, 26 July 1948, IIHF Minutes.

64. "Crowd Storms a Stadium," *The Manchester Guardian*, 17 February 1949; and "Eight Hockey Fans Hurt in Rush to See Sweden Tie Canada," *NYT*, 17 February 1949.

65. "Canadians Down Swedish Six, 8–0," *NYT*, 2 March 1954.

66. Quoted in Stark, *Folkhemmet på is*, 271. Translation by Stark.

67. Ibid., 266.

68. Ibid., 250–253.

69. Quoted in Stark, *Folkhemmet på is*, 261. Translation by Stark.

70. Ibid., 127.

71. A. Pedersen Dømmestrup, quoted in Keyser Nielsen, *Body, Sport, and Society in Norden*, 97.

72. Jouko Kokkonen, "Sports and Nationalism—United Forever?," *Motion: Sport in Finland*, I/2003, 8.

73. David Kirby, *A Concise History of Finland* (Cambridge: Cambridge University Press, 2006), 288.

74. Jari Lämsä, "Lions on the Ice: The Success Story of Finnish Ice Hockey," in *Nordic Elite Sport: Same Ambitions—Different Tracks*, eds. Svein S. Andersen and Lars Tore (Oslo: Universitetsforlaget, 2011), 158–159.

75. "Fast-Growing Tampere Is a Rival to the Finnish Capital," *NYT*, 14 March 1965.

76. Jouko Kokkonen, manuscript for *Koko kansan leijonat*, coauthored with Markku Jokisipilä and Kalle Rantala (Helsinki: Docendo, 2018).

77. "Swedish Hockey Star Earns $50,000 as Amateur," *NYT*, 9 February 1965; and Brundage to Hugh Weir, 5 November 1971; Jukka Uunila, Finnish Olympic Committee, to Artur Takac, 26 January 1972, and Hugh Weir to Takac, 25 October 1971, IOC Commissions and Committees—Eligibility, UILA Brundage.

78. Lämsä, "Lions on the Ice," 158–161; Stark, "How Swede It Is," 378–379; and Jyri Backman, *Ishockeyns amerikanisering: En studie av svensk och finsk elitishockey* (Malmö, Sweden: University of Malmö, 2018), 149–152.

79. Kingston, "The Organisation and Development of Ice Hockey during Childhood in the Soviet Union, Czechoslovakia, Sweden and Canada," chap. 2; and Lämsä, "Lions on the Ice," 158–164.

80. "West 'Digs' Hockey, Talks Up Pro Loop," *The Boston Globe*, 1 March 1960; "Winter Olympics TV Is Smashing Success," *The Boston Globe*, 24 February 1960; and *Detroit Free Press*, 28 February 1960.

81. "14,028 See Blues Gain 3-1 Decision," *NYT*, 7 March 1960.

82. Herb Goren, Press Liaison report for 1959–60, attached to NHL president's report, AO Smythe, 223-3-1-107. Jack McCartan, interview, 29 March 2019.

83. Ibid.
84. "Youth Hockey Is BIG in Bay State," *The Boston Globe,* 24 January 1965.
85. "Minnesota Has 18,000 Boys in Youth Hockey," *Minneapolis Star,* 28 December 1966.
86. Thomas J. Baerwald, "Forces at Work on the Landscape," in *Minnesota in a Century of Change: The State and Its People since 1900,* ed. Clifford E. Clark (St. Paul: Minnesota Historical Society Press, 1989), 20.
87. See Stephen Hardy and Andrew Holman, "Hockey Towns: The Making of Special Places in America and Canada," in *Putting it on Ice: Proceedings of the 2012 Hockey Conference,* eds. Lori Dithurbide and Colin Howell (December 2013), 42–45.
88. "Williard Ikola Talks, Bob Sansavere Listens," *Pioneer Press* (St. Paul), 2 March 2008, www.twincities.com/2008/03/02/willard-ikola-talks-bob-sansevere-listens/.
89. Jeffrey Manuel, *Taconite Dreams: The Struggle to Sustain Mining on Minnesota's Iron Range, 1915–2000* (Minneapolis: University of Minnesota Press, 2015).
90. See Patricia Cavanaugh, *Politics and Freeways: Building the Twin Cities Interstate System* (Minneapolis: University of Minnesota Center for Transportation Studies and Center for Urban and Regional Affairs, 2006).
91. M. Jeffrey Hardwick, *Mall Maker: Victor Gruen, Architect of an American Dream* (Philadelphia: University of Pennsylvania Press, 2010), 155–156.
92. Chad Montrie, "'A Bigoted, Prejudiced, Hateful Little Area': The Making of an All-White Suburb in the Deep North," *Journal of Urban History* (April 2017): 7–9.
93. US Department of Commerce, *1970 Census of Population and Housing: Census Tracts—Minneapolis-St. Paul, Minnesota, Standard Metropolitan Statistical Area* (Washington, DC: US Government Printing Office, 1972), Table P.1. www2.census.gov/library/publications/decennial/1970/phc-1/39204513p13ch01.pdf.
94. Bob O'Connor, interview, 29 August 2015.
95. John Hamre, "Why Is Edina Hockey So Successful?," *Let's Play Hockey!,* 25 February 2015, http://pointstreaksites.com/view/lph/news-1147/hamre-stored/why-is-edina-hockey-so-successful; "Pre-varsity Training Keys Edina's Success," *Minneapolis Tribune,* 22 February 1969, and "Booming Youth Program Rings Metro," *Minneapolis Star,* 22 December 1966.
96. "'There's No One Like Henry' for Warroad Hockey Boosters," *Pioneer Press* (St. Paul), 20 February 1969.
97. Game account is taken from assorted clippings in collections of the Warroad Historical Society.
98. E. M. Swift, "The Thrill of a Lifetime," *SI,* 7 March 1983, 80–94.
99. Nathan Wells, "2015 Minnesota Boys' High School Hockey Tournament Breaks Attendance Record," *SB Nation: College Hockey,* 7 March 2015, www.sbncollegehockey.com/high-school-hockey/2015/3/7/8167923/2015-minnesota-boys-high-school-total-attendance-record-135618.
100. Luděk Bukač, "Metodický dopis: Zkušenost z tréninku sovětských hokejových mužstev v přípravném období 1966–1967" (Prague: Ústřední výbor československého svazu tělesné výchovy, 1968).

101. Luděk Bukač, "Metodický dopis: Komplexní rozbor mistrovství světa a Evropy v ledním hokeji v Praze 1972" (Prague: Olympia, 1973).

102. Luděk Bukač and František Suchan, *Bukač: Moje hokejové století* (Brno: JOTA, 2018), 127.

103. Ibid., 118.

104. Vladimir Kostka, "The Czechoslovakian Youth Ice Hockey Training System," trans. Ladislav Hudak (unbound publication of Canadian Amateur Hockey Association, 1979), 1.

105. David Lukšů, *Žit jako Holík, Životné a hokejové zápasy Jaroslava Holíka* (Prague: Epocha, 2015), 142–144.

106. Documents and press coverage on the response to the August 1968 invasion, by sports officials and Czechoslovak athletes, are collected in OSA RFE 300-30-5, Czechoslovak Unit, Subject Files IV, box 15.

107. Informace o stavu vyšetřování trestních věcí v souvislosti s událostmi z 28, i.j.199; and Zpráva o bezpečnostní situaci na území ČSSR z 28. na 29. 3. 1969, 8 April 1969, A 10 (Sekretariát státního tajemníka MV ČSSR plk. JUDr. Jána Majera) i.j. 181, StBA.

108. Zpráva o bezpečnostní situaci na území ČSSR z 28. na 29. 3. 1969.

109. Ibid.; and Zpráva o situaci v Praze a jiných krajích v souvislosti s událostmi po hokejovém utkání ČSSR-SSSR v noci z 28. na 29. 3. 1969, A 34 (Hlavní správa kontrarozvědky Sboru národní bezpečnosti–II. správa SNB), i.j.3252A, StBA.

110. Oldřich Tůma, "'They Had No Tanks This Time and They Got Four Goals': The Hockey Events in Czechoslovakia in 1969 and the Fall of Alexander Dubček," in *The (Inter-Communist) Cold War on Ice: Soviet-Czechoslovak Ice Hockey Politics, 1967–1969*, Cold War International History Project Working Paper no. 69, ed. James G. Hershberg (February 2014), 31. See also the essays in the same publication by John Soares and Mikhail Prozumenschikov and the selected documents from Czechoslovak archives.

111. Fredrik Backman, *Us against You,* trans. Neil Smith (New York: Atria, 2017), 1.

112. Hardy and Holman, *Hockey: A Global History,* chap. 18.

CHAPTER FIVE. ON THE BRINK

1. See Donald Mackintosh and Donna Greenhorn, "Hockey Diplomacy and Canadian Foreign Policy," *Journal of Canadian Studies/Revue d'études canadiennes* 28, no. 2 (1993): 105–107.

2. Paper Presented by the Canadian Committee on International Hockey Negotiations, attachment to L. A. D. Stephens, Under-Secretary of State for External Affairs, to Canadian Embassy Moscow, 23 March 1972, LAC ExtRel, Cultural Affairs: Sports Competitions, 55-26-Hockey-1-USST-vol 2. On Canada's withdrawal from international hockey as prelude to the Summit Series, see Hardy and Holman,

Hockey: A Global History, 366–367; and Roy MacSkimming, *Cold War: The Amazing Canada-Soviet Hockey Series of 1972* (Vancouver: Greystone, 1996), chap. 1.

3. Ken Dryden, *Game Change: The Life and Death of Steve Montador, and the Future of Hockey* (Toronto: Signal, 2017), 30.

4. Stephen Smith, *Puckstruck: Distracted, Delighted, and Distressed by Canada's Hockey Obsession* (Vancouver: Greystone, 2014), 183.

5. "Everybody Likes Canada," *Montreal Gazette*, 2 September 1972.

6. Memo, Information Division, 21 June 1972. Cultural Affairs, Sports Competition: Hockey, External Affairs fonds, LAC ExtRel, RG25-A-3-c, Vol. 10921, File 55-26-HOCKEY-1-USSR.

7. Jack Ludwig, "Team Canada in War and Peace," *Maclean's*, December 1972, 32.

8. Ted Blackman, "Fearless Forecast: We'll Win," *Montreal Gazette*, September 1972.

9. "Boris Mikhaylov: 'Khotel udarit' kanadtsa kon'kom mezhdu nog. No ne dostal,'" *Sport Ekspress*, 2 September 2017, www.sport-express.ru/hockey/reviews/boris-mihaylov-hotel-udarit-kanadca-konkom-mezhdu-nog-no-ne-dostal-1303604/; Mikhailov, *Takova khokkeynaya zhizn*, 55.

10. Mikhailov, *Takova khokkeynaya zhizn*, 55.

11. "'Khokkei, kotoryi ne zabudetsya nikogda': 45 let nazad startovala Superseriya SSSR-Kanada," *Tass*, 1 September 2017, https://tass.ru/sport/4522544.

12. Mikhailov, *Takova khokkeynaya zhizn*, 55.

13. Ludwig, "Team Canada in War and Peace," 33.

14. "Hockey People, Fans Praise Russian Team," *Montreal Gazette*, 4 September 1972.

15. "A Dark Day: Sept. 2, 1972; When Pride Turned to Trauma," *Montreal Gazette*, 4 September 1972.

16. "Esposito Addresses the Nation," *1972SummitSeries.com*, www.1972summitseries.com/espospeech.html.

17. Jack Ludwig, *Hockey Night in Moscow* (Toronto: McClelland and Stewart, 1972), 75.

18. Jim Taylor, "Espo—A Night to Hit the Boos," *Vancouver Sun*, 9 September 1972.

19. Ludwig, *Hockey Night in Moscow*, 27.

20. "To Russia with Love," *Vancouver Sun*, 9 September 1972.

21. Scott Young, "A Sandwich Named Desire" (undated manuscript), 71. Notes—Hockey, AO Young, F 1134-6-0-48. Tarasov's original account of the conversation is in *Eto khokkei* (Moscow: Molodaya gvardiya, 1971), 164–165.

22. Young, "A Sandwich Named Desire," 72.

23. Dryden and MacGregor, *Home Game*, 193. See Neil Earle, "Hockey as Canadian Popular Culture: Team Canada 1972, Television and the Canadian Identity," *Journal of Canadian Studies* 30, no. 2 (1995): 107–123.

24. Looking at TV listings for Toronto during a random winter week in 1968, we find two international games in Winnipeg, two college games, and three Junior

A games, along with the Leafs on Wednesday and Saturday nights. "Sports Telecasts," *G&M,* 5 January 1968.

25. *Hockey Night in Canada* Audience Reports, fall 1970 and winter 1970/71, Glenbow IO, IM-13, box 11.

26. CBC Circular, TV and Radio Audience Ratings, 1971-75, Glenbow IO, IM-13, box 10.

27. Audience Data Reports, 1972-1973, Glenbow IO, IM-13, box 11.

28. Creative Research Group, "Toward an Understanding of the Perceptions of Toronto Hockey Fans: A Qualitative Assessment," October 1973, report prepared for MacLaren Advertising. Glenbow IO, IM-13, box 11.

29. Ibid., 13.

30. Following the mandate of the Broadcasting Act of 1958, which required licensed stations to provide service that was "basically Canadian in content and character," the Board of Broadcast Governors established quotas of 55 percent Canadian content for the whole day and 40 percent in the evening. The definition of "Canadian content" was slippery, however. For instance, baseball's World Series could be ruled Canadian, in the years before MLB had a team in Canada, because it was of general public interest. Rutherford, *When Television Was Young,* 104-107.

31. "One Way the CBC Can Stop Slide in NHL Ratings," *Toronto Star,* 2 January 1973. Clippings file. LAC CBC, RG 41, vol. 218.

32. Creative Research Group, "Toward an Understanding of the Perceptions of Toronto Hockey Fans," 11, 7.

33. For example, on April 17, 1958, 46 percent of viewers of the French broadcast were women, compared to 43 percent men (the remaining 11 percent were children). Ratings report on NHL Playoffs on Television, April 1958, AO Elliott, F 245-23-0-1126.

34. Hockey Night in Canada Audience Data, 1972-73, Glenbow IO, IM-13, box 11.

35. Survey of Viewers of 1965 Stanley Cup Playoffs, Edmonton, job files, AO Elliott, F 245-23-0 2044.

36. Memo, R. G. Reid to D. C. Twaits, 28 August 1972, TV and Radio Audience Ratings, 1971-75, Glenbow IO, IM-13, box 11.

37. Memo, D. C. Twaits to R. G. Reid, 31 August 1971, TV and Radio Audience Ratings, 1971-75, Glenbow IO, IM-13, box 11.

38. Imperial Oil Limited Long-Range Corporate Media Analysis, and *Hockey Night in Canada* Board Presentation Slides, February 1976; Glenbow IO, IM-13, box 9.

39. Waits to R. G. Reif, 15 January 1974 (copy), Glenbow IO, IM-13, box 9.

40. See Memos of D. G. Twaits, 22 January 1975 and 17 December 1975, Glenbow IO, IM-13, box 9.

41. Lyle Doering to Imperial Oil, 27 February 1976, *Hockey Night in Canada* Withdrawal—Letters and Replies, Glenbow IO, IM-13, box 9.

42. Finlay Payne, internal memo, 3 May 1976, LAC CBC, RG 41, vol. 876, file PG 7-7, pt. 3.

43. N. Garriock, internal memo, 6 May 1976, LAC CBC, RG 41, vol 876, file PG 7-7, pt. 3.
44. "Jocks on the Rocks," *Toronto Star,* 26 April 1980.
45. "Hockey—I Am.... A Research Report for Hockey Canada," prepared by Martin Goldfarb Consultants (April 1971), LAC HC, RG 29, vol. 2075, 54.
46. Ibid., 62.
47. Ibid., 298.
48. Saskatchewan Hockey Task Force, Final Report, submitted to Department of Culture and Youth, 17 April 1974, 6.
49. Ontario Hockey Council, *You and Your Child in Hockey* (Toronto: Ontario Ministry of Culture and Recreation, 1976), 9.
50. Ontario Hockey Council, *Minor Hockey in Ontario: Toward a Positive Learning Environment for Children in the 1980's* (Toronto: Ministry of Culture and Education), 6, 26.
51. Canadian Hockey Review, 1978–79 Minor-age Hockey Participation by Language Spoken in the Home, table 13 in National Participation Survey, LAC CHR, RG 29, vol. 2070.
52. Canadian Hockey Review, Discussion Paper on the Structure and Organization of Amateur Hockey in Canada (October 1979), 7. LAC CHR, RG 29, vol. 2070.
53. Ibid., 9.
54. "Hockey—I am.... A Research Report for Hockey Canada," table 11-1 (p. 56) and table 50-1 (p. 285).
55. Ontario Hockey Council, *Minor Hockey in Ontario,* 23, 25.
56. Peter Gzowski, *The Game of Our Lives* (Surrey, BC: Heritage House, 2004), 34.
57. *Toronto Star,* 22 May 1975.
58. Scott Young, "Fights on Ice," *SI,* 7 February 1955, 48. Young often repeated Smythe's quote in his own defenses of fighting. Archival evidence of Smythe's strategy of using fights to sell tickets and fire up his team is the letter he received from Frank Selke (13 January 1944), managing director of the Maple Leafs while Smythe was serving in the army. AO Smythe, F 223-3-1-102.
59. Conn Smythe, with Scott Young, *If You Can't Beat 'em in the Alley* (Toronto: McClelland and Stewart, 1981), 128.
60. William R. McMurtry, *Investigation and Inquiry into Violence in Amateur Hockey* (Toronto: Sports and Fitness Division, 1978), 20.
61. Michael D. Smith, "Towards an Explanation of Hockey Violence: A Reference Other Approach," *The Canadian Journal of Sociology/Cahiers canadiens de sociologie* 4, no. 2 (1979): 115.
62. Edmund W. Vaz, *The Professionalization of Young Hockey Players* (Lincoln: University of Nebraska Press, 1982), 140.
63. Smith, "Towards an Explanation of Hockey Violence," 114.
64. Ibid., 116.
65. "Team Canada humiliated by Russians," *G&M,* 25 April 1977.
66. Ibid.

67. The comments came from Al Strachan in the *Montreal Star,* Jean Acoin in the *Montreal Matin,* and Claude Larochelle in the *Quebec Le Soleil.* "Canada 'Savages' Take a Beating," *Los Angeles Times,* 26 April 1977.

68. First quote: Ann M. Johnston, Hamilton, to Iona Campagnolo, Minister of Fitness and Sport, 29 April 1977; second quote: Walter McGown, Gibsons, BC, to Campagnolo, 12 May 1977; third quote: B.J. Cermak, Ottawa, to Campagnolo, 19 April 1977. LAC CHR, RG 29, vol 2077.

69. Report by the Committee on International Hockey, to the Honourable Iona Campagnolo.

70. Roy MacGregor, "They Give Us Sex We Give Them Violence," *Maclean's,* 1 May 1974, 60.

71. Georges Larivière, *Canadian Hockey, vol. 1: Beginner's Program* (Vanier, ON: CAHA, Hockey Development Council, 1975), v.

72. MacGregor, "They Give Us Sex We Give Them Violence," 66.

73. See G.D. Alcorn, "Philosophy of the USSR Play," *Proceedings: National Coaches Certification Program, Level 5 Seminar* (Vanier, ON: CAHA, Hockey Development Council, 1973).

74. Dryden, "Introduction," in *Let's Play Better Hockey* (McDonald's/Hockey Canada, 1973). A best-selling training manual was *Howie Meeker's Hockey Basics* (Scarborough, ON: Prentice-Hall, 1973), by the *Hockey Night in Canada* analyst and former Maple Leafs forward.

75. Quoted in Murray Dryden, *Playing the Shots at Both Ends: The Story of Ken and Dave Dryden* (Toronto: McGraw-Hill Ryerson, 1972), 76.

76. Dryden recorded summaries of his conversations in the Soviet Union, Czechoslovakia, and Sweden on audio tapes, which were then transcribed. The single-spaced transcript, running over one hundred typed pages, is filed in the records of Hockey Canada as "Phone Interview with Gary Smith, July 16, 1973," without any explicit reference to Dryden's authorship. LAC CHR, RG 29, vol. 2075. Dryden summarized his visit to Europe in the article "To Russia with Love," *Maclean's,* 1 April 1974.

77. Mike Eaves, interview, 18 May 2018.

78. Lloyd Percival, *The Hockey Handbook,* rev. ed. (Vancouver and Toronto: Copp Clark/A.S. Barnes, 1957), 129.

79. Dave Dryden, interview, 12 July 2018; [Ken Dryden], "Phone Interview with Gary Smith, July 16, 1973."

80. Dave Dryden, interview, 12 July 2018.

81. Ed Willes, *The Rebel League: The Short and Unruly Life of the World Hockey Association* (Toronto: McClelland & Stewart, 2005), 6.

82. Quoted in Willes, *The Rebel League,* 180.

83. The background to Nedomanský's defection was reported in detail to Czechoslovak state security by an unnamed source, who was close to Nedomanský's parents. Report no. 47/74, O-StB Hodonín, 25 July 1974, OBŽ 115-11517 BN, StBA. See also Tal Pinchevsky, *Breakaway: From behind the Iron Curtain to the NHL— The Untold Story of Hockey's Great Escapes* (Mississauga, ON: Wiley, 2012), 9–12.

84. J. F. Ahearne, notice of suspension, 17 October 1974, IIHF Correspondence 1967–78, Archives of Sport Museum of Finland, Helsinki.

85. Bukač and Suchan, *Bukač: Moje hokejové století*, 228–229. Surveillance reports on Peter Ihnačák, found in KR-13173 VKR (reg. no. 6849) and OBŽ-11529 BN, StBA.

86. Bobby Hull, "Skills—A Priority in Canadian Hockey Deveopment," in *Proceedings, National Coaches Certification Program Level V Seminar*, Winnipeg, Manitoba, June, 1975 (Vanier, ON: Canadian Amateur Hockey Association, 1976), 1

87. Dave Dryden, interview, 12 July 2018.

88. Ray Kennedy, "A Nondecision Begs the Question," *SI*, 28 July 1975, 12.

89. The number of fights per game reached its peak in 1987–88, at 1.3 fights per game. http://dropyourgloves.com/Fights/FightsPerGameChart.aspx.

90. Willes, *The Rebel League*, 183.

91. On one of Salming's rough encounters with the Flyers, see Martin O'Malley, "Borje Salming, True Courage," *G&M*, 19 April 1976 (HHOF Clippings). Tobias Stark discusses Salming's importance in opening the NHL to European players in "'How Swede It Is': Börje Salming and the Migration of Swedish Ice Hockey Players to the NHL, 1957–2012," in *Constructing the Hockey Family: Home, Community, Bureaucracy and Marketplace*, eds. Lori Dithurbide and Colin Howell (Halifax, NS: St. Mary's University, 2012), 364–393.

92. Bobby Hull, "Skills—A Priority in Canadian Hockey Deveopment," in *Proceedings, National Coaches Certification Program Level V Seminar, Winnipeg, Manitoba, June, 1975* (Vanier, ON: Canadian Amateur Hockey Association, 1976), 4.

93. "Harvard Blasts Hockey Picture," *The Boston Globe*, 9 February 1962.

94. Ibid.

95. On the growth of big-time college sports, see Brian Ingrassia, *The Rise of Gridiron University: Higher Education's Uneasy Alliance with Big-Time Football* (Lawrence: University Press of Kansas, 2012).

96. Louis Benezet to J. L. Morrill, 13 March 1957, University of Minnesota Archives, President's Office, 1945–1978, box 228.

97. University of Minnesota administrators never trusted Armstrong; even though they were in the same conference, the Gophers refused to play a regular-season game against Denver for fourteen seasons. Mariucci claimed that this scheduling boycott was not his decision. He insisted that he wanted to play Denver, so that he could beat the Pioneers on the ice. John Gilbert, *Herb Brooks: The Inside Story of a Hockey Mastermind* (Minneapolis, MN: MVP Books, 2010), 47–48.

98. Murray Dryden, *Playing the Puck at Both Ends*, 54–57.

99. Mike Eaves, interview, 18 May 2018.

100. Minutes, WCHA Annual Meeting, 3–4 April 1971, UMNA Ath, box 17.

101. Burt Smith, circular to WCHA coaches, athletic directors, and faculty representatives, 9 February 1977, UMNA Ath, box 21.

102. "Brawl, More Than Loss, BU's Haunting Memory," *The Boston Globe*, 28 March 1976.

103. Gilbert, *Herb Brooks*, 33–35.

104. Gilbert, *Herb Brooks,* 46–47; and *Minneaspolis Tribune,* 13 March 1974.

105. "BU Harbors Bitter Memories," *The Boston Globe,* 29 March 1976.

106. "Pucksters Win National Title," *Minnesota Daily,* 26 March 1979, UMNA Ath, Hockey Clippings.

107. "BU Harbors Bitter Memories," *The Boston Globe,* 29 March 1976.

108. Brooks to Burt Smith, 28 September 1976, UMNA Ath, box 21.

109. Dan Levin, "Wisconsin on the Ice: Hullabaloo!," *SI,* 19 February 1973, www.si.com/vault/1973/02/19/576496/wisconsin-on-the-ice-hullabaloo.

110. E. M. Swift, "When You Say Winsconsin . . .," *SI,* 8 February 1982, 51.

111. Ibid., 48.

112. Mike Eaves recounted this conversation taking place in the one season Brooks was coach of the Utica Devils, 1991–92. Johnson had been diagnosed with brain cancer in August 1991, just after having won the Stanley Cup as coach of the Pittsburgh Penguins. He passed away that November.

113. John Harrington, interview, 4 August 2017.

114. "What a Great Day for Hockey!" *Edmonton Journal,* 7 December 1986, HHOF Clippings.

115. On players' difficulties with Brooks, see Wayne Coffey, *The Boys of Winter: The Untold Story of a Coach, a Dream, and the 1980 U.S Olympic Hockey Team* (New York: Three Rivers, 2005).

116. "'U' Hockey Practice: Almost as Rough as the Game Itself," *Minneapolis Tribune,* 4 December 1977.

117. "Big, Swift Wisconsin Tests BU," *The Boston Globe,* 16 March 1972.

118. Mike Eaves, interview, 18 May 2018. See also Coffey, *The Boys of Winter,* 76–77.

119. Gerald Eskenazi, "An Icy Challenge Starts," *NYT,* 2 August 1979.

120. William Oscar Johnson, "Of Gold and Gophers," *SI,* 10 December 1979, 60.

121. Tim Wendel, *Going for the Gold: How the U.S. Olympic Hockey Team Won at Lake Placid* (1980; reprint, Mineola, NY: Dover, 2009), 9.

122. "The Organizational Development of Hockey Canada," LAC HC, MG 28 I 263, vol 19.

123. Interview by Larry Regan with Jim McGregor and Rick Simmons, Pembroke, p. 27. Field Interview Transcripts, LAC CHR, RG 29, vol. 2068.

124. Creative Research Group, "Toward an Understanding of the Perceptions of Toronto Hockey Fans: A Qualitiative Assessment," 20. Glenbow IO, IM-13, box 11.

CHAPTER SIX. IN THE MONEY

1. Thomas E. Joiner Jr., Daniel Hollar, and Kimberly Van Orden, "Buckeyes, Gators, Super Bowl Sunday, and the Miracle on Ice: 'Pulling Together' Is Associated with Lower Suicide Rates," *Journal of Social and Clinical Psychology* 25, no. 2 (2006): 193.

2. Andrew C. Billings, James Angelini, and Paul J. MacArthur, *Olympic Television: Broadcasting the Biggest Show on Earth* (London: Routledge, 2017), 35–36. On American nationalism surrounding the Miracle on Ice, see Mary G. MacDonald, "Miraculous Masculinity Meets Militarization: Narrating the 1980 USSR-US Men's Olympic Ice Hockey Match and Cold War Politics," in *East Plays West: Sport and the Cold War*, eds. Stephen Wagg and David L. Andrews, 222–234 (New York: Routledge, 2007).

3. Monique Berlioux to Roone Arledge, 2 July 1980, IOC HA, JO-1986W-TVR/26; Minutes, IOC Executive Board, July–August 1984, 6; "Olympic Gold: How Networks Vied in Grueling Bidding for '88 Winter Games as Sarajevo Games Neared," *The Wall Street Journal*, 22 February 1984; and "ABC Moves to Protect Its Turf," *NYT*, 6 December 1983.

4. See Alan Abrahamson's reporting for the *Los Angeles Times*, in particular "Show the Money? IOC Keeps Finances Cloaked in Mystery," 30 July 2000.

5. Günther Sabetzki to IOC, 21 November 1985; and IOC-IIHF agreement, 31 October 1986, IOC HA, D-RM02/55.

6. IOC letters to René Fasel, 15 March and 20 March 1998, IOC HA, C-JO2-1998/010.

7. John Harrington, interview, 4 August 2017. On the family backgrounds of the players, see Coffey, *The Boys of Winter*.

8. Gerald Eskenazi, "Herb Brooks Takes His Style to Pros," *NYT*, 14 June 1981.

9. Helene Elliott, "Gold Medal Memories," *Newsday*, 1 February 1981.

10. Kathy Blumenstock, "The Flame Is Still Burning Brightly," *SI*, 10 March 1980, 16; "It's Been a Grind," *The Atlanta Constitution*, 13 March 1980; "This Flame Is Red Hot," *The Boston Globe*, 3 March 1980.

11. *Minneapolis Tribune*, 7 April 1980.

12. "Wird Startrainer Herb Brooks Trainer des HC Davos," *Walliser Volksfreund*, 31 March 1980; "Brooks to Coach Swiss Hockey," *NYT*, 27 April 1980; "Brooks Scans Horizon," *Minneapolis Tribune*, 12 January 1981.

13. Elliott, "Gold Medal Memories."

14. Ibid.; Phil Verchota, interview, 27 March 2019; and John Harrington, interview, 4 April 2019.

15. "Der Mann, der dem Schweizer Eishockey den Weg in die Moderne wies," *Neue Zürcher Zeitung*, 12 November 2018, www.nzz.ch/sport/der-mann-der-dem-schweizer-eishockey-den-weg-in-die-moderne-wies-ld.1435679.

16. "The Great Gretzky: He's Magic on Ice," *Chicago Tribune*, 29 March 1981; "Hail, the Great Gretzky," *Toronto Sun*, 30 March 1980, HHOF Clippings.

17. Playboy Interview: Wayne Gretzky, *Playboy*, April 1985, HHOF Clippings.

18. Ibid.

19. "Glen Sather—He Runs Gretzky & Co," *Chicago Tribune*, 1 May 1983.

20. "Sather: Brains behind Success of Hockey's Hottest Attraction," *G&M*, 7 May 1983.

21. "Sergei Makarov: 'Zala slavy dostoina vsia nasha piaterka,'" *KHL.ru*, 14 November 2016, www.khl.ru/news/2016/11/14/327901.html.

22. Gzowski, *The Game of Our Lives,* 191.
23. Doug Beardsley, *Country on Ice* (Toronto: PaperJacks, 1988), 111.
24. News from the *Edmonton Sun,* 7 and 8 August 1988.
25. Stephen Brunt, *Gretzky's Tears: Hockey, Canada, and the Day Everything Changed* (Toronto: Vintage Canada, 2010), 140.
26. *Edmonton Sun,* 11 August 1988.
27. Graham Hicks, "Jezebel Janet," *Edmonton Sun,* 10 August 1988.
28. "The Whole Story," *Edmonton Sun,* 12 August 1988.
29. Graham Hicks, "Eating Some Mighty Fine Tasting Crow," *Edmonton Sun,* 12 August 1988.
30. Earl McRae, "Gretzky was Synonymous with Canada," *Ottawa Citizen,* 11 August 1988.
31. Stephen Brunt, "The Gretzky Effect," *Report on Business Magazine,* April 1990, 79, HHOF Clippings.
32. Jenish, *The NHL—A Centennial History,* 292–293.
33. Player salaries are available from HockeyZonePlus NHL salary history database: www.hockeyzoneplus.com/. See also "Kurri Will Sign Deal with Milan," *Edmonton Journal,* 30 July 1990; and "Big Salaries Abound in Baseball," *The Indianapolis Star,* 18 October 1992.
34. "Off-Season a Shrinking Luxury for NHL Warriors," *G&M,* 8 August 1994.
35. Jack Falla, "A New Departure toward Arrival," *SI,* 28 March 1983, 38–47.
36. Ibid., 45.
37. "On Sports: Gypsy on the Balance Beam," *The Wall Street Journal,* 3 August 1984.
38. Falla, "A New Departure toward Arrival," 45.
39. "The Centre of NHL Attention American Sharpshooter Reaches Record Heights in Rookie Junior Campaign," *G&M,* 12 March 1983.
40. Brunt, *Gretzky's Tears,* 21.
41. Employment data by different economic sectors, 1991–2018, available at World Bank Open Data, World Bank Group, https://data.worldbank.org/indicator/SL.IND.EMPL.ZS.
42. "Detroit Firm Computes Big Hockey Future," *Montreal Gazette,* 9 February 1985.
43. "Computer Software Firm Plays High-Tech Hockey," *G&M,* 25 October 1983.
44. Ibid.
45. "Programmed for Success," *Windsor Star,* 15 November 1986.
46. "Scorecard," *SI,* 28 September 1981, 13.
47. "Detroit Firm Computes Big Hockey Future."
48. "Summer Hockey Is Paying Dividends," *Toronto Star,* 22 July 1985.
49. "Warming Up to Summer Hockey," *Detroit Free Press,* 28 June 1984.
50. "Summer Hockey Series Put Kids' Ambitions on Ice," *The Ottawa Citizen,* 14 July 1987.

51. Lou Vairo, interview, 14 June 2017; and Jane Leavy, "The Coach," *The Washington Post*, 5 February 1984.

52. On this trend in other children's activities, see Marie Winn, *Children without Childhood* (New York: Pantheon, 1983), 80–83.

53. Jay Coakley, "The Good Father: Parental Expectations and Youth Sports," *Leisure Studies* 25, no. 2 (April 2006): 153–163.

54. See Katherine S. Newman, *Declining Fortunes: The Withering of the American Dream* (New York: Basic Books, 1993).

55. "Girls Just Want to Play Hockey," *G&M*, 2 November 1985.

56. "Boyd's Love of Hockey Goes a Long Way," *Toronto Star*, 20 October 1987.

57. "For Youngest Granato, Birthright Is Realized," *St. Louis Post-Dispatch*, 14 December 1997; and "Talks Softly, Carries a Big Stick," *Chicago Tribune*, 26 January 1992.

58. Etue and Williams, *On the Edge*, 106.

59. Ibid., 44–50; and Avery and Stevens, *Too Many Men on the Ice*, 105–112.

60. Claudia Goldin, "The Quiet Revolution That Transformed Women's Employment, Education, and Family," *The American Economic Review* 96, no. 2 (2006): 19.

61. *The Wilson Report: Moms, Dads, Daughters, and Sports*, prepared by Diagnostic Research, presented by Wilson Sporting Goods and the Women's Sports Foundation (7 June 1988), 7–9, www.womenssportsfoundation.org/research/article-and-report/health/moms-dads-daughters-and-sports/.

62. Hall, *The Girl and the Game*, 171–172.

63. Abigail Hoffman, examination, 10 August 1985, *Blainey v. Ontario Hockey Association and Ontario Human Rights Commission*, 403, AO, Supreme Court of Ontario, Court of Appeals, C/A 630/85, bag 2 of 7 (hereafter *Blainey v. OHA*).

64. Lois Kalchman, examination, 29 August 1985, *Blainey v. OHA*, 435.

65. J. Thomas Riler, examination, 10 August 1985, *Blainey v. OHA*, 450. On players asking newspapers to be quiet, see Kalchman examination, 437.

66. Caroline Blainey, cross-examination, 6 September 1985, *Blainey v. OHA*, 466.

67. Etue and Williams, *On the Edge*, 161.

68. "Fight for Girls' Hockey Rights Led to Some Dark Corners," *Toronto Star*, 3 November 2017.

69. Ibid.

70. Brent Ladds, affidavit, *Blainey v. OHA*, 278.

71. Fran Rider, affidavit, *Blainey v. OHA*, 308.

72. Ladds, affidavit, *Blainey v. OHA*, 275.

73. Rider, affidavit, *Blainey v. OHA*, 302.

74. "Draft Threatens Junior Leagues WHA Baby Bulls Case Opened the Floodgates," *G&M*, 21 January 1984; and "Feud over Money Threatens to Split Hockey Bodies," *G&M*, 20 March 1980.

75. "Fight for Girls' Hockey Rights Led to Some Dark Corners."

76. Etue and Williams, *On the Edge*, 187.
77. Caroline Blainey, cross-examination, *Blainey v. OHA*, 463.
78. Caroline Blainey, affidavit, *Blainey v. OHA*, 63.
79. Rider, affidavit, *Blainey v. OHA*, 307–308.
80. Caroline Blainey, cross-examination, *Blainey v. OHA*, 470.
81. Caroline Blainey, affidavit, *Blainey v. OHA*, 58.
82. Daniel Damario, affidavit, *Blainey v. OHA*, 78.
83. J. A. Dubin, majority opinion, 17 April 1986, *Blainey v. OHA*, 49. On the decision, see "Girl Step Closer to Playing Hockey with Boys," *G&M*, 18 April 1986.
84. "Místo večeře sbalil kufry a utekl," *iROZHLAS.cz*, 1 May 2017, www.irozhlas.cz/sport/hokej/misto-vecere-sbalil-kufry-a-utekl-pribeh-emigranta-svobody-plnil-po-draftu_1705021045_sob.
85. Dominik Hašek with Robert Záruba, *Chytám svůj život* (Prague: Terra, 1999), 124.
86. Dominik Hašek, interview, 17 April 2018.
87. Minutes, Executive Committee, 10 May 1989, Ústřední výbor, Československého svazu tělesné výchovy, Slovak National Archive, box 123. See Vic Duke, "Perestroika in Progress? The Case of Spectator Sports in Czechoslovakia," *British Journal of Sociology* 41, no. 2 (1990): 145–156.
88. Declaration, 5 December 1989, Ústřední výbor, Československého svazu tělesné výchovy, Slovak National Archive, box 123; and Hašek, *Chytám svůj život*, 158–159.
89. Viktor Tikhonov, *Hokej na celý život*, trans. into Czech by Petr Feldstein (Prague: Olympia, 1988), 122.
90. Ibid., 25.
91. "Vladislav Tretiak: 'Tarasov skazal mne: "Polufabrikat, yesli vyzhivesh—budesh velikim!",'" *Sport Ekspress*, 25 April 2017, www.sport-express.ru/hockey/reviews/vladislav-tretyak-tarasov-skazal-mne-polufabrikat-esli-vyzhivesh-budesh-velikim-1247689/.
92. Igor Larionov, Jim Taylor, and Leonid Reizer, *Larionov* (Winnipeg: Codner, 1990), 35.
93. Ibid., 71.
94. Igor Larionov, "The Beautiful Game," *The Player's Tribune*, 23 February 2015, www.theplayerstribune.com/en-us/articles/miracle-on-ice-hockey-russia.
95. Larionov et al., *Larionov*, 37.
96. Igor Larionov, "V dolgu pered khokkeem . . . ," *Ogonyok*, no. 42 (1988), full text at "Otkrytoe pismo Larionova v zhurnale 'Ogonek,'" www.hockeyreview.ru/main/23027-otkrytoe-pismo-larionova-v-zhurnale-ogonek.html.
97. Reuters wire report, 27 January 1987, Subject Files—Sport, OSA, 300-85-12, box 278.
98. Reuters wirte report, 3 May 1989, Subject Files—Sport, OSA, 300-85-12: 278.
99. Robert Edelman, "A Surge from Below in Soviet Sport," *NYT*, 3 July 1989.
100. Fuks, "The Rebirth of *Dinamo Riga*," 22.

101. "Tikhonov i SSSR," *Kommersant/Ogonyok,* 11 August 2002, www.kommersant.ru/doc/2290622.

102. Katrina vanden Heuvel and Stephen F. Cohen, "Gorbachev on 1989," interview with Mikhail Gorbachev, 16 November 2009, *The Nation,* www.thenation.com/article/gorbachev-1989/; and Padraic Kenney, interview, *New Books Network,* 6 November 2009, https://newbooksnetwork.com/padraic-kenney-1989-democratic-revolutions-at-the-cold-wars-end/.

103. Tod Hartje, with Lawrence Martin, *From behind the Red Line: An American Hockey Player in Russia* (New York: Macmillan, 1992), 116–117.

104. Ibid, 151.

CHAPTER SEVEN. AROUND THE WORLD

1. "High-Speed Transition Game Key to Success in Today's NHL," *Ottawa Citizen,* 2 December 1991.
2. Hart Cantelon, "Have Skates, Will Travel: Canada, International Hockey, and the Changing Hockey Labour Market," in *Artificial Ice: Hockey, Culture, and Commerce,* eds. David Whitson and Richard Gruneau (Peterborough, ON: Broadview, 2006), 225.
3. Deutsche Eishockey League, 1997–1998, *Elite Prospects,* www.eliteprospects.com/league/del/1997-1998; and www.eliteprospects.com/team/119/adler-mannheim/1997-1998.
4. For league leaders and percentages of players by nationality, see pages for 1997–98 seasons in DEL, NLA, SHL, and Liiga at *Elite Prospects,* www.eliteprospects.com.
5. Mike DeAngelis, interview, 27 August 2015.
6. Dov Grumet-Morris, interview, 19 August 2015.
7. Backman, *Ishockeyns amerikanisering,* 162–164.
8. "Eishockey: Dollars oder Tränen," *Der Spiegel,* 12 September 1994, www.spiegel.de/spiegel/print/d-13686015.html.
9. Backman, *Ishockeyns amerikanisering,* 183–188 and 250.
10. Thomas Staggs, interview, 28 July 2016.
11. Michael Eisner, interview, 18 August 2016.
12. "Disney's Name Mighty Ducks Inspires Fans' Ire," *Orange County Register,* 20 March 1993.
13. "Poor Old Walt Must Be Spinning," *The Hamilton Spectator,* 15 March 1993.
14. "The Mighty What?," *Montreal Gazette,* 4 March 1993.
15. Quoted in Jim Silver, *Thin Ice: Money, Politics, and the Demise of an NHL Franchise* (Winnipeg: Fernwood, 1996), 38.
16. Julie Hatfield and Michael Saunders, "Hockey Jerseys: They're Cool off the Ice, Too," *The Boston Globe,* 21 March 1994. For a collection of rap videos featuring hockey jerseys, see "Rappers Wearing Hockey Jerseys in Music Videos," http://justagwailo.com/rappers.

17. Quoted in E. M. Swift, "Hot Not," *SI*, June 20, 1994, 40.

18. "Men of Teal in San Jose," *Los Angeles Times*, 26 April 1994; "Research Helps Sharks Get Sizable Bite of Gear Sales," *USA Today*, 23 January 1992; "San Jose Merchandise Prize Catch for Franchise," *Sporting Goods Business*, December 1991, 14.

19. "Licensed to Sell," *Sales and Marketing Management* 146, no. 10 (1994): 98; "Merchandise Sales Top $1 billion," *Montreal Gazette*, 26 September 1994; and "NHL-ers to Thaw Out Vintage Team Jerseys," *New York Post*, 5 August 2003.

20. Backman, *Ishockeyns amerikanisering*, 172–173. Translation by Tobias Stark.

21. Ibid., 171 and 197.

22. Christopher Stride, Jean Williams, David Moor, and Nick Catley, "From Sportswear to Leisurewear: The Evolution of English Football League Shirt Design in the Replica Kit Era," *Sport in History* 35, no. 1 (2015): 174.

23. Norm O'Reilly et al., "Merchandise Sales Rank in Professional Sport: Purchase Drivers and Implications for National Hockey League Clubs," *Sport, Business and Management: An International Journal* 5, no. 4 (2015): 311.

24. Richard Giulianotti, "Supporters, Followers, Fans, and *Flaneurs:* A Taxonomy of Specator Identities in Football," *Journal of Sport & Social Issues* 26, no. 1 (2002): 25–46.

25. David Beckerman, president of Starter Sportswear, quoted in Stuart B. Chirls, "Sports Logo Licensing Boom Keeps Growing," *Daily News Record*, 9 June 1988.

26. "Inhabited: Molson Centre Hockey Fan Comes First in New Arena," *G&M*, 15 March 1996.

27. Jay Weiner, *Stadium Games: Fifty Years of Big League Greed and Bush League Boondoggles* (Minneapolis: University of Minnesota Press, 2000), 93; John Pastier, "The Sporting Life," *Architectural Record*, August 1999; and "NHL Teams Score Big in the Suite Market," ALSD (Association of Luxury Suite Directors), 14 February 2012, https://alsd.com/content/nhl-teams-score-big-suite-market.

28. Dennis Coates and Brad R. Humphreys, "Can New Stadiums Revitalise Urban Neighbourhoods?," *Significance* 8, no. 2 (2011): 65–69; and Brad R. Humphreys, *The Economics of Professional Hockey* (Morgantown, WV: BRH Publishing, 2016), 199.

29. Weiner, *Stadium Games*, 149–157.

30. "Karmanos: They Love Him in Raleigh," *Hartford Courant*, 7 May 1997.

31. Peter Green, "Stockholm Scales Up Sphere," *Engineering News-Record*, 2 February 1989.

32. Shubert, *Architecture on Ice*, 216–217.

33. According to a 2010 study, 180,000–200,000 Slovak workers and students were living abroad, out of a total population of 5.4 million. Vladimír Baláž and Zuzana Kusá, *Social Impact of Emigration and Rural-Urban Migration in Central and Eastern Europe,* Final Country Report: Slovakia, prepared for European Commission DG Employment, Social Affairs and Inclusion (April 2012), https://ec.europa.eu.

34. Návrh koncepcie financovania SZĽH pre rok 1997/98, Slovenský zväz ľadového hokeja, Rady SZĽH, Slovak National Archive, box 2, A-2-10.

35. "European Attendance Ranking, 2018–19," *IIHF.com,* 15 March 2019, www.iihf.com/en/news/9527/european-attendance-ranking.
36. "Nordiques Bid Quebec Adieu," *Montreal Gazette,* 26 May 1995.
37. On economic and social changes in Winnipeg and Manitoba, see Gerald Friesen, *The West: Regional Ambitions, National Debates, Global Age* (Toronto: Penguin Canada, 1999), chap. 10.
38. Silver, *Thin Ice,* 58–60.
39. "This Love Affair Won't Die," *Winnipeg Free Press,* 16 May 1995.
40. "Hockey Love Means Having to Say Goodbye," *Winnipeg Free Press,* 3 May 1995.
41. Speeches by Premier Gary Filmon and John Loewen, 1 May 1995, Premier's Speeches, Archives of Manitoba, EC 0030, location Q 12456.
42. In 2007, Canadian hockey had 333,432 youth players, compared to 732,521 soccer players. Hockey numbers are taken from the IIHF Annual Survey of Players, from 1995–96 to 2008–09. Soccer registrations from 1994 to 2007 are taken from the Canadian Soccer Association's Strategic Plan, 2009–2013, www.canadasoccer.com/files/2008_CSA_StrategicPlanEN.pdf.
43. William Houston, "On the Air," part 11 of series "A Game in Crisis," *G&M,* 16 April 1998.
44. "Cherry on Top," *The Toronto Star,* 23 May 1993, HHOF Clippings. See Kristi Allain, "'A Good Canadian Boy': Crisis Masculinity, Canadian National Identity, and Nostalgic Longings in Don Cherry's Coach's Corner," *International Journal of Canadian Studies* 52 (2015): 107–132.
45. Don Gilmour, "Don Cherry Unleashed," *Saturday Night,* October 1992, 58, HHOF Clippings.
46. "Khokkei: Putin pointeresovalsia u Tretiaka," *Sport Ekspress,* 1 June 2006, www.sport-express.ru/newspaper/2006-06-01/7_1/.
47. Nina Poussenkova, "The Global Expansion of Russia's Energy Giants," *Journal of International Affairs* 63, no. 2 (2010): 103–124; and Richard Sakwa, "Putin and the Oligarchs," *New Political Economy* 13, no. 2 (2008): 185–191.
48. Quoted in Markku Jokisipilä, "World Champions Bred by National Champions: The Role of State-Owned Corporate Giants in Russian Sports," *Russian Analytical Digest,* no. 95 (6 April 2011), 9, http://css.ethz.ch/content/dam/ethz/special-interest/gess/cis/center-for-securities-studies/pdfs/RAD-95-8-11.pdf.
49. IIHF Survey of Players, 1995.
50. "Sych Slain; It's 'Life in Russia,'" *Los Angeles Times,* 23 April 1997; "Russian Ice Boss Aims to Return to Former Glory," *Toronto Star,* 15 August 1997.
51. Andrei Morozov, "Khokke ne vypolniaet plan Putina," *Profil,* 24 March 2008, 86–91, Universal Database of Russian Newspapers; "Vladimir Putin o khokkeye: 20 zaiavleniy premer-ministra Rossii," *Sports.ru,* 19 November 2011, www.sports.ru/tribuna/blogs/centre/199850.html.
52. Jokisipilä, "World Champions Bred by National Champions," 9–11.
53. "Vladimir Putin: 'Kontinentalnuiu khokkeinuiu ligu pridumal ia!,'" *Komsomolskaia pravda,* 22 July 2009, Universal Database of Russian Newspapers.

54. "Vladimir Putin o khokkeye: 20 zaiavleniy premer-ministra Rossii."
55. Fuks, "The Rebirth of *Dinamo Riga*," 63–66.
56. "It's Our Game, Too," *Toronto Star*, 7 January 2012.
57. The three oligarchs were Gennady Timchenko, Boris Rotenberg, and Roman Rotenberg. In 2019, they sold the team to Jari Kurri. See Elisabeth Braw, "Geopolitics Is Body Checking Putin's Hockey League," *Foreign Policy*, 1 April 2016.
58. "Fisher: Russia's KHL Is Good Hockey, but Bad Business," *Canwest News Service*, 18 October 2012.
59. When the KHL was founded, its marketing arm established KHL TV. In 2016, this branch of the league brought in revenue of 328 million rubles ($5 million). By contrast, the Finnish Liiga was earning $18.5 million in broadcast rights, while a new deal in 2017 brought each team in the Swedish Hockey League roughly $5 million in television money. "'Match TV' prinial shaibu," *Kommersant*, 11 July 2018, www.kommersant.ru/doc/3682465; "Incumbent Nelonen out of Race for Finnish Ice Hockey TV Rights," *Sportcal*, 27 April 2017, www.sportcal.com/News/FeaturedNews/110522.
60. "It's Our Game, Too."
61. Avery and Stevens, *Too Many Men on the Ice*, 92.
62. "Hockey Girls Want Ice Time," *Montreal Gazette*, 6 March 1995.
63. "They're Coming on Strong," *The Hamilton Spectator*, 28 October 1994.
64. Etue and Williams, *On the Edge*, 73–74.
65. In 2009, girls enrolled in the midget rank and below in Canada numbered 104,535, while 45,519 American girls age eighteen and below played the sport. "Male to Female Branch Registration Comparison," 1993–2009, Hockey Canada, http://cdn.hockeycanada.ca/hockey-canada/Hockey-Programs/Female/Downloads/Male-to-Female-Branch-Registration-Comparison.pdf; "USA Hockey Registration 1990–1991 through 2012–2013," USA Hockey, www.usahockey.com/membershipstats.
66. During the 1990s, participation in youth soccer in the United States grew from 1.6 to 3 million players, while total soccer registrations in Canada more than doubled to over 700,000. "Soccer by the Numbers: A Look at the Game in the United States," *NBC News*, 27 May 2015, www.nbcnews.com/storyline/fifa-corruption-scandal/soccer-numbers-look-game-u-s-n365601; and Canadian Soccer Association's Strategic Plan, 2009–2013, www.canadasoccer.com/files/2008_CSA_Strategic-PlanEN.pdf.
67. Women's Sports Foundation, *Go Out and Play: Youth Sports in America*, 2008, www.womenssportsfoundation.org/research/article-and-report/participation-opportunity/go-play-gender-equity-sports/; *Sport Participation Survey 2010*, Statistics Canada, February 2013, 9, http://publications.gc.ca/collections/collection_2013/pc-ch/CH24-1-2012-eng.pdf; *Teens in Sports in America*, Sports Goods Manufacturers Association report, 2001; and "Growth in Youth Sports Participation," *Journal of Physical Education, Recreation & Dance* 70, no. 9 (1999): 6.
68. Rebecca Huval, "Selling Sneakers with Feminist Poetry: An Interview with Janet Champ," *The Toast*, 27 April 2015, https://the-toast.net/2015/04/27/interview-with-janet-champ/.

69. See Leslie Heywood and Shari L. Dworkin, *Built to Win: The Female Athlete as Cultural Icon* (Minneapolis: University of Minnesota Press, 2003), chap. 2.

70. For a history of the legal and legislative challenges to Title IX, see Howard P. Chudacoff, *Changing the Playbook: How Power, Profit, and Politics Transformed College Sports* (Champaign: University of Illinois Press, 2017), chap. 5.

71. McKinley Boston to Sen. Don Samuelson, 31 January 1996, Women's Ice Hockey Task Force, 1997–1998, UMNA Ath, box 24. The University of Wisconsin was open in linking women's hockey, along with softball and rowing, to its struggle with Title IX compliance. "UW Board Vote Supports Women's Hockey Program," *Wisconsin State Journal* (Madison), 18 March 1998.

72. "OSU Women Prove They Can Play, Too," *Dayton Daily News*, 9 February 2000.

73. "Human Rights Case Going to Tribunal," *The StarPhoenix* (Saskatoon), 11 May 2006; and "School Settles Women's Hockey Complaint," *Calgary Herald*, 8 September 2007.

74. "Former Canadian Women's Hockey Coach Heads to the U.S. College Ranks," *The StarPhoenix* (Saskatoon), 2 June 1999.

75. Normand Chouinard, Sean Draper, Wade D. Gilbert, and Wayne Blann, "Athletic Scholarships for Canadian Hockey Players," *Journal CAHPERD* 65, no. 2 (1999): 34–36.

76. "Trends in the Participation of International Student-Athletes in NCAA Divisions I and II," NCAA.org, September 2018, www.ncaa.org/sites/default/files/2018RES_International_SA_charts_Sept2018_final_20180919.pdf.

77. "Power Shift Hits Women's College Hockey," *Star Tribune* (Minneapolis), 26 March 1999.

78. "UMD Women's Coach Gets the Last Laugh," *Star Tribune* (Minneapolis), 8 February 2000.

79. Patricia Elsmore-Sautter, interview, 18 August 2015.

80. "President Bush Greets Minnesota's Hockey Stars," *Pioneer Press* (St. Paul), 18 June 2003.

81. *Miller et al. v. Board of Regents of the University of Minnesota*, No. 0:15-cv-03740-RHKLIB (D. Minn. filed Sept. 28, 2015), http://stmedia.startribune.com/documents/MillerEtAlVUMBOR9_28_15.pdf. See also Erin Buzuvis, "Coaches in Court: Legal Challenges to Sex Discrimination in College Athletics," *Tennessee Journal of Race, Gender, & Social Justice* 6, no. 41 (2017).

82. "Trends in the Participation of International Student-Athletes in NCAA Divisions I and II."

83. Ibid.

84. Florence Schelling, interview, 4 February 2018.

85. Alena Polenská, interview, 31 July 2017. On conditions of European women's hockey in the 2000s, see Kajsa Gilenstam, Staffan Karp, and Karin Henriksson-Larsén, "Gender in Ice Hockey: Women in a Male Territory," *Scandinavian Journal of Medicine and Science in Sports* 18 (2008): 235–249.

86. Kim Martin Hasson, interview, 11 February 2018.

87. IOC Gender Equality Review Project, *Olympic.org*, March 2018, http://stillmed.olympic.org/media/Document%20Library/OlympicOrg/News/2018/03/IOC-Gender-Equality-Report-March-2018.pdf; and "III World Conference on Women and Sport," *Olympic.org*, 7–8 March 2004, http://stillmed.olympic.org/media/Document%20Library/OlympicOrg/Documents/Conferences-Forums-and-Events/Conferences/IOC-World-Conferences-on-Women-and-Sport/3rd-IOC-World-Conference-on-Women-and-Sport-Final-Report-Marrakech-2004.pdf.

88. "Five Questions with Angela Ruggiero," Women's Sports Foundation, 8 January 2013, www.womenssportsfoundation.org/education/five-questions-with-angela-ruggiero/.

89. Lois Kalchman, "Cost of Hockey Leaves Kids on Sidelines," *Toronto Star*, 25 March 1992; "Losing Sleep and Money—and Loving It," *Colorado Springs Gazette Telegraph*, 9 February 1992; "Kto ne igraet v khokkei," *The New Times*, 4 February 2008, Universal Database of Russian Newspapers; and "Die wichtigsten Spartipps für Hockey-Mütter," *Neue Zürcher Zeitung*, 8 December 2013, www.nzz.ch/sport/die-wichtigsten-spartipps-fuer-hockey-muetter-1.18200203.

90. "Is Kids' Hockey Too Expensive?," *Daily Gleaner* (Fredericton, NB), 24 September 2011.

91. Quoted in Jeannie S. Thrall, "Strategic Parenting: Making the Middle Class through Distinction and Discipline" (PhD diss., University of Michigan, 2010), 78. The term "orchestrated achievement" is Thrall's. Annette Lareau presents the concept of "concerted cultivation" in her book, *Unequal Childhoods: Class, Race, and Family Life* (Berkeley: University of California Press, 2003).

92. Coakley, "The Good Father: Parental Expectations and Youth Sports," 160.

93. Richard Gruneau, "Goodbye, Gordie Howe: Sport Participation and Class Inequality in the 'Pay for Play' Society," in *How Canadians Communicate, vol. 5: Sports*, eds. David Taras and Christopher Waddell (Edmonton, AB: AU Press, 2016), 223–246.

94. "Village's Simple Treasure Savoured Best at Night," *G&M*, 1 February 2003.

95. "The Best Game You Can Name?," *Toronto Star*, 3 February 2003; and "Village's Simple Treasure Savoured Best at Night."

96. Bobby Orr, *Orr: My Story* (New York: G. P. Putnam's Sons, 2013), 20.

97. Backman, *Us against You*, 420.

98. Mary Louise Adams, "The Game of Whose Lives? Gender, Race, and Entitlement in Canada's 'National' Game," in Whitson and Gruneau, *Artificial Ice*, 80. On the idyllic dream of outdoor hockey, see Blake, *Canadian Hockey Literature*, chap. 2.

99. Gzowski, *The Game of Our Lives*, 31.

EPILOGUE

1. The largest growth has come in Russia, where registrations increased by 86 percent over the last decade. The Czech Republic had a 22 percent growth in regis-

trations, and the United States 18 percent. IIHF Survey of Players, 2009–2010 Season; and IIHF Survey of Players, 2017–2018 Season, www.iihf.com/en/static/5324/survey-of-players.

2. On hockey in China, see "Chinese Hockey Expanding at an Astonishing Rate," *The Hockey Writers,* 27 February 2019, https://thehockeywriters.com/chinese-hockey-expanding-at-astonishing-rate/; "Chinese Ice Hockey Told to Improve to Justify Beijing 2022 Host Nation Spot," *Inside the Games,* 4 January 2019, www.insidethegames.biz/articles/1073832/chinese-ice-hockey-told-to-improve-to-justify-beijing-2022-host-nation-spot; and "The NHL, Seeking Fans in China, Calls in the Great One," *NYT,* 18 September 2018, www.nytimes.com/2018/09/18/sports/hockey/nhl-china-wayne-gretzky.html.

3. Branch, John. "Blood on the Ice," *NYT,* December 5, 2011, www.nytimes.com/2011/12/05/sports/hockey/derek-boogaard-blood-on-the-ice.html. Branch's book, based on the article series, is *Boy on Ice: The Life and Death of Derek Boogaard* (New York: Norton, 2014).

4. Dryden, *Game Change,* 314.

5. Ibid., 341.

6. Gary Bettman, testimony to House of Commons, Standing Committee on Health, Subcommittee on Sports-Related Concussions, 1 May 2019, www.ourcommons.ca/DocumentViewer/en/42-1/SCSC/meeting-11/evidence.

7. "For Noora Raty, a Continental Divide Is the Difference between Bronze and Gold," *The Washington Post,* 19 February 2018, www.washingtonpost.com/sports/olympics/for-noora-raty-a-continental-divide-is-the-difference-between-bronze-and-gold/2018/02/19/.

8. Ibid.

9. On the 2019 boycott, see Peter Donnelly, "North American Women's Ice Hockey Players Struggle for a League of Their Own," *The Conversation,* 9 June 2019, https://theconversation.com/north-american-womens-ice-hockey-players-struggle-for-a-league-of-their-own-117581; and the series of blog posts by Courtney Szto and Brett Pardy at the site *Hockey in Society,* https://hockeyinsociety.com/2019/04/07/myth-busting-part-1-no-one-wants-to-watch-womens-hockey/.

10. "Ilya Kovalchuk: 'U nas zabrali flag i gimn, no ne zabrali chest i sovest. Nado ekhat v Pkhenchkhan!,'" *Sport Ekspress,* 5 December 2017, www.sport-express.ru/olympics/pyeongchang2018/hockey/news/ilya-kovalchuk-u-nas-zabrali-flag-i-gimn-no-ne-zabrali-chest-i-sovest-nado-ehat-v-phenchhan-1344735/.

11. "Ataka shaiki Paunda: Doping v korlinge byl splanirovan zaraneie," *Championat,* 19 February 2018, www.championat.com/olympicwinter/article-3349889-olimpiada-2018-doping-v-kjorlinge-zagovor-provokacija-chto-delat.html.

12. "Alex Ovechkin Must Accept Missing Olympics, Russia Hockey Boss Says," *NBCSports.com,* 13 September 2017, https://olympics.nbcsports.com/2017/09/13/alex-ovechkin-vladislav-tretiak/. On other NHL players wanting to play in the Olympics, see "Will NHL Stars Defy League and Play in Olympics?," *SI.com,* 4 April 2017, www.si.com/nhl/2017/04/04/nhl-olympics-2018.

13. Szymon Szemberg, email, 30 July 2019.

14. Tony Keller, with Neville McGuire, "The New Economics of the NHL: Why Canada Can Support 12 Teams," April 2011, Mowat Centre for Policy Innovation, University of Toronto School of Public Policy and Government, munkschool.utoronto.ca/mowatcentre/wp-content/uploads/publications/19_the_new_economics_of_the_nhl.pdf.

15. "Blues-Bruins Stanley Cup Final Most-Watched in Four Years," *SportsMediaWatch*, 13 June 2019, www.sportsmediawatch.com/2019/06/stanley-cup-ratings-increase-blues-bruins-nbc/; "World Cup Final U.S. Ratings Fall from 2014," *Variety*, 17 July 2018, https://variety.com/2018/tv/news/world-cup-final-us-ratings-1202875655/.

16. "Viertelfinal-Aus beschert überragende TV-Quoten," *sport.de*, 24 May 2019, www.sport.de/news/ne3652000/eishockey-wm-viertelfinal-aus-von-deutschland-beschert-ueberragende-tv-quoten/; "Parad telezritelei: Chto smotreli v 2017-m," 26 December 2017, www.gazeta.ru/culture/2017/12/26/a_11539184.shtml; "Här är 2017 års mest sedda program," *Dagens Media*, 3 January 2018, www.dagensmedia.se/medier/rorligt/har-ar-2017-ars-mest-sedda-program-6891473; "Lejonen skapar VM-feber i tv-soffona," *HBL*, 24 May 2019, www.hbl.fi/artikel/lejonen-skapar-vm-feber-i-tv-soffornan-astan-25-miljoner-finlandare-tittade-pa-kvartsfinalen/.

17. "NHL Primes Pump for Future Talent with Transfer Fees," *USA Today*, 24 December 2012, www.usatoday.com/story/sports/nhl/2018/12/24/nhl-primes-pump-for-future-talent-with-transfer-fees/38791543.

18. Doo Jae Park, "'Hockey Is Not Your Stuff': The Racialized Athletic Identity of Korean Ice Hockey Players," *Hockey in Society*, 26 April 2017, https://hockeyinsociety.com/2017/04/26/hockey-is-not-your-stuff-the-racialized-athletic-identity-of-korean-ice-hockey-players/.

19. "Global Youth Team, League and Tournament Sports Market Is Expected to Reach USD 57.8 Billion by 2024," M2 Presswire, 24 September 2018.

20. Randi Griffin, email, 20 July 2019. On the absence of female coaches in hockey, see "Female Coaches Still Few, Doubted," *StarTribune* (Minneapolis), 6 January 2015.

21. Smith, *Puckstruck*, 82; see also Blake, *Canadian Hockey Literature*, 43.

22. Roy MacGregor, "Wally's Coliseum: The Melting of the Gretzky Backyard," in *Wayne Gretzky's Ghost and Other Tales from a Lifetime in Hockey* (Toronto: Random House Canada, 2011), 269; and "Outdoor Ice Rinks Melting into History," *CTV News* (November 20, 2015), www.ctvnews.ca/5things/flashback-friday-outdoor-ice-rinks-melting-into-history-1.2666100.

23. Stanley Kay, "Winter Is Going: How Climate Change Is Imperiling Outdoor Sporting Heritage," *SI*, 22 April 2019; "Canada's Outdoor Rinks Are Melting. So Is a Way of Life," *NYT*, 20 March 2018; and *RinkWatch*, www.rinkwatch.org.

24. Gopnik, *Winter*, 202.

BIBLIOGRAPHY

ARCHIVES
Canada

Archives of Manitoba, Winnipeg
Archives of Ontario, Toronto
Glenbow Museum Archives, Calgary
Hockey Hall of Fame Resource Centre, Toronto
Library and Archives Canada, Ottawa
University of Alberta Archives, Edmonton
University of Manitoba Archives, Winnipeg
University of Toronto Archives

Czech Republic

Archive of the National Museum, Prague
National Archive, Prague
Security Services Archive, Prague

Finland

Archives of Sport Museum of Finland, Helsinki

Hungary

Open Society Archives, Budapest

Slovakia

National Archive, Bratislava

Switzerland

International Ice Hockey Federation, Collected Minutes, Zurich
International Olympic Committee Historical Archives, Lausanne

United States

Minnesota State Historical Society, St. Paul
University of Illinois Archive, Champaign
University of Minnesota Archive, Minneapolis
Warroad (MN) Historical Society

PERIODICALS

Allgemeine Sport-Zeitung
Architectural Record
Argumenty i Fakty
The Atlanta Constitution
The Boston Globe
Calgary Herald
The Canadian Magazine
Canwest News Service
Chicago Tribune
Cleveland Call and Post
Colorado Springs Gazette Telegraph
Country Life Illustrated
The Courier (Davos)
Daily Gleaner (Fredericton, NB)
Daily News Record (New York)
Dayton Daily News
Detroit Free Press
Deutsche Allgemeine Zeitung
The Dominion Illustrated Monthly
Edmonton Journal
Edmonton Sun
Der Eissport/Der Eis- und Rollsport
Engineering News-Record
Foreign Policy
The Globe and Mail
The Hamilton Spectator
Hartford Courant
Illustrirte Sport Zeitung (Vienna)
Illustriertes (Österreichisches) Sportblatt

The Indianapolis Star
Jewish Exponent
Le Journal
Komsomolskaia pravda
Let's Play Hockey!
Los Angeles Times
Maclean's
The Manchester Guardian
Manitoba Free Press/Winnipeg Free Press
Minneapolis Star
Minneapolis Tribune
Montreal Gazette
Der Morgen (Vienna)
The Nation
National Post (Canada)
Neue Zürcher Zeitung
The New Times (Moscow)
The New York Times
Newsday
Orange County Register
Ottawa Citizen
Paris-soir
Pioneer Press (St. Paul)
Prager Tagblatt
Profil
Report on Business Magazine
Sales and Marketing Management
Saturday Night

Der Spiegel
Sport (Zurich)
Sport a hry (Prague)
Sporting Goods Business
Sports Illustrated
Star Tribune (Minneapolis)
The StarPhoenix (Saskatoon)
The Sun (Vancouver)
Der Tagesspiegel
The Times (London)
Toronto Evening Telegram
Toronto Star
Vancouver Sun
La Vie au grand air (Paris)
The Wall Street Journal
Walliser Volksfreund
The Washington Post
Windsor Star
Winnipeg Daily Tribune
Yunyi tekhnik (USSR)

WEBSITES

1972 Summit Series (1972SummitSeries.com)
British Pathé Historical Collection (britishpathe.com)
Canadian House of Commons (ourcommons.ca)
Canadian Parliamentary Historical Resources (parl.canadiana.ca)
Český Rozhlas (irozhlas.cz)
Championat (championat.com)
CIA Reading Room (cia.gov/library/readingroom)
The Conversation (theconversation.com)
Dagens Media (dagensmedia.se)
Elite Prospects (eliteprospects.com)
ESPN (espn.com)
Gazeta (gazeta.ru)
HBL (hbl.fi)
Hockey Canada (hockeycanada.ca)
Hockey in Society (hockeyinsociety.com)
The Hockey Writers (thehockeywriters.com)
iDnes (idnes.cz)
IIHF (iihf.com)
Inside the Games (insidethegames.biz)
IOC (olympic.org)
iSport (isport.cz)
KHL (khl.ru)
Kommersant (kommersant.ru)
Krasnaya Mashina (km1954.ru)
The Nation (thenation.com)
NBC Sports (nbcsports.com)
NCAA (ncaa.org)
New Books Network (newbooksnetwork.com)
Only a Game (wbur.org/onlyagame)
Pab Djon Donn (johndonne.ru)

The Players' Tribune (theplayerstribune.com)
Reuters (reuters.com)
Rink Watch (rinkwatch.org)
SBNation (sbnation.com)
Sport Ekspress (sport-express.ru)
Sport.de/NTV (sport.de)
Sports Illustrated (si.com)
Sports Media Watch (sportsmediawatch.com)
Sports.ru (sports.ru)
Statistics Canada (statcan.gc.ca)
Tass (tass.ru)
The Toast (the-toast.net)
Torontoist (torontoist.com)
US Census Bureau (www2.census.gov/library)
USA Hockey (usahockey.com)
USA Today (usatoday.com)
Variety (variety.com)
The Village (the-village.ru)
Women's Sports Foundation (womenssportsfoundation.org)
World Bank (worldbank.org)
Zolotaya Shaiba (zshr.ru)

BOOKS, ARTICLES, AND THESES

Adams, Carly. "Organizing Hockey for Women: The Ladies Ontario Hockey Association and the Fight for Legitimacy, 1922–1940." In *Coast to Coast: Hockey in Canada to the Second World War,* edited by John Chi-Kit Wong, 132–159. Toronto: University of Toronto Press, 2009.

———. "Troubling Bodies: 'The Canadian Girl,' the Ice Rink, and the Banff Winter Carnival." *Journal of Canadian Studies/Revue d'études canadiennes* 48, no. 3 (2014): 200–220.

Adams, Carly, and Jason Laurendeau. "'Here They Come! Look Them Over!' Youth, Citizenship, and the Emergence of Minor Hockey in Canada." In *Hockey: Challenging Canada's Game/Au-delà du sport national,* edited by Jenny Ellison and Jennifer Anderson, 111–124. Ottawa: Canadian Museum of History/University of Ottawa Press, 2018.

Adams, Mary Louise. *Artistic Impressions: Figure Skating, Masculinity, and the Limits of Sport.* Toronto: University of Toronto Press, 2011.

———. "The Game of Whose Lives? Gender, Race, and Entitlement in Canada's 'National' Game." In *Artificial Ice: Hockey, Culture, and Commerce,* edited by David Whitson and Richard Gruneau, 71–84. Peterborough, ON: Broadview, 2006.

Allain, Kristi. "'A Good Canadian Boy': Crisis Masculinity, Canadian National Identity, and Nostalgic Longings in Don Cherry's Coach's Corner." *International Journal of Canadian Studies* 52 (2015): 107–132.

Andersson, Torbjörn. "Bandy v. Ice Hockey in Sweden." *Sport in Society* 23 (2020).

Appadurai, Arjun. "Disjuncture and Difference in the Global Capital Economy." *Theory, Culture & Society* 7 (1990): 295–310.

Avery, Joanna, and Julie Stevens. *Too Many Men on the Ice: Women's Hockey in North America*. Victoria, BC: Polestar, 1997.

Backman, Fredrik. *Us against You*. Translated by Neil Smith. New York: Atria, 2017.

Backman, Jyri. *Ishockeyns amerikanisering: En studie av svensk och finsk elitishockey*. Malmö: University of Malmö, 2018.

Baerwald, Thomas J. "Forces at Work on the Landscape." In *Minnesota in a Century of Change: The State and Its People since 1900*, edited by Clifford E. Clark, 19–53. St. Paul: Minnesota Historical Society Press, 1989.

Baumann, Robert F. "The Central Army Sports Club (TsSKA): Forging a Military Tradition in Soviet Ice Hockey." *Journal of Sport History*, 15, no. 2 (1988): 151–166.

Beardsley, Doug. *Country on Ice*. Toronto: PaperJacks, 1988.

Bélanger, Anouk. "'The Last Game?' Hockey and the Experience of Masculinity in Québec." In *Sport and Gender in Canada*, edited by Philip White and Kevin Young, 293–309. Oxford: Oxford University Press, 1999.

Bennett, Paul W. "Training 'Blue-Blooded' Canadian Boys: Athleticism, Muscular Christianity, and Sports in Ontario's 'Little Big Four' Schools, 1829–1930." *Journal of Sport History* 43, no. 3 (2016): 253–271.

Berger, Carl. *Imperialism and Nationalism, 1884–1914: A Conflict in Canadian Thought*. Toronto: Copp Clark, 1969.

———. *The Sense of Power: Studies in the Ideas of Canadian Imperialism, 1867–1914*. 2nd ed. Toronto: University of Toronto Press, 2013.

Bidini, Dave. *The Tropic of Hockey: My Search for the Game in Unlikely Places*. Toronto: McClelland & Stewart, 2000.

Billings, Andrew C., James Angelini, and Paul J. MacArthur. *Olympic Television: Broadcasting the Biggest Show on Earth*. London: Routledge, 2017.

Blake, Jason. *Canadian Hockey Literature: A Thematic Survey*. Toronto: University of Toronto Press, 2010.

Boivin-Chouinard, Mathieu. *Chaïbou! Histoire du hockey russe, vol. 1: Des origines à la série du siècle*. Longueuil: Kéruss, 2011.

———. "Le hockey bourgeois est-il compatible avec la morale prolétarienne ? La naissance du hockey soviétique dans la complexité politique du stalinisme d'après-guerre." *Bulletin d'histoire politique* 22, no. 2 (2014): 53–76.

Bowman, Bob. *On the Ice*. London: Arthur Baker, 1937.

Branch, John. *Boy on Ice: The Life and Death of Derek Boogaard*. New York: Norton, 2014.

Brunt, Stephen. *Gretzky's Tears: Hockey, Canada, and the Day Everything Changed*. Toronto: Vintage Canada, 2010.

Buckner, Phillip, and R. Douglas Francis, eds. *Canada and the British World: Culture, Migration, and Identity*. Vancouver: University of British Columbia Press, 2006.

Bukač, Luděk. "Metodický dopis: Komplexní rozbor mistrovství světa a Evropy v ledním hokeji v Praze 1972." Prague: Olympia, 1973.

———. "Metodický dopis: Zkušenost z tréninku sovětských hokejových mužstev v přípravném období 1966–1967." Prague: Ústřední výbor československého svazu tělesné výchovy, 1968.

Bukač, Luděk, and František Suchan. *Bukač: Moje hokejové století*. Brno: JOTA, 2018.

Buma, Michael. *Refereeing Identity: The Cultural Work of Canadian Hockey Novels*. Montreal: McGill-Queen's University Press, 2012.

Buzuvis, Erin. "Coaches in Court: Legal Challenges to Sex Discrimination in College Athletics." *Tennessee Journal of Race, Gender, & Social Justice* 6, no. 41 (2017). https://trace.tennessee.edu/rgsj/vol6/iss1/4.

Cain, Louis P., and David D. Haddock. "Similar Economic Histories, Different Industrial Structures: Transatlantic Contrasts in the Evolution of Professional Sports Leagues." *The Journal of Economic History* 65, no. 4 (2005): 1116–1147.

Callaghan, Morley. "The Game That Makes a Nation" (1942). In *Words on Ice: A Collection of Hockey Prose*, edited by Michael P. J. Kennedy, 24–27. Toronto: Key Porter, 2003.

Cantelon, Hart. "Have Skates, Will Travel: Canada, International Hockey, and the Changing Hockey Labour Market." In *Artificial Ice: Hockey, Culture, and Commerce*, edited by David Whitson and Richard Gruneau, 215–236. Peterborough, ON: Broadview, 2006.

———. "Revisiting the Introduction of Ice Hockey into the Former Soviet Union." In *Putting It on Ice, vol. 2: Internationalizing "Canada's Game,"* edited by Colin D. Howell, 29–38. Halifax, NS: Saint Mary's University, 2011.

———. "The Social Reproduction of Sport: A Weberian Analysis of the Rational Development of Ice Hockey Under Scientific Socialism in the Soviet Union." PhD diss., University of Birmingham, 1981.

Carrier, Roch. *Our Life with the Rocket: The Maurice Richard Story*. Translated by Sheila Fischman. Toronto: Viking, 2001.

Chouinard, Normand, Sean Draper, Wade D. Gilbert, and Wayne Blann. "Athletic Scholarships for Canadian Hockey Players." *Journal CAHPERD* 65, no. 2 (1999): 34–36.

Chudacoff, Howard P. *Changing the Playbook: How Power, Profit, and Politics Transformed College Sports*. Champaign: University of Illinois Press, 2017.

Cleaver, Reginald. *A Winter-Sport Book*. London: Adam and Charles Black, 1911.

Coakley, Jay. "The Good Father: Parental Expectations and Youth Sports." *Leisure Studies* 25, no. 2 (April 2006): 153–163.

Coates, Dennis, and Brad R. Humphreys. "Can New Stadiums Revitalise Urban Neighbourhoods?" *Significance* 8, no. 2 (2011): 65–69.

Coffey, Wayne. *The Boys of Winter: The Untold Story of a Coach, a Dream, and the 1980 U.S Olympic Hockey Team*. New York: Three Rivers, 2005.

Cohen, Andrew. *Lester B. Pearson*. Toronto: Penguin Canada, 2008.

Collins, Tony. *The Oval World: A Global History of Rugby*. London: Bloomsbury, 2015.
Coupland, Douglas. *Souvenir of Canada*. Vancouver: Douglas & McIntyre, 2002.
Crefeld, Sven. *Gustav Jaenecke: Idol auf dem Eis*. Erfurt, Germany: Sutton, 2008.
Čupka, Milan, et al. *80 rokov slovenského hokeja*. Bratislava: Slovenský sväz ľadového hokeja, 2009.
Denault, Todd. *The Greatest Game: The Montreal Canadiens, the Red Army, and the Night That Saved Hockey*. Toronto: McClelland & Stewart, 2014.
Denning, Andrew. *Skiing into Modernity: A Cultural and Environmental History*. Berkeley: University of California Press, 2014.
Diamond, Dan, ed. *Total Hockey: The Official Encyclopedia of the National Hockey League*. New York: Total Sports, 1998.
Dowbiggin, Bruce. *The Stick: A History, a Celebration, an Elegy*. Toronto: Macfarlane, Walter & Ross, 2011.
Dryden, Ken. *The Game*, 30th anniversary edition. Chicago: Triumph, 2013.
———. *Game Change: The Life and Death of Steve Montador, and the Future of Hockey*. Toronto: Signal, 2017.
Dryden, Ken, and Cecil Eaves. *Let's Play Better Hockey*. McDonald's/Hockey Canada, 1973.
Dryden, Ken, and Roy MacGregor. *Home Game: Hockey and Life in Canada*. Toronto: McClelland & Stewart, 1989.
Dryden, Murray. *Playing the Shots at Both Ends: The Story of Ken and Dave Dryden*. Toronto: McGraw-Hill Ryerson, 1972.
Duke, Vic. "Perestroika in Progress?: The Case of Spectator Sports in Czechoslovakia." *British Journal of Sociology* 41, no. 2 (1990): 145–156.
Earle, Neil. "Hockey as Canadian Popular Culture: Team Canada 1972, Television and the Canadian Identity." *Journal of Canadian Studies* 30, no. 2 (1995): 107–123.
Edelman, Robert. *Serious Fun: A History of Spectator Sport in the USSR*. Oxford: Oxford University Press, 1993.
Eisenberg, Christiane. *"English Sports" und deutsche Bürger: Eine Gesellschaftsgeschichte*. Paderborn: Ferdinand Schöningh, 1999.
———. "'Not Cricket!' Sport in Germany, or How the British Model Fell into Oblivion." In *Britain as a Model of Modern Society? German Views*, edited by Arnd Bauerkämper and Christiane Eisenberg, 242–256. Augsburg, Germany: Wissner, 2006.
———. "Towards a New History of European Sport?" *European Review* 19, no. 4 (2011): 617–622.
Eto khokkei: Rasskazy, ocherki, chronikalnyie zametki, zabavnyie vydumannyie i nevydumannyie istorii i sluchai. Moscow: Molodaya gvardiya, 1971.
Etue, Elizabeth, and Megan K. Williams. *On the Edge: Women Making Hockey History*. Toronto: Second Story Press, 1996.
Fagan, Brian M. *The Little Ice Age: How Climate Made History*. New York: Perseus, 2000.
Ferry, Magnus, Jane Meckbach, and Håkan Larsson. "School Sport in Sweden: What Is It, and How Did It Come to Be?" *Sport in Society* 16, no. 6 (2013): 805–818.

Field, Russell. "A Night at the Garden(s): A History of Professional Hockey Spectatorship in the 1920s and 1930s." PhD diss., University of Toronto, 2008.
Fitsell, J. W. *Hockey's Captains, Colonels & Kings*. Erin, ON: Boston Mills Press, 1987.
Fosty, George and Darril. *Black Ice: The Lost History of the Colored Hockey League of the Maritimes, 1895–1925*. New York: Stryker–Indigo, 2004.
Friesen, Gerald. *The West: Regional Ambitions, National Debates, Global Age*. Toronto: Penguin Canada, 1999.
Fuks, Konstantin. "The Rebirth of *Dinamo Riga:* From the Glorious Soviet Past to the Kontinental Hockey League." MA thesis, University of Turku, 2013.
Fürst, Juliane. *Stalin's Last Generation: Soviet Post-war Youth and the Emergence of Mature Socialism*. Oxford: Oxford University Press, 2010.
Giddens, Anthony. *Runaway World: How Globalization Is Reshaping Our Lives*. London: Profile, 1999.
Gidén, Carl, Patrick Houda, and Jean-Patrice Martel. *On the Origin of Hockey*. Stockholm: Hockey Origin Publishing, 2014.
Gilbert, John. *Herb Brooks: The Inside Story of a Hockey Mastermind*. Minneapolis: MVP Books, 2010.
Gilenstam, Kajsa, Staffan Karp, and Karin Henriksson-Larsén. "Gender in Ice Hockey: Women in a Male Territory." *Scandinavian Journal of Medicine and Science in Sports* 18 (2008): 235–249.
Gitersos, Terry. "'Ça devient une question d'être maîtres chez nous': The Canadiens, Nordiques, and the Politics of Québécois Nationalism, 1979–1984." PhD diss., University of Western Ontario, 2011.
Giulianotti, Richard. "Supporters, Followers, Fans, and *Flaneurs:* A Taxonomy of Specator Identities in Football." *Journal of Sport & Social Issues* 26, no. 1 (2002): 25–46.
Goldblatt, David. *The Ball Is Round: A Global History of Soccer*. New York: Riverhead, 2008.
Goldin, Claudia. "The Quiet Revolution That Transformed Women's Employment, Education, and Family." *The American Economic Review* 96, no. 2 (2006): 1–21.
Gopnik, Adam. *Winter: Five Windows on the Season*. Toronto: Anansi, 2011.
Grant, George. *Lament for a Nation: The Defeat of Canadian Nationalism*, 40th anniversary edition. Montreal and Kingston: McGill University–Queen's University Press, 2005.
Gridasov, Stanislav. *Kristal'nyye lyudi*. Moscow: Pyatyy Rim, 2018.
Griswold, Robert. "The 'Flabby American,' the Body, and the Cold War." In *A Shared Experience: Men, Women, and The History of Gender*, edited by Laura McCall and Donald Yacovone, 323–334. New York: New York University Press, 1998.
"Growth in Youth Sports Participation." *Journal of Physical Education, Recreation & Dance* 70, no. 9 (1999): 6.
Gruneau, Richard S. "Goodbye, Gordie Howe: Sport Participation and Class Inequality in the 'Pay for Play' Society." In *How Canadians Communicate, vol. 5: Sports*, edited by David Taras and Christopher Waddell, 223–246. Edmonton, AB: AU Press, 2016.

Gruneau, Richard S., and David Whitson, eds. *Artificial Ice: Hockey, Culture and Commerce*. Peterborough, ON: Broadview Press, 2006.

Gruneau, Richard S., and David Whitson. *Hockey Night in Canada: Sport, Identities, and Cultural Politics*. Toronto: Garamond Press, 1993.

Guillen, Mauro F. "Is Globalization Civilizing, Destructive or Feeble? A Critique of Five Key Debates in the Social Science Literature." *Annual Review of Sociology* 27 (2001): 235–260.

Gut, Karel, and Gustav Vlk. *Světový hokej*. Prague: Olympia, 1990.

Gzowski, Peter. *The Game of Our Lives*. Surrey, BC: Heritage House, 2004.

Hall, M. Ann. *The Girl and the Game: A History of Women's Sport in Canada*. Toronto: University of Toronto Press, 2002.

Hansen, Kenth. "The Birth of Swedish Hockey: Antwerp 1920." *Citius, Altius, Fortius* 4, no. 2 (1996): 5–27.

Hanson, Stephen E. *Time and Revolution: Marxism and the Design of Soviet Institutions*. Chapel Hill: University of North Carolina Press, 1997.

Harder, Paul. "Developing World Championship Hockey in the USSR: The Inside Story, 1946–1972." MA thesis: Carleton University, 2004.

Hardwick, M. Jeffrey. *Mall Maker: Victor Gruen, Architect of an American Dream*. Philadelphia: University of Pennsylvania Press, 2010.

Hardy, Stephen, and Andrew Holman. *Hockey: A Global History*. Champaign: University of Illinois Press, 2018.

———. "Hockey Towns: The Making of Special Places in America and Canada." In *Putting It on Ice: Proceedings of the 2012 Hockey Conference*, edited by Lori Dithurbide and Colin Howell (December 2013).

Harris, Cecil. *Breaking the Ice: The Black Experience in Professional Hockey*. Toronto: Insomniac Press, 2003.

Hartje, Tod, with Lawrence Martin. *From behind the Red Line: An American Hockey Player in Russia*. New York: Macmillan, 1992.

Hašek, Dominik, with Robert Záruba. *Chytám svůj život*. Prague: Terra, 1999.

Haslinger, Josef. *Jáchymov*. Berlin: S. Fischer, 2011.

Heywood, Leslie, and Shari L. Dworkin. *Built to Win: The Female Athlete as Cultural Icon*. Minneapolis: University of Minnesota Press, 2003.

Holman, Andrew. "A Flag of Tendons: Hockey and Canadian History." In *Hockey: Challenging Canada's Game/Au-delà du sport national*, edited by Jenny Ellison and Jennifer Anderson, 25–44. Ottawa: Canadian Museum of History/University of Ottawa Press, 2018.

———, ed. *Canada's Game: Hockey and Identity*. Montreal: McGill-Queen's University Press, 2009.

Hughes, Jon. "'Im Sport ist der Nerv der Zeit selber zu spüren': Sport and Cultural Debate in the Weimar Republic." *German as a Foreign Language (GFL)* (2007): 28–45.

Humphreys, Brad R. *The Economics of Professional Hockey*. Morgantown, WV: BRH Publishing, 2016.

Igartua, José Eduardo. *The Other Quiet Revolution: National Identities in English Canada, 1945–71*. Vancouver: UBC Press, 2006.

Ingrassia, Brian. *The Rise of Gridiron University: Higher Education's Uneasy Alliance with Big-Time Football*. Lawrence: University Press of Kansas, 2012.

Jágr, Jaromír, with Tomáš Šmid, *Z Kladna do Ameriky: Vlastní životopis*. Prague: Gutenberg, 2011.

Jameson, Elizabeth, and Jeremy Mouat. "Telling Differences: The Forty-Ninth Parallel and Historiographies of the West and Nation." *Pacific Historical Review* 75, no. 2 (May 2006): 183–230.

Jenish, D'Arcy. *The NHL—A Centennial History: 100 Years of On-Ice Action and Boardroom Battles*. Toronto: Doubleday Canada, 2013.

Jensen, Erik N. *Body by Weimar: Athletes, Gender, and German Modernity*. Oxford: Oxford University Press, 2010.

Joiner, Thomas E., Jr., Daniel Hollar, and Kimberly Van Orden, "Buckeyes, Gators, Super Bowl Sunday, and the Miracle on Ice: 'Pulling Together' Is Associated with Lower Suicide Rates." *Journal of Social and Clinical Psychology* 25, no. 2 (2006): 179–195.

Jokisipilä, Markku. "Maple Leaf, Hammer, and Sickle: International Ice Hockey during the Cold War." *Sport History Review* 37 (2006): 36–53.

———. "World Champions Bred by National Champions: The Role of State-Owned Corporate Giants in Russian Sports." *Russian Analytical Digest* no. 95 (6 April 2011): 8–11.

Karas, Steffan. *100 Jahre Eishockey in Berlin: Faszination durch Tradition*. Berlin: Jeske/Mader, 2008.

Keller, Tony, with Neville McGuire. "The New Economics of the NHL: Why Canada Can Support 12 Teams." April 2011, Mowat Centre for Policy Innovation, University of Toronto School of Public Policy and Government. https://munkschool.utoronto.ca/mowatcentre/wp-content/uploads/publications/19_the_new_economics_of_the_nhl.pdf.

Kerk, John. "Curling." In *Skating*. London: Longmans, Green, 1892.

Kerr, Donald, and Deryck W. Holdsworth, eds. *Historical Atlas of Canada, vol. 3: Addressing the Twentieth Century, 1891–1961*. Toronto: University of Toronto Press, 1987.

Kidd, Bruce. "Muscular Christianity and Value-Centred Sport: The Legacy of Tom Brown in Canada." *Sport in Society* 16, no. 4 (2013).

———. *The Struggle for Canadian Sport*. Toronto: University of Toronto Press, 1996.

Kidd, Bruce, and John Macfarlane. *The Death of Hockey*. Toronto: New Press, 1972.

Kingston, George Edward. "The Organisation and Development of Ice Hockey during Childhood in the Soviet Union, Czechoslovakia, Sweden and Canada." PhD diss., University of Alberta, 1977.

Kirby, David. *A Concise History of Finland*. Cambridge: Cambridge University Press, 2006.

Kokkonen, Jouko. "Sports and Nationalism—United Forever?" *Motion: Sport in Finland*, I/2003, 8.

Kokkonen, Jouko, Markku Jokisipilä and Kalle Rantala. *Koko kansan leijonat.* Helsinki: Docendo, 2018.
Kostka, Vladimir. "The Czechoslovakian Youth Ice Hockey Training System." Translated by Ladislav Hudak. Unbound: Canadian Amateur Hockey Association, 1979.
———. *Útok v ledním hokeji.* Prague: Sportovní a turistické naklad, 1963.
Krüger, Arnd. "The Role of Sport in German International Politics, 1918–1945." In *Sport and International Politics: Impact of Fascism and Communism on Sport*, edited by Pierre Arnaud and Jim Riordan, 79–96. London: Routledge, 1999.
Lamb, H. H. *Climate, History, and the Modern World.* London: Methuen, 1982.
Lämsä, Jari. "Lions on the Ice: The Success Story of Finnish Ice Hockey." In *Nordic Elite Sport: Same Ambitions—Different Tracks,* edited by Svein S. Andersen and Lars Tore. Oslo: Universitetsforlaget, 2011.
Lanctôt, Gustave. "Past Historians and Present History in Canada." *The Canadian Historical Review* 22, no. 3 (September 1941): 241–253.
Lapierre, Emmanuel. "Le hockey est-il naturellement canadien ? Pour un débat sur le hockey et l'identité nationale." *Bulletin d'histoire politique* 22 (2014): 92–110.
Lappage, Ronald S. "Selected Sports and Canadian Society, 1921–1939." PhD diss., University of Alberta, 1974.
Lareau, Annette. *Unequal Childhoods: Class, Race, and Family Life.* Berkeley: University of California Press, 2003.
Larionov, Igor. "V dolgu pered khokkeem ...," *Ogonyok* 42 (1988) [full text at "Otkrytoe pismo Larionova v zhurnale 'Ogonek,'" www.hockeyreview.ru/main/23027-otkrytoe-pismo-larionova-v-zhurnale-ogonek.html].
Larionov, Igor, Jim Taylor, and Leonid Reizer. *Larionov.* Winnipeg: Codner, 1990.
Larivière, Georges. *Canadian Hockey, vol. 1: Beginner's Program.* Vanier, ON: CAHA, Hockey Development Council, 1975.
Laufer, Josef. *Hokej—můj osud.* Prague: Mladá fronta, 1960.
Leeworthy, Daryl. "Skating on the Border: Hockey, Class, and Commercialism in Interwar Britain." *Histoire sociale/Social History* 48 (2015): 193–213.
Lévesque, Jean. "Hockey et politique: jalons pour une historiographie raisonnée." *Bulletin d'histoire politique* 22, no. 2 (2014): 33–52.
Lewis, Robert W. *The Stadium Century: Sport, Spectatorship and Mass Society in France.* Manchester, UK: Manchester University Press, 2017.
Llewellyn, Matthew P., and John Gleaves. *The Rise and Fall of Olympic Amateurism.* Urbana: University of Illinois Press, 2016.
Lorenz, Stacy L. "'Bowing Down to Babe Ruth': Major League Baseball and Canadian Popular Culture, 1920–1929." *Canadian Journal of the History of Sport* 26, no. 1 (1995): 22–39.
———. "National Media Coverage and the Creation of a Canadian 'Hockey World': The Winnipeg-Montreal Stanley Cup Hockey Challenges, 1899–1903." *The International Journal of the History of Sport* 32 (2015): 2012–2043.
Lorenz, Stacy L., and Geraint B. Osbourne, "'Talk about Strenuous Hockey': Violence, Manhood, and the 1907 Ottawa Silver Seven-Montreal Wanderer Rivalry."

Journal of Canadian Studies/Revue d'études canadiennes 40, no. 1 (2006): 125–156.

Ludwig, Jack. *Hockey Night in Moscow*. Toronto: McClelland and Stewart, 1972.

Lukšů, David. *Žit jako Holík, Životné a hokejové zápasy Jaroslava Holíka*. Prague: Epocha, 2015.

Lukšů, David, and Aleš Palán. *Stanislav Konopásek: Hráč, který přežil*. Prague: Edice ČT, 2007.

———. *Vladimír Zábrodský: Skutečný příběh hokejové legendy*. Prague: Edice ČT, 2010.

Lunn, H. "Winter Sport in Switzerland." In Reginald Cleaver, *A Winter-Sport Book*, 28–36. London: Adam and Charles Black, 1911.

MacDonald, Mary G. "Miraculous Masculinity Meets Militarization: Narrating the 1980 USSR-US Men's Olympic Ice Hockey Match and Cold War Politics." In *East Plays West: Sport and the Cold War*, edited by Stephen Wagg and David L. Andrews, 222–234. New York: Routledge, 2007.

MacFarlane, Brian. *Proud Past, Bright Future: 100 Years of Canadian Women's Hockey*. Toronto: Stoddart, 1994.

MacGregor, Roy. *Wayne Gretzky's Ghost and Other Tales from a Lifetime in Hockey*. Toronto: Random House Canada, 2011.

Mackintosh, Donald, and Donna Greenhorn. "Hockey Diplomacy and Canadian Foreign Policy." *Journal of Canadian Studies/Revue d'études canadiennes* 28, no. 2 (1993): 96–112.

Macků, Jiří. *Kauza Zábrodský*. Prague: TYPO IP, 2005.

MacSkimming, Roy. *Cold War: The Amazing Canada-Soviet Hockey Series of 1972*. Vancouver: Greystone, 1996.

Manuel, Jeffrey. *Taconite Dreams: The Struggle to Sustain Mining on Minnesota's Iron Range, 1915–2000*. Minneapolis: University of Minnesota Press, 2015.

Martin, Lawrence. *The Red Machine: The Soviet Quest to Dominate Canada's Game*. Toronto: Doubleday, 1980.

Mason, Daniel S. "The International Hockey League and the Professionalization of Ice Hockey, 1904–1907." *Journal of Sport History* 25, no. 1 (1998): 1–17.

McKinley, Michael. *Hockey: A People's History*. Toronto: McClelland & Stewart, 2009.

———. *Putting a Roof on Winter: Hockey's Rise from Sport to Spectacle*. Vancouver: Greystone, 2002.

Meeker, Howie. *Howie Meeker's Hockey Basics*. Scarborough, ON: Prentice-Hall, 1973.

Melançon, Benoît. *The Rocket: A Cultural History*. Trans. Fred A. Reed. Vancouver: Greystone, 2009.

Metcalfe, Alan. *Canada Learns to Play: The Emergence of Organized Sport, 1807–1914*. Toronto: McClelland and Stewart, 1987 [and Toronto: Stoddart, 1994].

———. "Power: A Case Study of the Ontario Hockey Association, 1890–1936." *Journal of Sport History* 19, no. 1 (1992): 5–25.

Mikhailov, Boris. *Takova khokkeynaya zhizn*. Moscow: Eksmo, 2008.

Mills, Brian, and Rodney Fort. "League-Level Attendance and Outcome Uncertainty in U.S. Pro Sports Leagues." *Economic Inquiry* 52, no. 1 (2014): 205–218.

Montrie, Chad. "'A Bigoted, Prejudiced, Hateful Little Area': The Making of an All-White Suburb in the Deep North." *Journal of Urban History* (April 2017): 300–320.

Mott, Morris. "'An Immense Hold in the Public Estimation': The First Quarter Century of Hockey in Manitoba, 1886–1911." *Manitoba History* 43, no. 2 (2002)

———. "One Solution to the Urban Crisis: Manly Sports and Winnipeggers, 1900–1914." *Urban History Review* 12, no. 2 (1983): 57–70.

Mouton, Michelle. "Sports, Song, and Socialization: Women's Memories of Youthful Activity and Political Indoctrination in the BDM." *Journal of Women's History* 17, no. 2 (2005): 62–86.

Müller, Paul. "Die Entwicklung des Eishockeys in Davos (I)." *Davoser revue* 15 (February 1940): 79–103.

———. "Die Entwicklung des Eishockeys in Davos (II)." *Davoser revue* 15 (March 1940): 76–81.

Nathaus, Klaus. "Between Club and Commerce: Comparing the Organisation of Sports in Britain and Germany from the Late Nineteenth to the Early Twentieth Century." In *Cultural Industries in Britain and Germany: Sport, Music and Entertainment from the Eighteenth to the Twentieth Century*, edited by Christiane Eisenberg and Andreas Gestrich. Augsburg, Germany: Wissner, 2012.

National Collegiate Athletic Association. *Official Ice Hockey Guide*. New York: National Collegiate Athletic Bureau, 1953.

Newman, Katherine S. *Declining Fortunes: The Withering of the American Dream*. New York: Basic Books, 1993.

Nielsen, Niels Keyser. *Body, Sport, and Society in Norden: Essays in Cultural History*. Aarhus, Denmark: University of Aarhus Press, 2005.

Nielsen, Stefan. *Sport und Großstadt 1870 bis 1930: Komparative Studien zur Entstehung bürglicher Freizeitkultur*. Frankfurt am Main: Peter Lang, 2002.

Norberg, Johan R. "A Mutual Dependency: Nordic Sports Organizations and the State." *The International Journal of the History of Sport* 14, no. 3 (1997): 115–135.

Norton, Wayne. *Women on Ice: The Early Years on Women's Hockey in Western Canada*. Vancouver: Ronsdale Press, 2009.

Ontario Hockey Council. *You and Your Child in Hockey*. Toronto: Ontario Ministry of Culture and Recreation, 1976.

O'Reilly, Norm, et al. "Merchandise Sales Rank in Professional Sport: Purchase Drivers and Implications for National Hockey League Clubs." *Sport, Business and Management: An International Journal* 5, no. 4 (2015): 307–324.

Orr, Bobby. *Orr: My Story*. New York: G. P. Putnam's Sons, 2013.

Owram, Doug. *Born at the Right Time: A History of the Baby Boom Generation*. Toronto: University of Toronto Press, 1996.

Palmer, Scott W. *Dictatorship of the Air: Aviation Culture and the Fate of Modern Russia*. Cambridge: Cambridge University Press, 2006.

Parks, Jennifer. *The Olympic Games, the Soviet Sports Bureaucracy, and the Cold War: Red Sport, Red Tape*. Lanham, MD: Lexington, 2017.

Patton, B. M. *Ice-Hockey*. London: Routledge, 1936.

Pfister, Gertrud. "Cultural Confrontations: German *Turnen,* Swedish Gymnastics and English Sport—European Diversity in Physical Activities from a Historical Perspective." *Culture, Sport, Society* 6, no. 1 (2003): 61–91.

Pieterse, Jan Nederveen. *Globalization and Culture: Global Mélange.* Lanham, MD: Rowman & Littlefield, 2004.

Podnieks, Andrew, et al. *Kings of the Ice: A History of World Hockey.* Richmond Hill, ON: NDE, 2002.

Ponzio, Alessio. *Shaping the New Man: Youth Training Regimes in Fascist Italy and Nazi Germany.* Madison: University of Wisconsin Press, 2017.

Poulter, Gillian. *Becoming Native in a Foreign Land: Sport, Visual Culture and Identity in Montreal, 1840–85.* Vancouver: UBC Press, 2009.

Poussenkova, Nina. "The Global Expansion of Russia's Energy Giants." *Journal of International Affairs* 63, no. 2 (2010): 103–124.

Prozumenshchikov, Mikhail. "Soviet-Czechoslovak Ice Hockey Politics." In *The (Inter-Communist) Cold War on Ice: Soviet-Czechoslovak Ice Hockey Politics, 1967–1969,* Cold War International History Project Working Paper no. 69, edited by James G. Hershberg (February 2014): 91–109.

———. "Sports as a Mirror of Eastern Europe's Crises." *Russian Studies in History* 49, no. 2 (2010): 51–93.

Raleigh, Donald. *Soviet Baby Boomers: An Oral History of Russia's Cold War Generation.* Oxford: Oxford University Press, 2013.

Resch, Glenn. Oral history interview by Andrea Kaminsky. February 1976, Columbia University.

Riordan, James. *Sport in Soviet Society: Development of Sport and Physical Education in Russia and the USSR.* Cambridge: Cambridge University Press, 1977.

Riordan, James, and Victor Peppard. *Playing Politics: Soviet Sport Diplomacy to 1992.* Greenwich, CT: JAI Press, 1993.

Robidoux, Michael A. "Imagining a Canadian Identity through Sport: A Historical Interpretation of Lacrosse and Hockey." *Journal of American Folklore* 115, no. 456 (2002): 209–225.

———. *Men at Play: A Working Understanding of Professional Hockey.* Montreal: McGill-Queen's University Press, 2001.

Ross, J. Andrew. "Hockey Capital: Commerce, Culture, and the National Hockey League, 1917–1967." PhD diss., University of Western Ontario, 2008.

———. *Joining the Clubs: The Business of the National Hockey League.* Syracuse, NY: Syracuse University Press, 2015.

Rothe, Wolfgang. "When Sports Conquered the Republic: A Forgotten Chapter from the 'Roaring Twenties.'" *Studies in 20th Century Literature* 4, no. 1 (1979): 1–27.

Rubin, Evgenii. *Pan ili propal! Zhizneopisanie.* Moscow: Zakharov, 2000.

Rutherdale, Robert. "Fatherhood, Masculinity, and the Good Life During Canada's Baby Boom, 1945–1965." *Journal of Family History* 24, no. 3 (1999): 351–373.

Rutherford, Paul. *When Television Was Young: Primetime Canada 1952–1967.* Toronto: University of Toronto Press, 1990.

Sakwa, Richard. "Putin and the Oligarchs." *New Political Economy* 13, no. 2 (2008): 185–191.
Sejerstad, Francis. *The Age of Social Democracy: Norway and Sweden in the Twentieth Century*. Princeton, NJ: Princeton University Press, 2011.
Shubert, Howard. *Architecture on Ice: A History of the Hockey Arena*. Montreal and Kingston: McGill-Queen's University Press, 2016.
Silver, Jim. *Thin Ice: Money, Politics, and the Demise of an NHL Franchise*. Winnipeg: Fernwood, 1996.
Skille, Eivind Å. "Sport for All in Scandinavia: Sport Policy and Participation in Norway, Sweden and Denmark." *International Journal of Sport Policy and Politics* 3, no. 3 (November 2011): 327–339.
Smith, Bryan. *The Breakaway: The Inside Story of the Wirtz Family Business and the Chicago Blackhawks*. Evanston, IL: Northwestern University Press, 2018.
Smith, Michael D. "Towards an Explanation of Hockey Violence: A Reference Other Approach." *The Canadian Journal of Sociology/Cahiers canadiens de sociologie* 4, no. 2 (1979): 105–124.
Smith, Stephen. *Puckstruck: Distracted, Delighted, and Distressed by Canada's Hockey Obsession*. Vancouver: Greystone, 2014.
Smythe, Conn, with Scott Young. *If You Can't Beat 'em in the Alley*. Toronto: McClelland and Stewart, 1981.
Soares, John. "Complexity in Soviet-Czechoslovak Hockey Relations." In *The (Inter-Communist) Cold War on Ice: Soviet-Czechoslovak Ice Hockey Politics, 1967–1969*, Cold War International History Project Working Paper no. 69, edited by James G. Hershberg (February 2014): 4–11.
Stark, Tobias. *Folkhemmet på is: Ishockey, modernisering och nationell identitet i Sverige 1920–1972*. Malmö: idrottsforum.org, 2010.
———. "'How Swede It Is': Börje Salming and the Migration of Swedish Ice Hockey Players to the NHL, 1957–2012." In *Constructing the Hockey Family: Home, Community, Bureaucracy and Marketplace*, edited by Lori Dithurbide and Colin Howell, 364–393. Halifax, NS: Saint Mary's University, 2012.
———. "O Canada, We Stand On Guard for Thee: Representations of Canadian Hockey Players in the Swedish Press, 1920–2016." In *Hockey: Challenging Canada's Game/Au-delà du sport national*, edited by Jenny Ellison and Jennifer Anderson. Ottawa: Canadian Museum of History/University of Ottawa Press, 2018.
———. "The Pioneer, the Pal and the Poet: Masculinities and National Identities in Canadian, Swedish, and Soviet-Russian Hockey during the Cold War." In *Putting It on Ice, vol. 2: Internationalizing "Canada's Game,"* edited by Colin D. Howell. Halifax, NS: Gorsebrook Research Institute, Saint Mary's University, 2002.
Steger, Manfred B. *Globalization: A Very Short Introduction*, 2nd ed. New York: Oxford University Press, 2011.
———. *The Rise of the Global Imaginary: Political Ideologies from the French Revolution to the Global War on Terror*. New York: Oxford University Press, 2008.

Stride, Christopher, Jean Williams, David Moor, and Nick Catley. "From Sportswear to Leisurewear: The Evolution of English Football League Shirt Design in the Replica Kit Era." *Sport in History* 35, no. 1 (2015): 156–194.

Sund, Bill. "The Origins of Bandy and Hockey in Sweden." In *Putting It on Ice, vol. 2: Internationalizing "Canada's Game,"* edited by Colin D. Howell. Halifax, NS: Gorsebrook Research Institute, Saint Mary's University, 2002.

Surdam, David. *The Age of Ruth and Landis: The Economics of Baseball during the Roaring Twenties.* Lincoln: University of Nebraska Press, 2018.

Syers, Edgar Wood. "Skating and Skating Resorts." *The Winter Sports Annual, 1906–7.* London: Horace Cox, 1906.

Szemberg, Szymon, and Andrew Podnieks, eds. *World of Hockey: Celebrating a Century of the IIHF.* Bolton, ON: Fenn, 2007.

Szymanski, Stefan. *Money and Soccer: A Soccernomics Guide.* New York: Nation Books, 2015.

———. "A Theory of the Evolution of Modern Sport," with comment by Steven A. Riess, Arnd Krüger, and Malcolm MacLean. *Journal of Sport History* 35, no. 1 (2008): 1–64.

Tarasov, Anatoli. *Road to Olympus.* Richmond Hill, ON: Simon & Schuster of Canada, 1972.

Tebbutt, C. G. "Bandy," in *Skating and Figure Skating.* London: Longmans, Green, 1892.

Thordarson, Fred. "The Romance of the Falcons." 1932 manuscript, published in *The Icelandic Canadian* (Fall 1996): 5–19 and 32–35.

Theberge, Nancy. "It's Part of the Game: Physicality and the Production of Gender in Women's Hockey." *Gender and Society* 11 (1997): 69–87.

Thrall, Jeannie S. "Strategic Parenting: Making the Middle Class through Distinction and Discipline." PhD diss., University of Michigan, 2010.

Tikhonov, Viktor. *Hokej na celý život.* Translated into Czech by Petr Feldstein. Prague: Olympia, 1988.

Torrance, David E. "Instructor to Empire: Canada and the Rhodes Scholarship, 1902–39." In *Canada and the British World: Culture, Migration, and Identity,* edited by Phillip Buckner and R. Douglas Francis, 250–269. Vancouver: University of British Columbia Press, 2006.

Tretiak, Vladislav, with V. Snegirev. *The Hockey I Love.* Translated by Anatole Konstantin. Toronto: Fitzhenry & Whiteside, 1977.

Triet, Max. "Davos als Zentrum des Sports." In *Davos: Profil eines Phänomens,* edited by Ernst Halter. Zurich: Offizin, 1997.

Tůma, Oldřich. "'They Had No Tanks This Time and They Got Four Goals': The Hockey Events in Czechoslovakia in 1969 and the Fall of Alexander Dubček." In *The (Inter-Communist) Cold War on Ice: Soviet-Czechoslovak Ice Hockey Politics, 1967–1969,* Cold War International History Project Working Paper no. 69, edited by James G. Hershberg (February 2014), 12–34.

Vance, Jonathan F. W. *Death So Noble: Memory, Meaning, and the First World War.* Vancouver: UBC Press, 1997.

Vasiliev, Valerii. "Moi krestnyi otets." In *Trenery sedeyot rano,* edited by L. V. Rossoshik. Moscow: Terra-Sport, 2001.

Vaz, Edmund W. *The Professionalization of Young Hockey Players.* Lincoln: University of Nebraska Press, 1982.

Vigneault, Michel. "Montreal's Francophone Hockey Beginnings, 1895–1910." In *The Same but Different: Hockey in Quebec,* edited by Jason Blake and Andrew C. Holman. Montreal and Kingston: McGill-Queen's University Press, 2017.

———. "La naissance d'un sport organisé au Canada: le hockey à Montréal, 1875–1917." PhD diss., Université Laval, 2001.

Weiner, Jay. *Stadium Games: Fifty Years of Big League Greed and Bush League Boondoggles.* Minneapolis: University of Minnesota Press, 2000.

Weiss, Jessica. "Making Room for Fathers: Men, Women, and Parenting in the United States, 1945–1980." In *A Shared Experience: Men, Women, and the History of Gender,* edited by Laura McCall and Donald Yacovone. New York: New York University Press, 1998.

Wendel, Tim. *Going for the Gold: How the U.S. Olympic Hockey Team Won at Lake Placid.* Mineola, NY: Dover, 2009 [reprint; originally published in 1980].

Willes, Ed. *The Rebel League: The Short and Unruly Life of the World Hockey Association.* Toronto: McClelland & Stewart, 2004.

Winn, Marie. *Children without Childhood.* New York: Pantheon, 1983.

Wong, John Chi-Kit, ed. *Coast to Coast: Hockey in Canada to the Second World War.* Toronto: University of Toronto Press, 2009.

Wong, John Chi-Kit. *Lords of the Rinks: The Emergence of the National Hockey League, 1875–1936.* Toronto: University of Toronto Press, 2005.

Young, Scott. *Hello Canada! The Life and Times of Foster Hewitt.* Toronto: Seal Books, 1985.

———. *War on Ice: Canada in International Hockey.* Toronto: McClelland and Stewart, 1976.

GOVERNMENT DOCUMENTS

Blainey v. Ontario Hockey Association and Ontario Human Rights Commission. Supreme Court of Ontario, Court of Appeals, 1986. C/A 630/85.

Canada, Committee on International Hockey. Report to the Honourable Iona Campagnolo, Minister of State, Fitness and Amateur Sport. 1977.

McMurtry, William R. *Investigation and Inquiry into Violence in Amateur Hockey.* Toronto: Sports and Fitness Division, 1978.

Miller et al. v. Board of Regents of the University of Minnesota. 0:15-CV-03740-RHKLIB (D. Minn. 2015).

National Coaches Certification Program, Proceedings: Level 5 Seminar. Vanier, ON: CAHA, Hockey Development Council, 1973.

Ontario Hockey Council. *Minor Hockey in Ontario: Toward a Positive Learning Environment for Children in the 1980's*. Toronto: Ministry of Culture and Education, 1979.

———. *You and Your Child in Hockey*. Toronto: Ontario Ministry of Culture and Recreation, 1976.

Saskatchewan Hockey Task Force. Final Report, submitted to Department of Culture and Youth, 17 April 1974.

US Department of Commerce. *1970 Census of Population and Housing: Census Tracts—Minneapolis-St. Paul, Minnesota, Standard Metropolitan Statistical Area*. Washington, DC: US Government Printing Office, 1972.

US Department of the Interior, Heritage Conservation and Recreation Service. *The Third Nationwide Outdoor Recreation Plan: The Assessment*. Washington, DC: Heritage Conservation and Recreation Service, 1979.

INTERVIEWS

Marissa Brandt
Luděk Bukač
Matt Dalton
Mike DeAngelis
Dave Dryden
Mike Eaves
Michael Eisner
Randi Griffin
Dov Grumet-Morris
John Harrington
Dominik Hašek
Kim Martin Hasson
Jack McCartan
Bob O'Connor
Jim Paek
Caroline Park
Alena Polenská Mills
Patricia Sautter Elsmore
Florence Schelling
Thomas Staggs
Szymon Szemberg
Lou Vairo
Phil Verchota

INDEX

ABC Sports (American Broadcasting Corporation), 175–176
Alberta, 60, 116, 119, 182, 191, 196, 231; University of, 88, 165
Allan Cup, 59, 87, 117
Amateur Athletic Union of Canada, 89
amateurism, 45, 50–51, 53–54, 83, 89, 167, 207
American hockey 2–3, 95–96, 134–139, 162, 166–172, 174, 185–189; and girls and women, 191, 196, 227–228, 229–233, 241–242; players in NHL, 134, 135, 162, 177, 178, 179–180, 185, 187–188. *See also* United States
"Americanization" of hockey, Canadian views of, 48–49, 63–65, 83, 116–117, 117–119, 156–157, 181, 211, 220–221
Anaheim Ducks (Mighty Ducks of Anaheim), 211–212, 213, 223
Andersson, Mikael, 159, 161
Anschutz Entertainment Group, 12
Antwerp, Belgium, 34, 50–51, 52, 53, 59, 67
arenas: design of, 62, 69, 77, 131–132, 215–216, 217; construction in 1920s and 1930s, 62–63, 65, 69, 76–77, 79; construction in 1990s and 2000s, 211, 215–218, 220; in Europe, 66–67, 131–132, 208, 210, 216–218, 226
Arledge, Roone, 176
Armstrong, Murray, 166–167, 168, 231
Atlanta Flames, 164, 178
Austria-Hungary, 25, 34

baby boom/baby boomers, 93, 113, 174, 187, 190, 235
Backman, Fredrik, 143–144, 237
Ball, Rudi, 85–86
Bandy, 23–26, 25, 33, 35–38, 40, 41, 50, 52, 53, 55, 70, 99, 101, 103, 129, 130–131, 249
Banff Winter Festival, 60
Barron, John Augustus, 29
Baryshnikov, Mikhail, 164
baseball, 2, 11, 23, 28, 46, 59, 61, 118, 148, 192; Little League Baseball, 192; Major League Baseball, 65, 91, 140, 162, 184, 216; National League, 19, 42
basketball, 2, 6, 11, 60, 119–120, 138, 167, 171, 190, 192, 207, 242; National Basketball Association, 119, 207, 216, 242, 246; Women's Professional Basketball Association, 242
Beardsley, Doug, 182
Beijing, China, 18, 239; Kunlun Red Star, 239
Belak, Wade, 240
Belgium, 40, 50, 56
Bell, Bobby, 57, 76, 79, 84,
Belleville (Ontario) McFarlands, 113, 117
Berglund, Helge, 130
Berlin, Germany, 1, 12, 19, 35, 40, 53, 66, 67, 70, 74, 79, 85, 86, 97, 216, 225; East, 203; Wall, 199, 204; Berlin Eisbären, 12; Berlin Eislauf Verein, 35; Berlin Red-White, 85; Berliner Schlittschuhclub (Berlin SC), 35, 56, 66, 85; Berliner

Berlin, Germany *(continued)*
  Sportpalast, 66, 74, 79, 82, 85; Brandenburg SC, 85
Berlusconi, Silvio, 208, 210
Bern, Switzerland, 179; Bern SC, 208
Bettman, Gary, 5, 11, 207, 241
Blackman, Ted, 146, 148
Blainey, Caroline, 193, 196–197
Blainey, Justine, 193, *194,* 195–196, 243
Blake, Toe, 118
Bobrov, Vsevolod, 97, 100, 103, 125, 147
Bollettieri, Nick, 186
Bommes, Fred, 208
Boogaard, Derek, 240
Borden, Robert, 58
Bossy, Mike, 185
Boston, 7, 15, 42, 62, 95, 162, 188; Boston Bruins, 7, 51, 62, 63, *214,* 246; Boston Celtics, 119; Boston Garden, 62, 63, 80, *214,* 215; and girls' hockey, 191, 227; and youth hockey, 95, 96, 135; University, 168, 172
Boucha, Henry, 138, 161, 165
Bowe, William, 107
Bowman, Bob, 70
Bowman, Scotty, 188
Boyd, Stephanie, 190–191
Branch, John, 240
Brandt, Marissa, 7, 9
Bratislava, Slovakia, 12, 142, 225, 226
Brewer, Carl, 132, 149, 179
Brezhnev, Leonid, 141, 142
Brimsek, Frank, 135
Britain, 21, 28, 29, 31, 39, 50, 76, 77, 84, 86, *209,* 238, 239; British Empire, 27, 28, 30, 31, 32, 33, 58; British national hockey team, 70
British Broadcasting Corporation (BBC), 70
British Columbia, 31, 46, 60, 72, 76, 112, 168, 191, 227
Britt, Maj, 81
"Broad Street Bullies." *See* Philadelphia Flyers
Brooks, Herb, 4, 166, 168–169, 171–172, 177–179
Brown, Walter, 80
Brundage, Avery, 101, 110–111, 113, 125, 133
Buckna, Mike, 76, 79

Budapest, Hungary, 35, 40, 70
Buffalo, New York, 151, 188, 203; Buffalo Sabres, 161, 188
Bukač, Luděk, 101–102, 139–140, 160, 164
Bury Fen Club, 24
Bush, George W., 231
Bykov, Vyacheslav, 208

Calder, Frank, 63, 65
Calgary, Alberta, 31, 60, 116, 119, 178, 230; Calgary Flames, 32, 213; Calgary Stampeders, 87
California, 16, 118, 134, 183, 189, 211, 233; California Golden Seals, 162
Campagnolo, Iona, 158
Campbell, Clarence, 74, 96, 114, 116–117, 118, 126, 165
Canada: and baby boom, 93–94; and British Empire, 27–29, 31–32, 39–40; and climate change, 249; and Confederation, 27; cultural influence of hockey in, 10–11, 58–60, 92–95, 114–116, 145–146, 154–156, 181, 220–221, 236–237, 240; and cultural influence of United States, 64–65, 151, 183, 211; during 1960s, 114–115; early hockey in, 23, 26, 31–32; and economic relations to United States, 64, 65, 83, 119, 183, 219; and nationalism/national identity, 3–4, 10–11, 27–29, 30–32, 58–59, 61, 114–115, 119, 148, 152, 166, 181–182, 183, 221; origins of professional hockey in, 43–46, 47–48; and pond hockey, 236–237; popularity of hockey in, 5, 48–49, 71–73, 90–91, 113, 114, 150–153, 220–221, 246; radio and television in, 71–73, 92–93, 115, 150–153; and sports, 27–29, 31, 32–33, 59, 60, 64, 192, 221, 228; and Summit Series, 145–146, 147–149, 150, 159; and Wayne Gretzky, 180–183; women in, 152–153, 155–156, 191–192, 197, 228; and World War I, 58–59; and youth (minor) hockey, 93–95, 96, 157–158, 174, 188–190, 233–234, 236
Canada Cup, 201
Canadian Amateur Hockey Association (CAHA), 87–90, 93, 192; and relations

with international organizations, 53, 88–89, 112–113; and relations with NHL, 83, 89–92, 96, 116–119, 195
Canadian Broadcasting Corporation, 71–73, 150, 153
Canadian Charter of Rights and Freedoms, 193, 197
Canadian hockey, 23, 25–27, 30–32, 36–37, 101–102, 120, 140; and amateurism, 86–87, 111, 112–113; and calls for reform, 115–117, 154–156, 157–158, 159–161, 165–166, 172–173, 240; in Europe, 36–39, 40–41, 50–52, 113, 127–128, 129–130, 130–131; and hockey world, 11, 15, 30, 37–38, 50–51, 52–54, 112–114, 145, 158, 159–160, 221; and people of color, 31, 94, 155, 247; and player development/training, 91, 94, 96, 157–158, 159, 160–161, 172–173, 185; and strategy, 68–69, 91, 132, 148, 149, 156–157, 160; and women and girls, 59–61, 81, 94, 155–156, 190–191, 193–197, 227–228, 240; violence in, 15, 29–30, 132, 149, 156–158, 165; players in Europe, 7, 38–40, 50–51, 73–76, 79, 132, 179–180, 207–208, *209*, 240; players in United States, 43, 58, 63–65, 135, 166–168, 169, 171, 230, 231, 232
Canadian national team/representative team, men's, 6, 50–51, 53–54, 57–59, 73–74, 76, 96–97, 104–105, 110, 112, 126–127, 130, 133, 134, 145–146, 146–149, 158, 201, 226
Canadian national team, women's, 5, 229, 230, 232, 241, 242
Canadian Interuniversity Sport, 229, 230
Canadian Pacific Railway, 28, 31, 47
Canadian Women's Hockey League, 242
Carlson, Steve, 165
Carrier, Roch, 114, 237
Čáslavská, Věra, 141, 143
Carson, Jimmy, 188
Cattini, Ferdinand and Hans. *See* ni-Sturm
Central Army Sports Club, Moscow (CSKA or Red Army), 98, 100, 102, 103, 104, 111, 139, 153, 124–125, 200, 201, 202, 225
Chamonix, France, 66, *75*

Chelyabinsk, Russia, 121, 200
Chernyshev, Arkady, 103, 104, 121, 122, 125, 147
Cherry, Don, 15, 221
Chicago, Illinois, 3, 22, 48, 62, 63, 80, 139; Chicago Blackhawks, 48, 63, 80, 198; Chicago Bulls, 212; Chicago Cougars, 162, 165; Chicago Stadium, 62, 63, 218
China, 15, 206, 239, 247
Chronic Traumatic Encephalopathy (CTE), 240–241
Ciccarelli, Dino, 159, 161
Clarke, Bobby, 149
Cleveland, Ohio, 82, 92, 95, 96, 135; Cleveland Barons, 96
clubs, athletic, 34–36, 38, 41–42, 44–46
Cobalt (Ontario) Silver Kings, 44, 45, 47
college hockey: in Canada, 229, 230; in United States, 137, 162, 166–172, 176–177, 180, 186, 189, 229, 232, 242
Colorado College, 167
Colored Hockey League (Nova Scotia), 32
commercialization of hockey, 41, 62–63, 157, 188–189, 211–218, 234, 238, 246–247; in Canada, 43–46, 47–49, 63–65, 71–73, 152–153, 220–221; in Europe, 51, 55–56, 76–79, 120, 133, 199, 210, 213, 219; in United States, 42–43, 62–63, 178, 187
commercialization of sports, 20, 42, 111, 167, 174–175
communism/Communist Party: ideology and sports, 83, 99, 101–102, 109–110, 121–122, 140–141, 200, 203; in Czechoslovakia, 104–107, 109–110, 140–141, 143, 199; in Soviet Union, 97–99, 101–102, 121
Compuware Hockey, 187–188
Conan Doyle, Arthur, 54, 55
Cornell University, 160, 167–168, 218
Coubertin, Pierre de, 50
Craig, Jim, 172, 177, 178
Creighton, James, 23, 27, 30, 36, 49
curling, 21, 22, 27
CTV, 150
Czech lands (Bohemia and Moravia)/Czech Republic, 16, 25, 34, 143, *209*, 219, 224, 239, 246
Czech national team, men's, 38–39, 221, 247

Czechoslovakia, 17, 52, 70, *75,* 76, 86, 104–110, 112, 113, 133, 139–144, 160, 198–199; Communist takeover in, 104–105; Communist Party and sport in, 108–110, 164, 198–199; 1969 hockey demonstrations in, 142–143; 1989 revolution in, 199
Czechoslovak national team, 76, 104–105, 109–110, 112, 120, 140–142, 171; arrest and trial of, 105–108; and defections of players, 106–107, 164, 198
Czechoslovak state police (StB—Státní bezpečnost), 105, 106, 108, 141, 143, 164, 198

Dalhousie University, 40
Dallas, Texas, 189, 250; Dallas Stars, 213, 216
Dalton, Matt, 6–7, 8, 13
Datsyuk, Pavel, 226
Davos, Switzerland, 35, 54–55, *67,* 73, *75.* 79, 86, 104; HC Davos, 55–57, 66, 76, 178; and Spengler Cup, 56–57
DeAngelis, Mike, 208
Demitra, Pavol, 240
Denmark, *75,* 209
Denver, Colorado, 219; University of, 166–167, 168, 231
Detroit, Michigan, 95, 139, 186, 187, 188, 189, 191; Detroit Olympia, 62; Detroit Red Wings, 62, 91, 183, 213, 214–215
development of players, 16–17, 57, 84, 90, 91, 92, 100–101, 101–102, 103, 104, 111, 120, 122, 132, 133, 154–155, 160–161, 169, 189, 234, 242, 247
Dickson, Jeff, 77, 79, 80, 82, 86
Disney Corporation, 211–212
Djurgårdens IF (Stockholm), 35, 130
Drury, Herb, 51, 58
Dryden, Dave, 161–162, 165
Dryden, Ken, 10, 11, 68, 69, 91, 146, 160, 161, 168, 240–241
Dubček, Alexander, 141, 143
Dubin, Charles, 197, 243
Duggan, Tom, 62, 65, 211
Duluth, Minnesota, 3, 135, 250; University of Minnesota at (UMD), 229–233
Duquesne Gardens (Pittsburgh), 43, 62

Düsseldorf, Germany, *75,* 76, 216
Dwyer, Bill, 62, 63, 117
Dynamo sports clubs, 98; Dinamo Minsk, 224; Dinamo Riga, 99, 225, 226; Dynamo Berlin, 12; Dynamo Moscow, 100, 103, 125

Eagleson, Alan, 158
Eaves, Cecil, 160, 161, 168
Eaves, Mike, 161, 168, 172
Edina, Minnesota, 136–138; Edina High School Hornets, 137–138
Edmonton, Alberta, 12, 19, 47, 91, 174, 182–183; Edmonton Oilers, 15, 16, 165, 174, 181–183
Eisner, Michael, 211–212
Elvin, Arthur, 76–77, 86, 88
Eruzione, Mike, 1, 2, 172, 177
Esposito, Phil, 147, 148, 149, 181
Esso. *See* Imperial Oil
European hockey players in North America, 13, 15–16, 162–164, 165–166, 173, 174, 179, 184–185, 206–207, *209,* 221, 224, 225, 231, 232–233, 242
Eveleth, Minnesota, 135–136, 137, 138; Eveleth High School Golden Bears, 135–136; Eveleth Reds, 135
expense of hockey, 88, 93–94, 154, 188, 233–234, 236, 237

Falla, Jack, 185, 186
Faulkner, William, 91
Fédération Internationale de Football Association (FIFA), 11, 36, 222
Fedorov, Sergei, 206
Fetisov, Viacheslav, 201–203, 223, 225, 245
figure skating, 22, 25, 35, 36, 50, 55, 80–81, 84, 94, 176, 186, 191, 193
Filmon, Gary, 220–221
Finland, 86, 112, 113, 130–133, 135, 179, 224, 238, 239, 242, 246; bandy in, 70, 101, 130; social democracy in, 131, 139; sports culture in, 130–131, 133
Finnish hockey: domestic league (SM-liiga), 133, 179, 207–208, *209,* 210, 226; national team, 2, 112, 133, 221, 222, 226
Fleury, Lionel, 119

football: American, 2, 19, 29, 63, 64, 138, 167, 171, 177, 192, 229, 247; Canadian, 64, 221. *See also* rugby
Football Association (English), 19, 29, 41, 61
Forbes, Dave, 165
Forsberg, Peter, 206
France, 26, 37–38, 75, 76–79, 86, 104, 139, 209, 246
French Canadians, 10, 30–31, 32, 45, 58, 71, 155, 221, 237; and hockey broadcasts, 115, 150, 151; and Maurice Richard, 114–115; and Quiet Revolution, 114
Fribourg-Gottéron, HC, 208
Frölunda (Gothenburg), 130

Garmisch-Partenkirchen, Germany, 75, 85, 86, 88
Gazprom, 222, 223
German hockey, 12, 35, 38, 84–86; Deutsche Eishockey Liga, 207, 210, 213, 226; German national team, 76, 84, 85, 243
Germany, 52–53, 74, 75, 83–86, 209, 245; sport in, 34–36, 54, 83–85, 99; popularity of hockey in, 40, 50, 51, 56, 66, 85–86, 246
Germany, East (German Democratic Republic), 12, 109, 203
girls' hockey. *See* women and girls in hockey; youth hockey; youth sports
globalization: characteristics of, 14, 247; and sports, 11–13, 14–16, 18, 238, 248
Globe, Ericsson (Stockholm), 216, 218
Golden Puck tournament, 123–124
Goldsworthy, Bill, 148
Goodenow, Bob, 185
Gopnik, Adam, 11, 249
Gorbachev, Mikhail, 198, 202, 203–204
Gothenburg, Sweden, 126, 130; Frölunda, 130; IK Göta, 129
Granato, Cammi, 191
Green, Norm, 216
Green Line (Soviet national team), 201–202, 203
Gretzky, Brent, 187
Gretzky, Walter, 187, 249
Gretzky, Wayne, 15, 17, 180–184, 185, 187, 201, 213, 215, 246, 249; trade of, 182–183, 184, 212

Gridasov, Stanslav, 103, 104
Griffin, Randi, 7, 9, 13, 248
Grumet-Morris, Dov, 208
Gzowski, Peter, 156, 181, 237

Halifax, Nova Scotia, 23, 27, 36, 47, 58, 59
Hamburg, Germany, 33, 34, 35, 75, 85, 210
Hamilton, Ontario, 41, 63, 64, 219, 227; Hamilton Tigers, 63, 65, 117
Hardy, W. George, 88–90, 117
Harrington, John, 16, 171, 177, 179
Hartford (New England) Whalers, 3, 162, 174, 216
Hartje, Tod, 204
Harvard University, 7, 204, 230, 233
Hašek, Dominik, 13, 198–199, 218
Hay, Charles, 145
Hedberg, Anders, 163, 165
Helsinki, Finland, 12, 143, 149, 216, 225; Helsinki IFK, 132; Helsinki Jokerit, 179, 226
Henderson, Paul, 145, 147, 149, 150
Henie, Sonja, 79–81, 221
Hewitt, Foster, 71, 72, 145, 146
Hewitt, William A. (Billy), 52, 53, 61, 71, 88
hip-hop and hockey jerseys, 212
Hitler, Adolph, 74, 83, 85
Hockey Canada, 145, 147, 154, 156, 158, 159, 160, 171
Hockey Night in Canada, 113–114, 115, 173, 221; on radio, 71–73, 92–93; on television, 93, 150–153
hockey puck, 36–37, 38, 40, 49, 99
hockey stick, 24, 36–37, 38, 40, 99, 100, 123, 133, 156, 165, 198, 204, 234
Hoffman, Abby, 94, 191, 192, 228
Holst, Erika, 231
Howe, Gordie, 3, 13, 91, 95, 115, 134, 215, 236
Hull, Bobby, 114, 116, 126, 134, 147, 162–163, 165–166
Hull, Brett, 183
Humboldt, Saskatchewan, 94; Humboldt Broncos, 240
Hungary, 75, 239

Ice Capades, 80
Igloo, The (Pittsburgh), 184
Ihnačák, Peter, 164

Ikola, Willard, 137
Imperial Oil, 60, 71, 73, 114, 152–153
indoor rinks, 22, 23, 26, 36, 44, 46, 66–67, 69, 83, 85–86, 130, 132, 137; in Soviet Union/Russia, 102, 223
inquiries into Canadian hockey, 117, 155–156, 157, 158
International Ice Hockey Federation (Ligue Internationale de Hockey sur Glace), 5, 11, 16, 36, 52, 88, 119, 120, 140, 145, 164, 239; and Canadian hockey/NHL, 53, 113, 158, 207, 245; and different versions of hockey, 37, 40; and IOC, 7, 50, 53, 56, 113, 120, 176, 207. *See also* world championships
International Olympic Committee, 7, 11, 56, 114, 145, 175, 245; and amateurism, 53, 89, 111, 133; and commercialization of sports, 111, 133, 176, 207; and Soviet Union/Russia, 101, 110, 243; and women's sports, 233
Italy, 75, 83, 135, 210; hockey in, 208, *209*, 210

Jaenecke, Gustav, 31, 66, 79, 80, 85, 86
Jágr, Jaromír, 15–16, 206, 224
Jäkel, Ulf, 210
Japan, 5, 16, *209*, 248
Jerring, Sven, 130
jersey sales, 183, 212–215
Jesenice, Slovenia, 208
Joe Louis Arena (Detroit), 213, *214*.
Johnson, Bob, 169, *170*, 171–172
Johnson, Mark, 1, 172, 176, 178
Jokerit Helsinki, 179, 226
Jones, Janet, 182, 183
Juckes, Gordon, 116, 119

Karlsson, Lars, 159, 161
Karmanos, Peter, 187–188, 216
Kasatonov, Alexei, 201, 203
Kassel (Germany) Huskies, 213
Kenora (Ontario) Thistles, 44, 47
Kharlamov, Valeri, 149, 172
Khimik Voskresensk (Russia), 201
Khomutov, Andrei, 208
Kidd, Bruce, 14, 33, 48
Kiev (Ukraine) Sokol, 204

Kingston, Ontario, 27, 30, 31, 47, 147, 182
Kiruna, Sweden, 159
Klāvs, Edgars, 99
Kontinental Hockey League, 7, *209*, 223–226, 239, 240, 245
Konopásek, Stanislav, 76, 106, 107, 108
Korea, North, 6, 7–8, 10; cheerleaders from, 8
Korea, South, 5, 10, 239, 241, 243
Korean (South) national team, men's, 5, 6–7, 247
Korean (unified) team, women's, 5, 7–8, 9, 248
korobka, 122, 123
Korotkov, Pavel, 103, 104
Košice, Slovakia, 76, 142
Kostka, Vladimír, 140, 144
Kovalchuk, Ilya, 222, 243
Krutov, Vladimir, 201, 203
Kunlun Red Star, 239
Kurri, Jari, 174, 177, 181, 184
Kuzkin, Viktor, 123

lacrosse, 27, 59, 180, 190
Lafleur, Guy, 3, 16, 185, 215
LaFontaine, Pat, 185–186
Lamoriello, Lou, 202
Lanctôt, Gustave, 58
Larionov, Igor, 200, 201, 203; and *Ogonyok* article, 202
Larson, Reed, 168
Latvia, 75, 99–100, 225, 239
Laufer, Josef, 24, 38–39, 70–71
Laviolette, Jack, 45
Leksand, Sweden, 126
Lemaire, Jacques, 179
Lemieux, Mario, 184, 215
Le Mat, Raoul, 52
Lenardon, Norm, 127
Leningrad, USSR, 99 (see also St. Petersburg, Russia); SKA Leningrad, 160
Ligue Internationale de Hockey sur Glace. *See* International Ice Hockey Federation
Liiga. *See* Finnish hockey
Lindbergh, Pelle, 174
Lindsay, Ted, 91
Little Ice Age, 21, 26, 35

Little League Baseball. *See* baseball
Loicq, Paul, 56
Lokomotiv sports clubs, 98; Lokomotiv Yaroslavl, 11, 240
London, 19, 21, 50, 73, *75*, 77, 79, 81, 86, 87, 105, 106, 120; Prince's Skating Club, 40
Los Angeles, 3, 12, 15, 80, 91, 118, 183, 184, 211; Los Angeles Kings, 181, 183
Ludwig, Jack, 146, 147, 148
Lugano HC, 179
Luleå HF, 213
Luzhniki Stadium (Moscow), 121
Lynah Rink (Ithaca, NY), 218

MacGregor, Roy, 10, 159
MacLaren Advertising Company, 71, 150
Madison Square Garden: first (1879–1890), 66; second (1890–1925), 62; third (1925–1968), 61–63, 66, 77, 80, 82, 86, 91, 95, 134, 211
Magnus, Louis, 36
Makarov, Sergei, 181, 200, 201, 203
Maleček, Josef, 79
Malkin, Evgeni, 226
Malmö, Sweden, 216; Malmö Redhawks (Malmö IK), 208, 210, 213
Manitoba, 31, 47, 168, 219, 220; University of, 76
Mannheim, Germany, 85, 216; Mannheim Adler, 207
Mantegazza, Geo, 179
Maple Leaf Gardens, 62, 71, 80, 91, 116, 215, 218
Mariucci, John, 135, 166, 169
Martin Hasson, Kim, 233
Martinet, Jean, 108
Massachusetts, 13, 51, 95, 189
Matthews, Auston, 187
Mayasich, John, 136
Mayorov, Boris, 125
McCartan, Jack, 134, 162
McCrimmon, Brad, 240
McKinley, Michael, 23
McMurtry, Bill, 157
McNall, Bruce, 184
Medvedev, Alexander, 223, 225, 226
Memorial Cup, 87
merchandise, licensed, 212–214, 245

Mighty Ducks of Anaheim, 211–212, 213–214,
Michigan, 43, 44, 95, 185, 189, 191; University of, 137, 167; Michigan Tech University, 168
Mikhailov, Boris, 122–123, 147, 148
Mi'kmaq Indians, 36; Mi'kmaq sticks, 37
Milan, Italy, 56, 85, 208, 225; Devils Milano, 184, 208, 210
Miller, Shannon, 191, 229–231; firing of, 232–233
Minneapolis, Minnesota, 165; Minneapolis-St. Paul (Twin Cities), 4, 118, 135, 139; suburbs of, 136–137, 143
Minnesota, 3, 4, 7, 13, 16, 43, 51, 96, 135–139, 171, 177, 189, 227; Minnesota Fighting Saints, 162; Minnesota North Stars, 138, 161, 204; Minnesota Wild, 138; University of, 134, 166, 168–169, 172, 178, 229, 230, 242; University of, Duluth campus (UMD), 229–233
Minnesota State High School Hockey Tournament, 135–136, 137–139
minor-professional hockey, 80, 88, 89, 90, 91, 96, 117, 126, 172, 207, 215
Minsk, Belarus, 216; Dinamo Minsk, 224
"Miracle on Ice," 1–2, 3, 4, 175–178, 179, 189
Modrý, Bohumil, *105*, 106–108
Mogilny, Alexander, 203
Molson, David, 126
Montador, Steve, 240–241
Montreal, Quebec, 21, 23, 28, 30–32, 69, 114–115, 146, 148; Montreal Canadiens, 22, 45, 49, 61, 71, 82, 114–115, 119, 125–126, 150, 155, 160, 214–215; Montreal Forum, 60, 61, 116, 170, 198, 215, 218; Montreal Maroons, 64, 71, 82; Montreal Wanderers, 44–45, 48
Morrow, Ken, 178
Mortimore, George, 116
Müller, Paul, 55, 56, 57, 76
Munich, Germany, 53, *75*, 76, 85, 198, 210
Murphy, Margaret "Digit," 230
Muscular Christianity, 27–28, 32, 59

Näslund, Mats, 174, 177
National Collegiate Athletics Association (NCAA), 169, 171, 177, 229, 230, 231, 232, 246, 248

National Football League (NFL), 14, 63, 177, 216, 247, 248
National Hockey Association (NHA), 41, 45, 46
National Hockey League (NHL), 5, 15–17, 41, 134, 160, 172, 173, 198, *209*, 211, 221; as global league, 12, 207, *209*, 222, 223, 225, 226, 239; and relations with CAHA, 83, 89–90, 91, 92, 96, 116–117, 118–119, 195–196; and expansion of, 15, 61–62, 92, 116–119, 126, 162, 174; and Original Six era, 82–83, 90–93, 96, 113, 114–117; and Canadian national/representative teams, 145–149, 158; and business of, 43, 46, 62–65, 80, 89–90, 90–92, 94, 95, 114, 116, 125–126, 162, 174–175, 184–185, 207, 210, 211–218, 245–247; and power over hockey, 48, 64–65, 83, 90–92, 96, 154, 167, 220–221, 237, 241, 245–247; criticism of, 64, 65, 113, 115–117, 118–119, 143, 150–151, 157, 220–221, 247; on radio and television, 71–73, 92–93, 150–153, 246; Americans playing in, 134, 135, 162, 177, 178, 179–180, 185, 187–188; Europeans paying in, 127, 174, 198, 201, 203, 205, 206, 222, 223, 224, 225, 240, 243
National League of Professional Baseball Clubs, 19, 42
Nazi Germany/Nazis, 74, 82, 83, 97, 245; and sports, 83–84
Nedomanský, Václav, 164, 198
Netherlands, 21–22, 33, *75*, *209*
New Brunswick, 234, 236
New England, 23, 26, 238
New Hampshire, University of, 230
New Jersey Devils, 202
New York City, 3, 15, 21, 22, 61, 62, 63, 79, 80, 82, 134; New York Americans, 61, 62, 63, 82, 90; New York Islanders, 178, 185, 224; New York Rangers, 62, 64, 82, 95, 134, 151, 176, 178
Nilsson, Percy, 208, 210, 213
Nilsson, Ulf, *163*, 165, 180
ni-Sturm (HC Davos), 57, 79
NLA. *See* Swiss hockey
Nordic Europe, 101, 113, 126–133, 144, 213; and social democracy, 128–129, 133

North American players in Europe, 7, 38–40, 50–51, 73–76, 79, 132, 179–180, 207–209, 240
Nuremberg, Germany, 76; Nuremberg Ice Tigers (EC 80 Nuremberg), 213

Obama, Barack, 48
O'Brien, Ambrose, 45, 46, 47
Ohio State University, 229
Olympic Games: 1908 London, 50; 1920 Antwerp, 50–53, 57, 67, 130; 1924 Chamonix, 53, 57–58, 66; 1928 St. Moritz, 58; 1936 Garmisch-Partenkirchen, 70, 85, 88; 1948 St. Moritz, 94, 104, 107, 111; 1960 Squaw Valley, 134, 162; 1968 Mexico City, 141; 1972 Sapporo, 112, 172; 1980 Lake Placid, 1–4, 164, 175–179, 189; 1984 Sarajevo, 176, 200–201; 1988 Calgary, 159, 176, 202; 1988 Seoul, 176; 1996 Atlanta, 228; 1998 Nagano, 5, 176, 221, 228; 2006 Turin, 222, 231; 2010 Vancouver, 246; 2014 Sochi, 222; 2018 Pyeongchang, 5, 6, 8–10, *9*, 53, 97, 239, 241–242, 243–245, *244*, 247; 2021 Tokyo, 10; 2022 Beijing, 239, 247
oligarchs, Russian, 14, 222, 226, 243
Olson, Lynn, 227
Omsk, Russia, 233; Avangard Omsk, 224
Ontario: government inquiries into hockey, 117, 154, 156, 157; women's hockey in, 60, 61, 191, 227–228
Ontario Hockey Association, 29, 31, 60, 191
Ontario Supreme Court, 195, 197
Ontario Women's Hockey Association, 191–192
Original Six, 91, 212–213, 214
Örnsköldsvik, Sweden, 159
Orr, Bobby, 3, 17, 147, 180, 190, *214*, 237
Ottawa, Ontario, 27, 30, 31, 37, 43, 44, 47, 145, 146, 168, 228; Ottawa Senators (original), 43, 51, 64, 65, 82
Ouellette, Caroline, 231
Ovechkin, Alexander, 13, 222, 226, 243, 245
Oxford Canadians (Oxford University Ice Hockey Club), 39–40, 55–58, 73–74, *75*, 79, 114

Pacific Coast Hockey Association (PCHA), 41, 46, 48, 60, 63–64
Paek, Jim, 6
Paiement, Wilf, 158
Palais de Glace (Antwerp), 50–51, 67
Palais de Glace (Paris), 66
Palais des Sports. *See* Vélodrome d'Hiver)
Parliament, Canadian, 29, 58, 116, 118, 183, 241
parenting: and baby boom, 93, 94, 96; and contemporary sports, 186–188, 189–190, 191–192, 204, 206, 234–236; and girls in hockey, 190–191, 196, 242; and problems in hockey, 154–156, 221, 233, 249
Paris, France, 56, 66, 67, 75, 77–79, 81, 82, 86; Paris Club des Patineurs, 36, 40; Paris Racing, 79; Stade Français, 79
Parker, Jack, 168–169, 171, 172
Parkin, George, 28, 29, 40
Patrick, Frank, 43, 46, 48, 64
Patrick, Lester, 46, 48, 60, 64
Patrick, Lynn, 95
Pearson, Lester, 114, 116, 117, 118
peewee hockey. *See* youth hockey
Percival, Lloyd, 161
Peterborough, Ontario, 59, 190
Philadelphia, Pennsylvania, 118, 156, 174; Philadelphia Flyers, 153, 156, 165, 181, 214
Pittsburgh, Pennsylvania, 43, 63, 118, 135, 184; Pittsburgh Penguins, 6, 178, 184, 214; Pittsburgh Pirates, 62–63; Pittsburgh Steelers, 177
Plante, Jacques, 134
Plaster Rock, New Brunswick, 236–237, 238
Pocklington, Peter, 182–183
Poland, 70, 75, 109, 209
Polenská, Alena, 232, 248
Pond, The (Anaheim), 212
pond hockey, 23, 236–238
Prague, Czech Republic, 24, 35, 38–39, 40, 52, 66, 67, 68, 71, 73, 75, 76, 104–105, 106, 109, 164, 198, 199, 216, 225, 226; LTC Prague, 56, 76, 79, 100, 104, 107; Slavia Prague, 70, 76; 1969 demonstrations in, 140–143
Prince Edward Island, 72, 191
Prince's Skating Club (London), 40
professionalism, 41–44, 48, 51, 53, 76, 80, 83, 109, 111, 116, 133, 167, 179, 184, 188, 204–205, 207, 210, 232, 242, 248
Providence, Rhode Island, 7; Providence College, 230
Puchkov, Nikolai, 160
puck. *See* hockey puck
Putin, Vladimir: foreign policy of, 224, 243, *244;* and "national champions," 222, 223; and plans for KHL, 223–224, 245; and rehabilitation of Soviet past, 245

Quebec (province), 41, 60, 61, 71, 185, 186, *209;* and hockey broadcasts, 115, 150, 151, 152
Quebec City, 22, 44, 58, 59, 91; Quebec Nordiques, 174, 208, 219
Quebec International Pee-Wee Tournament, 248
Quiet Revolution, 114–115, 143

radio, 64, 70–73, 92–93, 115, 130, 138, 151, 182, 220
Radulov, Alexander, 224
Ramsey, Mike, 4
ratings: radio, 73, 92–93; television, 3, 5, 49, 113, 115, 120, 150–153, 173, 176, 197, 221, 241, 246
Räty, Noora, 242–243
recruiting, college hockey, 167, 169, 171, 196, 231, 232
Red Army. *See* Central Army Sports Club
"Red Machine." *See* Russian hockey; Soviet hockey
Regina, Saskatchewan, 59, 94; Regina Capitals, 63; Regina Pats, 159, 166
Renfrew, Al, 167
Resch, Glenn "Chico," 94
Rhodes Scholarships, 39–40, 74
Rice-Jones, Arthur, 73–74, 86–87, 186
Rice-Jones, Cecil, 86–87, 186
Richard, Maurice "Rocket," 13, 91, 114–115, 134, 181
Richmond (UK) Hawks, 73
Rickard, Tex, 62, 64, 65, 77, 211
Rider, Fran, 195, 196
Riga, Latvia, 222; Dinamo Riga, 99, 225, 226

Robertson, J. Ross, 29, 30
Rodnina, Irina, 202
Romania, 75, 109
Romanov, Nikolai, 98, 100
Rooth, Maria, 231
Rosa, Fran, 146
Roxborough, Henry, 60, 61
Royal Canadian Air Force Flyers, 104
rugby, 19, 26, 27, 29, 30–33, 35, 40–41, 64, 69, 70, 109
Ruggiero, Angela, 233
Russia, 5–6, 18, 25, 34, 104, 200, 240, 246; bandy in, 34, 35, 50, 99; economic development in, 98–99, 222, 223–224, 226; and foreign policy, 224–225, 243; oligarchs in, 14, 222, 226, 243. *See also* Soviet Union
Russian hockey, 7, 10, 11, 100, 102, 145, 222–226; and international sport, 5, 110, 177, 199, 222–223, 243, 245; as machine/robotic, 15, 97, 160; players in North America, 206, 207, 209, 222, 225, 231; national team, 5, 6, 17, 222, 225–226, 243, 245; and post-Soviet decline, 222, 223, 226. *See also* Kontinental Hockey League; Soviet hockey
Russian Women's Hockey League, 239
Ruth, Babe, 61, 62, 64
Rypien, Rick, 240

salaries, player, 43, 87; in NHL, 125, 184, 188, 215, 219, 220; in Europe, 112–113, 184; in Soviet Union, 112–113, 125; in KHL, 223
Salchow, Ulrich, 55
Salming, Börje, 127, 165, 236
Sandlin, Tommy, 160
San Francisco, California, 92, 118
San Jose, California, 49, 175; San Jose Sharks, 212, 213
Saskatchewan, 119, 154, 166, 168, 230, 231, 240; University of, 229
Saskatoon, Saskatchewan, 63, 219, 229; Saskatoon Sheiks, 63
Sather, Glen, 165, 181
Sault Ste. Marie, Ontario, 43
Sautter, Patricia, 231, 232, 235
Savin, Sergei, 99–100, 104

Schelling, Florence, 232, 242
Schneider, Buzz, 176, 179
scholarships: athletic, 17, 167, 189, 196, 229–230; Rhodes, 39–40, 74
Scotland, 21, 76
Seattle, Washington, 220; Seattle Metropolitans, 63; Seattle Pilots, 161
Selänne, Teemu, 206
Sellig, Max, 52
Sheehan, Bobby, 162
Shenkarow, Barry, 220
Shenzhen KRS Vanke Rays, 239
Shero, Fred, 165
shinny, 15, 23, 27, 92, 237
Shore, Eddie, 64, 80
Sikiö, Hanne, 231
Sinden, Harry, 146
skating, origins of, 21–22
Sjöberg, Lars-Erik, 163, 165
Slap Shot, 165
Slettvoll, John, 179
Slovakia, 52, 66, 76, 209, 219, 224, 226, 240
Slovenia, 208
SM-liiga. *See* Finnish hockey
Smythe, Conn, 61, 71, 126, 156, 157
social democracy, 133; in Sweden, 128, 130, 143; in Finland, 131, 132
Soviet hockey, 83, 119–126, 247; origins of, 97–104; in 1950s, 120–122; in 1960s, 121, 123–125; in 1970s, 158, 160; in 1980s and 1990s, 197–198, 199–203, 204; competition among coaches, 103–104, 125; concentration of talent in, 125, 200–201; domestic league, 100, 102–103, 125, 200; influence on North American hockey, 160–161, 165, 171–172, 184, 189; lack of equipment and rinks, 100, 102–103, 123, 146, 198, 204; as machine, 97, 122, 127, 132–133, 158, 200–201; players signing with NHL, 202–203; and strategy, 97, 103, 120, 127, 132, 147, 149, 161, 201; and training, 100–104, 111, 122, 125, 132–133, 146, 158, 161, 200–202, 204; and youth participation, 122–125. *See also* Russian hockey
Soviet Union (Union of Soviet Socialist Republics): collapse of, 5, 205, 206, 222–223, 225; and international sports,

98, 99, 101, 110–111, 145; and satellite states, 108–109, 110, 140–141, 203–204; and sports and ideology, 83, 98–99, 100, 101–102, 109, 121–122, 140, 200, 203, 204; and state-professional system, 83, 97–98, 100–101, 102, 109, 111, 112, 125, 133, 201; as world power, 2, 97–98, 206, 222. *See also* communism/Communist Party

Soviet national team, 96–97, 112–113, 125–126, 141–142, 158, 177, 198–203; in Summit Series, 145–147, 149

Spartak Moscow, 98, 103, 125, 226

speed skating, 5, 35, 55, 84

Spengler, Alexander, 54, 56

Spengler, Carl, 56

Spengler Cup, 56–57, 74, *75,* 79, 104, 106–107

St. Louis, Missouri, 65, 118, 183; St. Louis Blues, 183, 246

St. Moritz, Switzerland, *25,* 35, 40, 54, 55, *75*

St. Paul, Minnesota, 4, 135, 139, 162; St. Paul Civic Center, 218

St. Petersburg, Russia (Leningrad, USSR), 34, 35, 226

Stalin, Joseph, 97–99, 101, 102, 104, 105, 107, 109, 200, 202, 245; Stalinist rule, 109, 110, 139

Stalin, Vasily, 102, 103

Stanley, Isobel, 37

Stanley, Lord Arthur, 26, 36, 46, 211

Stanley Cup, 31–32, 41, 48–49, 114, 119, 156, 181, 183, 188, 213; as championship trophy of NHL, 48–49, 126; as influence in early hockey, 44, 46–47, 48; and television ratings, 150, 152, 153, 221, 246; trustees of, 46–48

Stasi, 12, 109

Šťastný brothers (Anton, Marián, Peter), 164, 174, 177, 198

Šťastný, Peter, 219

StB. *See* Czechoslovak state police

Stockholm, Sweden, 16, 24, 52, *75,* 103, 105, *129,* 130, 133, 141; Djurgårdens IF, 35, 130; Globe, 216–217; IFK Stockholm, 35; Olympic Stadium, 97, 130

Strobel, Eric, 176

Stuart, Hod, 43

Štvanice Winter Stadium (Prague), 71, 104

style of play, 51, 84, 112, 140, 144, 146, 163; in European hockey, 68–69, 163, 181; in North American hockey, 68–69, 91, 148, 171, 181; in Soviet hockey, 120, 172, 201; in Nordic hockey, 127–128, 133, 144; in contemporary hockey, 206, 247

Suchý, Jan, 141

Summit Series: background to, 145, 146–147, 154; reactions to, 147–149; effects of, in Canada, 146, 150, 152–154, 159–161

Sutherland, James, 59

Svoboda, Petr, 198

Sweden, 18, 34, 52, *75,* 86, 96, 105, 107, 112, 126–130; bandy in, 24, 70, 131; cost of hockey in, 17, 236; rinks and arenas in, 130, 217, 223

Swedish hockey, 104, 131, 159, 162–163, 179, *209;* domestic league (Elitserien/Swedish Hockey League), 133, 179, 207–208, 210; origins of, 52, 129–130; players in North America, 162–165, *163,* 173, 207, *209;* popularity of, 129–130, 213, 226; professionalism in, 133, 179; and social democracy, 133, 143, 236; women's national team, 8–9, 231

Swiss hockey, 15, 49, 51, 54–57, *209,* 242; domestic league (National League A), 179, 180, 187, 207–208, 224, 226; men's national team, 97, 178

Switzerland, 13, 17, 21, 37–38, 54–57, 74, *75,* 107–108, 112, 164, 179, 235, 242; bandy in, 24–26, 38; winter tourists in, 54–55, 57

Sych, Valentin, 223

Syers, Edgar Wood, 25, 26

Syers, Madge, 55

Szemberg, Szymon, 245

Tampere, Finland, 131; Hakametsä Ice Hall, *132*

Tarasov, Anatoli, 101–104, 111, 121, 122, 124, 125–126, 140, 144, 147, 149, 160, 171, 189, 198, 200

Taylor, Fred "Cyclone," 43

Tebbutt, William, 24, 25, 26

television: American programs in Canada, 151; and European hockey, 208, 213, 226; and female viewers, 151–152; and rights agreements for international hockey, 120, 175–176; and rights agreements with NHL, 153, 183, 215–216, 246. *See also* Canada; *Hockey Night in Canada*; ratings, television
Tikhonov, Viktor, 122, 200–203
Title IX, 192, 228, 231–233
Toronto, 6, 31, 48–49, 51, 60, 71, 93, 94, 150–151, 164, 193; Toronto Blue Jays, 49; Toronto Maple Leafs, 5, 49, 62, 64, 71, 80, 114, 115, 119, 127, 132, 149, 153, 157, 179, 215, 246; Toronto Raptors, 49, 246; Toronto Toros, 164; University of, 190
Torriani, Bibi. *See* ni-Sturm
Tragically Hip, The, 182
Trail, British Columbia, 72, 76; Trail Smoke Eaters, 112, 126–127
Tretiak, Vladislav, 1, 16, 103, 124, 146, 147, 200–201, 222, 223, 245
Troják, Ladislav, 76
Trudeau, Justin, 48
Trudeau, Pierre, 185
Tumba, Sven Johansson, 133
Turnbull, David, 74

United States, 3, 5, 14, 22, 40, 66, 71, 77, 80, 82, 125, 151; hockey in, 2, 3, 10, 12, 15, 16, 23, 41, 49, 88, 134, 156–157, 166–172, 238, 239; and Miracle on Ice, 175–177; NHL expansion in, 61–62, 64–65, 118–119; sports in, 63, 118, 185–188, 228–229, 230, 232–233; youth hockey in, 95–96, 134–139, 174, 187–190, 233, 235
United States national team, men's, 1–2, 50, 52, 58, 70, 77, 175–177
United States national team, women's, 228, 241–242
Upper Canada College (Toronto), 28, 29, 40
USSR. *See* Soviet Union

Vairo, Lou, 172, 189
Valascio (Ambrí, Switzerland), 218
Vancouver, British Columbia, 41, 46, 148, 149; bid for NHL franchise, 118; Vancouver Amazons, 60; Vancouver Canucks, 150, 198; Vancouver Millionaires, 64
Vaz, Edmund, 157
Vegas Golden Knights, 212
Vélodrome d'Hiver (Paris), 77–80, *78,* 82, 86
Verchota, Phil, 4, 176, 179
Victoria, British Columbia, 47, 59; Victoria Cougars, 64
Victoria Skating Rink (Montreal), 23, 30, 237–238
Vienna, Austria, 19, 33, 40, 53, 67, 74–76, 81, 120, 158, 198; Vienna Skating Club (Wiener Verein), 35, 56, 66, 67
violence in hockey, 29–30, 221; Americans to blame for, 15, 156–157; criticism of, 30, 148, 165–166, 240–241; during 1970s, 156–158; European views of, 126–128, 132–133, 147
Voskresensk, Russia, 200; Voskresensk Khimik, 201

Warroad, Minnesota, 137–138, 162
Watson, Blake, 76, 79
Wembley Arena (Empire Pool and Sports Arena, London), 70, 73, 76–77
Western Canada Hockey League, 64
Western Collegiate Hockey Association, 168, 169
Westmount Arena (Montreal), 69
Wickenheiser, Hayley, 191, 196, 230
Williamson, Murray, 172
Winnipeg, Manitoba, 12, 31–32, 47, 58, 59, 74, 86–87, 94, 148, 219–220; Winnipeg Falcons, 53, 59, 113; Winnipeg Jets (1972–1994), 162–163, 174, 181, 204, 219–221; Winnipeg Monarchs, 73–74; Winnipeg Victorias, 31, 47
winter: cultural meanings of, 21–23, 29, 237, 249–250; and climate change, 26, 54, 67, 83, 249
Wisconsin, 13; University of, 168–171, 230
women and girls in hockey: in Canada, 19, *20,* 59–61, 81, 94, 155–156, 190–197, 227–228, 240; in Europe, 81, 232–233, 241–242; in Finland, 242; in Olympics,

5, 7–10, 241; in United States, 191, 227–233
Women's Professional Basketball Association, 242
World Championships (IIHF), men's: 1931 Krynica, 70–71; 1935 Davos, 73, 74; 1947 Prague, 68, 104; 1949 Stockholm, 105, 107, 130; 1950 London, 105, 106; 1954 Stockholm, 96–97, 109, 130; 1957 Moscow, 122; 1961 Geneva and Lausanne, 112; 1963 Stockholm, 126, *129;* 1965 Tampere, 117, 131, *132;* 1967 Vienna, 120; 1969 Stockholm, 141–142; 1970 Stockholm, 120; 1971 Bern and Geneva, 112; 1977 Vienna, 158; 1985 Prague, 198–199; 1987 Vienna, 159, 198; 1989 Stockholm, 203; 2006 Riga, 222; 2007 Moscow, 222, 223; 2008 Halifax and Quebec City, 225
World Championship (IIHF), women's, 197, 231, 241, 242; 1990 Ottawa, 228
World Hockey Association (WHA), 147, 162–166, 173, 174, 181
World Pond Hockey Championships, 236, 238

Yakushev, Alexander, 103
Yaroslavl, Russia, 204; Yaroslavl Lokomotiv, 204
Yashin, Alexei, 224
year-round hockey, 16, 100, 132, 176, 188–189, 200–201, 248
Yegorov, Vladimir, 103, 104
Young, Scott, 118, 126
youth (minor) hockey: in Canada, 93–95, 157–158, 174; and participation of girls, 190–197; in the Soviet Union, 122–125; in the United States, 16, 95–96, 134–135, 137, 174, 187–188. *See also* Compuware Hockey; expense of hockey; year-round hockey
youth sports: and participation of girls, 191–193; specialization of, 234–236, 248: *See also* parenting
Yugoslavia, 17, *75,* 100, 155
Yzerman, Steve, 215

Zábrodský, Vladimir, 106, 108, 110
Zamboni, Frank, 80
Ziegler, John, 184
Zurich, Switzerland, 33, 51, 56–57, 76

Founded in 1893,
UNIVERSITY OF CALIFORNIA PRESS
publishes bold, progressive books and journals
on topics in the arts, humanities, social sciences,
and natural sciences—with a focus on social
justice issues—that inspire thought and action
among readers worldwide.

The UC PRESS FOUNDATION
raises funds to uphold the press's vital role
as an independent, nonprofit publisher, and
receives philanthropic support from a wide
range of individuals and institutions—and from
committed readers like you. To learn more, visit
ucpress.edu/supportus.

www.ingramcontent.com/pod-product-compliance
Lightning Source LLC
Chambersburg PA
CBHW031427160426
43195CB00010BB/645